# Organizational Theory

## A STRATEGIC PERSPECTIVE

# Organizational Theory

## A STRATEGIC PERSPECTIVE

**Donald L. Lester**
Middle Tennessee State University

**John A. Parnell**
University of North Carolina–Pembroke

ATOMIC PUBLISHING

Cincinnati, Ohio
www.atomicdog.com

# Organizational Theory:  A Strategic Perspective
## Donald L. Lester ~ John A. Parnell

**Executive Editors:**
Michele Baird, Maureen Staudt, and
Michael Stranz

**Marketing Manager:**
Mikka Baker

**Managing Editor:**
Kendra Leonard

**Marketing Coordinators:**
Lindsay Annett and Sara Mercurio

**Production/Manufacturing Manager:**
Donna M. Brown

**Production Editorial Manager:**
Dan Plofchan

**Rights and Permissions Specialists:**
Kalina Hintz and Bahman Naraghi

**Cover Image:**
© 2007 Atomic Dog

The Adaptable Courseware Program
consists of products and additions to
existing Thomson products that are
produced from camera-ready copy.
Peer review, class testing, and
accuracy are primarily the responsibility
of the author(s).

Organizational Theory / Donald L.
Lester and John A. Parnell – First
Edition

BOOK ISBN 1-592-60258-4
PACKAGE ISBN 1-592-60259-2

LCCN 2005935599

## International Divisions List

**Asia (Including India):**
Thomson Learning
(a division of Thomson Asia Pte Ltd)
5 Shenton Way #01-01
UIC Building
Singapore 068808
Tel:  (65) 6410-1200
Fax:  (65) 6410-1208

**Australia/New Zealand:**
Thomson Learning Australia
102 Dodds Street
Southbank, Victoria 3006
Australia

**Latin America:**
Thomson Learning
Seneca 53
Colonia Polano
11560 Mexico, D.F., Mexico
Tel (525) 281-2906
Fax (525) 281-2656

**Canada:**
Thomson Nelson
1120 Birchmount Road
Toronto, Ontario
Canada M1K 5G4
Tel (416) 752-9100
Fax (416) 752-8102

**UK/Europe/Middle East/Africa:**
Thomson Learning
High Holborn House
50-51 Bedford Row
London, WC1R 4L$
United Kingdom
Tel 44 (020) 7067-2500
Fax 44 (020) 7067-2600

**Spain (Includes Portugal):**
Thomson Paraninfo
Calle Magallanes 25
28015 Madrid
España
Tel 34 (0)91 446-3350
Fax 34 (0)91 445-621

*We dedicate this book to our families,*
*especially our wives,*
*Denise Lester and Denise Parnell.*

# Brief Contents

# Contents

## Part **3**    Internal Context of Organizations 71

# Part 4    Managing Organizational Processes 121

# Part 5    Future Challenges 167

Part **6**      Integrative Cases  199

# Preface

The goal of *Organizational Theory: A Strategic Perspective* is to make the study of organizational theory relevant to today's collegians. Strategic management and organizational behavior both trace their development back to organization theory. Hence, much value can be derived from the study and understanding of all facets of organizations, from structure and design, to technology, to culture and change.

Organization theory is a lively and engaging topic. This text presents the major theoretical perspectives that have contributed to our understanding of organizations in a very contemporary format. It is highly readable, presenting the concepts from a strategic perspective. Organization theory concepts are not only the foundation for understanding organizations, but also the basis for managing them effectively.

*Organizational Theory: A Strategic Perspective* is distinguished from other texts by two different features, both designed to facilitate the goal of making organization theory relevant to today's students. The first feature, Best Practices, identifies a modern, successful organization and discusses how it strategically manages some key concept of organizational theory. The second feature, Career Points, takes an important concept and relates it directly to what a student would be looking for in a full-time job. Both features are included in each chapter.

*Organizational Theory: A Strategic Perspective* also includes a number of discussions that distinguish it from other organizational theory texts. For example, Chapter 1 presents a brief summary of management history, highlighting its importance to the study and development of organization theory. This historical perspective serves as a backdrop for the discussion of many topics throughout the text. As a second example, Chapter 10 opens with a discussion of the relevance of the SCANS (Secretary's Commission on Achieving Necessary Skills) report, which details the needed skills and abilities of knowledge workers in today's technologically challenging business environment. These two examples illustrate the practical relevance of the text and the field. Reviewing management history reinforces the practical origin of organizational theory, and understanding the SCANS report underscores the relevance of certain skills and abilities if one is to be successful in a modern organization.

## Organization of the Book

The book has two major sections: text and cases. The text chapters are organized within the first five parts:

1. Introduction
2. Strategic Management
3. Internal Context of Organizations
4. Managing Organizational Processes
5. Future Challenges

Integrative cases are included in Part 6. Seven cases are featured, related to a variety of organizational theory concepts, such as culture, strategy, design, structure, and change. The cases include small and large, as well as for-profit and not-for-profit, organizations.

Other features of *Organizational Theory: A Strategic Perspective* include end-of-chapter quizzes, discussion questions, a glossary of terms and their definitions, and illustrations.

## Online and Print

*Organizational Theory: A Strategic Perspective* is available online as well as in print. The online version demonstrates how the interactive media components of the text enhance presentation and understanding. For example,

- Interactive chapter quizzes test your knowledge of various topics and provide immediate feedback.

- Clickable glossary terms provide immediate definitions of key concepts.

- Highlighting capabilities allow students to emphasize main ideas. They can also add personal notes in the margin.

- The search function allows students to quickly locate discussions of specific topics throughout the text.

- An interactive study guide at the end of each chapter provides tools for learning, such as interactive key-term matching and the ability to review customized content in one place.

Students may choose to use just the online version of the text, or both the online and print versions together. This gives them the flexibility to choose which combination of resources works best for them. To assist those who use the online and print versions together, the primary heads and subheads in each chapter are numbered the same. For example, the first primary head in Chapter 1 is labeled 1-1, the second primary head in this chapter is labeled 1-2, and so on.

The subheads build from the designation of their corresponding primary head: 1-1a, 1-1b, etc. This numbering system is designed to make moving between the online and print versions as seamless as possible.

Finally, next to a number of figures in the print version of the text, you will see an icon similar to the one below. This icon indicates that these figures in the online version of the text are interactive in a way that applies, illustrates, or reinforces the concept.

## Cases

Seven comprehensive cases are included in Part 6. Each case presents an overview of an organization, some for-profit and some not-for-profit, and details a specific situation it is facing. Students are encouraged to analyze the case studies based only on the information provided. The best way to learn how to deal with organizational problems and opportunities is to analyze a real organization and develop a list of alternative courses of action based on the information provided. Searching the Internet or reading articles about the organizations after the fact proves you can do research, but it does not improve decision-making skills.

## Supplements

Atomic Dog is pleased to offer a robust suite of supplemental materials for instructors using its textbooks. These ancillaries include a *Test Bank, PowerPoint® Slides,* and an *Instructor's Manual.*

The *Test Bank* for this book includes eighty questions in a wide range of difficulty levels for each chapter. The *Test Bank* offers not only the correct answer for each question, but also a rationale or explanation

for the correct answer and a reference—the location in the chapter where materials addressing the question content can be found.

A full set of *PowerPoint® Slides* is available for this text. This is designed to provide instructors with comprehensive visual aids for each chapter in the book. These slides include outlines of each chapter, highlighting important terms, concepts, and discussion points.

The *Instructor's Manual* for this book offers suggested syllabi for 10- and 14-week terms; learning objectives; lecture outlines and notes which correspond with the *PowerPoint Slides;* key terms; answers to the end-of-chapter review quizzes; critical thinking exercises; recommendations for multi-media resources such as films and websites; and teaching notes for the cases.

## Acknowledgments

### Case Authors

| | |
|---|---|
| *Walton Arts Center: Act 2* | John Todd<br>Donald D. White |
| *AstroTech Fuel Systems* | H. Richard Eisenbeis<br>Sue Hanks<br>Phil Sheehan |
| *I'm from the Government—and I'm Here to Help You* | Karl Borden<br>Jim Cooper |
| *AAA Construction: A Family Business in Crisis* | Donald L. Lester |
| *Kerrie's Challenge: Leading an Unpopular Change* | Kathleen Gurley<br>Assad Tavakoli |
| *The Zone Reorganization: Developing a Strategy for Managing Change* | Stuart Rosenberg |
| *Murata Chemicals* | Jeff Hicks<br>Padmakumar Nair<br>Celeste P. M. Wilderom |

### Reviewers

The authors would like to thank several reviewers for their suggestions and comments:

M. Suzanne Clinton, Cameron University

Hoyt Hayes, Columbia College

Jon Kalinowski, Minnesota State University

Richard J. Martinez, Baylor University

Mark W. Bestoso, Penn State Erie–The Behrend College

Lisa A. Burke, Louisiana State University–Shreveport

# About the Authors

## Donald L. Lester

Dr. Donald L. Lester is an Associate Professor of Management at Middle Tennessee State University. He was formerly the Chair of the Center for Entrepreneurial and Family Business Studies at Arkansas State University and Dean of the McAfee School of Business Administration at Union University in Jackson, Tennessee.

Dr. Lester's research interests include organizational theory topics such as organizational life cycle and generic strategies. He has published articles in several academic journals, currently serves on the editorial board of the *Journal of Management Development*, and has been a consultant to several organizations, including FedEx.

Dr. Lester earned B.S.E., M.B.A., and Ph.D. degrees from the University of Memphis.

## John A. Parnell

John A. Parnell presently serves as the William Henry Belk Distinguished Professor in Management at the University of North Carolina at Pembroke. He is the author of more than 150 basic and applied research articles, published presentations, and cases in strategic management and related areas. He earned B.S.B.A., M.B.A., and M.A. (adult education) degrees from East Carolina University, an Ed.D. from Campbell University, and his Ph.D. in strategic management from the University of Memphis.

Dr. Parnell's present research interests include such issues as competitive strategy, organizational culture, and strategic philosophy. Dr. Parnell was the recipient of a Fulbright Research Award in Egypt, and he has also lectured in a number of countries, including extensive recent involvement in China and Mexico.

# Introduction

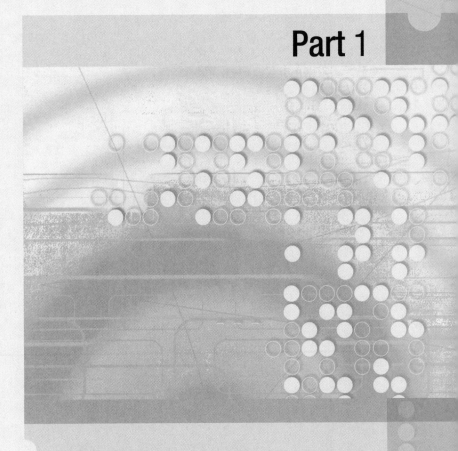

**1** Foundations of Organization Theory

# Foundations of Organization Theory

## Chapter Outline

## Key Terms

above-average returns

centralization

closed system

context

decentralization

formalization

hierarchy of authority

hypercompetitive environment

inputs

open systems

organizational culture

organizational structure

organizations

outputs

personnel ratios

professionalism

resource-based view

scientific management

specialization

subsystems

sustainable competitive advantage

**organizations** entities that gather people together into formal groups, providing the necessary structure, context, and culture to pursue common goals

**hypercompetitive environment** an environment that is global in nature, extremely competitive in terms of innovation, quality, and price, and fertile ground for alliances between competitors in order to amass large amounts of capital

**resource-based view** firms must base an evaluation of competitive strengths on their collection and use of valuable, rare, inimitable, and nonsubstitutable resources and strive to convert those resources into a sustainable competitive advantage

**sustainable competitive advantage** situation when a firm's strategy is unduplicated by competitors, allowing it to enjoy strategic benefits over an extended period of time

**above-average returns** returns on investment that are much higher than the average for the industry

**Organizations** gather people together into formal entities, providing the necessary structure, context, and culture to pursue common goals. They engage in business for profit (United Airlines), charitable pursuits (the United Way), governing (the United States), health care (United Healthcare), and many other worthy aspirations. Organizations are both needed and resented by their members in that they are useful as engines of progress, but are sometimes impediments to innovation and speed.

Organizations must operate in environments, some of which are stable, while others are more dynamic. The **hypercompetitive environment** in which many organizations find themselves today requires a strategic approach to management. Hypercompetition for organizations means an environment that is global in nature, extremely competitive in terms of innovation, quality, and price, and fertile ground for alliances between competitors in order to amass large amounts of capital.[1] Consider, for example, the cellular phone business. Cellular phones have gone global after saturating the market in Europe and the United States, moving into India, China, and other developed and emerging areas of the globe. Competition between service providers like Sprint and Verizon is fierce, and customers continue to demand new features, forcing rivals like Motorola and Nokia to innovate at breakneck speeds.

In the nonprofit arena, one of the most competitive environments is that of private higher education. Although not normally referred to as a global endeavor, the need for internationally diverse student populations requires private colleges to recruit foreign students and provide international exchange programs for their domestic students. And, while tuitions are rising fast, so is the number of available scholarships. The competition for resources has led to professional fund-raising, international recruiting programs, and millions of dollars spent annually on image and public relations issues by private colleges and universities.

In every business industry and nonprofit sector, competition for resources is at a zenith. According to a popular perspective, **resource-based view,**[2] firms must evaluate their base of resources and strive to convert those resources into a **sustainable competitive advantage.** This sustainable competitive advantage occurs when a firm creates a strategy that its competitors cannot duplicate, providing it strategic benefits over an extended period of time. The goal is to earn **above-average returns,**[3] that is, returns that are higher than the average for the industry. Chapter 2 provides a thorough discussion of the strategic management of organizations.

This chapter lays the foundation for the study of organizations. An understanding of how organizations work is necessary for their strategic management, their competitive sustainability, and their ability to earn above-average returns. The primary components of organizations are introduced, including their nature, their need for

Telecommunications resources help bring the global market into reach.

structure, and the importance of their design. A brief history of organization theory is presented for a clearer picture of the background information necessary to understand today's organizational challenges. Chapter 3 is devoted to understanding the external environment because strategically managing organizations requires a focus on the internal and external environments.

# 1-1 The Nature of Organizations

Organizations are constantly interacting with their environments, creating a need for extensive information. This interaction has led researchers to compare organizations to the biological concept of **open systems.** Just as organisms must interact with the elements of nature, including plants and other organisms, organizations must interact with the elements of their environments.[4] This environmental interaction involves various stakeholders that directly or indirectly benefit from the organization's operations, resources that must be garnered from the external environment, and the constant opportunities and threats that the environment produces.

The opposite of an open system is a **closed system,** where no interaction with other entities would be necessary. While no actual closed system is to be found in today's environment, some managers approach the operation of their organization as if it existed in a closed system. They do this by ignoring the environment's impact, focusing solely on improving internal operations. The advantage to this approach is that managers do not have to be concerned with environmental changes that might lead to lower sales, a lack of adequate resources, or some severe new governmental regulation. Unfortunately, strategic managers have found this approach to be unrealistic. Even organizations that prefer a very cost-efficient strategy that produces outputs at the lowest possible cost goods have found that ignoring the environment at best puts a firm at a competitive disadvantage and can, at worst, put it out of business.

To locate an example of ignoring the external environment we need look no further than the American automobile industry. During the energy crisis of 1973, gasoline was in short supply and relatively expensive compared to just a year or so earlier. Foreign automobile manufacturers took advantage of this development and gained valuable market share from American manufacturers who were slow to redesign their large, gas-guzzling models. General Motors, Ford, and Chrysler have never regained that lost market share.[5]

A business model that can be applied to almost any organization is depicted in Figure 1-1. This demonstrates a simple perspective of systems theory. The model of business is that inputs are transformed, or converted into outputs. These **inputs** are resources gathered from the open environment and are distributed back to that environment once they are turned into outputs. **Outputs** are the products and services that are produced through the value-added transformation process. Electronic Arts is an example of a company that fits this model. The thirtieth fastest growing business in America in 2004, Electronic Arts takes inputs such as creative knowledge, icons from the popular culture, and hardware and transforms them into exciting and realistic video games that are sold around the world.[6] Electronic Arts and its CEO, Larry Probst, have seen phenomenal growth as they negotiate licenses for movies that roll out several sequels (e.g., the Harry Potter series) and sports that continue to grow and attract more and more fans (Madden NFL).

The input → transformation → output model is simply demonstrated, but it is quite complicated for most modern organizations. There is tremendous competition

**open systems**  systems in which organizations interact with the elements of their environments

**closed system**  system in which organizations have no interaction with other entities

**inputs**  resources gathered from the open environment

**outputs**  the products and services that are produced through the value-added transformation process

**Figure 1-1**
*A Business System Model*

Box 1-1

### Career Point

#### The Business System Model

Innovation and speed are considered distinctive competencies of today's organizations that help set a firm apart from its competition. One way to promote and develop innovative activity within the context of a business is to understand creativity. Many people commonly refer to this trait as the ability to "think outside the box."

Figure 1-1 illustrates the business systems model, consisting of inputs, the transformation process, and outputs. Think of each of these three parts as important processes "boxes" of any organization. This is done to emphasize the idea of creativity, or thinking outside the box. Being able to step back from a problem to develop an innovative solution requires that you use mental imaging to picture yourself outside your firm's regular input-transformation-output processes in order to see the situation in an entirely different light. For example, suppose you were charged with the task of inventing a new soft drink. The market is full of different kinds of sodas, or carbonated drinks, and you have to invent a new one that will be so different that it will steal market share from other drinks already being sold. This is what happened when Slice was invented. Product researchers took fruit juice and added it to a soft drink to create a fresh new product that could utilize much of the old transformation process but create a new and exciting product.[7]

If you can learn to see problems or opportunities for your business from an objective perspective that is not completely influenced by your existing processes, you will be able to think outside the box. That is, you will be able to develop creative ways to make things happen that are not bound by existing technology or "the way we've always done it around here."

---

**subsystems** functional departments or divisions that are responsible for specific performance objectives of the organization

for inputs for many industries, requiring a subsystem of procurement specialists and human resource recruiters to be very knowledgeable of the organization's needs. As for the transformation process, several operational and support subsystems must operate in harmony and efficiency in today's environment. This transformation process must add value to the input in producing an output. Once outputs are produced and sent back into the environment as products or services, sales and marketing personnel function as another subsystem responsible for attracting market share. **Subsystems, therefore, are functional departments or divisions that are responsible for specific performance objectives of the organization.** The Career Point discussion (Box 1-1) suggests an innovative way of looking at the business system model.

## 1-2 Structure and Design of Organizations

**organizational structure** the formal establishment of reporting relationships, management responsibilities, and coordination of work

The work organizations are designed to do requires some formal and some informal structure or framework. **Organizational structure** refers to the formal establishment of reporting relationships, management responsibilities, and coordination of work. The activities of people working within organizations are most effective when they are coordinated and linked to the external environment. Proper coordination and cooperation are needed if organizational goals are to be met. Goal-setting and effectiveness are examined in Chapter 4.

### 1-2a Structural Dimensions of Organizations

**centralization** an organizational decision-making process whereby most substantial decisions are made by managers at higher levels within the organization

All organizations have various structural dimensions that describe their internal operational framework.[8] A brief description of the most common structural dimensions is provided below.

**decentralization** an organizational decision-making process whereby most decisions are made at the lowest possible levels in the organization

1.  **Centralization** and **decentralization**—Decisions of any importance are made at what level? Centralization occurs when decisions tend to be made at higher levels; decentralization occurs when they tend to be made at all levels of the organization.

2. **Hierarchy of authority**—What are the reporting relationships and how much span of control does any one manager have? Hierarchical organizations include those such as General Motors, a firm with 23 levels of hierarchy, constituting what might be referred to as a tall organizational structure.

3. **Formalization**—To what extent are decisions and procedures driven by established rules and policies? As will be detailed in Chapter 6, as organizations grow and develop, they tend to become more formal in their operational approach, promoting standardization and consistency. For example, a large national bank is very rule-driven to protect the interests of its customers and to ensure compliance with regulatory agencies. A small dry-cleaning operation, however, would rely on its employees' knowledge of the business rather than specific, written procedure manuals.

4. **Specialization**—How specific are job descriptions? The more limited in focus and content jobs are in an organization the more extensive the specialization. Again, at the dry-cleaners, employees may perform a variety of duties that are cross-functional in nature due to the lack of specialization. Conversely, at General Motors an employee's only task may be to install bumpers, just one of many tasks required to produce a new automobile.

Two other structural dimensions, professionalism and personnel ratios, have become more relevant in recent years. **Professionalism** refers to the amount of formal education and training needed by employees to do their jobs. It is high when several years of higher education are needed, as they are in a law firm. It is low when education is not really a factor in the hiring process, such as at a plant and garden nursery. **Personnel ratios** measure the percentage of people in different areas of the firm, such as administration, staff, and operations. The total number of employees is divided into the number of people in a certain area of the firm to arrive at the personnel ratio. For example, an organization with 1,000 employees where 50 are in administrative positions would have an administrative personnel ratio of 5% (50 ÷ 1000 = .05, or 5%). A smaller organization with 100 employees where 10 were involved in administration would have an administrative personnel ratio of 10% (10 ÷ 100 = .10, or 10%). This example demonstrates a bureaucratic concept that administrative ratios actually get smaller as organizations become larger. However, support staff and clerical ratios tend to develop in an opposite manner, growing larger as firms expand.

The Best Practices focus, Paradigm Solutions (Box 1-2), looks at a company trying to remain flexible and innovative while experiencing growth and the need for more formalization.

## 1-2b Context of Organizations

How organizations are structured varies a great deal depending on several issues of **context.** Context refers to the nature of the internal environment driving the organization and the external environment impacting the organization.[9] There is a natural overlap between both sets of factors. The internal factors of context include an organization's technology, size, culture, strategy, and goals. These factors interact with, impact upon, and are affected by the external environment in which a firm operates.

*Technology* describes the ways that organizations find to do something. It may include the use of machinery and equipment, production materials, computers, or skills and techniques necessary to take inputs and transform them into outputs. Some businesses need little technology due to the labor-intensive nature of their production process. A craftsman who makes decorative wooden objects utilizes raw materials such as wood, glue, nails, and so forth and combines those inputs with a specific knowledge of how to best perform the art of woodcarving. It is the craftsman's talent that converts the inputs into decorative outputs. Others, such as FedEx, depend on information technology and machines for their existence. For example, customers

**hierarchy of authority** the reporting relationships and the span of control of organizational members

**formalization** the extent that decisions and procedures are driven by established rules and policies

**specialization** describes how organizational tasks are divided; the more narrow the task, the more specialized the job

**professionalism** the amount of formal education and training needed by employees to do their jobs

**personnel ratios** measures of the percentage of people in different areas of the firm, such as administration, support staff, and operations

**context** the nature of the internal environment driving the organization and the external environment impacting the organization

## Box 1-2

utilize online accounts to ship and track packages through sophisticated technology designed and implemented by FedEx. The technology is not only integral to the operation of the company, but it is integrated with the customer's business, making FedEx a partner with its customers.

Organizational *size* refers simply to how large and how far-reaching are its operations. A small one- or two-person firm can only perform so much work due to its limited manpower. A large, multinational corporation, however, might have business dealings in more than 100 different countries, employing hundreds of thousands of people. Wal-Mart, the largest for-profit firm in the world, has more than 5,000 stores and more than 1.4 million employees.[11]

**organizational culture**
shared values and patterns of beliefs that are accepted and practiced by members of a particular organization

**Organizational culture** refers to the shared values and patterns of belief and behavior that are accepted and practiced by members of a particular organization. Other identifying traits of culture include rites, rituals, ceremonies, and values exhibited by the organization. Culture exists in groups, and it is developed so that they may cope with external adaptation and internal integration.[12]

*Strategy* and *goals* are difficult to separate since strategy is top management's plan on how its goals are going to be accomplished. Resource-based view, mentioned in the introduction to this chapter, proposes that rare and inimitable resources from the environment help build a sustainable competitive advantage that eventually earns a company above-average returns. However, obtaining such resources is very difficult. The strategy selected by an organization must have a good fit with the resources and capabilities it is able to obtain if its goals are to be accomplished.[13]

Several different types of organizational structure will be discussed in this book. From the simple structure with only one or two layers of management to the complex structure of a multinational firm, organizing assets and operations is essential. Some common forms of organization include functional structure, matrix structure, and divisional structure. Each will be discussed in detail in Chapter 5.

## 1-3 The Development of Organization Theory

Organization theory is a foundational field of study that, at one time or another, has included such diverse disciplines as strategy, human resource management, organizational behavior, and industrial engineering.[14] The development of several of these disciplines can be traced to early organizational theorists and management researchers. What really propelled the study of organizations was the appearance in the late 1800s and early 1900s of the large corporation, or big business.

Once the transportation systems of the world became sophisticated enough for large-scale commerce, large organizations came into being. Before the development of intercontinental railroads and the steam engine, very large organizations were not really needed. It was only when firms could do business internationally and consumers and goods could travel freely by automobile, train, or steamship that larger organizations became necessary. Another facilitator of the emergence of these large organizations was the development of industrial technologies in various industries that led to the realization of economies of scale, as per-unit costs of products and services were lowered over time as the volume of production increased.

As large organizations such as Standard Oil and Carnegie began to mature, problems that had to be addressed emerged. When large groups of people are thrown together in pursuit of commerce, there is always room for improvement. Some workers were exploited by the so-called "robber barons" who were amassing fortunes at the expense of women and children workers. Researchers in the areas of sociology and economics began to investigate this phenomenon of the new industrial giant, searching for ways to improve working conditions. In the more popular literature, Charles Dickens portrayed the poverty and ignorance that accompanied horrible working conditions in the factories of England. Karl Marx and Friedrich Engels promoted violence as a way for oppressed workers to rise up for their rights and overcome the chains of their owners/managers.

Yet, others began to preach and model efficiency,[15] a movement that has been described as **scientific management.** Scientific management was a method of discovering the best, most efficient way to perform tasks. Frederick Taylor tirelessly experimented with methods of production that were efficient and effective, allowing for the most output per person in every job. Taylor's work was supported and expanded by Frank and Lillian Gilbreth[16] and others.[17]

**scientific management**
a method of discovering the right way to perform tasks

The more researchers became interested in studying organizations, the greater the need became for a theory of management because organizations are made up of people, and people need goals, objectives, and training. Henri Fayol[18] proposed a set of guiding principles for managing an organization. Fayol, a French engineer who was managing director of a coal-mining and iron foundry combine, felt that all organizations needed managers and that people could learn the skill of management. His guiding management principles, which received much attention, were:

1.  Division of work—specialization of labor
2.  Authority—the right to give orders or to have power over others
3.  Discipline—workers should be respectful and obedient
4.  Unity of command—each employee should have only one supervisor
5.  Unity of direction—all members of a group work toward the same objective
6.  Subordination of individual interests to the general interest—individual interests were subordinate to the greater good of the organization
7.  Remuneration—methods of payment should be specified
8.  Centralization—the degree of centralization should vary depending on the circumstances of the organization
9.  Scalar chain or line of authority—there should be an actual chain of command from top to bottom
10. Order—a place for everything and everything in its place
11. Equity—practice kindliness and justice
12. Stability of tenure of personnel—orderly personnel planning
13. Initiative—employees should display energy for their jobs
14. Espirit de corps—build harmony and unity within the organization

Fayol was well respected as a business person and a thinker who initiated much discussion, research, and attention to the concept of management principles.[19]

Later, Mary Parker Follett suggested that goals for workers and employers should be compatible.[20] Her ideas proposed an integration of goals, rather than compromise or domination, because those two solutions only created further strife. Among other things, Follett also endorsed the concept of obeying the law of the situation and not relying simply on the power over someone or something. Whatever is required by the situation at hand should be the determinant of who gives the orders, not who has power over someone else.

Writing to a somewhat broader audience, Chester Barnard[21] advocated basing organizational research in social psychology, giving it a scientific background. Organizations were systems of coordinated human actions with three common elements: the willingness to cooperate, a common purpose, and communication. People willing to cooperate must forgo their own personal desires to pursue the organization's goals, they must share a common purpose in hopes of fulfilling their individual needs, and this must be facilitated through open and direct channels of communication.

One other organizational theorist who must be mentioned is Max Weber, the German sociologist. Weber wrote about the need for a rational basis for the organization and its management. His focus was on systematically and efficiently managing a large undertaking. He named this system the *bureaucracy.* Weber's bureaucracy included such elements as division of labor, hierarchy of authority, the need for formal qualifications, and an adherence to strict rules and controls.[22]

The real momentum for organizational research, however, was launched after World War II. Formal degree programs in business across America required academic instructors who, in turn, looked to organizations and management as legitimate research topics, eventually leading to a science of management, a notion strongly supported by Herbert Simon,[23] a Nobel laureate and pioneer in the field of organization theory. So, the teaching of organizations led to the study of organizations, which led to the formal development of organization theory.[24]

During the 1950s and early 1960s, subsets of organizational theory and management emerged, particularly organizational behavior and strategic management.[25] Organizational behavior is a discipline that studies how people respond to and act in organizations.[26] As a field of study, organizational behavior draws concepts from psychology, sociology, social psychology, and anthropology.

Strategic management originated after the Gordon-Howell report on business school curricula, published in 1959, recommended a capstone course for graduating business students that would integrate what they had learned in the various disciplines they had studied during their college careers.[27] This capstone course was called *business policy,* and from this beginning the course gradually expanded to become a strategic approach to managing organizations. Eventually, the course and the field became known as *strategic management.* As you can see, the study of management and organizations has progressed considerably since Fayol's principles were first outlined at the beginning of the twentieth century.

These fields provided specialization areas for research, journal outlets for topical areas, and more courses for the business curriculums. All organizations, be they for-profit or not-for-profit, benefit from the ongoing research into organizational behavior, strategic management, and organizational theory—research that is performed by academics and practitioners alike. The goal is to make organizations more productive and managers better at their jobs.[28]

# 1-4 Why Study Organizations?

The value of studying organizations is that through research, organizational theorists can provide theory, suggestions, and practical guidelines for current and future organizational managers. If the history of organizational study has proven anything, it is that both practitioners and researchers can learn from the past mistakes and successes of organizations.

Organizations are complicated entities because they involve people and systems, machinery and information, all of which must interact compatibly. The reason organizational theory is important to students is that they will most likely spend the rest of their lives involved in one or more organizations. For example, you are now part of a school of some sort, probably a college or university; you will become active in a business organization upon graduation (indeed, many of you already are); you have interests that lead to participation in other types of organizations, such as churches, charities, and clubs; and you may one day find yourself in another type of organization known as a retirement home. Organizations in an open society are unavoidable. If we are to be active participants in so many organizations, we should hope that they are properly managed and structured. This book strives to help its readers learn how to make organizations better.

# 1-5 The Organization of the Book

The book has been divided into six parts and twelve chapters. Following this introductory chapter, Part II focuses on strategic management. After a foundational look at strategic management in Chapter 2, all of Chapter 3 is devoted to managing the external environment. These two chapters then lead to the discussion of goals and effectiveness that comprises Chapter 4 (see Figure 1-2).

Part III discusses the internal context of organizations. All internal discussions begin with structure, the focus of Chapter 5. Structure and design lead to the organization life cycle and how organizations grow, which is discussed in Chapter 6. The internal section concludes with a discussion of organizational culture and ethics, two topics at the forefront of today's corporate scandals at such firms as Enron, Global Crossing, WorldCom, and Arthur Andersen.[29]

Part IV examines how to manage organizational processes, beginning with a fundamental presentation regarding decision making, power, and politics in Chapter 8. Next, Chapter 9 covers the topic of innovation, one of the key capabilities of today's leading businesses, and organizational change, something experienced by each and every organization during its history. Chapter 10 concludes this section with a look at technology, a driving force in every organization.

What future challenges lie ahead is the subject of Part V. How organizations learn and how they put that knowledge to work as a competitive advantage is the subject of Chapter 11. Chapter 12 concludes the text by delving into the fast-paced dynamics of our global environment, one that must be faced by large and small organizations alike.

As Figure 1-2 reflects, each section of the book tends to build on the last. We conclude with a group of cases that we believe demonstrates the need for practical, relevant research in organizational theory.

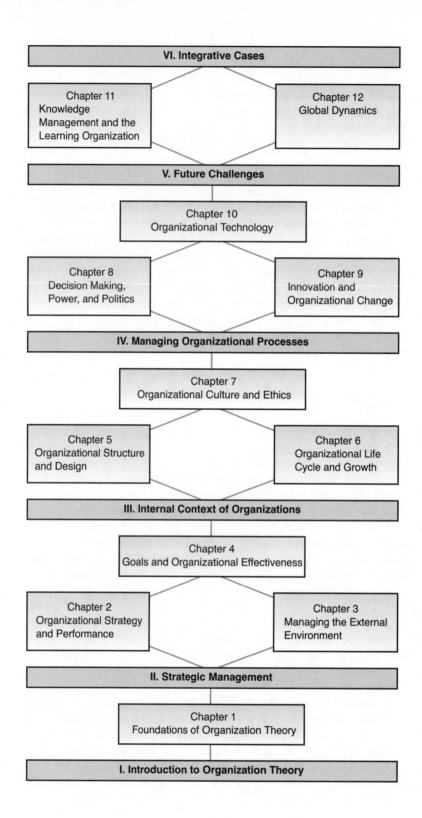

**Figure 1-2**
*Organization of the Book*

## Summary

Organizations gather people together into formal entities, providing the necessary structure, context, and culture to pursue common goals. Organizations are both needed and resented by their members in that they are useful as engines of progress, but are sometimes impediments to innovation and speed. They are open systems, constantly interacting with their external environments.

The work organizations are designed to do requires structure, which is the establishment of reporting relation-ships, management responsibilities, and implementation of strategy. How organizations are structured varies a great deal, depending on several issues of context. The internal factors of context include an organization's goals, strategy, culture, size, and technology.

The teaching of organizations in our colleges and universities led to the study of organizations, which led to the formal development of organization theory.

## Review Questions and Exercises

1. Why does modern society need organizations?

2. What is an example of a business organization that has achieved a sustainable competitive advantage and continues to earn above-average returns?

3. Using Figure 1-1, describe the actual business systems model of a business with which you are familiar. What are their inputs, transformation processes, and outputs?

4. Explain why smaller firms are less formalized and more centralized, while large firms are more formalized and less centralized.

5. What major inventions or developments in history facilitated the emergence of large, even multinational, organizations?

6. Select two of Fayol's guiding principles and explain why they are still very relevant today.

## Quiz

1. One approach to strategic management theory today is resource-based view.
   **True or False**

2. Above-average returns are earned by the lower performing firms in an industry.
   **True or False**

3. An open system is where organizations have no interaction with other entities in their external environment.
   **True or False**

4. A subsystem is a functional department or division responsible for specific performance objectives of the organization.
   **True or False**

5. Organizations that operate without very many policies and procedures are said to be formalized.
   **True or False**

6. Technology describes the set of tools, machines, computers, and people skills needed to transform raw inputs into valuable outputs.
   **True or False**

7. Organizations provide the necessary structure, context, and _____ for the pursuit of common goals.
   a. competition
   b. criticism
   c. culture
   d. conflict

8. The business system model includes all of the following, except
   a. entrepreneurship.
   b. outputs.
   c. transformation processes.
   d. inputs.

9. Which of the following terms describes the situation when most decisions in an organization are made at the highest level?
   a. formalization
   b. centralization
   c. decentralization
   d. empowerment

10. Internal factors of context include all of the following, except
    a. technology.
    b. size.
    c. culture.
    d. suppliers.

11. Which of Fayol's guiding principles refers to building harmony and unity within an organization?
    a. scalar chain of authority
    b. espirit de corps
    c. centralization
    d. authority

12. Two fields of management have emerged from the discipline of organization theory. They are
    a. psychology and anthropology.
    b. sociology and social psychology.
    c. organizational behavior and strategic management.
    d. economics and political science.

## Endnotes

1. R. D'Aveni, "Coping with Hypercompetition: Utilizing the New 7S's Framework," *Academy of Management Executive* 9, no. 3 (1995): 46-54.

2. J. Barney, "Firm Resources and Sustained Competitive Advantage," *Journal of Management* 17, no. 1 (1991): 99-120.

3. Barney, 1991.

4. L. von Bertalanffy, General Systems Theory (New York: Braziller, 1968).

5. A. Taylor, "U.S. Cars Come Back," *Fortune* 126, no. 11 (1992): 52-85. Also, see A. Taylor, "Why Toyota Keeps Getting Better and Better and Better, *Fortune* 122, no. 13 (1990): 66-79.

6. E. Florian, "Six Lessons from the Fast Lane," *Fortune* 150, no. 5 (2004): 146-156.

7. D. Kuratko and R. Hodgetts, *Entrepreneurship: Theory, Process, Practice* (Mason, OH: Thomson-Southwestern, 2004), 143.

8. R. Hall, *Organizations: Structures, Processes, and Outcomes* (Englewood Cliffs, NJ: Prentice-Hall, 1991).

9. D. Kuratko and R. Hodgetts, *Entrepreneurship: A Contemporary Approach*, 5th ed. (Orlando, FL: Harcourt College Publishers, 2001).

10. D. Pugh, "The Measurement of Organizational Structures: Does Context Determine Form?" *Organizational Dynamics* Spring (1973): 19-34.

11. J. Revel, "The Year of the Comeback," *Fortune* 149, no. 7 (2004): 289-435.

12. E. Schein, "Coming to a New Awareness of Organizational Culture," *Sloan Management Review*, Winter (1984): 3-16.

13. N. Venkataman and J. Camillus, "Exploring the Concept of 'Fit' in Strategic Management," *Academy of Management Review* 9, no. 3 (1984): 513-525.

14. H. Simon, "Comments on the Theory of Organizations," *American Political Review* 46 (1952): 1130-1139.

15. F. Taylor, *The Principles of Scientific Management* (New York: Harper & Row, 1911).

16. F. Gilbreth, *Primer of Scientific Management* (New York: Van Nostrand Reinhold Co., 1912); F. Gilbreth and L. Gilbreth, *Applied Motion Study* (New York: Sturgis and Walton Co., 1917).

17. J. Merkle, *Management and Ideology: The Legacy of the International Scientific Management Movement* (Berkeley: University of California Press, 1980).

18. H. Fayol, *General and Industrial Management*, trans. Constance Storrs (London: Sir Isaac Pitman and Sons, 1949).

19. D. Wren, *The Evolution of Management Thought* (New York: John Wiley & Sons, Inc., 1987), 183-184.

20. M. Parker Follett, *Creative Experience* (London: Longmans, Green and Company, 1924).

21. C. Barnard, *Organization and Management* (Cambridge, MA: Harvard University Press, 1948).

22. A. Henderson and T. Parsons, *Max Weber: The Theory of Social and Economic Organization* (New York: The Free Press, 1947).

23. H. Simon, "Comments on the Theory of Organizations," *American Political Science Review* 46 (1952): 1130-1139.

24. W. Starbuck, "Shouldn't Organization Theory Emerge from Adolescence?" *Organization* 10, no. 3 (2003): 439-452.

25. Starbuck, 2003.

26. J. George and G. Jones, *Understanding and Managing Organizational Behavior* (Reading, MA: Addison-Wesley, 1999), 3.

27. R. Gordon and J. Howell, *Higher Education for Business* (New York: Columbia University Press, 1959).

28. Starbuck, 2003.

29. B. McLean, "Why Enron Went Bust," *Fortune* 144, no. 13 (2001): 58-68.

# Strategic Management

## Part 2

# Organizational Strategy and Performance

**Chapter 2**

## Chapter Outline

## Key Terms

business-level strategy

business unit

competitive advantage

contingency theory

core competencies

corporate profile

corporate restructuring

corporate-level strategy

differentiation strategy

distinctive competence

divestment

downsizing

external growth

first-mover advantages

focus

functional strategies

generic strategies

growth strategy

industrial organization (IO)

industry

intended strategy

internal growth

liquidation

low-cost strategy

low-cost–differentiation strategy

realized strategy

related diversification

retrenchment strategy

stability strategy

strategic alliances

strategic group

strategic management process

strategy

synergy

turnaround

unrelated diversification

Organizations are most likely to succeed when their activities are integrated toward a common purpose. This does not occur automatically; it requires substantial fore-thought and planning. In other words, it requires a strategy. This chapter discusses the strategic planning process, as well as strategic alternatives available for each organization. Although the concepts presented herein have been developed with profit-seeking firms in mind, they can be equally applicable to public and private not-for-profit organizations that must compete in some way with other organizations or agencies.

**strategy**  top management's plans to attain outcomes consistent with the organization's mission and goals

The concept of an organizational strategy encapsulates the notion of planning for success. Specifically, a **strategy** refers to top management's plans to develop and sustain a competitive advantage so that the organization's mission is fulfilled. A strategy provides direction for the organization and can be identified by examining a pattern of decisions made by an organization's top managers. It is most likely to be effective when it is compatible with the organization's structure and culture—concepts that will be developed later in the text. Although strategy is discussed before structure and culture, all three dimensions are tightly intertwined.

A successful strategy is marked by four key distinctions. First, it does not simply emerge, but rather it is developed after top managers systematically evaluate both the organization's resources and external factors that can affect performance. Second, it is long term and future oriented—usually several years to a decade or longer—but built on knowledge about the past and present. Third, it is distinctively opportunistic, always seeking to take advantage of favorable situations that occur outside the organization. Finally, strategic thinking involves choices. Win-win strategic decisions are often possible, but most involve some degree of trade-off between alternatives, at least in the short run.

## 2-1  The Strategic Management Process

Ideally, a strategy is developed as part of a conscious activity led by an organization's top managers. The **strategic management process** also includes top management's analysis of the environment in which the organization operates prior to formulating a strategy, as well as the plan for implementation and control of the strategy. This process can be summarized in six steps:[1]

**strategic management process**  the continuous process of determining the mission and goals of an organization within the context of its external environment and its internal strengths and weaknesses, formulating and implementing strategies, and exerting strategic control to ensure that the organization's strategies are successful in attaining its goals

1. *External Analysis:* Analyze the opportunities and threats or constraints that exist in the organization's external environment.

2. *Internal Analysis:* Analyze the organization's strengths and weaknesses in its internal environment.

3. *Mission and Direction:* Reassess the organization's mission and its goals in light of the external and internal analyses.

4. *Strategy Formulation:* Formulate strategies that build and sustain competitive advantage by matching the organization's strengths and weaknesses with the environment's opportunities and threats. Consider the fit between the strategy and other organizational dimensions, such as the structure and the prevailing culture.

5. *Strategy Implementation:* Implement the strategies that have been developed. Make adjustments to the organizational structure, if feasible and relevant.

6. *Strategic Control:* Evaluate organizational effectiveness and engage in strategic control activities when the strategies are not producing the desired outcomes.

Although this process is simple and straightforward, complexities in the environment complicate the process, especially between the time a strategy is formulated and the time it is actually implemented. Henry Mintzberg introduced two terms to help clarify the shift that often occurs during this period. An **intended strategy** reflects what management originally planned and may be realized just as

**intended strategy**  the original strategy top management plans and intends to implement

it was proposed, but the intended strategy and the **realized strategy,** what management actually implements, usually differ.[2] Hence, the original strategy may be realized with desirable or undesirable results, or it may be modified as changes in the firm or the environment become known.

The gap between the intended and realized strategies usually results from unforeseen environmental or organizational events, better information that was not available when the strategy was formulated, an improvement in top management's ability to assess its environment, or strategic responses from competitors. As such, this gap can be minimized if top managers assimilate and process information about the organization's environment more effectively. It is not uncommon for such a gap to exist, creating the need for constant strategic action if a firm is to stay on course. Instead of resisting modest strategic changes when new information is discovered, managers should search for new information and be willing to make such changes when necessary.

A thorough discussion of each step of the strategic management process is beyond the scope of this text. However, many of the concepts presented in the text relate to one or more of these phases. The remainder of this chapter is concerned primarily with the theories that influence the process and the content of corporate and competitive strategies available to organizations.

## 2-2 Theories of Strategy

The strategic management process has been influenced by a number of theories and perspectives. Three of these are summarized in Table 2-1 and are discussed in this section.

**Industrial organization (IO)** economics, a branch of microeconomics, emphasizes the influence of the industry environment upon the organization. IO emphasizes that an organization must adapt to influences exerted by its **industry**—the collection of competitors that offer similar products or services—to survive and prosper. Following this logic, organizational performance is primarily determined by the structure of the industry in which it competes. Industries with favorable structures offer the greatest opportunity for high organizational performance.

IO logic can be seen in Michael Porter's frequently cited "five forces" model, discussed in greater detail in Chapter 3. Porter's model identifies five structural elements that influence industry profitability: existing rivalry, threat of substitutes, threat of new entrants, bargaining power of buyers, and bargaining power of suppliers.[3] These factors collectively determine the potential for profits in a particular industry. The model assumes that organizations are likely to perform well when they operate in industries with attractive structures.

The concept of adaptation is central to the IO perspective. In essence, an organization's performance and ultimate survival depend on its ability to adapt to external

**realized strategy** the strategy top management actually implements

**industrial organization (IO)** a view based in microeconomic theory that states that a firm's profitability is most closely associated with industry structure

**industry** a group of competitors that produces similar products or services

| **TABLE 2-1** | Theoretical Perspectives on Firm Performance | |
| --- | --- | --- |
| **Theoretical Perspective** | **Primary Influence on Organizational Performance** | **How Perspective Fits into the Strategic Management Process** |
| Industrial organization (IO) theory | Structure of the industry | Step 1: External Analysis |
| Resource-based theory | Firm's unique combination of strategic resources | Step 2: Internal Analysis |
| Contingency theory | Fit between the firm and its external environment | Step 3: Strategy Formulation |

forces rather than attempt to influence or control them. Strategies, resources, and competencies are assumed to be fairly similar among competitors within a given industry. If one organization deviates from the industry norm and implements a new, successful strategy, others will rapidly mimic the higher-performing organization by purchasing the resources, competencies, or management talent that have made the leading firm so profitable. Hence, strategic managers should seek to understand the nature of the industry and formulate strategies that feed off the industry's characteristics.[4]

In contrast to the IO perspective, resource-based theory views performance primarily as a function of an organization's ability to acquire and utilize its resources.[5] Although environmental opportunities and threats are important, an organization's unique resources comprise the key variables that allow it to develop a **distinctive competence,** distinguishing itself from its rivals, and creating a competitive advantage. Resources include all of a firm's tangible and intangible assets, such as capital, equipment, employees, knowledge, and information.[6] In many respects, an organization's resources define its capabilities, as an organization with strong research and development may also possess the capability to develop successful new products. Ultimately, this can create value and lead to greater performance.

Not all resources are equally valuable. If resources are to be used for *sustainable* competitive advantage—an organization's ability to enjoy strategic benefits and outperform the industry norm over an extended period of time—those resources must be valuable, rare (i.e., not easily obtained by rivals), not easily imitated, and without strategically relevant substitutes.[7] In other words, the most desirable resources are ones that are utilized by an organization in a way that competitors cannot easily match. Valuable resources contribute significantly to the organization's effectiveness and efficiency, rare resources are possessed by only a few competitors, and imperfectly imitable resources cannot be fully duplicated by rivals.

**Contingency theory** emphasizes the interaction between the organization and its environment. Within this perspective, the *fit* between an organization and its environment is the central concern. In other words, a strategy is most likely to be successful when it is consistent with the organization's mission, its competitive environment, and its resources. In effect, contingency theory represents a *middle ground* perspective that views organizational performance as the joint outcome of environmental forces and the firm's strategic actions. On the one hand, firms can become proactive by choosing to operate in environments where opportunities and threats match the firms' strengths and weaknesses.[8] On the other hand, should the industry environment change in a way that is unfavorable to the firm, its top managers should consider leaving that industry and reallocating its resources to other, more favorable industries.

Contingency theory is applied when a strategy is formulated. Strategic managers consider internal resources in light of external opportunities and threats and develop strategies that reflect a fit between the two. Hence, an effective strategy is not merely a good idea, but it is a strategy that capitalizes on the particular resources controlled by an organization and the environment in which the organization operates. In other words, an effective strategy fits the organization.

As has been demonstrated, each of these three perspectives has merit and has been incorporated into the strategic management process. The industrial organization view is prominent within the industry analysis phase, resource-based theory applies directly to the internal analysis phase, and contingency theory is seen in the strategy formulation phase. Hence, multiple perspectives are critical to a holistic understanding of an organization's strategy and its relationship with performance.[9]

## 2-3 Strategy at the Corporate Level

The complex notion of organizational strategy can be examined from three perspectives: firm (also called corporate), business (also called competitive), and functional. The **corporate-level strategy** reflects the broad strategic approach top management formulates for the organization. The **business-level strategy** outlines the

**distinctive competence**
unique resources, skills, and capabilities that enable an organization to distinguish itself from its competitors and create a competitive advantage

**contingency theory**
a perspective that suggests that the most profitable firms are likely to be the ones that develop the best fit with their environments

**corporate-level strategy**
the broad strategy that top management formulates for the overall organization

**business-level strategy**
a strategy formulated for a business unit that identifies how it will compete with other businesses within its industry

competitive pattern for a **business unit**—an organizational entity with its own mission, set of competitors, and industry. Top managers craft competitive strategies for each business (unit) to attain and sustain **competitive advantage,** a state whereby its successful strategies cannot be easily duplicated by its competitors.[10] **Functional strategies** are created at each functional level (e.g., marketing, finance, production, etc.) to support the business and corporate strategies.

There are two steps involved in developing the corporate strategy. The first step is to assess the markets or industries in which the firm operates and the second is to determine the appropriate size of the organization. In the first step, top management at the corporate level defines the **corporate profile** by identifying the specific industry (or industries) in which the organization will operate. Three basic profiles are possible: operate in a single industry, operate in multiple related industries, or operate in multiple, unrelated industries.

An organization that operates in a single industry can benefit from the specialized knowledge that it develops from concentrating its efforts on one business area. This knowledge can help the firm improve product or service quality and become more efficient in its operations. McDonald's, for instance, constantly changes its product line, while maintaining a low per-unit cost of operations by concentrating exclusively on fast food. Wal-Mart benefits from expertise derived from concentration in the retailing industry. Although involved in other businesses as well, Anheuser-Busch limits its scope of operations primarily to brewing, from which it derives more than 80 percent of its revenues and profits.[11] Firms operating in a single industry are more susceptible to sharp downturns in business cycles, however.

An organization may operate in multiple related industries to reduce the uncertainty and risk associated with operating in a single industry. An organization may diversify by developing a new line of business, or an organization with large, successful businesses may acquire smaller competitors with complementary product or service lines, a process known as **related diversification.** In some instances, however, a smaller firm may acquire a larger one, as was the case when Kmart acquired Sears in 2004. Size, of course, can be defined in a number of ways, including total revenues, number of employees or locations, or the physical size of facilities.

The key to successful related diversification is the development of **synergy** among the related business units. Synergy occurs when the two previously separate organizations join to generate higher effectiveness and efficiency than each would have generated separately. When there are similarities in product or service lines, relationships in the distribution channels, or complementary managerial or technical expertise across business units, synergy is most likely to result.

An organization may choose to operate in unrelated industries because its managers wish to reduce risk by spreading resources across several markets, thereby pursuing **unrelated diversification** by acquiring businesses not related to its core domain. Unlike related diversification, unrelated diversification is not about synergy. Unrelated diversification is pursued primarily to reduce risks that are associated with an organization that operates in only one area of business. Unrelated diversification, however, can make it more difficult for managers to stay abreast of market and technological changes in the various industries. In addition, they may unknowingly shift attention away from the organization's primary business in favor of less critical ones.

The second step involved in developing the corporate strategy is associated with the extent to which an organization seeks to increase its size. Simply stated, an organization may attempt to increase its size significantly, remain about the same size, or become smaller. These three possibilities are seen in three corporate strategies—growth, stability, and retrenchment (i.e., become smaller)—each of which is discussed in greater detail in Sections 2-3a, 2-3b, and 2-3c.

## 2-3a Growth Strategy

The **growth strategy** seeks to significantly increase an organization's revenues or market share. Growth may be attained in a variety of ways. **Internal growth** is

**business unit** an organizational entity with its own unique mission, set of competitors, and industry

**competitive advantage** a state whereby a business unit's successful strategies cannot be easily duplicated by its competitors

**functional strategies** strategies created at functional levels (e.g., marketing, finance, production, etc.) to support the business and corporate strategies

**corporate profile** identification of the industry(ies) in which a firm operates

**related diversification** a process whereby an organization acquires one or more businesses not related to its core domain

**synergy** situation that occurs when the combination of two organizations results in higher efficiency and effectiveness than would otherwise be achieved by the two organizations separately

**unrelated diversification** a process whereby an organization acquires businesses unrelated to its core domain

**growth strategy** a corporate-level strategy designed to increase profits, sales, and/or market share

**internal growth** a growth strategy in which a firm expands by internally increasing its size and sales rather than by acquiring other companies

**external growth** a growth strategy whereby a firm acquires other companies

accomplished when a firm increases revenues, production capacity, and its workforce, and can occur by growing a business or creating new ones. **External growth** is accomplished when an organization merges with or acquires another firm and can result in rapid growth. Mergers are generally undertaken to share or transfer resources and/or improve competitiveness by combining resources.

The attractiveness of merging with or acquiring another organization may seem intuitively obvious: two organizations join forces into a single one that possesses all the strengths of the individual firms. The key to successful mergers and acquisitions is often found in the ability to develop synergy. Some companies, like GE, are well known for their ability to acquire other companies and integrate them effectively. Opportunities for synergy are not always easy to identify, however. It is not uncommon for an organization to acquire a business and later discard it when the anticipated synergy is not attained.

When two organizations combine through a merger or acquisition to form a new organization, blending two distinct cultures can be difficult amidst the rumors of layoffs and restructuring that often accompany such transactions.[12] This is especially true when organizations across borders are involved. Although carmakers Chrysler and Daimler Benz merged to form DaimlerChrysler in 1998, complete cooperation between members from the two original organizations has been slow to develop. During the first few years of the merger, Mercedes executives closely guarded their technology from Chrysler for fear of eroding the Mercedes mystique. In 2003, the two divisions began to cooperate more closely when it began building the Crossfire, a Chrysler design with Mercedes components.[13]

**strategic alliances**

a corporate-level growth strategy in which two or more firms agree to share the costs, risks, and benefits associated with pursuing existing or new business opportunities; often referred to as partnerships

One alternative to pursuing a merger or acquisition is to form a close relationship with another organization without becoming part of the same firm. **Strategic alliances**—often called partnerships—occur when two or more firms agree to share the costs, risks, and benefits associated with pursuing existing or new business opportunities. Strategic alliances can be temporary, disbanding after a certain project is finished, or they can involve multiple projects over an extended period of time.[14] A strategic alliance can be particularly attractive when a project is so large that it strains a single company's resources or requires complex technology that no single firm possesses. Hence, firms with complementary technologies may combine forces, or one firm may contribute its technological expertise while another contributes its managerial or other abilities.[15] American carmakers General Motors (GM) and Ford have established strategic alliances with small manufacturers in emerging economies such as those in China and Russia. GM and Ford provide technological expertise to the alliance, whereas the producers in the host countries provide access and distribution to the local markets.

Strategic alliances have two major advantages over mergers and acquisitions. First, they minimize increases in bureaucratic, developmental, and coordination costs. Second, each company can share in the benefits of the alliance without bearing all the costs and risks itself. A key disadvantage of a strategic alliance, however, is that one partner in the alliance may offer less value to the project than other partners but may gain a disproportionate amount of critical know-how from the cooperation with its more progressive partners. In addition, the participating organizations may hesitate to share complete information and expertise with each other.

## 2-3b Stability Strategy

**stability strategy**

a corporate-level strategy intended to maintain a firm's present size and current lines of business

Although growth is intuitively appealing, it is not always the most effective strategy. The **stability strategy** seeks to keep the organization at roughly the same size. Growth may occur naturally but is typically limited to the level of industry growth. Stability enables the organization to focus its efforts on enhancing current activities, while avoiding costs associated with internal or external growth. An organization may adopt a stability strategy in leaner times and shift to a growth strategy when economic conditions improve. Stability can also be an effective strategy for a high performing organization, but it is not necessarily a risk-averse strategy.

Stability may be pursued instead of growth under at least four sets of circumstances:

1. Industry growth is slow or nonexistent. In this situation, one firm's growth must come at the expense of a rival. This can be particularly costly, especially when attacking an industry leader.[16]

2. Costs associated with growth exceed benefits. During the "cola wars" of the 1980s, PepsiCo and Coca-Cola spent millions to lure consumers to their cola brands, only to realize that the costs associated with securing this market share severely reduced profits.

3. Growth may place great constraints on quality and customer service, especially in small organizations known for their personal service and attention to detail.

4. Large, dominant organizations may not wish to risk prosecution for monopolistic practices associated with growth. American firms, for example, may be prohibited from acquiring competitors if regulators believe their combined market shares will threaten competitiveness. Even internal growth can be problematic at times, as was the case in the late 1990s through 2001 with Microsoft's costly defense against federal charges that the company unfairly dictated terms in the software industry.

## 2-3c  Retrenchment Strategy

Growth strategies and the stability strategy are generally adopted by healthy organizations. But when performance is disappointing, a **retrenchment strategy** may be appropriate. Retrenchment takes one or a combination of three forms: turnaround, divestment, or liquidation. A retrenchment strategy is often accompanied by a reorganization process known as corporate restructuring. **Corporate restructuring** includes such actions as realigning divisions in the firm, reducing the amount of cash under the discretion of senior executives, and acquiring or divesting business units.[17] Restructuring is not limited to organizations that perform poorly over an extended period of time. Even well-known, leading companies progress through product and economic cycles that require them to restructure on occasion. Fast-food giant McDonald's, for example, posted a fourth-quarter 2002 loss of $344 million, its first in 37 years. The firm responded with a restructuring plan that included opening fewer new stores, greater product and marketing emphasis on existing outlets, and a number of store closings in 2003 in the United States and Japan, its two largest markets.[18]

A **turnaround** seeks to transform the organization into a leaner, more effective firm and can include such actions as eliminating unprofitable outputs, reducing the size of the workforce, cutting costs of distribution, and reassessing product lines and customer groups.[19] Turnarounds are often accompanied by **downsizing**, the elimination of one or more hierarchical levels in an organization. Turnarounds are often preceded by changes in the external environment. In general, a turnaround is usually not as drastic a move as corporate restructuring, but the two terms are often used interchangeably in the business press.

Turnarounds involving layoffs are generally more difficult to implement than one might think. When layoffs are required, organizations must address their effects on both departing employees and those who remain with the organization, the "survivors." Employees may be given opportunities to voluntarily leave—generally with an incentive—to make the process as congenial as possible. The problem with this approach, however, is that those departing are often the top performers who are most marketable, leaving the organization with a less competitive workforce. When layoffs are simply announced, less competitive workers can be eliminated more easily, but morale is likely to suffer more.[20]

When layoffs are necessary, however, several actions may palliate some of the negative effects. Top managers should communicate honestly and effectively with all employees, explain why the layoffs are necessary and clarify how terminated employees were selected. Everyone, including the survivors, should be made aware of

**retrenchment strategy**
a corporate-level strategy designed to reduce the size of the firm

**corporate restructuring**
a corporate strategic approach that includes such actions as realigning divisions in the firm, reducing the amount of cash under the discretion of senior executives, and acquiring or divesting business units

**turnaround**  a corporate-level retrenchment strategy intended to transform the firm into a leaner and more effective business by reducing costs and rethinking the firm's product lines and target markets

**downsizing**  a means of organizational restructuring that eliminates one or more hierarchical levels from the organization and pushes decision making downward in the organization

Effective strategic planning at the corporate level requires strong teamwork and communication.

how departing employees will be supported. Employees should also be encouraged to take advantage of outplacement or other services available to them, and special efforts should be made to ensure that such programs are administered in a clear and consistent manner.[21] Although these measures will not eliminate all the harsh feelings associated with layoffs, they can help keep the process under control and minimize any negative repercussions that might occur.

**divestment**   a corporate-level retrenchment strategy in which a firm sells one or more of its business units

**Divestment**—selling one or more business units—may be necessary when an industry in which an organization competes is in decline, or when a business unit drains resources from more profitable units, is not performing well, or is not producing the desired synergy. In a well-publicized spin-off, PepsiCo divested its KFC, Taco Bell, and Pizza Hut business units into a new company, Tricon Global Restaurants, Inc., in 1997, in order to refocus PepsiCo's efforts on its beverage and snack food divisions. Tricon officially changed its name to Yum Brands in 2002 and has since acquired several other restaurant chains.

**liquidation**   a retrenchment strategy of last resort whereby a firm terminates one or more of its business units by selling its assets

**Liquidation** involves the sale of all the organization's assets and is the strategy of last resort. Liquidation results in a termination of the business and involves a divestment of *all* the firm's business units and should be adopted only under extreme conditions. Shareholders and creditors experience financial losses, employees eventually lose their jobs, suppliers lose a customer, and the community suffers an increase in unemployment and a decrease in tax revenues. Hence, liquidation should be pursued only when other forms of retrenchment are not viable.

## 2-4 Strategy at the Business Level

The corporate strategy does not address all of the strategic questions that an organization must face. Whereas the corporate strategy concerns the basic thrust of the firm—*where* top managers would like to lead the firm—the business strategy addresses the competitive aspect—*who* the business should serve, *what* needs should be satisfied, and *how* a business should develop core competencies and be positioned to satisfy customer needs.

**generic strategies**   strategies that can be adopted by business units to guide their organizations

**strategic group**   a select group of direct competitors who have similar strategic profiles

Although each business strategy is unique, the concepts of business strategy can be more easily presented by considering a limited number of **generic strategies** based on their similarities. Businesses adopting the same generic strategy comprise what is commonly referred to as a **strategic group**.[22] Because industry definitions and strategy assessments are not always clear, identifying strategic groups within an industry can be difficult. Hence, the concept of strategic groups can be used as a means of understanding and illustrating competition within an industry, but the limitations of the approach should always be considered.

The challenging task of formulating and implementing a generic strategy for each business unit is based on a number of factors. Selecting the generic approach is only the first step in formulating a business strategy.[23] It is also necessary to fine-tune the strategy and accentuate the organization's unique set of resource strengths.[24] Two generic strategy frameworks—one by Porter and one by Miles and Snow—serve as good starting points for developing business strategies. These are discussed in Sections 2-4a and 2-4b.

## 2-4a Porter's Generic Strategies

Michael Porter developed the most commonly cited generic strategy framework.[25] According to Porter's typology, a business unit must address two basic competitive concerns. First, managers must determine whether the business unit should **focus** its efforts on an identifiable subset of the industry in which it operates or seek to serve the entire market as a whole. For example, many specialty clothing stores in shopping malls adopt the focus concept and concentrate their efforts on limited product lines primarily intended for a small market niche. In contrast, most chain grocery stores seek to serve the mass market—or at least most of it—by selecting an array of products and services that appeal to the general public as a whole. Second, managers must determine whether the business unit should compete primarily by minimizing its costs relative to those of its competitors or by seeking to differentiate itself by offering unique and/or unusual products and services.

According to Porter, these two alternatives are mutually exclusive because differentiation efforts tend to erode a low-cost structure by raising production, promotional, and other expenses. Depending on the way strategic managers in a business unit address the first (i.e., focus or not) and second (low-cost, differentiation, or low-cost–differentiation) questions, six configurations are possible, as summarized in Table 2-2.

Businesses that compete with a **low-cost strategy** minimize costs by producing basic, no-frills products and services. Low-cost businesses often succeed by building market share through low prices, although some may charge prices comparable to rivals and enjoy a greater margin. Because customers are usually not willing to pay high or even average prices for basic products or services, it is essential that businesses using this strategy keep their overall costs as low as possible. Efficiency is a key to such businesses, as has been demonstrated by megaretailer Wal-Mart in recent years.

Low-cost businesses typically emphasize a low initial investment and low operating costs. They tend to purchase from suppliers who offer the lowest prices within a basic quality standard to minimize production expenditures. Most research and development efforts are directed at improving operational efficiency, and attempts are made to enhance logistical and distribution efficiencies. Such businesses tend to de-emphasize the development of new and improved products or services that might raise costs, as Aldi illustrates (see Box 2-1).

Effective business strategies take into account likely responses from competitors—just like a game of chess.

**focus** the concentration of strategic efforts on an identifiable subset of the industry in which it operates, as opposed to the market as a whole

**low-cost strategy** a generic business unit strategy in which a larger business produces, at the lowest cost possible, no-frills products and services industry-wide for a large market with a relatively elastic demand

| **TABLE 2-2** | Theoretical Perspectives on Firm Performance Configurations | | |
|---|---|---|---|
| | **Emphasis on Costs** | **Emphasis on Costs and Uniqueness** | **Emphasis on Uniqueness** |
| Concentration on a single subset of the market | Focus: low-cost strategy | Focus: low-cost–differentiation strategy | Focus: differentiation strategy |
| Attempt to serve the market as a whole | Low-cost strategy | Low-cost–differentiation strategy | Differentiation strategy |

### Best Practices
#### Delivering Value at Aldi

Aldi is an international retailer that offers a limited assortment of groceries and related items at the lowest possible prices. Aldi provides an excellent example of an organization whose functional operations are tightly coordinated around a single strategic objective—low costs.

Aldi minimizes costs a number of ways. Most products are private label, allowing Aldi to negotiate rock-bottom prices from its suppliers. Stores are modest in size; they are much smaller than that of a typical chain grocer. Aldi only stocks common food and related products, maximizing inventory turnover. The retailer does not accept credit cards, eliminating the 2–4 percent fee typically charged by banks to process the transaction. Customers bag their own groceries and must either bring their own bags or purchase them from Aldi at a nominal charge.

Aldi also takes an innovate approach to the use of its shopping carts. Customers insert a quarter to unlock a cart from the interlocked row of carts located outside the store entrance. The quarter is returned when the cart is locked back into the group. As a result, no employee time is required to collect stray carts unless a customer is willing to forgo the quarter by not returning the cart!

Aldi has grown to more than 5,000 stores in Europe, the United States, and Australia. Peruse the company website at www.aldi.com for more information on the retailer and its strategic approach. Which competitive strategy is Aldi implementing? How do Aldi's activities work together to support the strategy?

---

A cost leader may be more likely than other businesses to outsource a number of its production activities if costs are reduced as a result, even if modest amounts of control over quality are lost as a result. In addition, the most efficient means of distribution is sought, even if it is not the fastest or easiest to manage. Successful low-cost businesses do not emphasize cost minimization to the degree that quality and service decline excessively, which is an approach that can result in the production of cheap goods and services that nobody is willing to purchase.

**differentiation strategy**
a generic business unit strategy in which a business produces and markets to the entire industry products or services that can be readily distinguished from those of its competitors

**core competencies**
an organization's key capabilities and collective learning skills that are fundamental to its strategy, performance, and long-term profitability

Businesses that employ the **differentiation strategy** emphasize uniqueness, producing and marketing products or services that can be readily distinguished from those of their competitors. Differentiated businesses seek new product and market opportunities by leveraging advances in technology. Successful differentiation is typically linked to an organization's **core competencies,** which are its key capabilities and collective learning skills that are fundamental to its strategy, performance, and long-term performance. Ideally, core competencies should provide access to a wide array of markets, contribute directly to the goods and services being produced, and be difficult to imitate.

The potential for differentiation is, to some extent, a function of a product's physical characteristics. Tangibly speaking, it is easier to differentiate an automobile than bottled water. However, intangible differentiation can extend beyond the physical characteristics of a product or service to encompass everything associated with the value perceived by customers. As such, there are a number of prospective bases for differentiation, most notably product features (or the mix of products offered), including the objective and subjective differences in product attributes. Lexus automobiles, for example, have been differentiated on product features and are well known for their attention to detail, quality, and luxury feel. United and other airlines have attempted to differentiate their businesses by offering in-flight satellite telephone and email services.[26]

**low-cost–differentiation**
**strategy** a generic business unit strategy in which a business unit maintains low costs while producing distinct products or services industry-wide

Caution should be exercised when considering the combination of low-cost and differentiation strategies. As aforementioned, Porter contends a **low-cost– differentiation strategy** is not advisable and leaves a business "stuck in the middle" because differentiating a product generally drives up costs, eroding a firm's cost leadership basis.[27] In addition, a number of cost-cutting measures may be directly related to quality and/or other bases of differentiation. Following this logic, a business should choose *either* low-cost *or* differentiation, but not both.[28]

However, this is not necessarily the case, and the low-cost–differentiation strategy is a viable alternative for some businesses, although combining the two strategies can be difficult.[29] For example, some businesses begin with a differentiation strategy and integrate low costs as they grow, developing economies of scale along the way. Others seek forms of differentiation that also provide cost advantages, such as enhancing and enlarging the filter on a cigarette, which reduces the amount of costly tobacco required to manufacture the product, while also differentiating it from those of its competitors.

Fast-food giant McDonald's has combined low costs and differentiation effectively. The company was originally known for consistency from store to store, friendly service, and cleanliness. These bases for differentiation catapulted McDonald's to market share leader, allowing the firm to negotiate for beef, potatoes, and other key materials at the lowest possible cost. This unique combination of resources and strategic attributes has placed McDonald's in an enviable position as undisputed industry leader, although competition in this industry is intense.[30]

Changes in the mobile home industry in the United States also illustrate a link between low cost and differentiation. Traditionally, mobile homes have been positioned as an affordable housing option to low-income consumers. Indeed, about 22 million Americans, or 8 percent of the U.S. population, lived in manufactured housing in 2004. Sales approached almost 400,000 units per year in the late 1990s. However, they declined to about 131,000 units by 2003, a year in which about 100,000 units were repossessed from previous customers. Today, manufactured housing does not always represent a low-cost housing option. Manufacturers such as Clayton Homes responded to the hike in repossessions by targeting potential customers with higher incomes and offering homes with upscale features, such as Mohn faucets, porcelain sinks, a wood-burning fireplace, and even a high-definition television set.[31]

### 2-4b Miles and Snow's Generic Strategies

Porter's low cost-differentiation-focus framework is the most commonly cited approach to using strategies. However, a second commonly used framework for categorizing business-level strategies was developed by Miles and Snow; it considers four strategic types: prospectors, defenders, analyzers, and reactors.[32] *Prospectors* perceive a dynamic, uncertain environment and maintain flexibility to combat environmental change. Prospectors introduce new products and new services and design the industry. As such, prospectors tend to possess a loose structure, a low division of labor, and low formalization and centralization. Prospectors typically seek **first-mover advantages** derived from being first to market. First-mover advantages can be strong, as demonstrated by products widely known by their original brand names, such as Kleenex and ChapStick. Being first, however, is not always beneficial, and research has shown that competitors may be able to catch up quickly and effectively.[33] As a result, prospectors must develop expertise in innovation and evaluate risk scenarios effectively.

*Defenders* are almost the opposite of prospectors. They perceive the environment to be stable and certain, seeking stability and control in their operations to achieve maximum efficiency. Defenders incorporate an extensive division of labor, high formalization, and high centralization. The defender usually concentrates on only one segment of the market and stresses efficiency throughout the organization.

*Analyzers* stress stability and flexibility, attempting to capitalize on the best of the prospector and defender strategy types. Tight control is exerted over existing operations with loose control for new undertakings. The strength of the analyzer is the ability to respond to prospectors (or imitate them) while maintaining greater efficiencies in operations. An analyzer may follow a prospector's successful lead, modify the product or service offered by the prospector, and market it more effectively. In effect, an analyzer is seeking a "second mover" advantage, waiting to see which prospector moves are successful and then following suit as needed.[34]

**first-mover advantages**
benefits derived from being the first organization to offer a new or modified product or service

Copying successful competitors can be a successful strategy when the organization has the resources needed to effectively implement similar programs. After sales slumped in 2000 at Taco Bell, president Emil Brolick acknowledged its plans to model the restaurant after Wendy's, noting the rival's ability to gain market share without slashing prices. In 2001, Taco Bell began appealing to a more mature market with additional pricey items and fewer promotions. Although the product lines are substantially different, this approach has proven beneficial for Taco Bell.[35]

*Reactors* represent the fourth strategic type, lacking consistency in strategic choice and performing poorly. The reactor organization lacks an appropriate set of response mechanisms with which to confront environmental change. There is no strength in the reactor strategic type, and reactor organizations are generally encouraged to restructure and select one of the other three strategic approaches.

Successful implementation of a given strategy is contingent on a number of factors associated with the organization and its environment. One of these factors is the organization's human resources. This chapter's Career Point (Box 2-2) discusses the fit between one's personality and the organization's competitive strategy.

Porter's typology and Miles and Snow's typology represent different approaches to business strategies in organizations, but share some similarities. For example, Miles and Snow's prospector business is likely to emphasize differentiation, whereas the defender business typically emphasizes low costs. Miles and Snow's analyzer type also appears to resemble the low-cost–differentiation combination within Porter's framework. These tendencies notwithstanding, fundamental differences exist between the typologies. Porter's approach is based on economic principles associated with the cost-differentiation dichotomy, whereas the Miles and Snow approach describes the philosophical approach of the business to its environment.

Developing a successful business strategy requires both analysis and creativity.

Box 2-2

Does your personality fit better with one competitive strategy than with another? Perhaps it does. Consider Miles and Snow's generic strategy typology as an example. What kind of managers would be best suited for a prospector organization? Recall that the prospector seeks competitive advantage by being first with new products, services, or markets. By their nature, prospectors embrace the notion of risk. If you enjoy the fast pace of change, like new opportunities, are creative, and are not stressed by uncertainties associated with change, then a prospector organization might be an excellent fit.

Perhaps you are more analytical, less outgoing, and work well with numbers. Defender organizations seek competitive advantage by serving an established segment of the market very well. Defenders often do so by emphasizing efficiency of operations and cost controls.

Analyzers seek competitive advantage by balancing desires for innovation and cost controls. Analytical skills may also be highly important to professionals working in analyzer organizations. Flexibility is also a key attribute of analyzers.

In most instances, reactor organizations would not be attractive to any individuals. Regardless of strategy, most healthy organizations seek a balance of personality types, at least to some extent. However, people make an organization function and can contribute more when they can relate to or identify with the strategy it is pursuing. Perhaps you should consider how your personality type fits with the organization's strategy when you consider your next career move.

## 2-5 Strategy at the Functional Level

Strategic consistency throughout the organization can enhance prospects for success. After corporate- and business-level strategies have been developed, strategies should be formulated at the business unit's functional levels, such as those of marketing, finance, production, purchasing, human resources, and information systems. Functional strategies should support the implementation of the corporate- and business-level strategies. In doing so, each functional area should integrate its activities with those of the other functional departments because a change in one department can affect both the manner in which other departments operate, as well as the overall performance of the business unit.

Unfortunately, managers in each functional area often do not understand the interrelationships among the functions. For example, marketers who do not understand production may promise customers product features that the production department cannot readily or economically integrate into the product's design. In contrast, production managers who do not understand marketing may insist on production changes that result in relatively minor cost changes but fail to satisfy customer needs. In a similar vein, it is not worthwhile to launch a new advertising campaign emphasizing product quality while the production department is undergoing a massive effort to cut costs. For this reason, managers in all functional areas need to understand how the areas should integrate, and they should work together to formulate functional strategies that fit and support the business- and corporate-level strategies.

Functional strategies are formulated after the corporate and business strategies have already been established. However, examining the capabilities of the functional areas is still necessary when various corporate and business strategic options are being considered. For example, an airline considering expansion through additional international routes should consider factors such as the need for additional personnel and the organization's ability to finance additional airplanes *before* settling on the expansion plan as the preferred strategic option.

## Summary

Strategies are developed to integrate an organization's activities behind a common purpose. The process of strategic management is influenced by a number of perspectives, including industrial organization economics, resource-based theory, and contingency theory. The strategic management process includes external and internal analysis and the examination of mission and goals, as well as the formulation and implementation of strategies at three levels within the organization. Each of the three perspectives plays a distinct role in the strategic management process.

At the broad firm level, managers must identify the markets in which the organization will compete. In addition, they can attempt to increase the size of the organization through internal or external growth, seek to maintain stability, or pursue a reduction in size through retrenchment. At the business level, top managers formulate strategies to enable the business unit to compete effectively. Generic strategy frameworks can be used to illustrate the strategic approaches available. Porter's framework of business strategies includes low costs, differentiation, and focus. Miles and Snow's framework includes prospectors, defenders, analyzers, and reactors. Functional strategies are also developed for each business unit to support the business- and firm-level strategies.

## Review Questions and Exercises

1. What are the advantages and disadvantages of internal growth as opposed to growth through mergers and acquisitions?

2. Why would an organization adopt a stability strategy? Is a stability strategy a suboptimal approach for organizations over the long term?

3. Can low-cost and differentiation strategies be combined effectively? Why or why not?

4. How do strategies at the functional level integrate with those at the firm and business levels?

## Quiz

1. The growth strategy is always the most effective strategy for a healthy organization.
   **True or False**

2. Synergy occurs when the combination of two organizations results in higher effectiveness and efficiency than would otherwise be generated by them separately.
   **True or False**

3. Strategic alliances typically involve higher bureaucratic and developmental costs when compared to mergers and acquisitions.
   **True or False**

4. Corporate restructuring involves the acquisition of businesses unrelated to the organization's core.
   **True or False**

5. Organizations that employ the focus strategy produce and market to the entire industry products or services that can be readily distinguished from those of their competitors.
   **True or False**

6. The analyzer organization embodies characteristics of both prospector and reactor types.
   **True or False**

7. An organization seeking rapid growth should pursue
   a. internal growth.
   b. external growth.
   c. divestment of poor performing businesses.
   d. a restructuring strategy.

8. Which of the following is not a potential reason for selecting a stability strategy?
   a. The industry is not growing.
   b. Growth may place constraints on customer service.
   c. Costs associated with growth exceed its benefits.
   d. All of the above are potential reasons.

9. Organizations adopting the same generic business strategy are referred to as
   a. low-cost businesses.
   b. differentiated businesses.
   c. a strategic group.
   d. none of the above.

10. A no-frills product targeted at the market at large is consistent with
    a. the low-cost strategy.
    b. the differentiation strategy.
    c. the focus strategy.
    d. none of the above.

11. Analyzers
    a. seek first-mover advantages.
    b. control a distinct segment of the market.
    c. display some of the characteristics of both prospectors and defenders.
    d. do none of the above.

12. Functional strategies should
    a. be developed after corporate-level and business-level strategies have been formulated.
    b. be considered before corporate-level and business-level strategies are formulated.
    c. be integrated with corporate-level and business-level strategies.
    d. be all of the above.

## Endnotes

1. Based on P. Wright, M. Kroll, and J. A. Parnell, *Strategic Management: Concepts* (Upper Saddle River, NJ: Prentice Hall, 1998).

2. H. Mintzberg, "Opening Up the Definition of Strategy," in *The Strategy Process,* eds. J. B. Quinn, H. Mintzberg, and R. M. James, 14–15 (Englewood Cliffs, NJ: Prentice Hall, 1988).

3. M. E. Porter, "The Contributions of Industrial Organization to Strategic Management," *Academy of Management Review* 6 (1981): 609–620.

4. J. S. Bain, *Industrial Organization* (New York: Wiley, 1968); F. M. Scherer and D. Ross, *Industrial Market Structure and Economic Performance* (Boston: Houghton-Mifflin, 1990).

5. It has been argued that the resource-based perspective does not qualify as an academic theory. For details on this exchange, see R. L. Priem and J. E. Butler, "Is the Resource-Based 'View' a Useful Perspective for Strategic Management Research?," *Academy of Management Review* 26 (2001): 22–40; J. B. Barney, "Is the Resource-Based 'View' a Useful Perspective for Strategic Management Research? Yes," *Academy of Management Review* 26 (2001): 41–56.

6. J. B. Barney, "Looking Inside for Competitive Advantage," *Academy of Management Executive* 19 (1995): 49–61.

7. S. L. Berman, J. Down, and C. W. L. Hill, "Tacit Knowledge as a Source of Competitive Advantage in the National Basketball Association," *Academy of Management Journal* 45 (2002): 13–32.

8. E. J. Zajac, M. S. Kraatz, R. K. F. Bresser, "Modeling the Dynamics of Strategic Fit: A Normative Approach to Strategic Change," *Strategic Management Journal* 21 (2000): 429–453.

9. C. A. Lengnick-Hall and J. A. Wolff, "Similarities and Contradictions in the Core Logic of Three Strategy Research Streams," *Strategic Management Journal* 20 (1999): 1109–1132; O. E. Williamson, "Strategy Research: Governance and Competence Perspectives," *Strategic Management Journal* 20 (1999): 1087–1108.

10. I. M. Cockburn, R. M. Henderson, S. Stern, "Untangling the Origins of Competitive Advantage," *Strategic Management Journal* 21 (2000): 1123–1145.

11. Wright, Kroll, and Parnell, 1998.

12. M. A. Hitt, J. S. Harrison, and R. D. Ireland, *Mergers and Acquisitions: A Guide to Creating Value for Stakeholders* (New York: Oxford University Press, 2001).

13. N. E. Boudette, "At DaimlerChrysler, a New Push To Make Its Units Work Together," *Wall Street Journal*, March 12, 2003, A1, A15.

14. J. J. Reuer, M. Zollo, and H. Singh, "Post-Formation Dynamics in Strategic Alliances," *Strategic Management Journal* 23 (2002): 135–152.

15. T. E. Stuart, "Interorganizational Alliances and the Performance of Firms: A Study of Growth and Innovation Rates in a High-Technology Industry," *Strategic Management Journal* 21 (2000): 791–811.

16. K. G. Smith, W. J. Ferrier, C. M. Grimm, "King of the Hill: Dethroning the Industry Leader," *Academy of Management Executive* 15, no. 2 (2001): 59–70.

17. J. F. Weston, "Restructuring and Its Implications for Business Economics," *Business Economics* (January 1998): 41–46.

18. R. Gibson, "McDonald's Posts a Super-Size Loss, Lowers Growth Goals," *Dow Jones Newswires* release, January 23, 2003.

19. See M. Garry, "A&P Strikes Back," *Progressive Grocer* (February 1994) 32–38.

20. M. Murray, "Waiting for the Ax to Fall," *Wall Street Journal*, March 13, 2001, B1, B10.

21. *Purchasing,* "Some Specifics on How to Handle Layoffs," December 16, 1999, http://www.purchasing.com/article/CA148401.html.

22. T. D. Ferguson, D. L. Deephouse, and W. L. Ferguson, "Do Strategic Groups Differ in Reputation?" *Strategic Management Journal* 21 (2000): 1195–1214.

23. R. S. Kaplan and D. P. Norton, "Having Trouble with Your Strategy? Then Map It," *Harvard Business Review* 78, no. 5 (2000): 167–176.

24. C. Campbell-Hunt, "What Have We Learned about Generic Competitive Strategy? A Meta-Analysis," *Strategic Management Journal* 21 (2000): 127–154.

25. M. E. Porter, *Competitive Strategy* (New York: Free Press, 1980).

26. S. Carey, "United to Install In-Flight E-Mail By End of Year," *Wall Street Journal,* June 17, 2003, D1, D2; S. McCartney, "New In-Flight E-Mail Falls Short," *Wall Street Journal,* March 31, 2004, D1, D3.

27. Porter, 1980: 41.

28. Porter, 1980.

29. J. A. Parnell, "New Evidence in the Generic Strategy and Business Performance Debate: A Research Note," *British Journal of Management* 8 (1997): 175–181; J. A. Parnell, "Reframing the Combination Strategy Debate: Defining Different Forms of Combination," *Journal of Applied Management Studies* 9, no. 1 (2000): 33–54; C. W. L. Hill, "Differentiation versus Low Cost or Differentiation and Low Cost: A Contingency Framework," *Academy of Management Review* 13 (1988): 401–412.

30. R. Papiernik, "McDonald's Shows It Can Market Well with Numbers, Knack for Good Timing," *Nation's Restaurant News,* May 1, 2000, 15–16; J. F. Love, *McDonald's: Behind the Arches* (New York: Bantam Press, 1995).

31. J. R. Hagerty, "Mobile-Home Industry Tries to Haul Itself out of Big Slump," *Wall Street Journal*, March 30, 2004, A1, A12.

32. R. E. Miles and C. C. Snow, *Organizational Strategy, Structure, and Process* (New York: West, 1978); M. Forte, J. J. Hoffman, B. T. Lamont, and E. N. Brockmann, "Organizational Form and Environment: An Analysis of Between-Form and Within-Form Responses to Environmental Change," *Strategic Management Journal* 21 (2000): 753–773.

33. J. A. Matthews, "Competitive Advantages of the Latecomer Firm: A Resource-Based Account of Industrial Catch-Up Strategies," *Asia Pacific Journal of Management* 19 (2002): 467–488.

34. H. C. Hoppe and U. Lehmann-Grube, "Second-Mover Advantages in Dynamic Quality Competition," *Journal of Economics & Management Strategy* 10 (2001): 419–434.

35. J. Ordonez, "Taco Bell Chief Has New Tactic: Be Like Wendy's," *Wall Street Journal,* February 23, 2001, B1, B4.

# Managing the External Environment

## Chapter 3

## Key Terms

boundary-spanning
buffering
crisis
crisis management
Delphi technique
environmental scanning
gross domestic product (GDP)
imitation

industry life cycle
judgmental forecasting
macroenvironment
multiple scenarios
population ecology
time series analysis
uncertainty

An organization cannot function effectively unless its managers understand the forces outside of the organization that influence its performance and survival. There are two components of the organization's external environment: the industry—the collection of competitors that offer similar products or services—and the complex network of political-legal, economic, social, and technological forces known as the organization's **macroenvironment.** This chapter addresses each of these components.

# 3-1 The Organization's Industry

**macroenvironment**
the general environment that affects all business firms in an industry, which includes political-legal, economic, social, and technological forces

Each business unit operates among a group of companies that produce competing products or services known as an industry. Although there are usually some differences among competitors, each industry has "rules of combat" governing such issues as product quality, pricing, and distribution. This is especially true in industries that contain a large number of firms offering standardized products and services. For example, most service stations in the United States generally offer regular unleaded, mid-grade, and premium unleaded gasoline at prices that do not differ substantially from those at nearby stations. If a rival attempts to sell different grades, it may experience difficulty securing reliable sources of supply and may also confuse consumers by deviating from the standard.

In a perfect world, each organization would operate in one clearly defined industry. In the real world, however, many organizations compete in multiple industries, and it may be difficult to clearly identify the industry boundaries. As such, the concept of primary and secondary industries may be useful in defining an industry. A primary industry may be conceptualized as a group of close competitors, whereas a secondary industry includes less direct competition. The distinction between primary and secondary industry may be based on objective criteria such as price, similarity of products, or location, but it is ultimately a subjective call.

### 3-1a Porter's Five Forces Model

Industry factors have played a major role in the performance of many companies, with the exception of those that are its notable leaders or failures.[1] As such, one needs to understand these factors at the outset before delving into the characteristics of a specific firm. Michael Porter proposed a systematic means of analyzing an industry's potential profitability; this system is known as Porter's "five forces" model. As mentioned in Chapter 2, this model is based on IO economics and suggests that industry structure is the primary determinant of firm performance. According to Porter, an industry's overall profitability depends on five basic competitive forces, the relative weights of which vary by industry (see Figure 3-1). The forces include:

1. *The intensity of rivalry among incumbent firms:* Competition intensifies when a firm identifies the opportunity to improve its position or senses competitive pressure from other businesses in its industry, which can result in price wars, advertising battles, new product introductions or modifications, and even increased customer service or warranties.[2]

2. *The threat of new competitors entering the industry:* Unless the market is growing rapidly, new entrants intensify the fight for market share, lowering prices and, ultimately, industry profitability.

3. *The threat of substitute products or services:* Firms in one industry may be competing with firms in other industries that produce substitute products, offerings produced by firms in another industry that satisfy similar consumer needs but differ in specific characteristics.

4. *The bargaining power of buyers:* The buyers of an industry's outputs can lower that industry's profitability by bargaining for higher quality or more services and playing one firm against another.

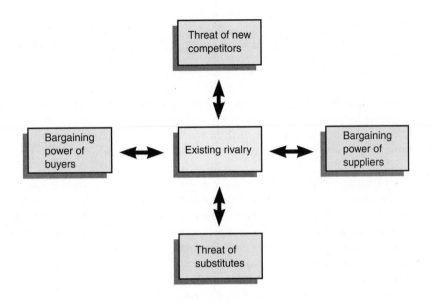

**Figure 3-1**
*Porter's Five Forces Model*

5. *The bargaining power of suppliers:* Suppliers can extract the profitability from an industry whose competitors may be unable to recover cost increases by raising prices.

Each of the five forces suggests that potential profits within an industry may be high, moderate, or low. Analyzing the five forces for an organization's industry can help managers understand the potential for superior performance within that industry. It does not guarantee high or low performance, as there are usually substantial performance differences among organizations in the same industry. Porter's five forces model, however, provides a useful framework for thinking about the effects an industry has on an organization.

There are other valid perspectives on organizations and industries besides Porter's view. As Porter suggests, organizations functioning in a given industry generally possess a number of similarities that are not typically shared by those in other industries. Fast-food restaurants, for example, tend to be labor intensive and cost conscious, with established systems to provide fast, efficient service to customers. However, new organizations may buck the trend from to time by taking different approaches designed to respond to changes in the environment more effectively. Whereas Porter's five forces model emphasizes similarities among organizations within an industry, the **population ecology** perspective emphasizes organizational diversity and adaptation.[3] According to this view, examining when and how organizations are formed, why new organizations might vary from existing ones, and ultimately why some survive when others fail leads to a better understanding of organizations. Some insight into this view can be obtained by considering the life cycle through which an industry passes.

**population ecology** a perspective on organizations that emphasizes the diversity among organizations that perform similar functions and utilize common resources

## 3-1b Industry Life Cycle

Like organizations, industries develop and evolve over time. Not only might the group of competitors within an organization's industry change constantly, but the nature and structure of the industry can also change as it matures and its markets become better defined. An industry's developmental stage influences the nature of competition and potential profitability among competitors.[4] In theory, each industry passes through five distinct phases of an **industry life cycle** (see Figure 3-2).

A young industry that is beginning to form is considered to be in the *introduction stage.* Demand for the industry's outputs is low because product and/or service awareness is still developing. Most purchasers are first-time buyers, and they tend to

**industry life cycle** the stages (introduction, growth, shakeout, maturity, and decline) through which industries are believed to pass

**Figure 3-2**
*The Industry Life Cycle*

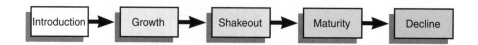

be affluent, risk tolerant, and innovative. Technology is a key concern in this stage because businesses often seek ways to improve production and distribution efficiencies as they learn more about their markets. Organizations emerging in this stage often attempt to capitalize on first-mover advantages, similar to the prospector strategy discussed in Chapter 2.

Normally, after key technological issues are addressed and customer demand begins to rise, the industry enters the *growth stage.* Growth continues during this stage but tends to slow as the market demand approaches saturation. Fewer first-time buyers remain, and most purchases tend to be upgrades or replacements. Some of the industry's weaker competitors may not survive. Those that establish distinctive competencies that can help distinguish them from their competitors tend to be the survivors.

*Shakeout* occurs when industry growth is no longer rapid enough to support the increasing number of competitors in the industry. As a result, an organization's growth is contingent on its resources and competitive positioning instead of a high growth rate within the industry. Marginal competitors are forced out, and a small number of industry leaders may emerge.

*Maturity* is reached when the market demand for the industry's outputs is completely saturated. Virtually all purchases are upgrades or replacements, and industry growth may be low, nonexistent, or even negative. Industry standards for quality and service have been established, and customer expectations tend to be more consistent than in previous stages. The U.S. automobile industry is a classic example of a mature industry. Firms in mature industries often seek new uses for their products or services or pursue new markets, often through global expansion. Because the field has become crowded and customers have become more sophisticated, many successful organizations begin to emphasize efficiencies in order to offer greater value.

The *decline stage* occurs when demand for an industry's products and services decreases and often begins when consumers begin to turn to more convenient, safer, or higher quality offerings from organizations in substitute industries. Some firms may divest their business units in this stage, whereas others may seek to "reinvent themselves" and pursue a new wave of growth associated with a similar product or service.

The life cycle model is a useful tool for evaluating an industry's development and the types of organizations that may be most likely to succeed. The key problem with the model, however, is that identifying an industry's precise position is often difficult, and not all industries follow these exact stages or at predictable intervals.[5] For example, the U.S. railroad industry did not reach maturity for many decades and extended over a hundred years before entering decline, whereas the personal computer industry began to show signs of maturity after only seven years.

# 3-2 The Organization's Macroenvironment

The second component within an organization's external environment is the macroenvironment, which consists of political-legal, economic, social, and technological forces (see Figure 3-3). Ultimately, the effects of these forces create opportunities and threats for an organization. In general, forces in the macroenvironment affect all competitors within a given industry, although the nature of the effects can differ among firms. For example, a sharp economic decline may threaten the livelihood of a luxury automobile manufacturer, while at the same time creating an opportunity for a carmaker with substantially lower costs.

**Macroenvironment**

Political-legal → Industry

Firm  Firm
Firm  **Firm**  Firm
Firm  Firm

Social

Economic →

Technological ←

**Figure 3-3**
*Macroenvironmental Forces*

Most organizations have little, if any, influence over the macroenvironment. On occasion, a large, dominant firm such as Wal-Mart may be able to exert some degree of influence over one or more aspects of the macroenvironment. For example, the giant retailer's political action committee contributed about $1 million to candidates and parties in the United States in both 2003 and 2004, presumably in an effort to influence regulation that might affect the organization.[6] However, most organizations must seek to join with others in trade and other associations in an attempt to exert some degree of influence on a particular factor in the macroenvironment.

Some factors may be placed neatly into one of these interrelated categories, whereas others may straddle two or more classes. For example, automobile safety has political-legal (e.g., legislation requiring that safety standards be met), social (e.g., consumer demands for safe vehicles), and technological (e.g., innovations that may improve safety) dimensions. For clarity concerns, however, each category of macroenvironmental forces is discussed separately in Sections 3-2a through 3-2d.

### 3-2a  Political-Legal Forces

Political-legal forces include such factors as the outcomes of elections, legislation, and judicial court decisions, as well as the decisions rendered by various commissions and agencies at every level of government. Military conflicts are also included in this arena and can influence how a number of industries operate, especially those with tight global ties. In 2003, for example, during the beginning of the war in Iraq, many American firms modified their promotional strategies, fearing that their television advertisements might be considered insensitive if aired alongside breaking coverage of the war. At the same time, others began to plan for meeting the anticipated future needs in Iraq for such products as cell phones, refrigerators, and automobiles. In late 2003, American firms began to compete vigorously for lucrative reconstruction contracts, while others prepared for increased business activity there in the coming years.[7]

Industries are often affected by legislation and other political events specific to their lines of business. For example, the Highway Traffic Safety Administration in the United States constantly tests cars and trucks sold in the U.S. and works with carmakers to improve safety performance.[8] Following the sharp declines in air travel in the United States in 2001, airlines on the verge of bankruptcy campaigned for and received $15 billion in government support in 2002 and an additional $2.9 billion in 2003.[9] All societies have laws and regulations that restrict or control business operations. Relatively speaking, free market-oriented nations such as the United States have fewer restrictions, but the level of regulation can be extensive in some areas. Many socialist nations have rigid guidelines for hiring and firing employees or establishing operations, and some require that a portion of what is produced in that country be exported to earn foreign exchange. These regulations are specific to each nation and create opportunities or pose threats to firms interested in operating across national boundaries.

### 3-2b Economic Forces

**gross domestic product (GDP)** the value of a nation's annual total production of goods and services

Every organization is affected by changes in the local, national, and/or global economies. The first economic consideration is that of the **gross domestic product (GDP),** the value of a nation's annual total production of goods and services. GDP growth among nations is often interrelated, but all nations do not experience the same rate of growth. For example, while GDP levels in the West were stagnant around the turn of the millennium, China's GDP grew at a staggering pace.[10]

Consistent GDP growth generally produces a healthy economy fueled by increases in consumer spending, whereas a decline signals lower consumer spending and decreased demand for goods and services. When GDP declines for two consecutive quarters, a nation's economy is generally considered to be in a recession. A recession is not detrimental for all organizations. For example, college and university enrollments often increase as undergraduate and graduate students seek to gain an advantage in a tight job market.[11] Unfortunately, it is difficult to forecast a recession in advance, and many recessions are identified only after they have occurred.

High inflation negatively affects most, but not all businesses. High rates raise many of the costs of doing business, and continued inflation can constrict the expansion plans of businesses and trigger governmental action, such as the case is when the U.S. Federal Reserve Board raises its discount rate during inflationary periods to slow economic growth. However, oil companies may benefit during inflationary times if the prices of oil and gas rise faster than the costs of exploration, refinement, and transportation. Sharp increases in the price of heating oil sparked a resurgence in the market for coal stoves in the winter of 2000–2001.[12]

Interest rates affect the demand for many products and services, especially high-ticket items whose costs are financed over an extended period of time, such as homes, automobiles, and appliances. At the consumer level, low short-term interest rates benefit retailers such as Wal-Mart and J.C. Penney because they also tend to lower rates on credit cards, thereby encouraging consumer spending. At the organizational level, high interest rates can hinder expansion efforts.

Organizations that transact a significant amount of business outside of its borders are especially vulnerable to changes in rates of exchange between the home and other currencies. When the value of the dollar increases relative to other currencies, for example, American organizations are at a competitive disadvantage internationally, as the prices of American-made goods rise in foreign markets. In addition, American manufacturers tend to locate more of their plants abroad and make

Recessions can be devastating for firms in many industries, but they are difficult to predict.

Abrupt changes in exchange rates can raise or lower prices of supplies and finished products shipped across borders.

purchases from foreign sources. During this time, American consumers are more likely to purchase products produced abroad, which are less expensive than goods produced at home.

### 3-2c  Social Forces

Social forces include such factors as societal values, trends, traditions, and religious practices and can substantially influence organizational performance. Social forces can vary widely among nations, especially as they are related to other factors. For example, smaller cars have been the vehicle of choice in European countries since the 1990s. In Europe, roads are narrower, gasoline is more heavily taxed, and fuel economy is a greater concern. In the United States, roads are wider, gasoline is less expensive, and fuel consumption does not play as strong a role in the purchase decision. As a result, American consumers tend to demand relatively larger vehicles, although increasing gasoline prices in 2005 could prompt some consumers to reconsider fuel economy in the purchase decision.[13] Fashion in China also offers another example, where styles reflect a mix of Asian, American, and European tastes.[14]

Social forces often reflect societal practices that have lasted for decades or even centuries. For example, the celebration of Christmas in the Western Hemisphere provides significant financial opportunities for card companies, toy retailers, confectioners, tree growers, and gift shops. Some retailers are happy just to break even during the year and generate their profits during the Christmas shopping season.

Societal trends also include demographic changes that can affect how organizations must function in order to succeed. Consider the United States as an example. The baby boom, which lasted from 1945 through the mid-1960s, initially created opportunities for baby apparel and diaper manufacturers, private schools, and even candy and snack makers. Later, as the baby boomers departed high school, universities grew at an astounding rate, and organizations had large applicant pools from which to select their employees. More recently, these baby boomers have begun shopping at home more and are spending heavily on health-care needs, leisure activities, and vacations.[15]

Today, the average American is older, busier, better educated, more technologically astute, and less likely to be a member of the Caucasian race than in previous years. This trend has affected consumer demand in areas such as personal computers and educational services and has prompted many organizations emphasizing the broad middle-age market to modify their strategic approaches to include either younger or older adults. For example, cosmetics maker Avon, confronted with a shrinking clientele, began to expand its appeal to the trendier sixteen- to twenty-four-year-old market in 2002.[16] J.C. Penney and Sears even opened stand-alone locations to provide easier access to customers too busy to plan a day at the mall.[17]

In many respects, social forces—more than other forces in the macroenvironment—have the greatest effect on organizations that produce goods for or provide services directly to consumers. Consider the American automobile industry as an example. Sport utility vehicles (SUVs) were first made in the 1990s and by the end of the decade had become the vehicle of choice for many suburban families. Auto manufacturers realized, however, that SUV patrons were willing to give up some of the rugged features associated with the SUV in exchange for the additional space and softer ride associated with the previously most popular class of vehicles known as the minivan. Ford responded by introducing a redesigned Explorer with three rows of seats, additional safety gadgets, and a softer ride.[18] By 2003, Ford, General Motors, and Nissan had begun to shift attention away from large SUVs to the vehicles they often termed "crossovers" or "active lifestyle wagons."[19]

Interestingly, however, the popularity of the SUV in the United States has been attacked on the grounds of another social force, environmental responsibility. Environmentalists charge that SUVs are simply too large and fuel inefficient, increasing the nation's dependence on external sources of oil, a reliance that may compromise the nation's ability to broker a lasting peace in the oil-rich Middle East. As a result, SUV manufacturers began to develop and produce more fuel-efficient hybrid (i.e., gasoline and electric) versions early in the twenty-first century.

One of the difficulties associated with social trends, however, is that they are often difficult to identify. In some cases, two trends may even appear to be at odds with each other. For example, American consumers have been sending a mixed message of "the celery stick and the double chocolate peanut swirl" for the past decade, confusing restaurants and packaged food producers alike. Fast-food restaurants responded by supersizing their meal combinations with extra fries and larger drinks, while at the same time expanding alternatives for items such as grilled chicken sandwiches and salads.[20] In 2004, Coca-Cola and PepsiCo began to emphasize smaller cans and bottles,[21] while McDonald's introduced low-carb menu items.[22]

During this same time, fast-food consumers began eating less often at Burger King, Pizza Hut, and Taco Bell, in favor of such outlets as Subway and Panera Bread, restaurants whose food many consumers perceived to be healthier. Although the traditional competitors responded with more salads and low-calorie, low-fat alternatives, their heavy and fried images have been difficult to overcome.[23] As these U.S. fast-food icons continue to expand abroad, restaurant chains from other parts of the world, most notably Latin America, are expanding into the United States.[24]

The health and fitness trend that emerged in the 1990s facilitated the growth in a number of fitness equipment manufacturers and sports drink producers, while hurting organizations in less health-friendly industries such as tobacco and liquor. In 2002, Anheuser-Busch launched Michelob Ultra, a low-carbohydrate beer, in an attempt to tap the health-conscious market,[25] while PepsiCo announced it would attempt to increase its sales of healthy snacks, including baked and low-fat offerings, to 50 percent of its total snack food sales.[26]

Shortly after 2000, concern about obesity in developed nations such as the United States and the United Kingdom became more prominent. Critics charge that sedentary lifestyles and unhealthy foods—such as those produced by many fast-food restaurants—have led to increases in diabetes, heart disease, and other medical problems associated with obesity. Some claim that food processors and fast-food restaurants such as McDonald's have contributed to this phenomenon by encouraging individuals to consume larger quantities of unhealthy foods.[27] Many consumers began to pursue low-carbohydrate diets to lose weight and improve overall health. As a result, many food producers and restaurants began catering to consumer interest in low-carb regimens as dieter concern shifted from fat content in foods to carbohydrate content. Unilever, for example, began promoting low-carb Skippy peanut butter, Wishbone dressing, and Ragu spaghetti sauce.[28]

Another prominent social trend in the early twenty-first century is related to technological advances associated with the Internet. During this time, many traditional retailers began to experience sales declines as more consumers shopped online. As a result, retailers began searching for new ways to attract prospective buyers to their stores, discovering that many consumers were less likely to frequent a traditional retailer unless it also provided some form of entertainment value. Bass Pro Shops, for example, increased its store traffic substantially by including such amenities as a large fish tank, live bats, and even a rock-climbing wall. Mall developers began to include activity zones in their facilities for such attractions as skating and fitness centers. This trend of mixing retailing with entertainment is expected to continue in the coming years.[29]

The tragic events of September 11, 2001 ("9-11"), also resulted in social changes that affect many organizations. Concerns over air travel safety have greatly influenced everything from flight routes to airline marketing strategies. After 9-11, Americans as a whole became more willing to accept inconveniences associated with their transactions if these inconveniences are associated with safety and security. Studies also suggest that investment and personal life strategies have become more conservative and reflective as a result of the tragedy.[30] Even churches are taking notice, as the 25 percent nationwide increase in attendance immediately following the events of September 11 had all but disappeared by the following year.[31]

General environmental concerns have also affected a number of organizations. These include the emphasis on socially responsible manufacturing and waste management practices, as well as concerns for saving private wetlands from business development.[32] Interest in both consumer recycling and the production of recyclable products heightened in the 1990s and has remained a key concern since then. Many analysts question consumer willingness to pay the higher prices typically associated with environmentally friendly products.[33]

## 3-2d  Technological Forces

Technological forces include scientific improvements and innovations that affect organizations. The rate of technological change can vary considerably among organizations and can affect operations in various ways. Many organizations have capitalized on advances in technology such as computers, satellites, and fiber optics to lower costs and serve their customers more effectively.

Technological change can also decimate existing organizations and even entire industries. Historical examples of such change include the shifts from vacuum tubes to transistors, from steam locomotives to diesel and electric engines, from fountain pens to ballpoint pens, and from typewriters to computers.[34]

On the consumer side, estimates of global Internet access in 2003 range from 600 to 800 million individuals, the vast majority of whom reside in the United States, Canada, Europe, or Asia. Many Americans now shop online; frequent online shoppers tend to be male, married, and college educated, between eighteen and forty years of age.[35] Online retail spending for 2003 is estimated at $52 billion, with an average annual growth rate through 2007 estimated at 21 percent.[36] Indeed, the widespread use of the Internet over the past decade is arguably the most pervasive technological force affecting business organizations since the dissemination of the personal computer.

The effects of the Internet are most profound in some industries, such as brokerage houses, where online companies have demonstrated huge gains in the market, or the travel industry, where the number of flights, hotels, and travel packages booked over the past decade has skyrocketed. The Internet has also spawned the advent of online banking, a much less costly means of managing transactions. As such, by 2002, a number of major banks and creditors had begun encouraging customers to pay bills online by offering free software, elimination of fees, and even sweepstakes entries with each transaction.[37] Indeed, the Internet has had a major effect on virtually every industry in the developed world.

# Box 3-1

## *Career Point*

### Gleaning Career Insight from the Macroenvironment

What can macroenvironmental forces tell you about career opportunities with a particular organization? Sometimes they can tell you a great deal. Consider the automobile and fast-food industries as examples.

Governments heavily regulate the automobile industry for safety and fuel economy. Most consumers finance vehicle purchases, so sales of new cars typically decline when interest rates are high and increase when rates are low. Consumer tastes are constantly evolving in areas such as fuel economy, vehicle size preferences, and the like. Technological change to promote increased fuel economy via hybrid gas/electric or even hydrogen power is on the horizon.

Regulations in the fast-food industry are not as heavy as in the automobile industry, although there are concerns for cleanliness and safety. The industry is also less susceptible than the automobile industry to economic conditions. The evolution of consumer tastes is also an issue, although the concerns are associated with taste, health, and food preparation. Technology has improved the efficiency of operations in a number of fast-food restaurants but does not appear to be the driving force in firm success or failure.

What do these environmental factors tell us about careers in the auto and fast-food industries? The greater role played by technology in the auto industry suggests that competitors will need a significant number of highly trained and well-compensated engineers and research and development specialists to keep pace, whereas fast-food outlets will likely concentrate on hiring large numbers of less skilled workers. The link between auto sales and interest rates suggests that the auto industry is more cyclical and restructurings might be more common than in fast-food restaurants. Of course, changing consumer tastes suggest that decision makers in both industries need to remain abreast of changes in consumer preferences.

---

It is difficult to overestimate the effect of advances in technology on strategic planning.

Consider the Internet's effect on the airline industry as an example. As Internet usage spread, many consumers began to purchase their airline tickets online instead of utilizing the traditional intermediary, a travel agency. As airlines began investing in this much more efficient means of ticketing in the 1990s, they started to trim commissions paid to travel agencies for booking their flights. In 2003, the major U.S.-based airlines eliminated commissions altogether for most tickets sold in the United States. Although many travel agencies moved aggressively to incorporate Internet technology and revamp their businesses, others did not survive.[38]

Technology has also prompted changes in customer service. For example, many of the touch-tone consumer hotlines of the 1990s were replaced in the following few years by virtual agents that answer calls and use speech recognition technology to either resolve a question or transfer the customer to a real person for additional assistance. Studies suggest that these systems improve response time by as much as 40 percent. Whereas some consumers appreciate the increased speed and are enamored by many agents' use of accents and even flirtatious personalities, others feel awkward about talking to a computer "pretending" to be a person. Interestingly, some American companies have addressed this frustration by utilizing fewer technology-based systems and transferring incoming calls to their consumer hotlines and technical support centers directly to representatives in countries such as India, where labor costs are much lower.[39]

The influence of technology on organizations is discussed in greater detail in Chapter 10. There is much to be learned by examining each of the macroenvironmental forces in greater detail. Box 3-1 discusses how assessing trends in the macroenvironment—including political-legal, economic, social, and technological forces—can provide insight into one's personal career decisions.

# 3-3 Managing Environmental Uncertainty

Managers must develop systems to address confusion concerning the availability of appropriate information about the organization's environment. Ideally, top managers are well aware of the variety of external forces that influence an organization's activities. **Uncertainty** occurs when decision makers lack current, sufficient, reliable information about their organization and cannot accurately forecast future changes. In reality, however, decision makers in any organization must be able to make decisions when environmental conditions are uncertain. Some organizations, such soft drink bottlers, are typically marked by lower levels of uncertainty. Top managers in other organizations, such as biotech and aerospace firms, tend to encounter higher levels of uncertainty.

Environmental uncertainty as perceived by decision makers is influenced by three key characteristics of the organization's environment. First, the environment may be classified along a simple-complex continuum. Simple environments have relatively few external factors that influence the organization, and the strength of these factors tends to be low. Complex environments are marked by numerous external factors, some of which can have a major influence on the organization. Of course, many organizations fall between these two extremes.

Second, the environment may be classified along a stable-unstable dimension. Stable environments are marked by a slow pace of change in the nature of external influences. Unstable environments are characterized by rapid change, such as when competitors constantly modify strategies, consumer tastes change quickly, or technological forces are developing constantly.

Finally, environmental uncertainty is a function of the quality or richness of information available to decision makers.[40] This is a key concern in emerging economies where reliable data on market demand, economic forces, and consumer preferences may not be readily available. In developed nations, however, information sources such as business publications, trade associations, and governmental agencies tend to be more developed.

Considering these three environmental characteristics, uncertainty is lowest in organizations whose environments are simple and stable, and where the quality of available information is high. In contrast, uncertainty is highest in organizations whose environments are complex and unstable and where the quality of information is low.[41] At the one extreme, many governmental entities in developed countries may be the most simple and stable. Although governments can restructure and budgets may change from year to year, the pace of change is relatively slow, and such entities are usually not influenced as greatly by external forces as many for-profit organizations. In contrast, organizations whose core is tied closely to technology tend to experience the greatest complexity and instability. Following the terrorist attacks of September 11, 2001, airlines could be added to this category because of increased regulatory pressure and fears of further attacks.

Organizations in environments marked by low uncertainty are managed differently than those marked by high uncertainty. When uncertainty is low, for example, greater formality and established procedures can be implemented to improve efficiency. When uncertainty is high, however, procedures are difficult to develop because processes tend to change more frequently. In this situation, decision makers are often granted more freedom and flexibility so that the organization can adapt to its environment as it changes or as better information on the environment becomes available.

A number of techniques are available for managing uncertainty in the environment. The first consideration, however, is whether the organization should concentrate on adapting to its environment or attempting to influence it. The adaptation perspective suggests than an organization is unable to substantially influence factors

**uncertainty** a state whereby decision makers lack current, sufficient, reliable information about their organization and cannot accurately forecast future changes in its external environment. As such, this approach is consistent with industrial organization as discussed in Chapter 2.

Alternatively, the influence perspective assumes that an organization can either influence its environment—a difficult task for all but large firms—or by strategic choice reduce the level of uncertainty in the environment. Influencing the environment can take many forms, such as operating only in a highly predictable niche of the market, forming strategic alliances to expand a customer base, or forming a joint venture to investigate new technologies without having to go it alone. For example, a restaurant may select a more expensive location on a well-traveled highway to reduce uncertainty associated with traffic flow at a less expensive, more remote site.

Most organizations choose an approach between the two extremes, adapting in areas where top managers are unable to influence the environment and operating only in certain domains of the environment when this is possible. Southwest Airlines, for example, reduces competitive uncertainty by concentrating on small- to medium-size airports and reduces global political uncertainty by operating flights only within the United States. At the same time, however, Southwest adapts to consumer tastes and economic conditions by keeping tickets affordable and easy to purchase online or by telephone.

Organizations may take other techniques to managing uncertainty. One is **buffering,** a common approach whereby organizations establish departments to absorb uncertainty from the environment and thereby buffer its effects.[42] Purchasing departments, for example, perform a buffering role by stockpiling resources for the organization in case they become scarce.

Another technique is **imitation,** an approach whereby the organization mimics the strategy and structure of a successful key competitor. Organizations that imitate their competitors reduce the risk of making poor strategic decisions. As such, this can be an attractive approach, especially when an organization is struggling and when the competitor it mimics is highly successful. Imitation can restrict an organization's ability to develop its own distinctive competence, however.

Aside from these techniques, enhancing the quality and quantity of information available to an organization and the ability to disseminate it to decision makers is a key concern. Improving the organization's ability to predict future environmental changes and respond to unanticipated crisis events is also important. These issues are discussed in greater detail in Sections 3-4, 3-5, and 3-6.

## 3-4 Environmental Scanning

Keeping abreast of changes in the external environment that affect the organization presents a key challenge to managers. **Environmental scanning** refers to collecting and analyzing information about relevant trends in the external environment. A systematic environmental scanning process organizes the flow of current information relevant to organizational decisions while providing decision makers with an early warning system for changes in the environment. Because members of an organization often lack critical knowledge and information, they may scan the environment by interacting with outsiders, a process known as **boundary-spanning.**

Environmental scanning by nature is future oriented. Unfortunately, however, the results of environmental analysis are often too general or uncertain for specific interpretation.[43] Hence, the need for *effective* environmental scanning to produce relevant information is critical.[44]

Environmental scanning can be viewed as a continuous process.[45] Top managers must plan for and identify the type of information the organization needs to support decision making. A system for obtaining this information is then developed. Information is collected, analyzed, and disseminated to the appropriate decision makers. Their feedback concerning the usefulness and timeliness of the information should influence the type of information required by the organization. Figure 3-4 includes a summary of this process.

**buffering** a process for managing uncertainty whereby an organization establishes departments to absorb uncertainty from the environment

**imitation** an approach to managing uncertainty whereby the organization mimics the strategy and structure of a successful key competitor

**environmental scanning** collecting and analyzing information about relevant trends in the external environment

**boundary-spanning** the interaction by members of an organization with outsiders in order to obtain information relevant to the organization

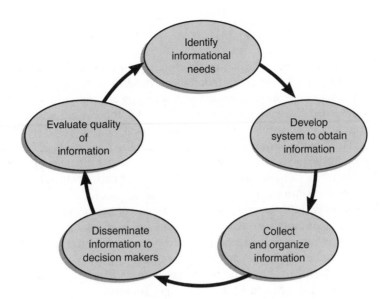

**Figure 3-4**
*Environmental Scanning Process*

Large organizations may engage in environmental scanning activities by employing one or more individuals whose sole responsibility is to obtain, process, and distribute important environmental information to its decision makers. These individuals constantly review articles in trade journals and other periodicals and watch for changes in competitor activities. Alternatively, however, organizations may contract with a research organization that offers environmental scanning services and provides them with real-time searches of published material associated with their organizations, key competitors, and industries. In contrast, decision makers at many smaller organizations must rely on trade publications or periodicals such as the *Wall Street Journal* to remain abreast of changes that may affect their organizations.

A potential lack of objectivity can be a concern when decision makers evaluate environmental information, because they selectively perceive their environment through the lens of their own experiences and organization. Managers with expertise in various functional areas tend to be more interested in and elevate information pertaining to their functions. For example, marketing managers may see the need for immediate changes in the marketing strategy to respond to changes in products offered by competitors, whereas operations managers may argue for the immediate implementation of a new cost-reducing technology.[46]

Interestingly, environmental scanning often identifies relationships among key industry influences in two or more forces. For example, heightened consumer concerns for automobile safety—a social force—could foster legislative action—a political-legal force—to require that automobile manufacturers add side airbags to all vehicles within a five-year period, an action that may be facilitated by improved manufacturing techniques—a technological force. Environmental scanners should be less concerned about classifying external activities as one force or another and more concerned about obtaining timely, accurate information for organizational decision makers.

Today, a key problem created by environmental scanning is often one of determining which information available warrants attention. Consider that it is not uncommon for a major American organization to be referenced in over a thousand news stories in a given week. Deciding which stories to read can be a daunting task.

For small organizations and for those competing in global markets, however, a greater problem might be the lack of reliable information on environmental conditions and trends. In China, for example, research house Euromonitor International reported that 23 billion liters of soft drinks were consumed in 2002, whereas a Coca-Cola study concluded the level to be 39 billion liters.[47] Discrepancies such as this can create great difficulties for decision makers.

# 3-5 Forecasting the Environment

It is important for decision makers in an organization not only to understand how the environment affects an organization today, but also how it may influence the organization in the future. As such, environmental scanning activities are most useful when they not only reveal current conditions, but also aid in forecasting future trends and changes. A number of forecasting techniques can be used, four of which are discussed briefly here.

**Time series analysis** attempts to examine the effects of historical trends such as population growth, technological innovations, or changes in disposable personal income on key organizational variables such as firm costs, sales, profitability, and market share. Time series analysis incorporates such factors as seasonal fluctuations, weather conditions, and holidays to the firm's performance, and can often reveal the effect of economic cycles on organizational performance. Time series analysis is most useful when trends can be quantified (e.g., temperature, population) and are believed to be developing at a consistent pace.

The **Delphi technique** is often employed when specialized expertise is required to forecast the future.[48] If the trend to be forecasted lies within a particular field, then experts in the area can be identified and independently surveyed about the likelihood and nature of the trend, as well as its prospective effect on the organization. After the initial results from experts are tabulated, they are redistributed to a panel of experts for follow-up assessments until a consensus about the trend is reached.

When relationships between variables are complex, difficult to identify, or cannot be adequately quantified, an organization may utilize **judgmental forecasting,** the use of a variety of sources including customers, suppliers, or trade associations to provide qualitative information about future trends. For instance, sales representatives may be asked to forecast sales growth based on their knowledge of customers' expansion plans. Surveys may also be mailed to suppliers or trade associations to obtain their judgments on specific trends. Data is then compiled into a composite forecast. Although judgmental forecasting effectively obtains input from a variety of sources, it is often difficult to draw clear conclusions due to the qualitative nature of the input and the variety of sources that might be employed in the data collection process.

In **multiple scenarios,** managers formulate several competing descriptions of future events and trends.[49] In doing so, strategic managers are required to identify the key forces in the environment, determine how they are interrelated, estimate their influence on future events, and ask "what if . . ." questions with each scenario. Decision makers then develop contingency plans that usually specify trigger points such as changes in sales or competitor activity that initiate the implementation-particular aspects of a plan.[50]

In practice, managers may utilize a combination of methods to predict environmental changes that will affect their organizations. There is no consensus on the most

**time series analysis**
an empirical forecasting procedure in which certain historical trends are used to predict variables such as a firm's sales or market share

**Delphi technique** a forecasting procedure whereby experts are independently and repeatedly questioned about the probability of some event's occurrence until consensus is reached regarding the particular forecasted event

**judgmental forecasting**
a forecasting procedure whereby employees, customers, suppliers, and/or trade associations serve as sources of qualitative information regarding future trends

**multiple scenarios** a forecasting procedure in which management formulates several plausible hypothetical descriptions of sequences of future events and trends

Forecasting the business environment can be like forecasting the weather—basic trends are easy to spot, but specific and precise forecasts are not always accurate.

effective forecasting method, and most experts agree that each method can be useful in the appropriate situation.

# 3-6 Crisis Management

Forecasting methods are primarily used to project market conditions and performance levels that are at least somewhat predictable. Unfortunately, however, a **crisis,** a disruption that physically affects an organization, its basic assumptions, or its core activities can face any organization.[51] How an organization addresses a crisis may determine its ultimate survival. Although a crisis can be initiated by factors internal or external to the organization, there are often multiple factors involved. **Crisis management** refers to the process of planning for and implementing the response to a wide range of negative events that could severely affect an organization.

### 3-6a Types of Crises

The terrorist attacks of September 11, 2001, highlighted the need for organizations to anticipate, prepare for, and respond to crisis events.[52] For some organizations, the attack resulted not only in the tragic loss of a substantial number of employees, but also in a loss of key facilities and data.[53] Bioterrorism—the use of biological agents for terrorist purposes—has become a major concern for top executives. One recent survey reported that approximately two-thirds of executives are not confident that their organizations would be safe in the event of a biological or chemical attack, even though 80 percent of the organizations in question have crisis management plans in place.[54]

Of course, terrorism is but one crisis that can affect an organization. In addition, a number of other potential organizational crises should be considered, such as fires and other natural disasters, economic crises (e.g., extortion, boycotts, bribery), information crises (e.g., computer system sabotage, copyright infringement, counterfeiting), and political unrest such as urban riots.[55] The effects of crises on an organization can vary widely around the world and can be especially traumatic in emerging nations where organizations may be less likely to have the resources and infrastructure to deal with crises.[56]

In addition to the events of September 2001, a number of large organizations have faced major crises at some time during the past few decades. In 1984, for example, gas leaked from a methyl isocyanate tank at a Union Carbide plant in Bhopal, India, killing approximately 3,800 persons and totally or partially disabling about 2,700 more. Officials later learned that the leak occurred when a disgruntled employee sought to spoil a batch of the chemical by adding water to the storage tank. The incident was reported to officials at company headquarters in the United States after a 12-hour delay, an event which sparked a widespread view that Union Carbide was negligent and was covering up details. India's Supreme Court later provided a $470 million settlement for victims and their families.[57]

In 1989, the Exxon Valdez tanker hit a reef in Prince William Sound, Alaska, spilling approximately 250,000 barrels of oil. Although there was no loss of human life, the loss of animal and bird life was extensive, and the negative press was damaging. The company's untested crisis management plan said such a spill could be contained in five hours, but the company did not implement the plan for two days. Exxon eventually spent about $2 billion to clean up the spill and another $1 billion to settle legal claims associated with the disaster.[58]

In 2003, The New Delhi Center for Science and Environment published a report asserting that local samples of Pepsi and Coke products contained pesticide residues at 30 times the acceptable limits in Europe. India's Parliament stopped serving the beverages and India nationalist activists in Allahabad smashed bottles and vandalized the property of a Coke distributor. Daily sales dropped by about one-third in less than two

**crisis** any disruption that physically affects an organization, its basic assumptions, or its core activities

**crisis management** the process of planning for and implementing the response to a wide range of negative events that could severely affect an organization

### Best Practices

#### Crisis Management at McDonald's

It is usually easier to locate examples of ineffective or nonexistent crisis management practices in organizations than it is to identify examples of successful crisis planning. Fast-food giant McDonald's has not always been noted for its success in this area, but demonstrated effective crisis management in 2004.

In April of that year, McDonald's chief executive Jim Cantalupo died suddenly from a heart attack. Less than six hours later, the McDonald's board of directors named president and chief operating officer Charlie Bell as his successor. The board had already intended for Bell to succeed Cantalupo at some point, but its quick, decisive action quelled many fears about the future of the leading fast-food chain. Hence, the board not only made a quick decision, but it had already thought about and planned for succession.[59]

McDonald's response highlights the importance not only of planning for CEO succession, but also of preparing for unexpected medical emergencies, especially with regard to top executives. Many experts suggest that a firm's board should always be prepared for an unexpected loss of the top two executives in their firms, and that they should not even fly on the same aircraft.

weeks, further curtailing efforts by the soft drink giants to spawn consumption of a product in a country where the average resident consumes less than one soft drink per month. The soft drink giants questioned the methodology and credentials of the group's laboratory, a response that did little to palliate the adverse effect of the crisis.[60]

### 3-6b The Crisis Management Process

The key to managing crises effectively is to plan in advance. As such, it is helpful to view crisis management as a three-step process. *Before the crisis,* organizations should develop a crisis management team to develop and plan for worst-case scenarios and define standard operating procedures that should be implemented prior to any crisis event. For example, top managers anticipating labor unrest at a company facility may hire additional security guards or contract with a private agency to provide additional security.

Proactive organizations that continually assess their vulnerabilities and threats and develop crisis management plans tend to be adequately equipped when a crisis occurs. Proper preparation requires research of the literature, of the industrial sector, and of the company itself. Information is needed to properly prepare for the crisis events. When managers understand which crisis events are more likely to occur, they can plan for the event more effectively and foster a business culture that is ready to meet the challenge if and when a crisis occurs.[61] Box 3-2 illustrates how one well-known firm was well prepared when a faced with a crisis.

*During the crisis,* an organizational spokesperson should communicate effectively with the public to minimize the effect of the crisis. For example, after being unprepared when Tylenol capsules laced with cyanide killed seven people in 1982, Johnson & Johnson prepared more effectively and responded to a 1986 lacing incident by acknowledging the crisis with the public and instructing all consumers to return products for a refund.[62] Presentations to the public should be prompt, honest, professional, and conducted through a single person or office.

*After the crisis,* communication with the public should continue as needed, and the cause of the crisis should be uncovered. Understanding the cause can help executives minimize the likelihood that the crisis will occur again and improve preparation for the crisis if it does.[63]

## Summary

Each organization is affected by factors in its external environment, including the collection of competitors known as the industry. Porter's five forces model offers a framework for evaluating the industry's structure and its influence on the organization.

In addition to the industry, each organization is affected by four sets of forces in its macroenvironment. Political-legal forces include various forms of legislation and judicial rulings, such as the decisions of various commissions and agencies at all levels of government. Economic forces include the effects of factors such as inflation, interest rates, and exchange rates. Social forces include traditions, values, societal trends, and a society's expectations of business. Technological forces include such factors as the Internet, as well as scientific improvements and innovations that affect firm operations and/or products and services in a given industry.

Environmental scanning is the process of researching and analyzing macroenvironmental changes so that managers can consider this information when making decisions. Understanding the present state of an organization's environment is only part of the process, however. It is also important to understand how changes might influence an organization in the future. A number of forecasting techniques, including time series analysis, the Delphi technique, judgmental forecasting, and multiple scenarios, can assist in assessing how future trends may affect firms in a particular industry.

Unfortunately, some environmental events are difficult to predict and can have substantial effects. Therefore, each organization should form a crisis management team and consider various crisis scenarios as part of its effort to remain abreast of changes in the environment.

## Review Questions and Exercises

1. How might the concept of primary and secondary industries be applied to a fast-food restaurant such as McDonald's?

2. In what industry life cycle stage would you classify the airline industry? How might this stage affect some of the strategic decisions made by a particular airline within the industry?

3. Using your college or university as an example, explain how political-legal, economic, technological, and social forces have affected its operations over the past decade.

4. What steps should your college or university officials take to prepare the institution for potential crises?

## Quiz

1. It is common for a single organization to influence a macroenvironmental force.
   **True or False**

2. The expansion of a religion in an emerging country is an example of a social force.
   **True or False**

3. Reading business publications can serve as a means of environmental scanning.
   **True or False**

4. Judgmental forecasting involves compiling and averaging the opinions of top executives in an industry.
   **True or False**

5. Crisis management refers to efforts made to eliminate the possibility that the organization can be affected negatively by unforeseen events.
   **True or False**

6. Crisis management involves a series of steps that can be taken before a crisis occurs, while it is occurring, and after it has passed.
   **True or False**

7. Porter's five forces model
   a. determines the level of performance for organizations in an industry.
   b. identifies the five activities an organization must perform to be successful.
   c. outlines the industry forces under an organization's direct control.
   d. does none of the above.

8. Market demand for an industry's outputs is completely saturated when an industry enters which stage of the industry life cycle?
   a. introduction
   b. growth
   c. shakeout
   d. maturity

9. Technological forces often
   a. decimate an entire industry.
   b. spawn new industries.
   c. vary substantially among industries.
   d. do all of the above.

10. When organizations cope with uncertainty by establishing departments to absorb uncertainty from the environment, its managers are involved in a process called
    a. coordination.
    b. buffering.
    c. forecasting.
    d. multiple scenarios.

11. Surveying experts about the likelihood of a certain trend or its effect on organizational performance is known as
    a. time series analysis.
    b. the Delphi technique.
    c. judgmental forecasting.
    d. multiple scenarios.

12. A crisis management team should be developed
    a. before a crisis occurs.
    b. while a crisis is occurring.
    c. after a crisis has occurred.
    d. during none of the above stages.

## Endnotes

1. G. Hawawini, V. Subramanian, and P. Verdin, "Is Performance Driven by Industry- or Firm-Specific Factors? A New Look at the Evidence," *Strategic Management Journal* 24 (2003): 1–16.

2. J. R. Graham, "Bulletproof Your Business Against Competitor Attacks," *Marketing News* (March 14, 1994): 4–5; J. Hayes, "Casual Dining Contenders Storm 'Junior' Markets," *Nation's Restaurant News,* March 14, 1994, 47–52.

3. M. Hannon and J. Freeman, "The Population Ecology of Organizations," *American Journal of Sociology* 82 (1977): 929–964.

4. C. W. Hofer, "Toward a Contingency Theory of Business Strategy," *Academy of Management Journal* 18 (1975): 784–810; G. Miles, C. C. Snow, and M. P. Sharfman, "Industry Variety and Performance," *Strategic Management Journal* 14 (1993): 163–177.

5. T. Levitt, "Exploit the Product Life Cycle," *Harvard Business Review* 43, no. 6 (1965): 81–94.

6. J. Cummings, "Wal-Mart Opens for Business in a Tough Market," *Wall Street Journal,* March 24, 2004, A1, A15.

7. C. Cummins, "Business Mobilizes for Iraq," *Wall Street Journal,* March 24, 2003, B1, B3; J. A. Trachtenberg and B. Steinberg, "Plan B for Marketers," *Wall Street Journal,* March 20, 2003, B1, B3; N. King, Jr., "The Race to Rebuild Iraq," *Wall Street Journal,* April 11, 2003, B1, B3.

8. S. Power, "New Rollover Test Could Lead to Safer SUVs," *Wall Street Journal,* October 8, 2003, D1, D7.

9. D. Sevastopulo, "US Airlines 'Are On Life Support'," *Financial Times,* October 2, 2003, 15.

10. M. Wolf, "Why Europe Was the Past, the U.S. is the Present and a China-Dominated Asia the Future of the Global Economy," *Financial Times,* September 22, 2003, 3.

11. J. E. Hilsenrath, "America's Pricing Paradox," *Wall Street Journal,* May 16, 2003, B1, B4.

12. R. G. Matthews, "Coal Stoves Are Hot Again," *Wall Street Journal,* January 30, 2001, B1.

13. J. B. White and D. Gautier-Villars, "Little Cars, Lots of Tricks," *Wall Street Journal,* October 2, 2002, B1, B3.

14. G. Kahn and A. Galloni, "Fashion's China Syndrome," *Wall Street Journal,* June 16, 2003, B1, B5.

15. K. J. Marchetti, "Customer Information Should Drive Retail Direct Mail," *Marketing News* (February 28, 1994): 7.

16. S. Beatty, "Avon Is Set to Call on Teens," *Wall Street Journal,* October 17, 2002, B1, B3.

17. K. Stringer, "Abandoning the Mall," *Wall Street Journal,* March 24, 2004, B1, B6.

18. J. B. White, G. L. White, and N. Shirouzu, "Drive for Lower Floors, Softer Rides Results in Domestic-Looking SUVs," *Wall Street Journal Interactive Edition,* January 4, 2001.

19. J. Ball, "Detroit Revs Up the Wagon," *Wall Street Journal,* January 7, 2003, B1, B3.

20. S. Ellison and B. Steinberg, "To Eat, Or Not to Eat," *Wall Street Journal,* June 20, 2003, B1, B4.

21. B. McKay, "Downsize This!" *Wall Street Journal,* 27 January 27, 2004, B1, B5.

22. S. Leung, "McDonald's Makeover," *Wall Street Journal,* January 28, 2004, B1, B10.

23. S. Leung, "Fleeing from Fast Food," *Wall Street Journal,* November 11, 2002, B1, B3; S. Leung and R. Lieber, "The New Menu Option at McDonald's: Plastic," *Wall Street Journal,* November 26, 2002, D1, D2.

24. T. Bouza and G. Sama, "America Adds Salsa to Its Burgers and Fries," *Wall Street Journal,* January 2, 2003, A1, A12.

25. C. Lawton, "Anheuser Tries Low-Carb Beer to Tap Diet Buzz," *Wall Street Journal,* September 13, 2002, B1, B2.

26. B. McKay, "Pepsico Challenges Itself to Concoct Healthier Snacks," *Wall Street Journal,* September 23, 2002, A1, A10.

27. N. Buckley, "Have Fat, Will Sue," *Financial Times,* December 13–14, 2003, W1–W2.

28. S. Ellison and D. Ball, "Now Low-Carb: Unilever's Skippy, Wishbone, Ragu," *Wall Street Journal,* January 14, 2004, B1–B2.

29. D. Starkman, "Retail Riddle: Is Shopping Entertainment?" *Wall Street Journal,* January 22, 2003, B1, B6.

30. "How September 11 Changed America," *Wall Street Journal,* March 8, 2002, B1.

31. K. McLaughlin, "The Religion Bubble: Churches Try to Recapture Their 9/11 Crowds," *Wall Street Journal,* September 11, 2002, D1, D6.

32. J. Carlton, "Saving Private Wetlands," *Wall Street Journal,* November 13, 2002, B1, B6.

33. G. A. Fowler, "'Green' Sales Pitch Isn't Helping to Move Products off the Shelf," *Wall Street Journal,* March 6, 2002, B1.

34. P. Wright, M. Kroll, and J. A. Parnell, *Strategic Management: Concepts* (Upper Saddle River, NJ: Prentice Hall, 1998).

35. Scarborough Research, "Almost Half of Internet Users Are Buying Products or Services Online," November 28, 2000, http://www.find-articles.com/p/articles/mi_m0EIN/is_2000_Nov_28/ai_67371649.

36. M. Pastore, "Young Americans Take Their Spending Online," September 19, 2000, http://www.clickz.com/stats/ sectors/demograph-ics/article.php/5901_463961; Nua Internet Surveys, "Online Retail Spending to Soar in the U.S." January 15, 2003, *Web Metro News & Internet Statistics,* www.webmetro.com/news1detail1.asp?id=868.

37. M. Higgins, "Honest, the Check Is in the E-Mail," *Wall Street Journal,* September 4, 2002, D1, D4.

38. N. Harris and S. Carey, "Delta Ends Commissions for Most Travel Agents," *Wall Street Journal Interactive Edition,* March 15, 2002; J. Costello, "Travel Agents Blast Decision to Cut Commissions in U.S." *Wall Street Journal Interactive Edition,* March 25, 2002.

39. J. Spencer, "Virtual Phone Reps Replace the Old Touch-Tone Menus; Making Claire Less Irritating," *Wall Street Journal,* January 21, 2002, D1, D4.

40. W. H. Starbuck, "Organizations and Their Environments," in *Handbook of Industrial Psychology,* ed. M. D. Dunnette, 1069–1123 (Chicago: Rand McNally, 1976).

41. R. B. Duncan, "Characteristics of Perceived Environments and Perceived Environmental Uncertainty," *Administrative Science Quarterly* 17 (1972): 313–327.

42. J. D. Thompson, *Organizations in Action* (New York: Transaction Publishing, 2003).

43. K. Kumar, R. Subramanian, and K. Strandholm, "Competitive Strategy, Environmental Scanning, and Performance: A Context Specific Analysis of Their Relationship," *International Journal of Commerce & Management* 11 (2001): 1–33.

44. J. R. Groom and F. David, "Competitive Intelligence Activity Among Small Firms," *SAM Advanced Management Journal,* 66, no. 1 (2001): 12–29.

45. J. Herring, "The Future of Competitive Intelligence: Driven by Knowledge-Based Competition," *Competitive Intelligence Magazine* 6, no. 2 (2003): 5.

46. D. F. Jennings and J. R. Lumpkin, "Insights Between Environmental Scanning Activities and Porter's Generic Strategies: An Empirical Analysis," *Journal of Management* 18 (1992): 791–803.

47. G. Kahn, "Chinese Puzzle: Spotty Consumer Data," *Wall Street Journal,* October 15, 2003, B1, B10.

48. G. Rowe and G. Wright, "The Delphi Technique as a Forecasting Tool: Issues and Analysis." *International Journal of Forecasting,* 15 (1999): 353–375; P. Ayton, W. R. Ferrell, and T. Stewart, "Commentaries on 'The Delphi Technique as a Forecasting Tool: Issues and Analysis' by Rowe and Wright." *International Journal of Forecasting,* 15 (1999): 377–381.

49. L. Fahey and V. K. Narayanan, *Macroenvironmental Analysis for Strategic Management* (St. Paul, MN: West, 1986): 215.

50. C. D. Pringle, D. F. Jennings, and J. G. Longenecker, *Managing Organizations: Functions and Behaviors* (Columbus, OH: Merrill, 1988): 114.

51. J. Burnett, *Managing Business Crises: From Anticipation to Implementation* (Westport, CT: Quorum, 2002).

52. D. N. Greenberg, J. A. Clair, and T. L. Maclean, "Teaching Through Traumatic Events: Uncovering the Choices of Management Educators as They Respond to September 11th," *Academy of Management Learning & Education Journal* 1, no. 1 (2002): 38–54.

53. J. W. Greenberg, "September 11, 2001: A CEO's Story," *Harvard Business Review* 80, no. 10 (2002): 58–64; P. T Hart, L. Heyse, and A. Boin, "New Trends in Crisis Management Practice and Crisis Management Research: Setting the Agenda," *Journal of Contingencies & Crisis Management* 9, no. 4 (2001): 181–188.

54. *Business Wire,* "BioTerrorism Response Plans Doubted; Organizations Feel Vulnerable Despite Contingency Planning, According to Survey at International Biosecurity Summit," November 26, 2002.

55. A. H. Miller, "The Los Angeles Riots: A Study in Crisis Paralysis," *Journal of Contingencies and Crisis Management* 9, no. 4 (2001): 189–199; C. Pearson and I. Mitroff, "From Crisis Prone to Crisis Prepared: A Framework for Crisis Management," *Academy of Management Executive,* 7, no. 1 (1993): 48–59.

56. J. A. Parnell, W. R. Crandall, and M. L. Menefee, "Management Perceptions of Organizational Crises: A Cross-Cultural Study of Egyptian Managers," *Journal of the Academy of Strategic and Organizational Leadership* 1, no. 1 (1997): 8–19.

57. Bhopal.com Information Center (accessed November 26, 2002), www.bhopal.com

58. A. Tanneson and L. Weisth, "FT Report: Mastering Leadership," *Financial Times,* November 22, 2002.

59. C. Hymowitz and J. S. Lublin, "McDonald's CEP Tragedy Holds Lessons, *Wall Street Journal,* April 20, 2004, B1, B8; R. Gibson and S. Gray, "Death of Chief Leaves McDonald's Facing Challenges," *Wall Street Journal,* April 20, 2004, A1, A16.

60. J. Slater, "Coke, Pepsi Fight Product-Contamination Charges in India," *Wall Street Journal,* August 15, 2003, B1, B4.

61. L. Barton, *Crisis in Organizations II* (Cincinnati: South-Western Publishing Co., 2001); R. R. Ulmer, "Effective Crisis Management Through Established Stakeholder Relationships," *Management Communication Quarterly* 14 (2001): 590–615.

62. P. Shrivastava, I. I. Mitroff, D. Miller, and A. Miglani, "Understanding Industrial Crises," *Journal of Management Studies* 25 (1988): 205–303.

63. Special thanks to John E. Spillan, Ph.D., The Pennsylvania State University, DuBois Campus, for his insight and suggestions concerning the role of crisis management in the strategic management of organizations.

# Goals and Organizational Effectiveness

## Chapter 4

## Chapter Outline

## Key Terms

agency problem

balanced scorecard

best practices

CEO duality

competitive benchmarking

concurrent control

corporate governance

diversification

employee stock ownership plan (ESOP)

feedback control

feedforward control

formal organization

goals

informal organization

leveraged buyout (LBO)

mission

objectives

organizational capacity

organizational control

organizational effectiveness

stakeholders

takeover

top management team

It has been said many times that, "if you don't know where you're going, any road will get you there." This admonition is true for organizations. Its leaders must understand and articulate the desired results from organizational activities if they expect them to be successful. This chapter discusses three key considerations to help leaders identify where an organization should be headed: (1) setting the mission, goals, and objectives; (2) conceptualizing organizational effectiveness and determining how to measure it; and (3) initiating organizational control when the organization is not as effective as it should be.

# 4-1 The Organization's Mission, Goals, and Objectives

Organizations are more likely to function effectively when their purpose and resources are well understood by their members. Toward this end, a mission, goals, and objectives should be developed for each organization. The **mission** is the reason for the firm's existence. The organization's **goals** represent the desired general ends toward which efforts in the organization are directed. **Objectives,** sometimes called operative goals, are specific, and often quantified, versions of goals. Unlike goals, objectives are verifiable and specific, and are developed so that managers can measure performance.

**mission** the reason for an organization's existence; the mission statement is a broadly defined but enduring statement of purpose that identifies the scope of an organization's operations and its offerings to the various stakeholders

**goals** desired general ends toward which efforts are directed

**objectives** specific, verifiable, and often quantified versions of a goal

An organization's mission, goals, and objectives should be intertwined. For example, the mission of a fast-food restaurant chain might be to "provide high-quality food with consistent and rapid service to consumers in the southeastern United States at a profit." Management may establish a goal "to expand the size of the organization by adding new outlets." From this goal, a number of specific objectives may be derived, such as "to increase the number of stores by 20 percent each year for the next five years." The restaurant chain may have another goal, "to be known as the innovative leader in the industry." On the basis of this goal, one of the specific objectives may be "to have 15 percent of sales each year come from seasonal offerings or new products developed during the preceding two years."

As is apparent, the mission is generally viewed as enduring and long term in nature. At the other end of the spectrum, objectives are seen as short term with a fixed duration. In this respect, goals fit neatly between the mission and objectives, but the length of their duration can vary depending on context. Broadly speaking, *short-term goals* look about a year into the future, *intermediate-term goals* look about three to five years into the future, and *long-term goals* look six to ten years down the road. The notion of short, intermediate, and long with respect to the duration of goals is relative, however.

It is important to distinguish the concepts of mission, goals, and objectives from the concept of strategy. Whereas the mission, goals, and objectives emphasize the desired ends of organizational activity at various levels, the strategy connotes the organizational approach that will be taken to achieve the ends. The concepts are related and may even use some of the same language, but they should be differentiated.

It is also important to note the fine line between goals and objectives in contemporary business expression. Some leaders may even use the terms interchangeably. Although it is necessary to understand the key principle behind the distinction between terms—the need to incorporate measures into the equation—the use of different terms is not necessarily problematic as long as everyone in the organization understands their meanings.

Objectives are typically set in a number of areas. Most notably, organizations usually develop performance objectives utilizing measures such as profit, market share, and stock price. Managers often develop objectives for improvements in areas such as productivity, innovation and new product development, product quality, resource attainment, employee welfare, and social responsibility.

Without verifiability and specificity, objectives will not provide clear direction for the organization. For example, if a manager states a departmental objective as "increases average order size to existing customers," it will not always be easy to tell whether or not the department has been successful. Would the department be successful if the average order increased by only one percent while inflation rose by five percent? Would the department be successful if the average order increased by 10 percent but 15 percent of the customers switched to competitors? Without specifics, individuals are left to debate success or failure based on their own perspectives of what happened and why.

Interestingly, specific and verifiable objectives can also lead to debates over the appropriateness of the measures used. For example, if the previous objective was revised to "increase sales to existing customers by 10 percent," some might argue that sales representatives will have an incentive to ignore new customers in an effort to meet the stated objective. Hence, it is conceivable that pursuit of the objective could actually work against other departmental goals. Simply stated, a sales rep could pursue one objective at the expense of another. For this reason, it is essential that objectives not only be specific and verifiable, but that the most appropriate measures are selected.

## 4-2 The Case for Goals and Objectives

It has been argued that setting goals and objectives can be an arduous, cumbersome, and time-consuming process. However, goals and objectives are necessary for three main reasons. First, they provide direction, guidance, and legitimacy for the organization. Without such guidance, employees will determine for themselves what they should do, why they should do it, and how their activities fit into the larger picture of organizational survival. For example, clerks at a department store's customer service desk often make decisions concerning whether customers without receipts or returning damaged goods should receive refunds. Without goals and objectives that embody the activities of the department, different clerks will inevitably make inconsistent judgments when faced with similar situations.

Second, goals create unity across functional and geographical units of the organization. Without organizational goals, units divided by function or geography are more likely to move in different directions and compete for resources instead of working together toward a common purpose. The existence of goals does not guarantee that a common purpose will be achieved, but it improves the likelihood that it will be pursued.

Customers typically have contact with members of different departments within an organization. In many cases, these members may be located in different geographical locations. When each member of the organization, regardless of department or location, understands its goals, a higher level of consistency is likely to be achieved.

Third, goals and objectives motivate employees by encouraging workers to work toward their attainment. They set benchmarks for employee performance and challenge them to put forth maximum effort to reach them. When operational objectives are set for a 1 percent defect rate, for example, production workers can monitor success or failure easily and may be motivated to produce higher quality goods in an effort to meet the objective.

An organization's leadership should be proactive in developing its goals and objectives. At first glance it might appear that all organizations have goals and that most are well understood by their members. Unfortunately, this is not the case. In some organizations, goals are inferred but never specified because decision makers do not take the time to identify them. Goals emerge anyway in these organizations—at least to some extent—as individual members of the organization seek to identify ends toward which activity should be directed.

The problem with allowing goals to emerge is twofold. First, the goals that develop, either explicit or implicit, might not be appropriate for the organization.

Box 4-1

## Career Point

### Organizational Goals and Career Goals

What are your career goals? Should you be concerned about your organization's mission, goals, and the like? It depends on the company.

Organizations often disseminate a mission, goals, values, and other written statements as a means of guiding the firm's strategic and daily activities. An organization whose mission is "to provide customers with a level of value unsurpassed by any competitors" is setting guidelines for its decision makers. If value to the customer is at the forefront, then managers must determine whether the ultimate customer value associated with any activity will surpass the costs incurred. These activities can include anything from production and equipment purchase decisions to how much is budgeted for employee travel.

Unfortunately, many organizations create elaborate goals and mission statements as a formality or gimmick.

In the former case, everything is filed away at company headquarters and decisions are not affected. In the latter case, statements such as "the customer is king" or "our goal is zero defects" are plastered throughout the organization, but employees soon learn that objectives have not been set to measure whether or not the goals are being attained. In this situation, published goals can actually have a negative effect, as employees not only widely ignore the goals, but they have the impression that the organization lacks any serious direction.

Ideally, it is best to work for an organization whose goals are clearly defined, serve as real guidelines for decisions, and are compatible with individual goals. When you consider employment with an organization, you should ask not only for a short list of company goals, but you should ask how the organization is pursuing them.

Consider an electronics components manufacturer as an example. Without strong leadership, the goals that evolve might emphasize the retention of two or three key customers because they account for a large percentage of revenues and members of the organization have become accustomed to working with them in the past. It is possible, however, that the organization might be better suited to reduce its dependence on these prime customers by cultivating additional accounts. Without forethought and planning, goals aimed at expanding the reach of the organization are not likely to develop.

Second, if goals are allowed to emerge, it is likely that competing sets of goals will evolve for different factions within the organization. The goals developed by production employees will probably concern production issues, those developed by the sales department will probably emphasize revenue generation, and so on. Hence, without central leadership in the development of goals, an organization can easily end up with counterproductive or contradictory goals.

In sum, managers should understand the importance of goals and objectives and should seek to develop them in a proactive manner. Goals and objectives that are clear and appropriate for an organization can play a great role in improving its effectiveness. When goals or objectives are unclear, inconsistent, or simply do not exist, however, organizational effectiveness is likely to suffer as a result. Organizational goals can also be important when assessing one's career goals, as outlined in Box 4-1.

## 4-3 Goals and Stakeholders

**stakeholders** individuals or groups who are affected by or can influence an organization's operations

Establishing a mission, goals, and objectives may appear to be a noncontroversial task. However, various **stakeholders**—individuals or groups who are affected by or can influence an organization's operations—have different perspectives on the purpose of an organization and can complicate the process. As a result, the task can become quite complex.

Top managers are responsible for establishing and communicating a vision for the organization that integrates the views of the various stakeholders. Hence, decision makers of profit-seeking organizations should be concerned not only with the shareholders' primary objective of profits, but also with attaining the goals of other stakeholders as well.[1] Ultimately, the mission, goals, and objectives that eventually emerge should balance the pressures from the different stakeholder groups.

Various stakeholders often have different, even conflicting goals for an organization.[2] This occurs because each stakeholder group—including stockholders, members of the board of directors, managers, employees, suppliers, creditors, and customers—views the organization from a different perspective. Table 4-1 suggests what some of the goals might be for key stakeholders in a typical organization.

It is easy to see how stakeholder goals can conflict with one another. Following Table 4-1, for example, shareholders are generally interested in maximum profitability, whereas creditors are more concerned with long-term survival so that their loans will be repaid. Customers wish to purchase high-quality products at the lowest possible prices, whereas the general public may seek to require a firm to incorporate costly measures to cut pollution, a move that can ultimately cause the organization to raise prices. In addition, some individuals may be represented by disparate stakeholder groups. For example, employees may own shares of stock in a firm and also purchase its products. Top managers must reconcile these differences while pursuing its own set of goals, which typically includes quality of work life and career advancement.

Organizations create value for various parties, including employees through wages and salaries, shareholders through profits, customers through value derived via its goods and services, and even governments through taxes. Organizations, however, should not seek to maximize the value delivered to any single stakeholder at the expense of the goals of other groups.[3] Those that do so may enjoy desirable short-term results but can jeopardize their long-term survival and profitability. For example, an organization that emphasizes the financial interests of shareholders over the monetary needs of employees can alienate employees, motivating the top performers to seek employment elsewhere, thereby threatening the continued performance of the organization. Likewise, establishing long-term relationships with suppliers may restrict the organization's ability to remain flexible and change suppliers when necessary so that it can offer innovative products to customers. Top

| TABLE 4-1 | Suggested Goals of Stakeholders |
|---|---|
| **Stakeholders** | **Goals** |
| Customers | The organization should provide high-quality products and services at the most reasonable prices possible. |
| General public | The organization should provide goods and services with minimum environmental costs, increase employment opportunities, and contribute to social and charitable causes. |
| Suppliers | The organization should establish long-term relationships with suppliers and purchase from them at prices that allow the suppliers to remain profitable. |
| Employees | The organization should provide good working conditions, equitable compensation, and opportunities for advancement. |
| Creditors | The organization should maintain a healthy financial posture and a policy of on-time payment of debt. |
| Shareholders | The organization should produce a higher-than-average return on equity. |
| Board of directors | Current directors should be retained and should be shielded from legal liability. |
| Managers | The organization should allow managers to benefit financially from the growth and success of the company. |

Balancing the views of stakeholders can be a challenging process.

management is charged not only with the task of resolving opposing shareholder demands, but also with doing so in a manner conducive to long-term success for the organization.[4]

Balancing the various goals of an organization's stakeholders can be difficult. In a publicly traded organization, for example, top managers and the board of directors are primarily accountable to the firm's shareholders. As such, top managers are responsible for generating financial returns, and board members are in charge of oversight of the firm's management. Some have argued, however, that this traditional *shareholder-driven* perspective is too narrow, and that financial returns are actually maximized when a *customer-driven* perspective is adopted, a view that is consistent with the marketing concept.[5] In other words, an organization should not focus on generating profits per se, but on satisfying customers, a process that ultimately increases profits in the long term. Consumer advocate and frequent U.S. Presidential candidate Ralph Nader has argued for more than thirty years that large corporations must be more responsive to customers' needs.[6]

## 4-4 The Agency Problem

Ideally, top management should attempt to maximize the return to shareholders on their investment while simultaneously satisfying the interests of other stakeholders. However, because absentee owners (i.e., the shareholders) in publicly held firms hire professionals to manage their organizations, some experts question the extent to which these managers pursue profits for the organization rather than seeking to satisfy their own personal goals.[7] In many instances, managers' goals of greater salaries and stability may be in direct opposition to shareholders' goals of high organizational performance. For this reason, it is not uncommon to see successful small organizations seeking to stay small so the owner can remain personally in charge of the major business decisions.

**agency problem** a situation in which a firm's top managers (i.e., the agents of the firm's owners) do not act in the best interests of the shareholders

The **agency problem** refers to a situation in which a firm's managers—the agents of the owners—do not always act in the best interests of the shareholders. The extent to which the problem adversely affects most organizations is widely debated, and factors associated with the problem can vary from country to country.[8] Indeed, some argue that management primarily serves its own interests, whereas others contend that managers share the same interests as the shareholders. These two perspectives are briefly discussed in sections 4-4a and 4-4b.

### 4-4a Management Serves Its Own Interests

According to one perspective, top managers tend to make decisions that ultimately increase their own salaries and other rewards. Hence, top managers are likely to grow their firms even if growth is not the optimal strategy because executive salaries tend to be higher in larger firms.[9]

**diversification** the process of acquiring companies to increase a firm's size

Executives may also pursue **diversification,** increasing the size of their firms by acquiring other companies. Diversification not only increases a firm's size but may also improve its survivability by spreading risk among business units operating in different markets. However, diversification pursued only to spread risk is generally not in the best interest of shareholders since they always have the option of reducing their financial risks by purchasing shares in other corporations.[10] This perspective does not suggest that top managers are unconcerned with firm performance, but rather that top managers may deemphasize it when personal considerations are also involved in a decision.

The extent to which this perspective is accurate can create an advantage for relatively small, entrepreneurial organizations whose owners actively manage the firm. Because owners and managers are one and the same, no agency problem exists. For

this reason, such organizations may be able to compete aggressively and successfully with their larger rivals, especially if they concentrate their efforts on limited domains within a given market.

### 4-4b Management and Stockholders Share the Same Interests

Because managers' livelihoods are directly related to the success of an organization, one can argue that managers generally share the same interests as the stockholders. Because management rewards rise with firm performance, managers by definition are most concerned with organization performance, not individual concerns. Many experts argue that managerial jobs are structured in ways that force managers to attempt to enhance profits.[11]

### 4-4c Resolving the Agency Problem

Historically, the agency problem was not a concern in the early years of the industrial revolution. During that time, owners and their family members served as active supervisors. Organizations tended to be small and ownership was not typically dispersed. When nonfamily members were secured as managers, they were usually watched closely by an owner. Hence, the agency problem became pervasive only when the corporate form of ownership became more widely spread.

Today, the debate over whether top managers are primarily concerned with their firms' returns or their own interests continues. Most managers, however, acknowledge truth in both perspectives. In reality, differences in perspective are a matter of degree. It is also likely that the degree to which the agency problem exists is related to factors such as the industry in which an organization competes, the size of the firm, and even its position in the organizational life cycle.

Ultimately, resolving the different perspectives of the agency problem is a philosophical and experiential endeavor. Some managers may argue that a serious agency problem exists while others in the same organization may not perceive the problem to be significant. Regardless of perspective, manager and shareholder goals may be easily aligned when managers also own part of a firm. Hence, one of the most common suggestions for aligning the goals of top management and those of shareholders is to award shares of stock or stock options to top management, transforming professional managers into shareholders. Many companies have adopted **employee stock ownership plans (ESOPs)** to distribute shares of the company's stock to managers and other employees over time. Box 4-2 discusses employee ownership in one firm in detail.

Stock option plans and high salaries may bring the interests of top management and stockholders closer together.[12] Top executives must deliver high performance

**employee stock ownership plan (ESOP)** a formal program that transfers shares of stock to a company's employees

## Best Practices
### Employee Ownership of American Firms

The National Center for Employee Ownership (NCEO) publishes a list it calls the *Employee Ownership Top 100,* including U.S.-based firms that are at least 50 percent employee-owned through an ESOP, stock purchase plan, or other broad-based ownership plans.

Florida-based Publix Super Markets is one of the largest firms on the list. The grocery chain operates about 800 stores in Florida, Alabama, Georgia, South Carolina, and Tennessee. Publix ownership is distributed to employees through ESOPs and stock purchase plans. Almost 100,000 employees are shareholders,

comprising almost two-thirds of the total number of shareholders for the firm.

Although a significant portion of the company is owned by nonemployees, Publix circumvents some of the concerns associated with the agency problem by distributing ownership widely among its employees. Because they are both managers and owners, decision makers have an incentive to act in the best interest of the shareholders.

Interestingly, four of the top ten employee-owned companies as of 2004 are grocery chains. In addition to Publix, Hy-Vee, Price Chopper, and Brookshire Brothers are also on the list.

for the organization in order to protect their salaries and option plans. Research supports this notion, suggesting that as managerial stock ownership rises, the interests of managers and shareholders begin to converge to some extent.[13] Many organizations pursue compensation models designed to bring the two sides together, such as those that emphasize stock options and profit sharing for managers instead of fixed pay levels.

## 4-5 Organizational Effectiveness

**organizational effectiveness**
the extent to which an organization utilizes its resources effectively to accomplish its goals and objectives

**organizational capacity**
an organization's ability to remain effective and sustain itself over the long term

The concepts of goals and objectives—as well as the agency problem—assume that the outcomes of an organization's activities can be readily understood. The idea of organizational performance is primarily associated with financial and market-oriented measures. Organizational effectiveness is an elusive, broader term and can mean different things to different people. We define **organizational effectiveness** as the extent to which an organization utilizes its resources effectively to accomplish its goals and objectives. Although traditional metrics such as profits, market share, and stock price are useful in assessing organizational effectiveness, other factors such as productivity, creativity, and human capital are also considered.

The notion of organizational effectiveness cannot be fully understood without also recognizing its relationship to organizational resources. **Organizational capacity** refers to an organization's ability to remain effective and sustain itself over the long term. It is possible for an organization to be highly effective with limited capacity, although this is typically not the case. In practice, organizations seek to acquire valuable resources to build capacity and ultimately improve effectiveness.

There are many ways top managers can foster organizational effectiveness. First, its leaders can build trust and autonomy among its members. Trust leads to increased autonomy and free sharing of information and ultimately greater job satisfaction, organizational commitment, and personal performance.[14] Second, its leaders can create a productive and supportive work environment, including factors such as comfortable and sufficient office space, ergonomic awareness, and an emphasis on training and development. Of course, there are costs associated with these activities, and they should be taken into account. However, the costs can be offset in many cases by improvements in effectiveness. Third, its leaders can build capacity. Pressures to meet short-term financial goals often relegate capacity building to a back seat position.

Many organizations invest capital only in outcomes that they can immediately measure or quantify. Instead, these organizations should invest in activities and resources that can serve as the foundation for *long-term* organizational effectiveness.

### 4-5a Measuring Organizational Effectiveness

Although concepts such as organizational effectiveness and capacity are broad enough to assist managers in communicating about their organizations, both are notoriously difficult to measure. For this reason, some managers emphasize only basic financial and accounting measures such as return on assets and sales growth. One problem with this approach is that each measure tells only a piece of the story. Astute managers examine multiple measures—some nonfinancial—when evaluating an organization's outcomes. In general, performance is associated with profit measures whereas organizational effectiveness is considered with other factors as well.

Because individual measures of performance and effectiveness can provide a limited snapshot of the firm, a number of companies have begun using a **balanced scorecard** approach. In this technique, measurement is not based on a single quantitative factor, but on an array of quantitative and qualitative factors, such as return on assets, market share, organizational capacity, customer loyalty and satisfaction, speed, and innovation.[15]

**balanced scorecard**
an approach to measuring performance or organizational effectiveness based on an array of quantitative and qualitative factors, such as return on assets, market share, organizational capacity, customer loyalty and satisfaction, speed, and innovation

Four primary perspectives are inherent within the balanced scorecard approach. The *financial perspective* is concerned with traditional performance measures such as profitability, return on investment, and improvement in stock price. The *customer perspective* considers such factors as customer service, loyalty, and satisfaction. The *learning and growth* perspective evaluates such areas as the degree to which an organization is engaged in continuous improvement and is able to retain its most valuable human resources. The *internal business process perspective* emphasizes the value an organization delivers to its customers and shareholders.[16]

The balanced scorecard is concerned not only with the traditional performance measures as captured in the financial perspective, but also with broader, "softer" measures that can be easily overlooked when a firm is focused solely on short-term financial performance. Interestingly, one can argue that high marks along the other three perspectives can position the organization for superior financial performance in the long term. The key to employing a balanced scorecard is to select a combination of performance measures tailored specifically to the organization. In other words, each organization's members should develop a reasonable number of simple measures that collectively reflect the organization's effectiveness.[17]

Another problem with measuring organizational performance is that one measure can be pursued to the detriment of another. The common goals of growth and profitability represent an example of this phenomenon. Many firms pursue growth by investing in research and development focused on improving existing products or developing new ones or by slashing prices to gain customers. Either approach tends to reduce profits, at least in the short term. This reality was reflected in Ford's decision to cut North American production early in the twenty-first century and sacrifice market share in order to enhance profits. Ford's market share declined from about 22 percent in 2001 to below 19 percent in 2004, but profits increased steadily during this same period.[18]

One approach to measuring organizational effectiveness involves the examination of three key organizational processes: (1) controlling the external environment, (2) maintaining efficiency within operations, and (3) fostering innovation.[19] Specific goals can be developed to move the organization toward greater effectiveness in each of these realms.

Controlling the external environment is difficult for any organization to do, especially smaller ones. The key to effective control, however, is the ability of a firm to secure the resources to produce and market its products or services. As such, traditional performance indicators such as stock price, market share, revenue growth, and

Production efficiency can be measured by examining indicators such as units per time period, cost per unit, and defective rates.

return on assets may be used to reflect the control dimension. Managers may set goals such as increasing profits or market share as means of pursuing effectiveness in control.

Maintaining efficiency is concerned with more technical issues. Within this realm, managers are concerned with an organization's ability to produce a high quantity and quality of products or services relative to the amount of input it consumes. As such, managers should evaluate changes in technology on a continuous basis to reduce costs and increase quality. Organizations measure efficiency by such indicators as quality, production costs, and customer service. Managers may set goals such as reducing product defects, cutting delivery time, and improving customer satisfaction as means of pursuing efficiency.

Whereas efficiency is primarily related to improving existing products, services, and processes, innovation involves the identification of new and better ones. As such, managers can foster innovation by developing the organization's human, physical, and organizational resources. Innovative firms minimize conflict, support worthy initiatives, and empower employees to make better decisions. As such, indicators such as rate of new product development and employee coordination are often used to reflect an organization's level of innovation.

Although it is not difficult to identify prospective indicators for each of the three processes, measuring them is far from easy, especially for innovation. For example, developing new products is an activity generally presumed to reflect innovation with a firm. However, it is difficult to determine precisely how many new products should be developed within a given time period. In addition, managers should also consider the ultimate success or failure of new product introductions, as well as the costs to develop and move them to market.

The interrelationships among these three broad measures—control, efficiency, and innovation—cannot be overstated. For example, an organization that excels in control by securing the appropriate resources may be in a better position to utilize them to produce more efficiently or to create new products or services. Hence, managers who wish to emphasize excellence in one realm should realize that they may be sacrificing excellence in the other two.

## 4-6 Controlling Organizational Effectiveness

**organizational control**
determining the extent to which organizational effectiveness is attained and taking corrective measures to improve effectiveness if needed

**Organizational control** consists of determining the extent to which organizational effectiveness is attained and taking corrective measures to improve effectiveness if needed. Organizational control is similar to but broader than strategic control, which emphasizes the extent to which strategies are effective. Whereas strategies at various levels may emphasize a limited number of goals, organizational control is concerned with a broader array of issues and processes.

Organizational control can be exerted through three primary means. Control can be exerted through strategic control, from the board of directors through proper oversight, and from outside of the organization via takeover. Control measures taken by managers within the organization are usually more effective and efficient. These measures are summarized in Table 4-2 and discussed in greater detail in Sections 4-6a, 4-6b, and 4-6c.

## 4-6a Exercising Control within the Organization

Organizational control within the organization is generally concerned with the strategy of the organization. Although control may be instituted at other management levels, it is usually the chief executive and/or members of the **top management team** who initiates it. The chief executive is the individual ultimately responsible for the organization's management but rarely acts alone. In most organizations, a *team* of top-level executives—including members of the board of directors, vice presidents, and various line and staff managers—is also involved. Most top executives build a top management team to add different perspectives and improve decision quality.[20]

Organizational control from within the organization can be initiated in a number of ways. One is **competitive benchmarking**—the process of measuring a firm's performance against that of the top performers, usually in the same industry. After determining the appropriate benchmarks, goals can be set to meet or exceed them. **Best practices**—processes or activities that have been successful in other organizations—may be adopted as a means of improving performance.

Benchmarking tends to occur most frequently at the top of an organization, but it can also occur at middle and lower management levels. At the top level, factors such as profitability, market share, and revenue growth may be applied. The most appropriate performance benchmarks are those associated with the strategy's success and those over which the organization has control. The importance of specificity cannot be overstated, however. For example, if market share is identified as a key indicator of the success or failure of a growth strategy, a specific market share should be identified, based on past performance and/or industry norms. Without specificity, it is difficult to assess the effectiveness of a strategy after it is implemented.

The data required to set benchmarks is often readily available. For example, *Fortune* magazine annually publishes the most- and least-admired American corporations with annual sales of at least $500 million in such diverse industries as electronics, pharmaceuticals, retailing, transportation, banking, insurance, metals, food,

**top management team** the team of top-level executives—including members of the board of directors, vice presidents, and various line and staff managers—all of whom play instrumental roles in managing the organization

**competitive benchmarking** the process of measuring a firm's performance against that of the top performers, usually in the same industry

**best practices** processes or activities that have been successful in other organizations

| | **TABLE 4-2** | Sources of Organizational Control |
| --- | --- | --- |

| Level | Nature of Organizational Control | Emphasis of Control |
| --- | --- | --- |
| Within the management ranks of the organization | Strategic control | Ensure that strategies at all levels (firm, business, and functional) contribute to organizational effectiveness and that organizational divisions are properly managed. |
| Board of directors | Strategic and organizational oversight | Ensure that firm-level strategies contribute to organizational effectiveness and that top managers represent the wishes of the shareholders. |
| Outside of the organization | Takeovers | Outsiders acquire the organization and implement major changes to improve effectiveness. |

Exercising strategic control requires that anticipated performance be compared to actual performance.

motor vehicles, and utilities. Corporate dimensions are evaluated along factors such as quality of products and services, innovation, quality of management, market share, financial returns and stability, social responsibility, and human resource management effectiveness. Publications such as *Forbes, Industry Week, Business Week,* and *Industry Standard* also provide performance scorecards based on similar criteria. Although such lists generally include only large, publicly traded companies, they can offer high-quality strategic information at minimal cost to the strategic managers of all organizations, regardless of size. Published information on areas such as quality, innovation, and market share can be particularly useful measures.

*Consumer Reports* is also an excellent source of product quality data, evaluating hundreds of products from cars to medicine each year. Because *Consumer Reports* accepts no advertising, its evaluations are relatively free of bias, rendering it an excellent source of quality product information. Even if *Consumer Reports* does not review an organization's products or services, its managers can still gain insight on the quality of products and services produced by competitors, suppliers, and buyers.

Specific published information may also exist for organizations in select industries. One of the best known is the "Customer Satisfaction Index" released annually by J.D. Power and Associates for the automobile industry. A survey of new-car owners each year examines such variables as satisfaction with various aspects of vehicle performance; problems reported during the first 90 days of ownership; ratings of dealer service quality; and ratings of the sales, delivery, and condition of new vehicles.[21] Numerous Internet sites—such as Virtualratings.com—offer quality ratings associated with a number of industries for everything from computers to university professors.

An organization's top managers may seek to change how activities are performed, both formally and informally. The **formal organization**—the official structure of relationships and procedures used to manage organizational activity—can facilitate or impede a firm's success. When problems occur, it may be necessary to implement changes within the existing formal organization or consider changing it altogether.

For minor and less complex problems, managers can implement changes within the formal organization before an activity begins, while it is occurring, and after an activity has already occurred. It is generally desirable to institute a control measure as early as possible. A **feedforward control** anticipates problems and is initiated prior to an occurrence of an activity. For example, most major airlines have instituted preventative maintenance programs designed to reduce flight delays and crashes.

**formal organization**
the official structure of relationships and procedures used to manage organizational activity

**feedforward control**
a measure that anticipates problems and is initiated prior to an occurrence of an activity

A **concurrent control** seeks to correct a problem while it is occurring. Supervision is a common means of exercising concurrent control. Even when constant direct supervision is not required, managers often walk around their departments from time to time to learn about potential problems in their early stages.

Although it is best to anticipate a problem and correct it before it occurs—or at least while it is occurring—this is not always possible. A **feedback control** seeks to correct a problem after it has occurred and prevent it from happening again. For example, a task force may be appointed to investigate contributing factors to a major breakdown in a production facility in order to correct problems and reduce the chance that the breakdown occurs again.

When problems are acute, however, changing the organization's structure may be desirable, as discussed in Chapter 5. Substantial structural changes cannot be easily implemented and typically require a large amount of training and development. Top managers at firms undertaking such changes often underestimate the complications associated with transforming their organizational structures into a more complex matrix structure.

In contrast to the formal organization, the **informal organization** refers to the norms, behaviors, and expectations that evolve when individuals and groups come into contact with one another.[22] The informal organization is dynamic and flexible and does not require managerial decree to change. When top executives use the formal organization effectively, the informal organization tends to reinforce the formal organization and promote the same values. However, when the organization's value system is unclear or even contradictory, the informal organization will ultimately develop its own set of values and rewards. For example, every organization claims to reward high job performance. However, when promotions and pay increases go to individuals who have the greatest seniority (regardless of performance level), employees will lose motivation and develop their own set of informal rules concerning what will and will not be rewarded.

Managers at all levels must recognize that they can *influence,* but cannot control, the informal organization. Interestingly, the most effective means of influencing the informal organization is to develop and promote a formal organization dysfunctional when it develops means to address inconsistencies in the formal organization.[23]

## 4-6b Corporate Governance and the Board of Directors

**Corporate governance** refers to the board of directors, institutional investors (e.g., pension and retirement funds, mutual funds, banks, and insurance companies, among other money managers), and large shareholders known as block holders who monitor organizational strategies and performance to ensure effective management. Boards of directors and institutional investors are generally the most influential in a typical governance system. Because institutional investors own more than half of all shares of publicly traded firms, they tend to wield substantial influence. Block holders tend to hold less than 20 percent of all firm shares, so their influence is proportionally less than that of institutional investors.[24] Nonetheless, both institutional investors and block holders are in a position to influence decision making to an extent that few individual shareholders can.

Boards often include both inside (i.e., firm executives) and outside directors. Insiders bring company-specific knowledge to the board, whereas outsiders bring independence and an external perspective. Over the past several decades, the composition of the typical board has shifted from one controlled by insiders to one controlled by outsiders, allowing board members to oversee managerial decisions more effectively.[25] Furthermore, when additional outsiders are added to insider-dominated boards, CEO dismissal is more likely when corporate performance declines,[26] and outsiders are more likely to pressure for corporate restructuring.[27]

Many experts argue that one organization's board members should limit their service on other boards. In the 1990s, the number of corporate board members with

**concurrent control** a measure that seeks to correct a problem while it is occurring

**feedback control** a measure that seeks to correct a problem after it has occurred and prevent it from happening again

**informal organization** the norms, behaviors, and expectations that evolve when individuals and groups come into contact with one another

**corporate governance** the board of directors, institutional investors, and block holders who monitor firm strategies to ensure managerial responsiveness

memberships in other boards began to increase dramatically. With outside directors of the largest 200 firms commanding an average of $152,000 in cash and equity in 2001, a number of companies became concerned about both potential conflicts of interest and the amount of time each individual can spend with the affairs of each company. As a result, many companies have begun to limit the number of board memberships their own board members may hold. By 2002, approximately two-thirds of corporate board members at the largest 1,500 U.S. companies did not hold seats on other boards.[28] This change has been underscored by the Sarbanes-Oxley Act of 2002, which requires that firms include more independent directors on their boards and make new disclosures on internal controls, ethics codes, and the composition of their audit committees on annual reports. A number of analysts have noted positive changes among boards because of this legislation in terms of both independence and expertise.[29]

Boards of directors are composed of officials elected by the shareholders and are responsible for monitoring activities in the organization, evaluating top managers, and establishing the broad strategic direction for the firm. As such, boards are responsible for selecting, compensating, and replacing the chief executive officer, advising top management on strategic issues, and monitoring managerial and company performance as representatives of the shareholders. A number of critics charge, however, that board members do not always fulfill their legal roles.[30] The CEO nominates board members and expects them to support his or her strategic initiatives. The board members often receive generous compensation, and they may have a tendency not to challenge the status quo to improve their prospects for a long-term appointment.[31]

When insiders control boards, a rubber stamp mentality can develop, whereby directors do not aggressively challenge executive decisions as they should. This is particularly true when the CEO also serves as chair of the board, a practice known as **CEO duality**.[32] Insider board members—especially those who report to the CEO—may be less willing to exert control when the CEO also serves as chair of the board. In the absence of CEO duality, however, insiders may be more likely to contribute to board control.

**CEO duality**    a situation in which the CEO also serves as the chair of the board

Pressure on directors to acknowledge shareholder concerns has increased over the past two decades. The major source of pressure in recent years has come from institutional investors. By virtue of the size of their investments, they wield considerable power and are more willing to use it than ever before.

However, some board members have played effective stewardship roles. Many directors strongly promote the best interests of the firm's shareholders, as well as those of various other stakeholder groups as well. By conscientiously carrying out their duties, effective directors can ensure that management remains focused on company performance.[33]

A number of recommendations have been made on how to promote effective governance. It has been suggested that outside directors be the only ones to evaluate the performance of top managers against established mission and goals, that all outside board members should meet alone at least once annually, and that boards of directors should establish appropriate qualifications for board membership and communicate these qualifications to shareholders. It is important for institutional shareholders, institutions, and other shareholders to act as owners and not just investors,[34] to avoid interfering with day-to-day managerial decisions, and to evaluate the performance of the board of directors regularly.[35]

### 4-6c Takeovers

When shareholders conclude that the top managers and ineffective board members are mismanaging the firm, institutional investors, block holders, and other shareholders may sell large portions of their shares, substantially lowering the market price of the company's stock.[36] Depressed prices often lead to a **takeover,** a purchase of a controlling quantity of a firm's shares by an individual, a group of investors, or another organization. Takeovers may be attempted by outsiders or insiders (i.e., managers), and may be friendly or unfriendly. A friendly takeover is one in which the prospective buyer(s) work with the board to negotiate a transaction. In contrast, an unfriendly takeover is one in which the target firm resists the sale. In this instance, one or more individuals may purchase enough shares in the target firm to force a change in top management or to manage the firm themselves. Interestingly, groups that seek to initiate unfriendly takeovers often include current or former firm executives.

In many cases, sudden takeover attempts rely heavily on borrowed funds to finance the acquisition, a process referred to as a **leveraged buyout (LBO).** LBOs strap the company with heavy debt and often lead to a partial divestment of some of the firm's subsidiaries or product divisions to lighten the burden.[37] Top managers often become wary of LBOs if share prices drop precipitously, thereby enabling would-be investors to acquire the firm at a lower cost.

Corporate takeovers provide a system of checks and balances often required to initiate changes in ineffective management. Proponents argue that the threat of LBOs can pressure managers to operate their firms more efficiently.[38] However, the debt created by a takeover can cause management to pursue activities that are expedient in the short run but not best for the firm in the long run. In addition, the extra debt required to finance an LBO tends to increase the likelihood of bankruptcy for a troubled firm.[39]

**takeover** the purchase of a controlling quantity of shares in a firm by an individual, a group of investors, or another organization; takeovers can be friendly or unfriendly

**leveraged buyout (LBO)** a takeover in which the acquiring party borrows funds to purchase a firm

## Summary

An organization's mission outlines the reason for its existence. A clear purpose provides managers with a sense of direction and can guide all of the organization's activities. Goals represent the desired general ends toward which organizational efforts are directed. However, managers, shareholders, and board members do not always share the same goals. Top management must attempt to reconcile and satisfy the interests of each group of stakeholders.

The concept of organizational effectiveness evaluates the extent to which an organization accomplishes its goals and objectives. Measuring organizational effectiveness is a complex process that should include a number of factors, not only accounting and financial performance measures. One approach, the balanced scorecard, evaluates other dimensions of performance beyond the financial realm.

When effectiveness is not attained, control measures are necessary. Organizational control can be initiated from within the organization's management ranks, through its board of directors, or from outside of the organization through takeovers. Generally speaking, control closest to the source of the problem is the most desirable.

## Review Questions and Exercises

1. Do missions often change over time? Should missions remain constant? Why or why not?

2. What is organizational effectiveness, and how is it measured?

3. Why do stakeholders in the same organization often have different goals? Would it not be best if they shared the same goals? Explain.

4. Which control form—feedforward, concurrent, or feedback—is most desirable? Which is most effective? Explain.

## Quiz

1. Mission statements are specific and often quantified versions of objectives.
   **True or False**

2. If an organization is profitable, it is balancing the needs of the various stakeholders.
   **True or False**

3. The agency problem refers to the balancing act an organization must exhibit when attempting to satisfy customer needs.
   **True or False**

4. Although diversification often reduces organizational effectiveness, managers may pursue the strategy because it can also reduce the risk of firm failure.
   **True or False**

5. Feedforward controls seek to correct a problem while it is occurring.
   **True or False**

6. Most boards of directors include both inside and outside directors.
   **True or False**

7. The reason for the firm's existence is known as
   a. the vision.
   b. the mission.
   c. organizational objectives.
   d. organizational goals.

8. Which of the following is not an example of a stakeholder?
   a. customers
   b. suppliers
   c. employees
   d. none of the above

9. Measures taken to anticipate and prevent a problem before it occurs are called
   a. feedforward controls.
   b. concurrent controls.
   c. feedback controls.
   d. all of the above.

10. The board of directors is responsible for
    a. selecting the CEO.
    b. determining the CEO's compensation package.
    c. overseeing the firm's strategies.
    d. all of the above.

11. The purchase of a controlling quantity of a firm's shares by an individual, a group of investors, or another organization is known as
    a. a leveraged buyout.
    b. a takeover.
    c. a hostile acquisition.
    d. none of the above.

12. Leveraged buyouts can
    a. strap the company with a large amount of debt.
    b. serve as a system of checks and balances.
    c. lead to the sale of company assets.
    d. do all of the above.

## Endnotes

1. R. Jacob, "The Search for the Organization of Tomorrow," *Fortune* 125, no. 10, (1992): 93.

2. A. L. Friedman and S. Miles, "Developing Stakeholder Theory," *Journal of Management Studies* 39 (2002): 1–22.

3. H. A. Simon, "On the Concept of Organizational Goal," *Administrative Science Quarterly* 9 (1964): 1–22; J. Pfeffer and G. Salancik, *The External Control of Organizations* (New York: Harper & Row, 1978).

4. R. M. Cyert and J.G. March, *A Behavioral Theory of the Firm* (Englewood Cliffs, NJ: Prentice-Hall, 1963); J. G. March and H. A. Simon, *Organizations* (New York: John Wiley & Sons, 1958).

5. S. I. Wu and C. Wu, "A New Market Segmentation Variable for Product Design-Functional Requirements," *Journal of International Marketing and Marketing Research* 25 (2000): 35–48.

6. For an example of his early work, see R. Nader, *Unsafe at Any Speed: Design and Dangers of the American Automobile* (New York: Grossman, 1964).

7. B. M. Staw and L. D. Epstein, "What Bandwagons Bring: Effects of Popular Management Techniques on Corporate Performance, Reputation, and CEO Pay," *Administrative Science Quarterly* 45 (2000): 523–556.

8. K. Ramaswamy, R.Veliyath, and L. Gomes, "A Study of the Determinants of CEO Compensation in India," *Management International Review* 40 (2000): 167–191.

9. J. E. Richard, "Global Executive Compensation: A Look at the Future," *Compensation and Benefits Review* 32, no. 3 (2000): 35–38.

10. D. J. Teece, "Towards an Economic Theory of the Multiproduct Firm," *Journal of Economic Behavior and Organization* 3 (1982): 39–63.

11. C. R. Weinberg, "CEO Compensation: How Much Is Enough?" *Chief Executive* 159 (2000): 48–63.

12. J. Child, *The Business Enterprise in Modern Industrial Society* (London: Collier-Macmillan, 1969).

13. S. L. Oswald and J. S. Jahera, "The Influence of Ownership on Performance: An Empirical Study," *Strategic Management Journal* 12 (1991): 321–326.

14. R. M. Kanter, *Men and Women of the Corporation* (New York: Perseus, 1993).

15. R. Kaplan and D. Norton, *The Balanced Scorecard: Translating Strategy Into Action* (Boston: Harvard Business School Press, 1996); R. Kaplan and D. Norton, *The Strategy Focused Organization* (Boston: Harvard Business School Press, 2001).

16. Kaplan and Norton, 1996; Kaplan and Norton, 2001.

17. M. L. Frigo, "Strategy and the Balanced Scorecard," *Strategic Finance* 84, no. 5 (2002): 6–8; E. M. Olson and S. F. Slater, "The Balanced Scorecard, Competitive Strategy, and Performance," *Business Horizons* 45, no. 3 (2002): 11–16.

18. J. B. White and N. Shirouzu, "At Ford Motor, High Volume Takes Backseat to Profits," *Wall Street Journal,* May 7, 2004, A1, A12.

19. R. R. Rojas, "A Review of Models for Measuring Organizational Effectiveness Among For-Profit and Nonprofit Organizations," *Nonprofit Management and Leadership* 11, no. 1 (2000): 97-104; L. Galambos, "What Have CEOs Been Doing?" *Journal of Economic History* 18 (1988): 243-258.

20. T. K. Das and B. Teng, "Cognitive Biases and Strategic Decision Processes: An Integrative Perspective," *Journal of Management Studies* 36 (1999): 757-778; M. A. Carpenter, "The Implications of Strategy and Social Context for the Relationship Between Top Team Management Heterogeneity and Firm Performance," *Strategic Management Journal* 23 (2002): 275-284.

21. A. Taylor III, "More Power to J. D. Power," *Fortune* 125, no. 10 (1992): 103-106.

22. D. Krackhardt and J. R. Hanson, "Informal Networks: The Company Behind the Chart," *Harvard Business Review* 71, no. 4 (July–August 1993): 104-111.

23. G. A. Miller, "Culture and Organizational Structure in the Middle East: A Comparative Analysis of Iran, Jordan and the USA," *International Review of Sociology* 11 (2001): 309-324; H. Kahalas, "How Competitiveness Affects Individuals and Groups Within Organizations," *Journal of Organizational Behavior* 22, no. 1 (2001): 83-85.

24. S. Chen and K. W. Ho, "Blockholder Ownership and Market Liquidity," *Journal of Financial & Quantitative Analysis* 35 (2000): 621-633; J .J. McConnell and H. Servaes, "Additional Evidence on Equity Ownership and Corporate Value," *Journal of Financial Economics* 27 (1990): 595-612.

25. W. J. Salmon, "Crisis Prevention: How to Gear Up Your Board," *Harvard Business Review* 71 (1993): 68-75.

26. See B. Hermalin and M. S. Weisbach, "The Determinants of Board Composition," *Rand Journal of Economics* 19, no. 4 (1988): 589-605; E. F. Fama and M. C. Jensen, "Separation of Ownership and Control," *Journal of Law and Economics* 26 (1983): 301-325; M. S. Weisbach, "Outside Directors and CEO Turnover," *Journal of Financial Economics* 20 (1988): 431-460.

27. P. A. Gibbs, "Determinants of Corporate Restructuring: The Relative Importance of Corporate Governance, Takeover Threat, and Free Cash Flow," *Strategic Management Journal* 14 (1993): 51-68.

28. P. Plitch, "Ready and Able?" *Wall Street Journal,* February 24, 2003, R3, R5; J. S. Lublin, "More Work, More Pay," *Wall Street Journal,* February 24, 2003, R4, R5.

29. N. Dunne, "Adding a Little Muscle In the Boardroom," *Financial Times,* October 10, 2003, I.

30. J. H. Morgan, "The Board of Directors Is No Longer Just a 'Rubber Stamp,'" *TMA Journal* 19, no. 5 (1999): 14-18.

31. B. R. Baliga and R. C. Moyer, "CEO Duality and Firm Performance," *Strategic Management Journal* 17 (1996): 41-53; P. Stiles, "The Impact of Board on Strategy: An Empirical Examination," *Journal of Management Studies* 38 (2001): 627-650.

32. S. Finkelstein and R. D'Aveni, "CEO Duality as a Double-Edged Sword," *Academy of Management Journal* 37 (1994): 1079-1108.

33. M. S. Mizruchi, "Who Controls Whom? An Examination of the Relation Between Management and Board of Directors in Large American Corporations," *Academy of Management Review* 8 (1983): 426-435.

34. C. Wohlstetter, "Pension Fund Socialism: Can Bureaucrats Run the Blue Chips?" *Harvard Business Review* 71 (1993): 78.

35. J. A. Conger, D. Finegold, and E. E. Lawler III, "Appraising Boardroom Performance," *Harvard Business Review* 76, no. 1 (1998): 136-148.

36. P. Wright and S. Ferris, "Agency Conflict and Corporate Strategy: The Effect of Divestment on Corporate Value," *Strategic Management Journal* 18 (1997): 77-83.

37. S. Perumpral, N. Sen, and G. Noronha, "The Impact of LBO Financing on Bank Returns," *American Business Review* 20, no. 1 (2002): 1-5.

38. M. C. Jensen, "The Eclipse of the Public Corporation," *Harvard Business Review* 67 (September–October 1989): 61-74; P. H. Pan and C. W. L. Hill, "Organizational Restructuring and Economic Performance in Leveraged Buyouts," *Academy of Management Journal* 38 (1995): 704-739.

39. R. B. Reich, "Leveraged Buyouts: America Pays the Price," *New York Times Magazine* (January 29, 1989): 32-40.

# Internal Context
of Organizations

**Part 3**

# Organizational Structure and Design

**Chapter 5**

## Chapter Outline

## Key Terms

bureaucracy
flat organization
functional structure
geographic divisional structure
horizontal growth
horizontal structure
information asymmetry
information symmetry
integration

matrix structure
organizational differentiation
product divisional structure
profit center
span of control
subunit orientation
tall organization
vertical growth

The first step in completing a task is to determine *how* it will be done. This can be a simple process when the task is routine and does not involve more than one or a few individuals. When multiple tasks are involved and many individuals are required to complete them, however, the process can become tedious and complex. Many organizations invest considerable time, energy and resources to ensure that it is structured accordingly so that this process is managed properly.

To some extent, each organization approaches this task differently. The end result is referred to as the organizational structure, the grouping of tasks, activities, and responsibilities within an organization. An organization is most likely to succeed when its structure is aligned with its strategy. When alignment is not present, managers can redesign the strategy or structure, or both, to achieve a fit and improve effectiveness.

This chapter discusses organizational structure in greater detail, with an emphasis on key considerations and broad categorizations that describe the major approaches to formalizing a system whereby work gets done. The chapter closes with considerations managers should make when designing or modifying such a system for their organizations.

# 5-1 Organizational Structure

Most new organizations start small with an owner/manager and a few employees. Neither an organizational chart nor a formal assignment of responsibilities is necessary because each employee performs multiple tasks and the owner/manager is involved in all aspects of the business. This form of organization is often called a simple structure.

New organizations survive if there is sufficient demand for their products or services. As an organization grows to meet this demand, a more permanent division of labor forms. The owner/manager, who once was involved in nearly all functions of the enterprise, begins to play more of a leadership role, and additional employees lead and participate in specialized functions. At some point, however, top management must constantly evaluate the effectiveness of the evolving system of coordinating tasks. Modifying this system is usually necessary for the organization to operate efficiently and effectively as it grows and faces new challenges. A formal means by which work is coordinated develops; this is known as the organizational structure.

The organizational structure exists to provide control and coordination for the organization. It designates formal reporting relationships, defines the number of levels in the hierarchy,[1] and can be seen in an organizational chart such as the one depicted in Figure 5-1. Difficult decisions must be made because there may be logical reasons for organizing work in different ways. For example, work can be organized by function so employees can work only in their areas of specialty, by product so decisions about products can be made in an integrated fashion, or along geographical lines so decisions can be tailored to meet the unique needs of each geographical region. The organizational structure should not be seen as restrictive, however, as individuals can and should work across it when necessary. Nonetheless, there is no single best structure, and the one selected for any organization will have its own set of benefits and challenges. It is typical for many large organizations to change structures frequently as their environments change.

## 5-1a Bureaucracy

Many characteristics of modern organizational structures can be traced to German sociologist Max Weber's notion of bureaucracy about a century ago. Weber defined **bureaucracy** as an organizational structural form with highly specific rules and standard operating procedures. Weber emphasized that employees cannot be held accountable for their actions in a bureaucracy as long as they act in accordance with these clearly defined rules.[2]

**bureaucracy** an organizational structural form with highly specific rules and standard operating procedures

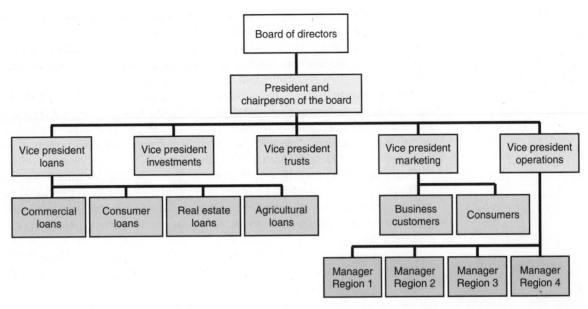

**Figure 5-1**
*Security Bank Organization Chart*

Weber proposed six principles of bureaucratic structure (see Table 5-1). First, Weber's theory states that bureaucracy is founded on the authority a person possesses because of the position he or she holds in an organization. This rational-legal authority legitimizes an individual's role within the organization and grants him or her the right to make decisions and direct others.

Second, positions are based on technical competency, not social status or kinship. In Weber's day, many managerial positions were awarded solely to relatives of other managers and not on the basis of expertise. Weber envisioned an organization where such factors were not a consideration. It would operate as effectively as possible because each position would be filled by the best qualified individual.

Third, individuals responsible for managing and completing tasks should be clearly specified. Responsibility for anything done in an organization should be assigned to one or more individuals, with nothing left to chance. Such a system would ensure that every task would be completed in an efficient and timely manner.

Fourth, from the bottom of the organization up, each office should be responsible to another at the next highest level. This chain of command specifies reporting relationships and ensures that employees have a single immediate superior.

Fifth, rules and procedures should be developed to govern organizational behavior. There should be no questions about what should be done in a certain situation.

| TABLE 5-1 | Weber's Principles of Bureaucratic Structure |
|---|---|

1. A bureaucracy is founded on the concept of rational-legal authority, the authority a person possesses because of his or her position within the organization.
2. Organizational roles are held on the basis of technical competence, not social status or kinship.
3. A role's task responsibility and decision-making authority and its relationship to other rules should be clearly specified.
4. The organization of roles in a bureaucracy is such that each lower office in the hierarchy is under the control and supervision of a higher office.
5. Rules, standard operating procedures, and norms should be used to control the behavior and the relationship between roles in an organization.
6. Administrative acts, decisions, and rules should be formulated and put in writing.

Rather, individuals can consult rules and standard operating procedures to determine how each task should be performed.

Finally, these rules—as well as other top-level decisions—should be put in writing. Doing so increases accuracy and consistency across employees' performance over time. Not doing so leaves individual behavior to chance.

It is difficult to argue with Weber's key principles. Most notably, Weber argued for an authority based on a rational-legal perspective whereby subordinates are obedient to a superior because of the authority that the position—not the individual—commands. Employees are hired for technical competence and operate within a formal system where rules are clear and in writing.

Today, the word *bureaucracy* carries a negative connotation and conjures ideas of inefficiency. This is not always justified, however, and characteristics of Weber's bureaucracy can be seen in almost every organization. As we shall see, a number of different structures have been developed to modify, but not completely reject, Weber's original ideas.

Whether or not Weber's principles are followed, an effective structure should facilitate the transfer of accurate and timely information throughout the organization. Effective *vertical* communication is required so that employees throughout the organization understand the direction in which top management is headed, and so that top managers understand the key concerns and issues faced by employees at all levels of the organization. The chain of command—also referred to as the organizational hierarchy—defines reporting relationships to foster such communication. A vertical information system may be developed to share information produced at one level of the organization with decision makers at other levels.

Effective *horizontal* communication is required so that employees in different functional areas and units can work together as needed to support the mission and goals of the organization. It is helpful when a structure provides for a lot of direct contact among employees in different areas. This contact can occur when members of the organization work together on project teams. Some organizations even develop departments or appoint individuals whose specific responsibility is to foster effective communication across the organization. In addition, the information system aforementioned can also facilitate information sharing across the organization.

Before specific structural options can be presented in detail, however, the following key concepts must be discussed: vertical and horizontal growth, centralization and decentralization, and differentiation and integration. As shall become clear, trade-offs are often required to put these concepts into practice. It is the nature of the trade-offs that ultimately determine an organization's structure. These concepts will be discussed in Sections 5-1b, 5-1c, and 5-1d.

### 5-1b Vertical and Horizontal Growth

**vertical growth** an increase in the number of levels, or in the height of the organization's hierarchical chain of command

**span of control** the number of employees reporting directly to a given manager

**tall organization** an organization characterized by many hierarchical levels and a narrow span of control

**flat organization** an organization characterized by relatively few hierarchical levels and a wide span of control

**Vertical growth** refers to an increase in the number of the organization's levels of management, or hierarchy. The number of employees reporting to each manager in the hierarchy represents that manager's **span of control.** A **tall organization** is composed of many hierarchical levels, each with relatively fewer reporting relationships and a narrow span of control. In contrast, a **flat organization** has few levels in its hierarchy, each with relatively more reporting relationships and a wide span of control.

Researcher John Child noted that the average number of hierarchical levels for an organization with 3,000 employees is seven.[3] Consequently, one might consider such an organization with fewer than seven hierarchical levels to be flat, and one with more than seven to be tall. In practice, flat and tall are relative terms, however. As such, we often speak of specific organizations as relatively flat or relatively tall. In this section, however, we compare and contrast the two extreme ends of the continuum. Most organizations fall somewhere in the middle.

Because tall organizations have a narrow span of control, authority tends to be relatively centralized and managers in such organizations exercise a relatively high degree of control over their subordinates. Authority is more decentralized in relatively flat organizations because managers have broad spans of control and must therefore grant more flexibility to their employees to keep work flowing at an appropriate pace. Because decisions are more likely to be made at lower levels in flat organizations, employees are usually less specialized and are more empowered to make decisions.

Both tall and flat organizations have certain advantages. Tall, centralized organizations foster more effective coordination and communication throughout the various levels in the hierarchy. Planning is relatively easy to accomplish because all employees are centrally directed. As such, tall organizational structures may be best suited for environments that are relatively stable and predictable. Nonetheless, the notion of a tall organization is not in vogue today and many experts believe that employees should be empowered to make decisions as much as possible.

Flat structures also have their advantages and have become more popular among scholars and practitioners. Administrative costs tend to be lower in flat organizations because fewer hierarchical levels require fewer managers and support personnel. Decentralized decision making also gives managers more authority, which may increase their satisfaction and motivation.[4] Increased freedom in decision making can also encourage innovation and new ideas. Hence, flat structures are often best suited to more dynamic environments, such as those in which most Internet businesses operate. Decision quality tends to improve when decisions are made at the level closest to the point where they will be implemented.

**Horizontal growth** refers to an increase in the breadth of an organization's structure. Although the owner, managers, and a few employees may perform all of the functions in a new business, each function expands as the organization grows so that no one individual can be involved in all of the company's functions. The structure of the organization is broadened to accommodate the development of more specialized functions. Owners and managers who are unable to let go of former realms of responsibility during this time are often referred to disparagingly as micromanagers.

Growth in organizations usually adds organizational layers and increases bureaucracy. As a result, a large organization may become both inefficient and incapable of meeting the needs and expectations of its customers. Top management often responds by instituting a more **horizontal structure**—one with fewer hierarchies. A horizontal approach facilitates decision making by empowering employees who are close to the customer.

The organizational restructuring so pervasive throughout the 1980s and 1990s has often involved forming a more horizontal structure through downsizing. Additionally, employee layoffs often occur to reduce costs and eliminate some of the bureaucracy that invariably accompanies multiple organizational layers. As layers are reduced, decision making becomes more decentralized.

Organizations occasionally seek to downsize for the specific purpose of eliminating part of the workforce so that it can be rebuilt in a different manner. A downsizing may occur after an acquisition if there are substantial cultural differences between the two organizations and the acquiring firm wishes to reorient the new combined workforce.

Interestingly, downsizing often does not lead to greater efficiency, especially in the long term. Studies suggest that only about one-half of downsized firms actually lower costs, and many also suffer declines in productivity.[5] In some cases, cuts are applied equally to all departments. As a result, both efficient and inefficient departments lose employees without regard to performance level. In other cases, cost reductions are sought through attractive buyouts offered to relatively high-paid, long-time employees. The result, however, can be a severe loss of critical experience within the employee base.

Positive changes in the formal organization created by downsizing can lead to dysfunctional consequences in the informal organization. Employees who survive the cuts are typically less loyal to the organization and may seek employment elsewhere,

**horizontal growth**
an increase in the breadth of an organization's structure

**horizontal structure**
an organizational structure with fewer hierarchies designed to improve efficiency by reducing layers in the bureaucracy

figuring that they might be cut next. Hence, downsizing can help an organization improve its effectiveness, but its long-term ramifications must be seriously considered before it is adopted.[6]

## 5-1c Centralization and Decentralization

When one organization owns another, the extent to which a firm's managers are involved in the operations of its businesses or to which a given manager tends to directly govern the activities of those below him varies from one firm to another. Involvement is sometimes seen as a stabilizing force and is welcomed by those in business units. However, a number of business unit managers refer to the corporate office in a less than positive light and may view such involvement as interference or stifling to innovation and rapid decision-making.

When effective, corporate involvement in the activities of its business units can improve business performance.[7] Some firms have diversified into unrelated businesses and tend to operate in a relatively decentralized fashion. When decentralization occurs in a firm that controls more than one business unit, the firm is likely to employ small corporate staffs and allow the business unit managers to make most of their own strategic and operating decisions, including such functional areas such as purchasing, inventory management, production, finance, research and development, and marketing. When decentralization occurs in a stand-alone organization, most significant decisions are made at the lowest possible level in the organization.

Alternatively, firms with multiple business units often follow a centralization pattern and make most of the strategic decisions concerning the business units at corporate headquarters. This is especially true when the business units are related, in which case centralization can improve efficiencies and help the business units learn from each other.

When centralization occurs in a stand-alone organization, most significant decisions are made at the top level. For example, top managers must determine the extent to which middle and lower-level managers will be empowered to make their own decisions. Centralizing authority improves consistency across the organization but ultimately results in decisions not made by the individual with the best information. In practice, however, most organizations operate between these two extremes and are constantly struggling to achieve an appropriate balance.

Organizations that are relatively centralized make many functional (e.g., marketing, finance, and production) decisions at the top level. Centralization, however, can also be inefficient, either when a firm attempts to control the activities of a diverse array of business units or when leaders of a stand-alone organization do not allow their managers to function without tight controls.[8]

## 5-1d Differentiation and Integration

**Organizational differentiation** (not to be confused with the differentiation strategy) refers to the means by which organizational activities are grouped into subunits and by which hierarchies are established to manage them. Differentiation identifies areas of authority and reporting relationships and establishes a division of labor to improve organizational effectiveness. The means by which an organization is differentiated is elaborated in the organizational chart.[9]

At first glance one might think that high differentiation is desirable because it improves clarity, specialization, efficiency, and productivity. However, this can also lead to a **subunit orientation** whereby individuals identify and communicate almost completely with those in their divisions, not the organization as a whole.[10] Hence, differentiation can actually work against **integration,** a state whereby individuals identify with the organization and actively work with and learn from each other to achieve organizational goals.

**organizational differentiation** the means by which organizational activities are grouped into subunits and by which hierarchies are established to manage them

**subunit orientation** a state whereby individuals identify and communicate almost completely with those in their divisions, not the organization as a whole

**integration** a state whereby individuals identify with the organization and actively work with and learn from each other to achieve organizational goals

| TABLE 5-2 | Broad Categorizations of Organizational Structure | |
|---|---|---|
| | **Differentiation** | **Integration** |
| Centralization | Functional structure | Weber's bureaucracy |
| Decentralization | Divisional structure (product or geographical) | Matrix structure |

Managers must strike balances between centralization and decentralization and between differentiation and integration that fit with the mission and strategy of the organization. For this reason, identifying one or two optimal structures is neither possible nor desirable. Rather, four alternative structures—functional, product divisional, geographical divisional, and matrix, discussed in Sections 5-2 through 5-5—may be adopted to meet the needs of the organization.

Broadly speaking, the four alternative structures, as well as Weber's notion of bureaucracy, can be classified along dimensions of centralization-decentralization and differentiation-integration. Table 5-2 provides such a categorization as a precursor to Sections 5-2 through 5-5.

## 5-2 Functional Structure

The initial growth of an organization often requires that it be organized along functional areas. In the **functional structure,** each subunit of the organization engages in organization-wide activities related to a particular function, such as marketing, human resources, finance, or production, as depicted in Figure 5-2. Managers are grouped according to their expertise and the resources they use in their jobs.

A functional structure has a number of advantages. It can improve specialization and foster the development of economies of scale by grouping together employees who perform similar tasks. When functional specialists interact frequently, improvements and innovations for their functional areas are more likely to occur. Such innovations may not otherwise happen without a mass of specialists organized within

**functional structure**  a form of organizational structure whereby each subunit of the organization engages in firm-wide activities related to a particular function, such as marketing, human resources, finance, or production

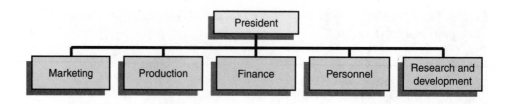

**Figure 5-2**
*A Partial Example of Functional Structure*

the same unit. In addition, working closely on a daily basis with others who share one's functional interests also tends to increase job satisfaction and decrease turnover.

Because of its ability to group specialists and promote economies of scale, this form tends to address cost and quality concerns well. However, the functional structure also has its disadvantages. Because the business is organized around functions rather than around products or geographic regions, pinpointing the responsibility for profits or losses can be difficult. For example, a decline in sales could be directly linked to problems in any of a number of departments, such as marketing, production, or purchasing. Members of these departments may point the finger at other departments when performance declines, and it may be difficult to determine exactly where the problem lies.

In addition, a functional structure is prone to interdepartmental conflict by fostering a narrow perspective of the organization among its members. Managers in functional organizations tend to view the firm totally from the perspective of their field of expertise. In many cases, they might associate their positions more with their functional area of expertise than with the organization. For example, the marketing department might see a company problem as sales related, whereas the human resources department might view the same challenge as a training and development concern.

Communication and coordination across functional areas are often difficult because each function tends to have its own perspective and vernacular. The research and development (R&D) function, for example, tends to focus on long-term issues, whereas the production department generally emphasizes the short run. Grouping individuals along functional lines minimizes communication across the functions and can result in different languages for different departments.

In sum, the functional structure can serve as a relatively effective and efficient means of controlling and coordinating activities. However, there has been a growing emphasis on customer service and speed in recent years, challenges that the functional structure may not be as well equipped to address. Depending on the specific issues facing an organization, a division along product or geographical lines may be more appropriate.

## 5-3 Product Divisional Structure

**product divisional structure**
a form of organizational structure whereby the organization's activities are divided into self-contained entities, each responsible for producing, distributing, and selling its own products

The **product divisional structure** divides the organization's activities into self-contained entities, each responsible for producing, distributing, and selling its own products or services. Each division has its own functional areas, such as R&D, marketing, and finance. This structure is often adopted when an organization has several distinct product or service lines. For example, a software developer may organize along three product lines: business, productivity, and educational applications.

The product divisional structure has a number of advantages. Rather than emphasizing functions, it emphasizes product lines, resulting in a clear focus on each product category and a greater orientation toward customer service. Pinpointing the responsibility for profits or losses is also easier because each product division becomes a **profit center**—a well-defined organizational unit headed by a manager accountable for its revenues and expenditures. The product divisional structure is also ideal for training and developing managers because each product manager is, in effect, operating his or her own business. Hence, product managers develop general management skills, an end that can be accomplished in a functional structure only by rotating managers from one functional area to another.[11]

The product divisional structure also has its disadvantages. Because product divisional firms generally have multiple departments performing the same function, total expenses are likely to be higher than if only one department were necessary. The coordination of activities at headquarters also becomes more difficult, as top management finds it harder to ensure consistency among the various departments. This problem can become substantial in large organizations with dozens of product divisions. Finally, because each product manager emphasizes his or her own product area, product managers tend to compete for resources instead of working together in the best interest of the company.

## 5-4  Geographic Divisional Structure

When a firm's operations are dispersed among various locations, organizations may employ a **geographic divisional structure,** whereby activities and personnel are grouped by specific geographic locations. This structure may be used on a local basis (i.e., a city may be divided into sales regions), on a national basis (i.e., Southern region, mid-Atlantic region, Midwest region), or even on an international basis (i.e., North American region, Latin American region, Asian region, Western European region). Figure 5-3 illustrates such a structure. The primary impetus for the geographic divisional structure is the existence of two or more distinct markets that can be segmented easily along geographical lines.

There are two key advantages to organizing geographically. First, products and services may be tailored more effectively to the legal, social, technical, or climatic differences of specific regions. For example, relatively small, 220-volt appliances may be appropriate for parts of Asia where living quarters tend to be limited and the American 110-volt system is not used. In addition, insurance companies are often organized along state and national boundaries because of legal differences. Second, producing or distributing products in different locations may give the organization a competitive advantage. Many firms, for example, produce components in countries that have a labor cost advantage and assemble them in countries with an adequate supply of skilled labor.

The disadvantages of a geographic divisional structure are similar to those of the product divisional structure. Efficiency may be reduced as more functional personnel are required because each region has its own functional departments. Coordination of company-wide functions is often more difficult, and area managers may emphasize their own geographic regions to the exclusion of a company-wide viewpoint.

**profit center**  a well-defined organizational unit headed by a manager accountable for its revenues and expenditures

**geographic divisional structure**  a form of organizational structure in which jobs and activities are grouped on the basis of geographic location—for example, Northeast region, Midwest region, and Far West region

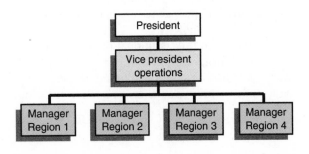

**Figure 5-3**
*A Partial Example of Geographic Divisional Structure*

Organizing along geographical lines can help firms meet location-specific needs in the marketplace more effectively.

# 5-5 Matrix Structure

In a general sense, the functional and divisional structures—both product and geographical—can be viewed as opposites ends of a continuum. The traditional demands for quality and price may pull an organization toward the functional end, whereas demands for service and speed may pull the organization toward the divisional end. To address these demands, organizational leaders may settle on one of the two poles or may attempt to position the organization between the extremes. One such approach, the matrix structure, was designed to balance the two and has gained considerable popularity in recent years.

Unlike the other structures that are characterized by a single chain of command, the **matrix structure** is a combination of the functional and product divisional structures. Hence, personnel within the matrix have two (or more) supervisors: a functional boss and a project boss. Some individuals may be assigned to more that one team at the same time, as Figure 5-4 illustrates. For one project, a project manager might pull together some members of the organization's functional departments. After the project is completed, the personnel in the project return to their functional departments.

The matrix structure is most commonly used in organizations facing a high rate of technological change, such as software development, management consulting, engineering, and telecommunications. Because of its complexity, the matrix structure is seen only in a relatively small number of organizations. However, recent developments in network technology have helped managers in many matrix organizations overcome some of the confusion and duplication that can accompany the structure. As such, matrix approaches are likely to continue to expand, especially in industries governed by technology.

A variation to the traditional project form of the matrix structure is reflected in the form of organization pioneered by Procter & Gamble (P&G) in 1931. At P&G, each individual product has a brand manager. Like a project manager, the brand manager pulls various specialists as needed from functional departments. Each brand

**matrix structure**   a form of organizational structure that combines the functional and product divisional structures

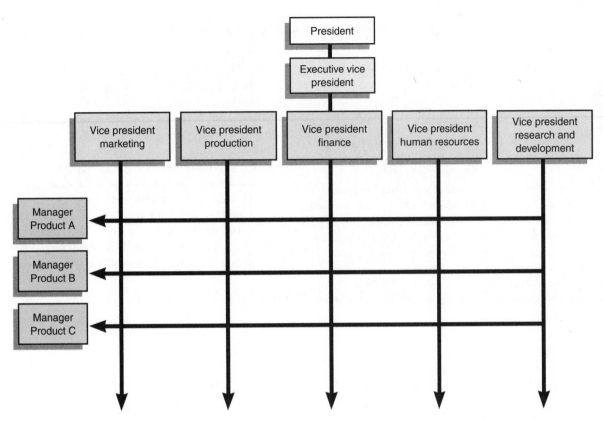

**Figure 5-4**
*Matrix Organizational Structure*

manager reports to a category manager, who is in charge of all related products in a single category. The category manager coordinates the advertising and sales efforts to reduce competition among P&G products. Interestingly, P&G continues to modify its brand management approach as the environment changes, and has recently undergone a shift toward a more global orientation.[12] Please see Box 5-1.

The matrix structure offers four key advantages. First, by combining the functional and product divisional structures, a firm can enjoy many of the advantages of both forms. Second, a matrix organization is flexible because employees may be transferred with ease between projects with different time frames. Third, a matrix permits lower-level functional employees to become heavily involved in important projects and gain valuable experience. Finally, top management in a matrix is freed from day-to-day involvement in the operations of the enterprise in order to focus on strategic leadership.

The matrix also has a number of disadvantages. First, because coordination across functional areas and across projects is so important, employees spend considerable time in meetings exchanging information, ultimately growing the bureaucracy and raising personnel costs. Second, matrix structures are characterized by considerable conflict, both between project and functional managers over budgets and personnel, and among the project managers themselves over similar resource allocation issues. Finally, reporting to two managers simultaneously violates a basic premise of management, the idea that each employee should report to only one superior. This can create role conflict when different bosses provide conflicting instructions.

Working in a matrix organization is not for everyone, however. This issue is discussed in greater detail in Box 5-2 on page 85.

Box 5-1

## Best Practices
### Brand Management at P&G

Proctor & Gamble is famous for developing an alternative to the functional structure known as brand management in 1931. The shift was initiated when a young manager working on an advertising campaign for Camay soap became frustrated that competitors were not limited to soaps from Palmolive and Lever, but also included other P&G products such as Ivory. The manager, Neil McElroy, argued that each brand should have its own manager supported by a team of individuals devoted solely to the brand. As such, each product would be targeted to different consumer markets. Executives at P&G were impressed with McElroy's suggestion and initiated a massive structural change in the organization.[13]

Success of the brand management concept helped catapult McElroy's career, which eventually included the position of CEO at the firm. McElroy believed that the role of a brand manager is to determine what consumers want (i.e., conduct marketing research) and give it to them. Interestingly, his perspective on marketing can be seen as a forerunner to the idea of a competitive strategy based on differentiation, as well as what is commonly referred to today as the marketing concept.

Since that time, many consumer products firms around the world have developed their own deviations of the brand management structure.

# 5-6  A Structural Revolution

During the past two decades, rapid changes in technology have caused many organizations to modify their existing structures to meet the challenges of dynamic environments. These organizations have engaged in a process economists refer to as disaggregation and reaggregation.[14] The economic basis for this transformation was proposed by Nobel laureate Ronald Coase in what is called *Coase's law:* A firm will tend to expand until the cost of organizing an extra transaction within the firm becomes equal to the cost of carrying out the same transaction on the open market.[15] In other words, large firms exist because they can perform most tasks—raw material procurement, production, human resource management, sales, and so forth—more efficiently than those tasks would otherwise be performed if they were outsourced to the open market.

However, recent technological advances, most notably the development of the Internet, have reduced the costs of these transactions for all firms. As a result, progressive firms have placed less emphasis on performing all of the required activities themselves and have partnered with enterprises outside the organization to manage many of the functions that were previously handled in house. Whereas *outsourcing* refers to specific agreements associated with a single task, *partnering* implies a longer term commitment associated with more complex activities.

The development in Internet technology and subsequent disaggregation and reaggregation has fostered a shift toward structures that are more flexible and responsive to customer needs. Five specific changes have contributed to this shift (see Table 5-3). The first is a movement toward **information symmetry**, a state whereby all parties to a transaction share the same information concerning that transaction. **Information asymmetry**—when one party has information that another does not—is the primary reason why many markets that might otherwise tend toward pure competition remain marginally competitive. Organizations often seek to promote information asymmetry and utilize the information edge to their own advan-

**information symmetry**
situation that occurs when all parties to a transaction share the same information concerning that transaction

**information asymmetry**
situation that occurs when one party has information that another does not

tage. Automobile retailers, for example, rarely post their absolute bottom line prices on their vehicles. Consumers are generally left to haggle with a number of dealers to estimate the true wholesale cost of the vehicle and the value of various options and accessories. The lack of consumer knowledge, as well as the lack of time and expertise required to obtain the information desired, results in higher selling prices for many of the retailers.

The second change is that the Internet now acts as a distribution channel for nontangible goods and services. Consumers can purchase items such as airline tickets, insurance, stocks, and computer software online without the necessity of physical delivery. For largely tangible goods and services, businesses can often distribute the intangible portion, such as product and warranty information, online.

Third, the Internet offers numerous opportunities to improve the speed of the actual transaction, as well as the process that leads up to and follows it. Consumers and businesses alike can research information twenty-four hours a day. Orders placed online can potentially be processed immediately. Software engineers in the United States can work on projects during the day and then pass their work along to their counterparts in India who can continue work while the Americans sleep.

| TABLE 5-3 | Strategic Dimensions of the Internet |
|-----------|--------------------------------------|

1. Movement toward information symmetry
2. The Internet as a distribution channel
3. Premium on speed
4. Potential for interactivity
5. Potential for cost reduction and cost shifting

Fourth, the Internet provides extensive opportunities for interactivity that would otherwise not be available. Consumers can discuss their experiences with products and services on bulletin boards or in chat rooms. Firms can readily exchange information with trade associations that represent their industries. Users can share files with relative ease.

Finally, the Internet provides many businesses with opportunities to minimize their costs—both fixed and variable—and thereby enhance flexibility. Information can be distributed to thousands or millions of recipients without either the expense associated with the mail system or the equipment required to do so. The virtual storefront does not necessarily require an actual facility and may reduce transaction costs through automated online ordering systems, although this is not always the case.

It is difficult to overstate the effects that the Internet, and specifically the process of disaggregation and reaggregation, have had on the structures of many organizations. In many respects, a partner can be viewed as an extension of the organization, although it is not officially part of the organization. Partner capabilities and limitations are fast becoming as important as internal strengths and weaknesses. Although these changes are more pronounced in some markets than in others, the development of the Internet economy has significantly changed the nature of almost every organization.

## 5-7 Which Structure Is Best?

As previously noted, there is no single best way to structure an organization. The most effective structure depends on a number of considerations, including the organization's strategy. When strategy and structure are aligned, organizational effectiveness is more likely to be attained. For example, the functional structure is better equipped to promote production efficiency, thereby supporting the implementation of a low cost competitive strategy. In contrast, a divisional structure may be more appropriate for an organization emphasizing differentiation. The relationships are generalities, however, and the appropriate strategy-structure alignment is different for each organization.

In many cases, the structures discussed herein are combined to create an approach uniquely tailored to the strategic needs of the organization. Figure 5-5 illustrates such a combination structure. It is interesting to note that a number of organizations combine two or more of the structures according to the specific needs of the firm and the philosophy of its top executives. Yum Brands, for example, has a division for each of its domestic restaurant holdings (i.e., KFC, Pizza Hut, Taco Bell, Long John Silver's, and A&W Restaurants). Another division, however, is based on geography and includes units in all three of the restaurant brands located outside the United States. Hence, implementing a single, pure structure is not necessary.

In addition, when a firm has multiple business units, it is not necessary that all of them adopt the same structure. If some of the firm's business units operate in relatively dynamic environments while others compete in relatively stable environments, structural differences may be necessary.

Top managers can consider five basic issues to assess the alignment between an organization's structure and its strategy (see Table 5-4).[16] The first issue concerns the compatibility of the existing structure with the strategy and market orientation of the organization. For example, the product divisional structure may be more appropriate than the functional structure for firms operating in multiple industries. If an organization is seeking a growth strategy, a product divisional or geographic divisional structure may not be advisable. The matrix structure may be more appropriate when an organization seeks differentiation through personalized service and complex problem solving.

Second, decision makers should consider the number of hierarchical levels in the organization. Flatter organizations, with relatively fewer hierarchical levels and

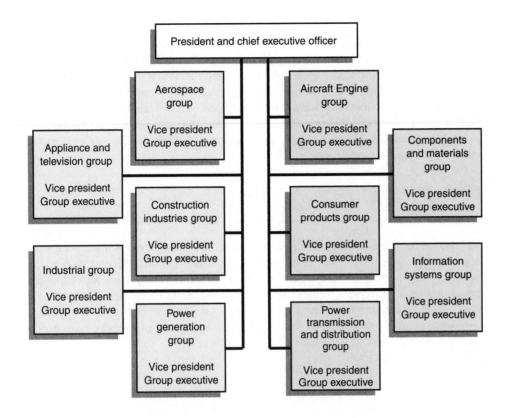

**Figure 5-5**
*A Partial Example of a Combination Structure*

wider spans of control, tend to work more effectively in dynamic environments, whereas taller organizations may operate more effectively in stable, more predictable environments.

Third, the organization should consider the extent to which the structure permits the appropriate grouping of activities. For instance, customers may be confused when they are contacted by multiple sales representatives for the same company, each representing a different product line. In addition, it is difficult to hold a product divisional manager fully responsible for product sales when he or she has no control over either the development or the production of the product.

Fourth, decision makers should consider the extent to which a given structure promotes effective coordination. For example, a firm with multiple related businesses usually requires greater coordination of its business unit activities than a stand-alone organization operating in a single industry. As an organization becomes more complex, however, coordinating activities becomes more difficult, especially in organizations with related businesses.

Fifth, organizational leaders should consider the extent to which the structure allows for appropriate centralization or decentralization of authority. The appropriate level of centralization or decentralization depends on a number of factors, one of which is organizational size. In general, very large organizations tend to be more decentralized than very small ones, simply because it is difficult for the CEO of a very

| TABLE 5-4 | Considerations When Selecting a Structure |
|---|---|

1. Strategy of the organization
2. Number of hierarchical levels
3. Structure's ability to group activities effectively
4. Structure's ability to promote coordination
5. Structure's ability to appropriate desired degree of centralization

large company to stay abreast of all of the organization's operations. In addition, firms with large numbers of unrelated businesses tend to be relatively decentralized, whereby corporate-level management determines the overall corporation's mission, goals, and strategy, and lower-level managers make the actual operating decisions. Organizations in dynamic environments must be relatively decentralized so that decisions can be made quickly, whereas organizations in relatively stable environments can be managed more systematically and centrally because change is relatively slow and fairly predictable. In such cases, most decisions are routine, and procedures can often be established in advance.

## Summary

Organizational structure refers to the means through which work is coordinated in an organization. The structure of an organization can greatly influence organizational effectiveness. An organization's structure is founded on the philosophical considerations of vertical and horizontal growth, centralization and decentralization, and differentiation and integration. In general, managers may choose to structure the organization around functions, products, or geography, or they may choose a matrix approach.

There is no single best structure. Each has its own advantages and disadvantages related to factors such as communication, coordination, specialization, and efficiency. However, organizational structures have evolved to become more flexible and customer oriented during the past two decades as a result of a process known as disaggregation and reaggregation.

## Review Questions and Exercises

1. How do organizational structures develop? Why is the concept of organizational structure so important to managing organizations?

2. Explain the concepts of centralization and decentralization. When might each be appropriate for an organization?

3. What forms of organizational structure are available to strategic managers? What are the primary advantages and disadvantages of each?

4. What are the primary issues that should be considered when selecting a structure for the organization?

## Quiz

1. A flat organization is composed of many hierarchical levels and narrow spans of control.
   **True or False**

2. Span of control refers to the amount of confidence one manager has in his or her subordinates.
   **True or False**

3. A flat organization has relatively many levels in the hierarchy.
   **True or False**

4. Integration refers to the means by which organizational activities are grouped into subunits and by which hierarchies are established to manage them.
   **True or False**

5. The concept of a brand manager is consistent with the functional structure.
   **True or False**

6. Informational asymmetry occurs when one individual has information another does not.
   **True or False**

7. The formal means by which work is coordinated in an organization is called
   a. the organizational dynamic.
   b. the organizational domain.
   c. the organizational culture.
   d. none of the above.

8. An increase in the breadth of an organization's structure is known as
   a. centralization.
   b. decentralization.
   c. horizontal growth.
   d. vertical growth.

9. The notion of a profit center is consistent with which form of organizational structure?
   a. functional structure
   b. product divisional
   c. geographic divisional structure
   d. matrix structure

10. Which structure is likely to be appropriate when products or services must be tailored to meet the needs of specific groups in different locations?
    a. functional structure
    b. product divisional
    c. geographic divisional structure
    d. matrix structure

11. Which form of organizational structure is actually a combination of two other forms?
    a. functional structure
    b. product divisional
    c. geographic divisional structure
    d. matrix structure

12. Which of the following is not a consideration when selecting a structure?
    a. number of hierarchical levels
    b. strategy of the organization
    c. desired degree of centralization
    d. all of the above

## Endnotes

1. J. Hagel, "Fallacies in Organizing Performance," *The McKinsey Quarterly* 2 (1994): 97–108. Also see J. Child, *Organization: A Guide for Managers and Administrators* (New York: Harper & Row, 1977): 10.

2. M. Weber, *Theory of Social and Economic Organization* (New York: Free Press, 1997).

3. Child, 1977.

4. L. G. Love, R. L. Priem, and G. T. Lumpkin, "Explicitly Articulated Strategy and Firm Performance Under Alternative Levels of Centralization," *Journal of Management* 28 (2002): 611–627.

5. M. Farrell and F. T. Mavondo, "The Effect of Downsizing Strategy and Reorientation Strategy on a Learning Orientation," *Personnel Review* 33 (2004): 383–403; C. R. Littler and P. Innes, "The Paradox of Managerial Downsizing," *Organization Studies* 25 (2004): 1159–1184.

6. D. Rigby, "Look Before You Lay Off," *Harvard Business Review* 80, no. 4 (2002): 1–2; I. Suarez-Gonzalez, "Downsizing Strategy: Does It Really Improve Organizational Performance?" *International Journal of Management* 18 (2001): 301–307.

7. S. Chang and H. Singh, "Corporate and Industry Effects on Business Unit Competitive Position," *Strategic Management Journal* 21 (2000): 739–752.

8. S. Hill, R. Martin, and M. Harris, "Decentralization, Integration and the Post-Bureaucratic Organization: The Case of R&D," *Journal of Management Studies* 37 (2000): 563–585; C. Hales, "Leading Horses to Water? The Impact of Decentralization on Managerial Behaviour," *Journal of Management Studies* 36 (1999): 831–851.

9. Child, 1977.

10. P. R. Lawrence and J. W. Lorsch, *Organization and Environment* (Boston: Harvard University, 1967).

11. P. Wright, M. Kroll, and J. A. Parnell, *Strategic Management: Concepts* (Upper Saddle River, NJ: Prentice Hall, 1998).

12. J. Neff, "The New Brand Manager," *Advertising Age* 70, no. 46 (1999): 2–3; B. Dumaine, "P&G Rewrites the Marketing Rules," *Fortune* 122, no. 45 (1989): 34–48; A. Swasy, "In a Fast-Paced World, Procter & Gamble Sets Its Store in Old Values," *The Wall Street Journal*, September 21, 1989, 1; Z. Schiller, "No More Mr. Nice Guy at P&G—Not by a Long Shot," *Business Week*, February 3, 1992, 54–56.

13. T. K. McCraw, J. H. Franklin, and A. S. Eisenstadt, *American Business, 1920-2000: How It Worked* (Wheeling, IL: Harlan Davidson, 2000)

14. T. Malone and R. J. Laubaucher, "The Dawn of the E-Lance Economy," *Harvard Business Review* 76, no. 5 (1998): 144–152; D. Tapscott, D. Ticoll, and A. Lowy, *Digital Capital: Harnessing the Power of Business Webs* (Boston: Harvard Business School Press, 2000).

15. R. Coase, *The Firm, The Market, and The Law* (Chicago: University of Chicago Press, 1990).

16. Wright, Kroll, and Parnell, 1998.

# Organizational Life Cycle and Growth

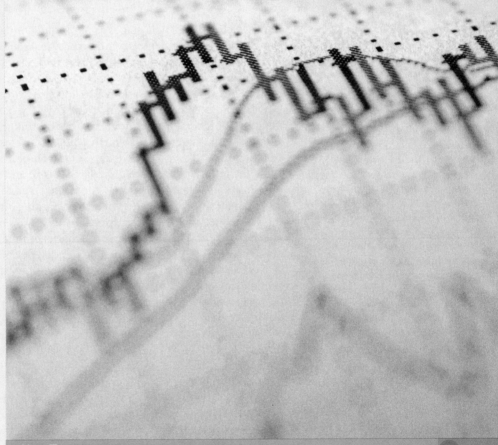

## Chapter Outline

## Key Terms

factors that determine life cycle stage

five-stage organization life cycle

life cycle stages

organization life cycle

self-directed work teams

organization life cycle
the pattern that describes the
birth, growth, maturity, and
decline of organizations

This book is about organizations and the important role they play in modern society. In this chapter, organizations will be compared to living organisms in a manner similar to the approach followed in the biological sciences. Human beings go through a predictable pattern of birth, growth, maturity, and decline. In a similar manner, but with some very different twists, so do organizations.

This pattern that describes the birth, growth, maturity, and decline of organizations is known as the **organization life cycle.** All organizations are born, or come into existence, at some particular point in time. They proceed to get older, sometimes much larger, and more complicated to manage over time. Eventually, all organizations die, or cease to exist. Some organizations remain relatively small for their entire lives, such as a two-person accounting partnership, while others grow to become multinational in scope, such as Microsoft. This evolution of growth and development and what factors determine that growth are the focus of this chapter.

# 6-1 Factors That Determine Life Cycle Stage

factors that determine life
cycle stage   factors that
include situation, which refers
to the overall makeup of the
firm, including its size, number of owners or shareholders,
how customers influence decisions, the heterogeneity of its
markets, and so forth; decision-making style, or how decisions are made in organizations and how participatory
that process is; structure,
which refers to how a firm
establishes its reporting relationships, divides responsibilities, and organizes itself for
operations; and strategy, which
is top management's plan to
attain its desired outcomes for
the organization based on its
mission and goals

Hanks[1] defined life cycle stages as a "unique configuration of variables related to organization context, strategy, and structure." Specifically, four **factors that determine life cycle stage** have been identified.[2] These identifying factors are strategy, structure, decision-making style, and organizational situation. To understand life cycle is to know how these activities and structures change over time.

Organizational situation refers to the overall makeup of the firm, including its size, number of owners or shareholders, how customers influence decisions, the heterogeneity of its markets, and so forth. Age and size can also play a role in life cycle development. However, age and stage of development are actually poorly correlated.[3] Some organizations are born quite large in size and scope of operations,[4] while other organizations remain in an early life cycle stage for decades without ever growing much larger than they were when they began. Some large organizations are so centrally managed that they may appear as if they are much smaller. In addition, stages of development have no prescribed lengths of time, as some are passed through rapidly and some are prolonged for an extended period of time.[5]

Decision-making style refers to how decisions are made in an organization. Decision making can be very centralized at the top, or it can be decentralized to the level of the individual manager, self-directed work team, or single employee, depending on the circumstance. These differences depend upon degrees of participation, as decision making tends to become more participative as organizations develop.[6] Also of importance to understanding life cycle stage is whether decisions are future oriented, innovative, or defensive.

Organizational structure is concerned with how reporting relationships are organized. It will vary from simple to complex, departmental to divisional, and informal to formal. Of particular importance in considering structural issues are information processing procedures, decentralization of authority, and departmental differentiation. Each of these three issues becomes more complex through the first four phases of the life cycle.[7]

The fourth factor is strategy, top management's plan to attain its desired outcomes for the organization based on its mission and goals. Organizations operating in any environmental sector need a defined and clearly articulated strategy to accomplish goals. Even nonprofit organizations such as charities, associations, and foundations struggle to succeed without a defined strategy. As the discussion in Chapter 2 detailed, there are two commonly accepted strategic typologies used to describe the primary strategy of an organization. Porter's[8] typology categorizes firms based on an emphasis on low cost, differentiation, or a combination of the two. According to Porter, firms may choose to operate only in a niche market, or they may try to appeal to the entire market available for their products or services. Miles and Snow developed the second typology.[9] It identifies four strategic groups that operate in most industries. They include prospectors, analyzers, defenders, and reactors.

Prospectors perceive a dynamic environment and attempt to be first movers in new product markets. Defenders operate in perceived stable environments, focusing on maximum efficiency in a single market sector. Analyzers try to merge the best practices of prospectors and defenders into a combination strategy where tight control is exerted over existing operations while leaving some flexibility for new undertakings. Reactors have no real strategic bent, choosing to react to changes in the market only when forced to by more progressive competitors.

Research conducted by the authors of this textbook demonstrates that another important determining factor of life cycle stage is information processing. Information processing improves and becomes more sophisticated as an organization grows and develops. In fact, in a recent study, the level of sophistication of information processing proved to be the strongest indicator of a firm's life cycle stage.[10]

# 6-2 The Five-Stage Model of Organization Life Cycle

The life cycle model that has the most support in the literature is a five-stage model based on the work of several researchers.[11] This model, known as the **five-stage organization life cycle,** is presented in Table 6-1. Although management researchers have suggested several other models that have anywhere from three to ten stages, the five-stage model most thoroughly and most succinctly demonstrates organizational life. Models with fewer stages tend to overgeneralize and models with more stages tend to be overly specific.

## 6-2a Stage One: Existence

Known as the entrepreneurial[12] or birth stage, existence[13] marks the beginning of organizational development. The focus is on viability, or simply identifying a sufficient number of customers to warrant the existence of the organization. Decision making and ownership are in the hands of one or a few individuals. Organizations in this stage tend to enact or create[14] their own environments.

**five-stage organization life cycle** includes the following stages: existence, the first or birth stage when firms first come into being; survival, the second stage of development where firms can remain for an indefinite period of time, begin to grow quickly becoming much larger, or fail to progress at all and go out of business; success, the third stage of development characterized by maturity of operations, bureaucracy, large size and scope; renewal, the fourth stage of development, in which mature organizations attempt to return to a leaner form, renewing growth and becoming more flexible and responsive to customers; and, decline, the fifth stage, in which organizations tend to focus inward with power and politics playing a major role in hampering growth and development

| **TABLE 6-1** | Five-Stage Life Cycle Characteristics | | | |
|---|---|---|---|---|
| **Life Cycle Stage** | **Situation** | **Structure** | **Decision-Making Style** | **Strategy** |
| **Existence** < 10 years old | Small; young; homogenous | Informal; simple; owner-dominated | Centralized; trial and error | Prospector/differentiation |
| **Survival** > 15% growth | Medium-sized environment; more competitive | Functional; some formality | Some delegation; begin formal information processing | Analyzer/differentiation |
| **Success** < 15% growth | Heterogeneous environment; larger size | Formal; bureaucratic; functional | Reliance on internal information processing | Defender/low cost |
| **Renewal** > 15% growth | Very heterogeneous environment; very large | Divisional; some matrix | Sophisticated controls; formal analysis in decision making | Analyzer/combination; differentiation; low cost |
| **Decline** No growth | Homogeneous and competitive environment | Formal; bureaucratic; mostly functional | Moderate centralization; less sophisticated information processing | Reactor/low cost |

Most firms in this stage are small, sometimes totally operated by only one person. However, as we noted earlier, in today's competitive environment, many new or young organizations are actually quite large.[15] Workers grinding out long hours and wearing many hats characterize the existence stage. Sufficient funds are not available for the owner to hire specialists in every area of operations. Organizational members must share responsibilities for the work, and, in some cases, perform duties with which they might not be very familiar. As organizations grow in size, this specialization issue is diffused as individuals with very specific skills are hired to fill needed roles.

An organization in the existence stage is Room to Grow in Paragould, Arkansas. This company buys and sells preworn baby clothes and maternity wear, children's toys, and baby furniture. The owner, Renee Dwyer, is unsure of the long-term direction of her company, experimenting with different product lines to try to find the right mix for her clients.

### 6-2b  Stage Two: Survival

As firms move into the survival stage, they seek to grow,[16] develop some formalization of structure,[17] and establish distinctive competencies, or special abilities that separate them from their competitors.[18] Goals are formulated routinely in this stage, with the primary goal being the generation of enough revenue to continue operations and finance sufficient growth to stay competitive.[19]

As the scope of an organization's operations increases, so does its division of labor. Job descriptions that were very general in the existence stage become more specific and narrow in the survival stage. Another necessary ingredient to growth is more management, or a greater degree of supervision, as founders release total control and empower other managers to assist them in directing specific areas of operations. In years past, organizations would simply add managers for each functional area, such as finance, marketing, and operations, and those managers would add more managers to their staffs for different, more narrowly defined, areas of their responsibility.

**self-directed work teams**
a group of workers acting as a team who come together to perform tasks and take responsibility for performing work as a unit rather than having an individual supervisor

Some modern organizations, however, attempt to manage growth through teams of people, sometimes referred to as **self-directed work teams,**[20] rather than simply adding more managers. These teams hire and fire team members, divide responsibilities for the work, and collaborate on important operational decisions.

The survival stage provides several interesting alternatives: Some organizations grow large and prosper well enough to enter stage three, some hit and miss, earning marginal returns in some fiscal cycles, and others fail to generate sufficient revenue to survive. This is the stage in which many older, but smaller, organizations find themselves. They never garner enough market share to become major players in their industries, but their niche is strong enough to maintain operations for an extended period of time. An example of a survival stage company is AAA Construction, Inc. featured as a case study in this textbook (see Case D). AAA never became a large or mature firm due to the desire of its founder to stay small and controllable without adding layers of managers. The company managed to make profits some years while failing to in others. Yet, AAA managed to stay in business for almost forty years.

### 6-2c  Stage Three: Success

Commonly called maturity by many organizational theorists,[21] the success stage represents an organizational form where formalization and control through bureaucracy are the norm. This formalization is manifested in specific written job descriptions, the adoption of official policies and procedures, standardization of work and a division of labor, and hierarchical reporting relationships. A common problem in this stage is what U.S. businesses have long referred to as red tape, a condition of wading through layers of organizational structure to get any new idea or product initiated.

Such organizations have passed the survival test, growing to a point that they may seek to protect what they have gained instead of targeting new territory. The top management team focuses on planning and strategy, leaving daily operations to middle managers.

Most organizations in this stage have large operational scopes. Managing organizations of this size requires a certain amount of bureaucracy.[22] Simply put, bureaucracy is an organizational form that permits the routine, systematic accomplishment of organizational activities, ensuring consistency, efficiency, and effectiveness. Bureaucracy is necessary for the management of large-scale functions. Imagine the difficulty of carrying out all the necessary jobs related to managing the Social Security Administration. Every citizen has to be tracked, their contributions to the fund collected for many years, and their eventual draw upon their eligible retirement date executed. A systematic, very organized, and regimented bureaucracy is suited to this work. Delegation of duties is extensive, job specialization is high, and operations are systematic. However, it is this emphasis on routine efficiency and effectiveness that leads many organizations to become stagnant, lacking innovation and creativity.

## 6-2d  Stage Four: Renewal

The renewing organization displays a desire to return to a leaner time[23] when its size was smaller and it could act much faster. Firms in the renewal stage are trying to recapture a spirit of collaboration and teamwork that foster innovation and creativity. This creativity is sometimes facilitated through the use of a matrix structure, and the creativity is focused on serving the needs of customers. Decision making is very much decentralized. The organization is still large and bureaucratic, but organizational members are encouraged to work within the bureaucracy without adding to it.

Firms enter renewal by choice, hoping to move from the middle of the pack in their industry to become an industry leader. As smaller, more nimble organizations begin to steal market share, older and larger firms find they must revolutionize their operations if they are to remain competitive. IBM found itself in this situation in the early 1990s, as new technology firms focused on niches in the information technology sector began to erode IBM's position. In 1993, new CEO Lou Gerstner staged a dramatic turnaround for IBM by refocusing attention on the customer and integrating the company's various operational divisions to better serve customer needs. Gerstner's renewal of IBM was a much-publicized success story in American business. He has since retired and turned the reins of IBM over to Sam Palmisano. It is Palmisano's job to make sure IBM doesn't become stagnant and lose its newfound competitive edge.[24]

## 6-2e  Stage Five: Decline

Firms may exit the life cycle at any stage by dying, or going out of business. The decline stage, however, is frequently the trigger for this demise. The decline stage is characterized by politics and power[25] as organizational members become more concerned with personal goals than they are with organizational goals. For some organizations, the inability to meet the external demands of a former stage has led them to a period of decline where they experience a lack of profit and a loss of market share. Control and decision making tend to return to a handful of people, as the desire for power and influence in earlier stages has eroded the viability of the organization.

Decline can be reversed in organizations, but it is not an easy task. In many cases a new CEO who is not encumbered by the baggage of having spent many years at the firm is needed. Strategies for turnaround were discussed in Chapter 2. The Career Point discussion in Box 6-1 provides advice for job seekers by making a prospective employing organization's life cycle stage relevant. Discover how you can determine through personal research the life cycle stage of an organization, matching its determining characteristics to your personal job preferences.

Box 6-1

The next time you begin a job search, whether it's to start your new career or seek a career change, put the life cycle concept to work. Based on your personality, in what type of organization would you be most happy and productive?

If you enjoy informal cultures, wearing several different hats, making quick decisions based on limited information, and the challenge of building a new organization on scarce resources, a start-up business may be what you're looking for. Conversely, if a more formal culture is to your liking, where decisions are procedure driven, job descriptions are very specific, and reporting relationships clearly established, you will be more happy working in a mature organization. You may also prefer the challenge of a fast-paced, can't-keep-up-with-demand kind of growth atmosphere.

Take the time to research firms before you interview so that your decision to accept or decline an offer will be as informed as possible. This knowledge is more than just an understanding of the job's salary and benefits. Try to ascertain how long the firm has been in business, where it ranks in its industry, what its history of growth and innovation are, and why it continually leads or lags behind others in its industry. Consult online research sites, *Fortune* magazine, industry newsletters, stock reports from financial analysts, or any other resource that might help you better understand a potential employer's stage of development.

Organizations in every stage of the life cycle can be found in most industries. Understanding the concept of organizational life cycle will help you discern which kind of organization you are dealing with and whether or not it is the right place for you depending on where you are in your career path.

## 6-3 Practical Application of Life Cycle Theory

Understanding the life cycle model has important implications for managers. Each stage of development encompasses pitfalls to be avoided and opportunities to be taken advantage of. The four factors that determine life cycle (see Table 6-1) take on different dimensions as organizations grow and develop. Knowing when to make changes, such as increased delegation or adding formalization of structure, can allow managers to navigate difficult competitive waters strategically.

As organizations grow and become more complex, several crises, or trigger points, are encountered by top management. How these trigger points are managed determines the future growth and development of the organization. The first real trigger point managers encounter must be dealt with before the business is launched. Founders must ask "Can we deliver our product or service to enough customers to make our business viable?" If the answer is yes, a new firm is born, or comes into existence.

As the new business moves through its early development, this preexistence question is answered. Either the new business begins to prosper, or it quickly goes out of business. If it prospers, a new set of challenges emerges, which usually lead to the next trigger point. Top management must face this question: "Can the development of some distinctive competencies and some formalization provide the impetus for rapid growth?" A positive determination in this regard compels management to position the firm for a transition to the survival stage gradually. The key to this progression is solving the crisis of leadership.[26] Founders and technical entrepreneurs are sometimes ill equipped to handle multiple employees and the day-to-day grind of managing a business. Their interests often lie in creating new products/services or adding new customers. Yet, the rapid growth needed to move into the survival stage is not possible without a steady hand of leadership, either from the founder or from a hired manager.

Box 6-2

## Best Practices

### Life Cycle—FedEx

If you closely study organizations, you discover that all of them are born, grow (to some extent), and eventually die. Some, however, manage to avoid death by renewing themselves before decline has rendered them noncompetitive. One such firm is FedEx.

Fred Smith, the founder of FedEx, remains its leader and its heart and soul nearly 32 years after its founding. At each critical juncture in its history when FedEx could have easily become complacent or have gone into decline, Smith found a way to reenergize his organization and its people. In 1977, with weight limits forcing him to fly his Dasault Falcon jets from Memphis to California and back twice a night, Smith lobbied Congress to pass legislation allowing him to fly larger cargo planes.

When the Asian transportation market began to boom, Smith purchased the primarily cargo airline, Flying Tigers, to secure landing rights at major Asian airports. Flying Tigers had been in business primarily in Asia since the end of World War II. When organizations began to look for cost-cutting measures due to intense competition in nearly every industry, FedEx introduced a logistics management service, relieving manufacturers, wholesalers, and retailers of excessive transportation overhead. And, with its archrival, UPS, taking over Mail Boxes Etc. to gain a stronger foothold in the retail shipping sector, Fred Smith countered by buying Kinko's.

FedEx has continued to find ways to grow its business year after year. Although it has become a large, international organization ($24 billion in revenue), its emphasis on technology innovation and implementation has established a competitive advantage that has been hard for others to overcome. For the thirty-two years of its existence, FedEx has never been in decline.[27]

---

Firms that find themselves in survival have several options. Some founders desire to disengage, leaving daily operations of their organizations to others while they pursue different career options or other activities, such as early retirement or politics. Other founders, such as FedEx's Fred Smith (see Box 6-2), choose to grow their firms as rapidly as possible, sinking all profits and financing options into fueling future growth. Other founders choose to keep their firms fairly stable, almost stagnant, in size and market share, ensuring the business is at a level they can successfully manage without adding extra layers or different managers. For firms that choose rapid growth and have the product or service to appeal to a broad market, the second crisis occurs. The crisis is the need for delegation. Rapid growth cannot be managed by a single individual. The business becomes too complex as it divides and multiplies, constantly taking on new markets and new customers.

The trigger points and crises experienced in each stage of the organizational life cycle are depicted in Figure 6-1.

For those founders who choose the second option of growth, the next trigger point eventually emerges: "Are we large enough that we need a bureaucratic form where formalization and control are paramount if we are to protect the market position we have established?" An affirmative answer to this question forces a transition to the success stage.

Organizations that begin as small or at least not very large entities in the existence stage become large, formal, and tightly controlled by the success stage. They typically have sales in the hundreds of millions, or billions, and serve markets that are geographically dispersed and diverse. The sheer size of the organization makes managing it difficult. Over time, firms in the success stage begin to experience slower growth, well below the 15% or greater level that they were accomplishing in the survival stage. Newer, more innovative firms enter their industry and steal market share. Some companies cannot overcome the next major crisis, the burden of red tape and bureaucratic gridlock, and they eventually fall into the decline stage. Others face the competitive threat and honestly address the next trigger point, which causes them to ask themselves: "Has the effort to protect market share resulted in an inability, through the development of our own innovative activities, to capture new

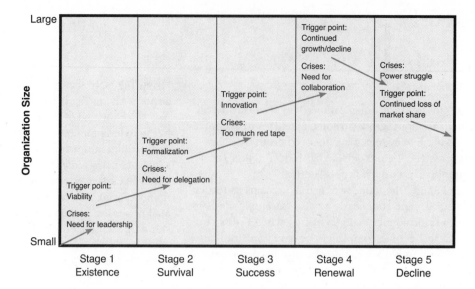

**Figure 6-1**
*Crises and Trigger Points
of Organizational Life Cycle
Stages*

domains?" If the answer for the concerned company is yes, a progression to renewal is possible.

In many cases, the really excellent companies operating in the global business arena are to be found in this life cycle stage. These organizations have learned how to manage extensive operations across countries and continents without losing the entrepreneurial spirit on which they were initially founded. Annual growth in revenues returns to the 15% or greater level that had been experienced during the survival stage before the stagnation of the success stage set in. The company recaptures its innovative know-how and extends its life span for many years to come. Three options are available to renewal firms. First, they can continue to grow, sometimes at the 15% annual pace previously described. Second, their growth can slow to a level below 15% that typically defines a renewal organization, sending them back into the success stage. Third, the renewal firm can actually begin to lose market share and plunge into decline.

For the decline organization, a return to growth is imperative. Power struggles and politics tend to dominate a firm in decline. Responding to this crisis of power and internal politics is essential if a decline organization is to return to either a renewal or

Firms of all sizes utilize private air travel to improve customer/supplier relations, investigate new markets, and/or prompt operational speed and efficiency.

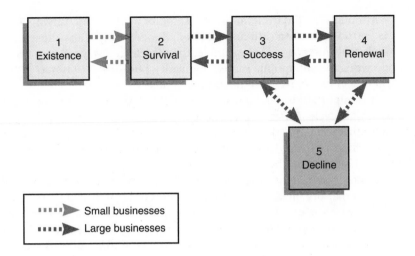

**Figure 6-2**
*Five-Stage Life Cycle Model*

success stage. The trigger point is how to reverse the loss of market share that has developed over time, usually because the firm has not responded to market changes.

The entrepreneurship literature has established that small firms grow through delegation and empowerment. Founders who are not obsessed with power and control enable other managers and employees to expand and develop individual units of the firm, contributing to overall growth. In contrast, large organizations that have become overstaffed and nonresponsive to market conditions can be revitalized by astute managers who understand the factors that are diminishing the firm's competitiveness.

Figure 6-2, which shows a five-stage life cycle model, illustrates the flexibility managers have in strategically managing the life cycle of their organizations. **Life cycle stages** can be experienced progressively, or they can be experienced in a more disjointed fashion. According to the figure's depiction, small businesses never progress past the second, or survival, stage. For organizations that experience problems in certain stages, operations can sometimes be retrenched to allow the organization to return to a past stage.

**life cycle stages** identifiable periods of the life of an organization that have distinct characteristics

## 6-4 Industry Life Cycle versus Organizational Life Cycle

Each business operates among a group of companies that produce competing products or services known as an industry. Like firms, industries develop and evolve over time. Not only might the group of competitors within a firm's industry change constantly, but the nature and structure of the industry can also change as it matures and its markets become better defined. An industry's developmental stage influences the nature of competition and potential profitability among competitors.[28] In theory, each industry passes through five distinct phases of an industry life cycle.

The five stages of the industry life cycle are detailed in Chapter 3. They include introduction, growth, shakeout, maturity, and decline. As you can see, these stages are similar to the organizational life cycle, but they are not the same. The introduction stage involves the beginning of a new industry. Demand for the industry's outputs is low, and technology is a key concern. Growth refers to the time of rising customer demand for an industry. As growth begins to wane, a shakeout occurs where growth is no longer rapid enough to support the increasing number of competitors in the industry. Marginal competitors are forced out. In the maturity stage, the market demand for the industry's outputs is saturated. Most purchases are upgrades of existing products. And, finally, the decline stage occurs when demand for an industry's products and services decreases.

Although the life cycle model is useful for analysis, identifying an industry's precise position is often difficult, and not all industries follow these exact stages or at predictable intervals.[29] For example, the bicycle industry fell into decline some years ago when the automobile gained popularity, but society's interest in health and physical fitness has rejuvenated the bicycle industry.

It is important to distinguish between the life cycle of an organization and an industry life cycle. For example, organizations do not go through a shakeout period because that term only defines a stage of an industry's development that refers to firms not being able to stay competitive in a certain industry and eventually having to leave the industry for another or go out of business completely.

Another important difference between industry life cycle and organizational life cycle is that organizations in varying stages of growth will be found in most industries regardless of what life cycle stage the industry finds itself. Put another way, most industries contain organizations or firms that individually are in different stages of growth than the industry itself. For example, in the United States, FedEx and UPS dominate the increasingly mature overnight package delivery business. Both firms are also mature. A new entrant in that industry is DHL, a firm that had not competed on a very wide basis in the United States until very recently. DHL's U.S. division is certainly in an early stage of development, but it is hoping to steal market share from UPS and FedEx in a rapid fashion, becoming larger and more mature as market share and operations increase.

Some mature or even declining industries, such as the steel industry, appear to be composed of mostly mature businesses. However, occasionally a new competitor with a better process or product will make inroads in a mature industry while still in an early stage of development. Just the opposite is also possible, as an older, more mature business will be found trying to compete in a new, introductory industry, such as when IBM entered the personal computer (PC) market in the 1981, four years after Apple introduced the first PC.[30]

## 6-5 Family Businesses

An often overlooked aspect of organizational theory is the importance of family owned and operated businesses. Most organizational theory textbooks fail to make mention of family businesses. Yet, family business researchers are carving a niche for themselves in this area of management research that is critical to growth of knowledge in the field. Family businesses are responsible for between 40 and 60% of the gross national product of the United States.[31]

A family business can be defined as a firm where the ownership and management are concentrated within a single family unit.[32] In the age of corporate scandals and serious problems with corporate governance and unethical behavior, the family business promises something better. The stewardship of resources and the value of a family ownership and control system have been demonstrated over and over, and the emphasis on the value of the family legacy exemplified through the family business makes decision making a much more serious duty than might be found in some sectors of public-corporate America.[33]

Family businesses can also achieve superior performance from three other perspectives. First, family ownership has the ability to show higher levels of concern for organizational employees than some corporate-managed businesses, preserving the humanity of the workplace. Second, family managers are in business for the long term and can manage their firms based on long-term growth. Third, because the family's reputation is many times directly related to the business, family firms tend to emphasize quality and value.[34]

The relevance of family business to organizational life cycle research is that family businesses span all stages of the life cycle, from existence to decline. However, many family firms fail to carry on past the first generation. Approximately 67 percent of family businesses do not survive under the family's ownership beyond the founder's tenure. Only about 12 percent make it to the third generation.[35] One of the goals of life cycle research is to identify common problems encountered at each stage by firm managers in an effort to provide solutions to these problems for future organizations.

Another important aspect to family business research is the growing number of jobs being created by small and family businesses in the United States. Since 1993, more than twenty million new jobs have been created by small businesses, while corporate employment fell by six million.[36] In the fast-paced global marketplace of today's competitive environment, the largest company in the world, Wal-Mart, still has substantial ownership and input by its founding family, the Waltons.[37]

## Summary

The organizational life cycle describes the pattern of development of organizations from birth to eventual decline and death. Factors that determine life cycle stage include situation, structure, decision-making style, strategy, and, most recently, information-processing capability. A model divided into five stages, including existence, survival, success, renewal, and decline, reflects the commonly accepted view of most organizational researchers.

The value of life cycle research is that it provides organizational managers with a set of characteristics that describe each stage of development. Managers can fine-tune operations, make changes in structure, delegate, or make whatever changes are necessary to prolong the life of their organizations once they understand the stage their firm is in and what might be prohibiting growth.

## Review Questions and Exercises

1. Discuss how smaller, younger organizations are different from larger, older organizations.

2. Describe the three options available to organizations during the survival stage. Give an example of a firm you are familiar with that is in the survival stage and describe which option its owners seem to be following.

3. List the five stages of the organizational life cycle and briefly define each one.

4. How can an organization that finds itself in a slow-growth period such as success return to a leaner, more customer-focused stage such as renewal?

5. Discuss the practical value of studying the organizational life cycle.

6. Contrast the industry life cycle with the organizational life cycle.

## Quiz

1. The organization life cycle describes the growth and development of an industry.
   **True or False**

2. Firms in the survival stage can grow to be large, can stay about the same size for an indefinite period of time earning marginal returns, or they can fail and go out of business.
   **True or False**

3. A common characteristic of the success stage is a condition known as red tape, where organizational members have to follow very specific, bureaucratic procedures.
   **True or False**

4. Firms that are in decline seem to focus primarily on their customers, staying ahead of their competition, and working toward continuous improvement and innovation.
   **True or False**

5. Situation, a factor determining life cycle stage, is defined as the overall makeup of a firm, including size, number of owners, how customers influence decision making, heterogeneity of markets, and so forth.
   **True or False**

6. A primary difference between the industry life cycle model and the organizational life cycle model is the inclusion of a shakeout stage in the industry model.
   **True or False**

7. The organizational life cycle model includes all of the following stages, except
   a. success.
   b. decline.
   c. survival.
   d. entrepreneurship.

8. Firms in the success stage of the life cycle model of organizations exhibit all of the following characteristics, except
   a. formalization.
   b. small size.
   c. hierarchy of control.
   d. bureaucracy.

9. The primary crisis experienced by organizations in the existence stage is
   a. need for delegation.
   b. power struggles.
   c. need for leadership.
   d. too much red tape.

10. Firms in the decline stage are likely to follow which strategy(ies)?
    a. prospector/differentiation
    b. reactor/low cost
    c. analyzer/combination low-cost–differentiation
    d. defender/low cost

11. The primary factors that determine life cycle stage include all of the following, except
    a. CEO tenure, or time in office.
    b. strategy.
    c. situation.
    d. decision-making style.

12. A firm that is growing slowly in revenue each year, has been in business for many years, has a broad scope of operations across several continents, and emphasizes strict adherence to policy and procedures is in the _____ stage of the organizational life cycle.
    a. existence
    b. survival
    c. renewal
    d. success

13. Since 1993, small and family businesses have created _____ new jobs.
    a. five million
    b. ten million
    c. twenty million
    d. thirty-five million

14. Family businesses have the opportunity for superior performance due to all but which of the following features?
    a. lack of family ownership
    b. preserving the humanity of the workplace
    c. focusing on the long run
    d. emphasizing quality and value

# Endnotes

1. S. Hanks, "An Empirical Examination of the Organizational Life Cycle in High Technology Firms" (doctoral dissertation, University of Utah, 1990).
2. D. Miller and P. Friesen, "A Longitudinal Study of the Corporate Life Cycle," *Management Science* 30, no. 10 (1984): 1161–1183.
3. G. Lippit and W. Schmidt, "Crises in Developing Organizations," *Harvard Business Review* 45, no. 6 (1967): 102–112.
4. W. Starbuck, "Shouldn't Organization Theory Emerge from Adolescence?" *Organization* 10, no. 3 (2003): 439–452.
5. K. Cameron and D. Whetton, "Perceptions of Organizational Effectiveness over Organizational Life Cycles," *Administrative Science Quarterly* 26, no. 4 (1981): 525–544; R. Miles and W. Randolph, "Influence of Organizational Learning Styles on Early Development," in *The Organizational Life Cycle,* ed. J. Kimberly and R. Miles, 44–62 (San Francisco, CA: Jossey-Bass Publishers, 1980).
6. P. McNamara and C. Baden-Fuller, "Lessons from the Celltech Case: Balancing Knowledge Exploration and Exploitation in Organizational Renewal," *British Journal of Management* 10, no. 4 (1999): 291–307.
7. Miller and Friesen, 1984.
8. M. Porter, *Competitive Strategy* (New York: The Free Press, 1980).
9. R. Miles and C. Snow, *Organizational Strategy, Structure, and Process* (New York: McGraw-Hill, 1978).
10. D. Lester, J. Parnell, and S. Carraher, "Organizational Life Cycle: A Five-Stage Empirical Approach," *International Journal of Organizational Analysis* 11, no. 4 (2003): 337–352.
11. Lester, Parnell, and Carraher, 2003; Miller and Friesen, 1984.
12. R. Quinn and K. Cameron, "Organizational Life Cycles and Shifting Criteria of Effectiveness: Some Preliminary Evidence," *Management Science* 29, no. 1 (1983): 33–41.
13. N. Churchill and V. Lewis, "The Five Stages of Small Business Growth," *Harvard Business Review* 6, no. 3 (1983): 30–50.
14. A. Bedeian, "Choice and Determinism: A Comment," *Strategic Management Journal* 11, no. 7 (1990): 571–573.
15. Starbuck, 2003.
16. I. Adizes, "Organizational Passages: Diagnosing and Treating Life Cycle Problems," *Organizational Dynamics* 8, no. 1 (1979): 3–24; A. Downs, "The Life Cycle of Bureaus," in *Inside Bureaucracy,* ed. A. Downs, 269–309 (San Francisco, CA: Little, Brown, & Co. and Rand Corporation, 1967).
17. Quinn and Cameron, 1983.
18. Miller and Friesen, 1984.
19. Churchill and Lewis, 1983.
20. J. Pearce II and E. Ravlin, "The Design and Activation of Self-Regulating Work Groups," *Human Relations* 11 (1987): 751–782.
21. Quinn and Cameron, 1983.

22. M. Weber, *The Theory of Social and Economic Organizations,* trans. A. M. Henderson and T. Parsons (New York: The Free Press, 1947).

23. Miller and Friesen, 1984.

24. D. Kirkpatrick, "The Future of IBM," *Fortune* 145, no. 4 (2002): 60-68; D. Kirkpatrick, "Breaking up IBM," *Fortune* 126, no. 2 (1992): 44-58.

25. H. Mintzberg, "Power and Organization Life Cycles," *Academy of Management Review* 9, no. 2 (1984): 207-224.

26. L. Greiner, "Evolution and Revolution as Organizations Grow," *Harvard Business Review* 50, no. 4 (1972): 37-46.

27. D. Lester, "An American Entrepreneur Manages across the Life Cycle," *Journal of Business & Entrepreneurship* 16, no. 1 (2004): 104-118.

28. C. W. Hofer, "Toward a Contingency Theory of Business Strategy," *Academy of Management Journal* 18 (1975): 784-810; G. Miles, C. C. Snow, and M. P. Sharfman, "Industry Variety and Performance," *Strategic Management Journal* 14 (1993): 163-177.

29. T. Levitt, "Exploit the Product Life Cycle," *Harvard Business Review* 43, no. 6 (1965): 81-94.

30. D. Kirkpatrick, 1992.

31. J. Chua, J. Chrisman, and L. Steier, "Extending the Theoretical Horizons of Family Business Research," *Entrepreneurship, Theory, & Practice* 27, no. 4 (2003): 331-338.

32. P. Sharma, J. Chrisman, and J. Chua, *A Review and Annotated Bibliography of Family Business Studies* (Norwell, MA: Kluwer Academic Publishers, 1996).

33. E. Poza, *Family Business* (Mason, OH: Thomson-Southwestern, 2004).

34. P. Davis, "Realizing the Potential of the Family Business," *Organizational Dynamics* 12 (1983): 53-54.

35. Poza, 2004.

36. J. Glover, "Labor Day 2000: A Small Business Celebration," *The Small Business Advocate* (September 3, 2000).

37. A. Serwer, "The Waltons: Inside America's Richest Family," *Fortune* 150, no. 10 (2004): 87-116.

# Organizational Culture and Ethics

## Chapter Outline

## Key Terms

cultural strength
culture
ethical relativism
integrative social contracts view of ethics
justice view of ethics
managerial ethics
religious view of ethics

rights view of ethics
self-interest view of ethics
social obligation
social responsibility
social responsiveness
utilitarian view of ethics
values-based management

**culture** the commonly held values and beliefs of a particular group of people

There is a way things are done in every organization. Long-term members understand it well and newcomers tend to learn it quickly. Organizational theorists refer to this phenomenon as organizational or corporate culture. **Culture** refers to the commonly held values and beliefs of a particular group of people,[1] and the concept of organizational culture reflects the application of the culture concept to members of an organization.

The concept of organizational culture is based on the observation from anthropology that unique norms of behavior develop for groups of individuals who spend a considerable amount of time together. Originally the term was used to describe behaviors within geographical boundaries, such as the British, French, or Chinese cultures. Organizational theorists have applied the concept to the study of organizations. Organizational culture (also called corporate culture) refers to the shared values and patterns of belief and behavior that are accepted and practiced by the members of a particular organization.[2] As we shall see, the organizational culture can greatly influence the success or failure of the organization.

Standards and expectations for ethics and social responsibility are often intertwined with an organization's culture. Managers and employees are expected to act in appropriate ways or consider certain criteria when making decisions. As such, the notions of ethics and responsibility are inseparable from that of organizational culture. Sections 7-2 and 7-3 discuss ethics and responsibility in detail.

# 7-1 Organizational Culture

Although it can be traced to the 1940s, the concept of organizational culture became popular in the 1980s when scholars and executives began searching for reasons to explain recent Japanese business successes.[3] They coined terms such as "Theory Z" to describe the type of cultures that are common to Japanese organizations.[4] Hence, an *organizational* culture is influenced by the prevailing *national* culture, although the two concepts should be distinguished.

An organization's culture exists at two levels. At the *surface level,* one can observe specific behavior of the culture, such as accepted forms of dress and rituals or ceremonies. These artifacts reflect a deeper, *underlying level* that includes shared values, belief patterns, and thought processes common to members of the organization.[5] The underlying level is the most critical to understand. Because it cannot be seen, it is often inferred by studying the surface level.

Because each organization develops its own unique culture, even organizations within the same industry and city will exhibit distinctly different ways of functioning. The organizational culture enables a firm to adapt to environmental changes and to coordinate and integrate its internal operations.[6] Ideally, the values that define a culture should be clear, easy to understand by all employees, embodied at the top of the organization, and reinforced over time. *Adaptive cultures* are innovative and encourage initiative, whereas *inert cultures* are conservative and encourage maintenance of existing resources.

An organizational culture provides members with a sense of belonging and identity within the organization. All organizations have cultures, although some are more pervasive than others. When a culture is well understood and managed, conflicts are handled more efficiently, knowledge is transferred more effectively, turnover is reduced, and teamwork is enhanced. Because culture unifies members of an organization around a set of beliefs and behaviors, it can be a powerful help or hindrance in efforts to facilitate change.

The first and most important influence on an organization's culture is its founder or founders. The founder's core values and business beliefs serve as the foundation for the organization's activities.[7] For instance, the primary influence on McDonald's culture was the fast-food company's founder, Ray Kroc. Although he passed away in 1984, his philosophy of fast service, assembly line food preparation, wholesome image, cleanliness, and devotion to quality are still central facets of the organization's culture.[8] Likewise, Sam Walton's influence on the Wal-Mart culture can still be seen today even though he passed away a number of years ago.

Whether allowed to evolve on its own or skillfully managed, the organization's culture serves as the basis for many day-to-day decisions in an organization. For example, members of an organization whose culture values innovation are more likely to invest the time necessary to develop creative solutions to complex problems than their counterparts in organizations whose culture values short-term cost containment.

Deal and Kennedy identified four key dimensions of culture.[9] *Values* constitute the beliefs central to the culture. *Heroes* are individuals within the organization who embody the values. *Rites and rituals* (or ceremonies) are symbolic events that influence the culture within organizations. The *culture network* includes the informal hierarchy and communication systems that develop in any organization. Identifying these four dimensions for any organization can help determine why decisions are made.

Views and assumptions about an organization's distinctive competence comprise one of the most important elements of culture when an organization is formed and begins to develop. For example, historically innovative firms are likely to respond to a sales decline with new product introductions, whereas companies whose success is based on low prices may respond with attempts to lower costs even further.[10] However, it is possible to modify the culture over time as the environment changes, rendering some of the culture obsolete and even dysfunctional.

Sometimes there is considerable agreement among an organization's members concerning its values, norms, and behavior. At other times, however, this is not the case. **Cultural strength** refers to the extent to which organizational members agree about the importance of certain values.[11] Strong cultures—such as 3M's strong emphasis on innovation and Southwest Airlines's strong emphasis on delivering value in a friendly manner—can lead to success, but a culture strong in all respects may not be appropriate for all organizations. Colleges and universities, for example, value diversity of thought and expression among faculty and students. As such, a culture strong in the sense that all members place a high value on freedom of expression and differences of opinion may be appropriate. However, a culture strong in the sense that all members agree on various perspectives may not be appropriate.

**cultural strength** the extent to which organizational members agree about the importance of certain values

It is essential that an organization's culture be aligned with its strategy. For example, an organization whose environment is rapidly changing may craft a new strategy that makes sense from financial, product, and marketing points of view. Implementing the strategy may be problematic, however, because it requires significant changes in assumptions, values, and ways of working.[12] All things considered, changing an organization's strategy is often easier than changing its culture, and both are often required for organizations to be successful.[13]

Organizations with strategically appropriate cultures—such as PepsiCo, Wal-Mart, and Shell—tend to outperform those whose cultures do not fit as well with their strategies. Successful firms tend to develop cultures that emphasize three key groups of stakeholders: customers, stockholders, and employees. Note that the point is *not* that these corporations have strong cultures, but that the culture must be appropriate to that firm's strategy and must contain values that can help the firm adapt to environmental change.[14]

Because culture reflects the past, changes in the environment can necessitate changes in an organization's culture.[15] Conservative organizations do not become aggressive and entrepreneurial simply because they have formulated new goals and plans, but because they embark on a substantial effort to modify the culture—the way things are done.[16]

It should be noted that cultural considerations do not end at the organizational level. Subcultures can develop in any organization and tend to be more prevalent when the organization is relatively large and its culture is relatively weak. Shared values and beliefs in a subculture can be based on commonalities within departments or divisions, such as functional expertise, geography, or differences in national culture.

## 7-1a Categorizing Culture

Each organization has a different culture. It is difficult to categorize cultures along similarities lest the uniqueness be lost in the discussion. Nonetheless, it is useful to identify broad characterizations of cultures as a means of better understanding how they influence organizational effectiveness. One way to do so is to consider four broad categorizations on the basis of the organization's primary internal and external characteristics. From an internal perspective, the key issue for the organization is the extent to which its strategic focus is internal or external. From an external perspective, the key issue for the organization is whether the environment necessitates flexibility or stability. In broad terms, these key issues suggest four categories of culture, as depicted in Figure 7-1.

The *adaptation culture* emphasizes an external strategic focus through change and flexibility. Innovation and creativity are highly valued and encouraged. The organization remains flexible so that its members can adapt to changes in the environment as they occur. Organizations with an adaptation culture seek not only to adapt to the needs of the external environment, but also to influence it.

The *mission culture* emphasizes an external strategic focus through stability. Leaders in such organizations place a great value on developing a shared understanding of the mission and vision. The mission culture is often best suited for organizations pursuing a focus strategy, as stability is achieved through concentration on only one specific segment of the market.

The *involvement culture* emphasizes an internal strategic focus through change and flexibility. Organizations with involvement cultures view performance as emanating from satisfied employees who are well equipped with ample resources to do their jobs. Employees are encouraged to become involved as instigators of change in the organization.

The *bureaucratic culture* emphasizes an internal strategic focus through stability. Consistency and predictability are valued by the organization's members. Business is conducted in a methodical manner following established rules and procedures in order to sustain a stable environment. The bureaucratic culture is often seen as less effective than other cultures because it does not allow members of the organization to tailor solutions to the individual needs of customers.

Should managers attempt to promote an organizational culture consistent with only one category or should they draw from multiple categories? The answer is not always clear. On the one hand, it can be argued that an organization's strategy should have both an internal and an external focus, and that a balance of stability and flexibility might be appropriate for most environments in which organizations operate. Following this logic, one might reject the notion of a clearly defined culture and attempt to create a culture that reflects each of the competing internal and external perspectives.

On the other hand, however, effective organizational leadership requires choices and accepts the fact that some paths will be taken and others will be avoided. It is rarely possible to produce products or services in all recognized categories for all segments of the market equally well. When an organization's mission and strategies are clearly defined, it is logical that a culture whose values reflect the mission and strategies will be most appropriate. Hence, the key issue is the *fit* between the organization's culture and other characteristics of the organization. The fit between the organization's culture and individual preferences is also a key consideration, as discussed in Box 7-1.

**Figure 7-1**

*Categories of Organizational Culture*

Source: Adapted from D. R. Denison and A. K. Mishra, "Organizational Culture and Effectiveness," *Organization Science* 6 (2001): 204–223.

| Strategic Emphasis | | Flexibility | Stability |
|---|---|---|---|
| | External | Adaptation culture | Mission culture |
| | Internal | Involvement culture | Bureaucratic culture |

**Environmental Emphasis**

## Box 7-1

### *Best Practices*

#### The Individual–Organization Fit

Do you like to dress casually, set your own hours, and make a lot of the decisions that affect your professional life? Or do you prefer a highly defined structure with clear sets of responsibilities and hierarchical decision making? Characteristics such as these describe an organization's culture. Studies suggest that many individuals leave one job for another because of differences in the organizational culture.

Business analytics software leader SAS is known for a highly unusual corporate culture, one that reflects a people-centeredness and promotes high loyalty and low turnover. Developing and promoting a culture can be costly, however. SAS's Cary, North Carolina, headquarters includes two on-site child-care centers, an employee health-care center, wellness programs, and even a 77,000 square foot recreation and fitness facility.*

SAS has been included in the list of Best Companies for Working Mothers thirteen times and is frequently listed on *Fortune*'s "100 Best Companies to Work for in America." SAS's ability to recruit and retain highly marketable, talented, and creative professionals can be attributed to its ability to develop a company that is too good to leave.

* SAS web page, http://www.sas.com/corporate/worklife/index.html, accessed 6/23/04.

### 7-1b Managing Culture

It is difficult to change an organization's culture. It often evolves on its own and is affected by a number of factors outside of the control of organizational leaders. The culture can be managed, however, so that it begins to reflect a desired set of values over a period of time.

According to researcher Edgar Schein, leaders can manage and shape the organization's culture in at least five ways.[17] The first way is to systematically pay attention to areas of the business believed to be of key importance to the strategy's success. Employees notice where leaders invest time and resources and are likely to incorporate the values and practices they observe into their own behavior. The leader may take steps to accomplish this goal formally by measuring and controlling the activities of those areas, or less formally by making specific comments or questions at meetings. These specific areas should be ones identified as critical to the firm's long-term performance and survival, and may include such areas as customer service, new product development, or quality control.

The second means involves the leader's reactions to critical incidents and organizational crises. The way a CEO deals with a crisis or important occurrence in an organization, such as declining sales or technological obsolescence, can emphasize norms, values, and working procedures, or even create new ones. When Saturn's chief executive chose to destroy a group of vehicles produced with faulty coolant instead of simply draining the radiators, a strong pro-quality message was sent to its workers.

The third means is to serve as a deliberate role model, teacher, or coach. Employees take notice of what a CEO does, both on and off the job. When a CEO models certain behavior, others in the organization are likely to adopt it as well. For example, chief executives who give up their reserved parking place and park among the line workers send a message about the importance of status in the organization.

The fourth means is the process through which top management allocates rewards and status. Leaders communicate their priorities by consistently linking pay raises and promotions, or the lack thereof, to particular behaviors. Rewarded behavior tends to continue and become ingrained in the fabric of the organization. Policies that reward seniority, for example, support a culture in which loyalty, not necessarily high performance or innovation, is highly valued.

The fifth means of shaping the culture is to modify the procedures through which an organization recruits, selects, promotes, and terminates employees. An organization's culture can be perpetuated by hiring and promoting individuals whose values are similar to those of the firm and whose beliefs and behaviors more closely fit the organization's changing value system. The easiest way to affect culture over the long term is to hire individuals who possess the desired cultural attributes.

In sum, an organization's culture can be changed, but modification is generally a difficult, time-consuming process. Leaders should seek to modify the culture in a positive direction (i.e., one that is appropriate for the organization). However, they should also recognize their limitations in institutionalizing steep cultural changes over a short period of time.

# 7-2 Managerial Ethics

**managerial ethics** an individual's responsibility to make business decisions that are legal, honest, moral, and fair

Inherent in an organization's culture is a set of expectations concerning ethical behavior and decision making. **Managerial ethics** refers to an individual's responsibility to make business decisions that are legal, honest, moral, and fair. Unethical behavior in organizations can result in costly government fines and penalties when it involves a violation of the law. However, the greater costs incurred by organizations engaging in such practices are indirect, such as the loss of reputation, the departure of top employees, lost customers, and greater government regulation.[18] Most managers and scholars agree that organizational decisions should be made in an ethical manner. Difficulties arise when the concept of managerial ethics is examined in greater detail, however, as competing definitions and perspectives can have a great bearing on what would be considered as ethical or unethical.

### 7-2a Ethical Relativism

**ethical relativism** the idea that ethics is based on accepted norms in a culture

Two contextual issues should be considered at the beginning of this discussion. The first is the frequently debated notion of **ethical relativism,** the idea that ethics is based on accepted norms in a culture. Most ethical relativists would argue, for example, that bribery is unethical in the United States and most Western nations where the practice is generally viewed as inappropriate. In contrast, bribery is ethical in other parts of the world where the practice is a generally accepted means of getting things done. Hence, according to the ethical relativist, the culture defines the ethics.

Strict opponents of ethical relativism argue that actions are either ethical or unethical without consideration to cultural acceptance. They would argue that bribery might be an accepted practice in some parts of the world, but not necessarily for the right reasons. Following this logic, allowing a culture to define ethics would result in a society where the ethical nature of all decisions is negotiable and clear standards of right and wrong cannot be established.

Ethical dilemmas in organizations are not always easy to resolve.

Although the debate between ethical relativists and their opponents is real and legitimate, most decision makers balance these contrasting views in practice. Most managers who embrace ethical relativism, for example, would acknowledge that certain actions in organizations—such as stealing from a coworker or defrauding a customer—are simply unethical in any culture. Likewise, most managers who eschew ethical relativism would acknowledge that other actions—such as giving a small gift of appreciation to a major customer—are more complex and might be ethical in some cultures but not in others.

The second contextual issue involves the resolution of ethical disputes. If a decision maker determines that a course of action is ethical, for example, should a subordinate be required to implement the action if the subordinate believes the action is unethical? In general, managers or other employees should not be required to perform activities inconsistent with their ethical convictions concerning the role that they may be expected to play in firm activities. From a practical perspective, however, employees should consider their ethical views when evaluating employment and pursue positions that do not inherently run counter to those views. The ethics test in Figure 7-2 provides food for thought concerning both of these issues.

| | | | | | | | Strongly Agree | | | |
|---|---|---|---|---|---|---|---|---|---|---|
| Strongly Disagree | -0- | | -1- | | -2- | | -3- | | | |
| | | | | | | | -0- | -1- | -2- | -3- |

1. Employees should not expect to inform on their peers for wrongdoings. ☐ ☐ ☐ ☐

2. There are times when a manager must overlook contract and safety violations in order to get on with the job. ☐ ☐ ☐ ☐

3. It is not always possible to keep accurate expense account records; therefore, it is sometimes necessary to give approximate figures. ☐ ☐ ☐ ☐

4. There are times when it is necessary to withhold embarrassing information from one's superior. ☐ ☐ ☐ ☐

5. We should do what our managers suggest, though we may have doubts about it being the right thing to do. ☐ ☐ ☐ ☐

6. It is sometimes necessary to conduct personal business on company time. ☐ ☐ ☐ ☐

7. Sometimes it is good psychology to set goals somewhat above normal if it will help to obtain a greater effort from the sales force. ☐ ☐ ☐ ☐

8. I would quote a "hopeful" shipping date in order to get an order. ☐ ☐ ☐ ☐

9. It is proper to use the company 800 line for personal calls as long as it's not in company use. ☐ ☐ ☐ ☐

10. Management must be goal oriented; therefore, the end justifies the means. ☐ ☐ ☐ ☐

11. If it takes heavy entertainment and twisting a bit of company policy to win a large contract, I would authorize it. ☐ ☐ ☐ ☐

12. Exceptions to company policy and procedures are a way of life. ☐ ☐ ☐ ☐

13. Inventory controls should be designed to report "underages" rather than "overages" in goods received. ☐ ☐ ☐ ☐

14. Occasional use of the company's copier for personal or community activities is acceptable. ☐ ☐ ☐ ☐

15. Taking home company property (pens, tape, paper, etc.) for personal use is an accepted fringe benefit. ☐ ☐ ☐ ☐

Total score: _____

If your score is:

|  |  |
|---|---|
| 0 | Prepare for canonization ceremony |
| 1–5 | Bishop material |
| 6–10 | High ethical values |
| 11–15 | Good ethical values |
| 16–25 | Average ethical values |
| 26–35 | Need moral development |
| 36–44 | Slipping fast |
| 45 | Leave valuables with warden |

**Figure 7-2**
*An Ethics Test*

### 7-2b Perspectives on Ethics

**utilitarian view of ethics**
perspective suggesting that anticipated outcomes and consequences should be the only considerations when evaluating an ethical dilemma

**self-interest view of ethics**
perspective suggesting that benefits of the decision maker(s) should be the primary considerations when faced with an ethical dilemma

**rights view of ethics**
perspective that evaluates organizational decisions on the extent to which they protect basic individual rights

What constitutes ethical behavior can be viewed in a number of ways, six of which are discussed here (see Table 7-1). The **utilitarian view of ethics** suggests that anticipated outcomes and consequences should be the only considerations when evaluating an ethical dilemma. The primary shortcoming associated with this approach, however, is that a decision may have multiple consequences, some of which may be positive, others negative, and still others undetermined. For example, a decision to lay off 10 percent of an organization's work force will harm those who lose their jobs but may help shareholders by increasing the projected returns on their investments. The long-term effect of the layoff could be positive if the organization emerges as a more competitive entity or negative if employee morale suffers and productivity declines. Hence, the utilitarian view is not always easy to apply.

The **self-interest view of ethics** suggests that benefits of the decision maker(s) should be the primary considerations. This view assumes that society will likely benefit when its individual members make decisions that are in their own best interest. As Smith and Friedman argued, firms that attempt to maximize their returns within the legal regulations of society behave ethically. This perspective limits ethical concerns to the consideration of short-term financial benefits for the organization.

However, self-interest can be viewed from a narrow, short-run perspective or from a broader, long-term perspective. It can be argued that one who always promotes his or her short-term interests at the expense of others will suffer greater loss in the long term. For example, firms whose managers construct loopholes in their product or service warranties to promote short-term profits can ultimately alienate their customers. Hence, ethical behavior has long-term profit considerations.

The **rights view of ethics** evaluates organizational decisions based on the extent to which they protect basic individual rights, such as a customer's right to privacy and an employee's right to a safe work environment. The key shortcoming of this approach, however, is that it is possible to protect individual rights at the expense of group progress or productivity.

The rights view is generally inferred when legislation prohibiting various forms of employee discrimination is considered. Such legislation often seeks to protect the rights of current or prospective employees even if organizations must incur costs to safeguard them. From an ethical standpoint, proponents of antidiscrimination legislation often desire a bias-free workplace but invoke a different view of ethics when evaluating the proposed law.

| TABLE 7-1 | Six Common Views of Ethical Decision Making | |
|---|---|---|
| **View of Ethics** | **Primary Strength** | **Primary Weakness** |
| Utilitarian | Decisions are based on actual outcomes. | A decision often has multiple outcomes, some positive, others negative, and even some undetermined. |
| Self-interest | Promotes freedom, initiative, and personal responsibility. | Decisions best for an individual could be devastating to a group. |
| Rights | Ensures that the rights of all involved are protected. | It is possible to protect individual rights at the expense of group benefits. |
| Justice | Decisions are made in a consistent manner because they are based on existing rules and procedures. | Rules and procedures must be developed in advance, a timely and imperfect process. |
| Integrative social contracts | Situational factors are emphasized. | Clear standards of right and wrong are deemphasized. |
| Religious | Clear standards of right and wrong are emphasized. | There may be different interpretations of religious principles in different areas and among different groups. |

The **justice view of ethics** suggests that all decisions will be made in accordance with preestablished rules or guidelines. Employee salaries may be administered by developing a formula that computes salary based on level of experience, amount of training, years of experience, and previous job evaluations. The key shortcoming associated with the justice view is that it requires decision makers to develop rules and procedures for every possible anticipated outcome, an arduous task indeed.

The **integrative social contracts view of ethics** suggests that decisions should be based on existing norms of behavior, including cultural, community, or industry factors. Although this perspective emphasizes the situational influences on a particular decision, it deemphasizes the need for clear standards of right and wrong devoid of the situation.[19]

The **religious view of ethics** is based on personal or religious convictions. In the United States, the Judeo-Christian heritage has formed a distinct notion of ethics, whereas Islam, Hinduism, and other religions comprise the majority viewpoint in many other nations. From the Christian perspective, for example, individuals should behave in ways that benefit others, treating other people as one would wish to be treated.[20] In one respect, the religious perspective counters the integrative social contracts view because it emphasizes clear principles of right or wrong with limited regard to situational variables. Needless to say, however, the religious view would result in markedly different ethical perspectives across cultures.

It should be noted that various additional ethical perspectives exist. Some have rich philosophical underpinnings, such as those traced to Aristotle or the famous eighteenth-century philosopher Immanuel Kant. Others are based in contemporary business thought and provide a broader framework for decision making that extends beyond ethical considerations. One such perspective, the stakeholder approach, suggests that organizational decisions should balance the interests of the organization's stakeholders (i.e., those groups that have a stake in the organization, such as employees, customers, suppliers, the community, etc.). Hence, the views presented in this chapter represent the major perspectives and do not comprise an exhaustive list.

It is also worth noting that most decisions are made without considering an ethical perspective on which they are based. For example, decision makers rarely speak of whether an organizational decision should be made from a justice view or an integrative social contracts view. In most cases, managers evaluate alternatives and make a decision. As such, some of the perspectives applied may be subconscious.

Of the major approaches, research suggests that the utilitarian view is the most commonly applied perspective in organizations.[21] It should be emphasized, however, that these views of ethical decision making are not always mutually exclusive. Further, it is likely that most managers employ a combination of ethical perspectives when making decisions. This is especially true when organizations are faced with decisions whose ethical dimensions are not always clear. In 2003 for example, the Recording Industry Association of America launched several hundred lawsuits against teenagers and college students in an effort to emphasize the notion that swapping copyrighted music files via the Internet is against the law. Critics charged that suing kids is both bad business and unethical, while industry executives argued that the law is clear and that widespread violations are taking a serious toll on its member firms.[22]

## 7-2c Overcoming Ethical Dilemmas

The ethical imperatives of other decisions may be easier to identify, however. For example, some organizations and individuals indiscriminately send unwanted, bulk emails (spam) to the public, including unwanted direct response advertisements of pornography sites, mortgage and investment services, and the like. One study suggested that spam cost American corporations $9 billion in 2002 due to loss of worker productivity, consumption of bandwidth and other technological resources, and the use of technical support time. Although this largely illegal practice is

**justice view of ethics** perspective suggesting that all decisions will be made in accordance with preestablished rules or guidelines

**integrative social contracts view of ethics** perspective suggesting that decisions should be based on existing norms of behavior, including cultural, community, or industry factors

**religious view of ethics** perspective that ethical dilemmas should be evaluated by considering personal or religious convictions

deplored by most industry groups and Internet users, enforcement is a complicated legal endeavor.[23]

Why do some organizations portray a pattern of unethical business practices? Anand and Ashforth identified six commonly used rationalization tactics to explain this behavior.[24] First, individuals *deny responsibility,* rationalizing that they have no other choice but to participate in unethical behavior. One employee may contend that the practice is directly associated with another's responsibility.

Second, individuals *deny injury,* suggesting that the unethical behavior did not really hurt anyone. This perspective defines behavior only as unethical if directly injured parties can be clearly identified and then the perpetrator hesitates to acknowledge the injury.

Third, individuals *deny rights of the victims,* rationalizing that the victims deserved what they got. This perspective rationalizes unethical behavior when competitors or other related parties are alleged to be involved in at least the same level of corruption.

Fourth, individuals engage in *social weighting* by making carefully controlled comparisons. One way this is done is by character assassination of those suggesting that a particular pattern of behavior is unethical. If those condemning us are corrupt—the argument goes—then how much credence can be given to their arguments? Another way this is done is by selectively comparing the unethical action to others whose actions are purported to be even more unethical. For example, falsifying an expense account for meals not eaten on a business trip is not considered a major offense when compared to someone who falsifies expenses for an entire business trip that never occurred.

Fifth, individuals can *appeal to higher values* by suggesting that justification of the unethical behavior is due to a higher order value. In this sense, one might argue that it is necessary to accept some degree of lower-level unethical behavior in pursuit of ethical responsibility at a higher level. For example, one sales rep who is brought in to help resolve a dispute between a customer and another sales rep may deny the legitimate claims of the customer, rationalizing that loyalty among sales representatives is a higher order value.

Finally, individuals may invoke the *metaphor of the ledger,* arguing that they have the right to engage in certain unethical practices because of other good things they have done. For example, a manager on a business trip may justify padding a travel expense account because she has already done more than her share of traveling in recent months.

Improving the ethical stance of an organization is not easy, however. Treviño and Brown identified five commonly held myths concerning ethics in organizations.[25] These myths and accompanying realities are summarized in Table 7-2. In concert,

| TABLE 7-2 | Myths and Realities of Organizational Ethics |
| --- | --- |
| **Myth** | **Reality** |
| 1. Ethical decision making is easy. | Ethical decision making is a complex process. |
| 2. Unethical behavior can be traced to a limited number of bad apples in an organization. | Unethical behavior can be a systemic part of the organization's culture. |
| 3. Ethics can be managed by developing formal ethics codes and programs. | Formal codes and programs are helpful, but ethical expectations must be part of the culture and fabric of the organization. |
| 4. Ethical leadership is really about leader morality and honesty. | Leader morality and honesty is a good start, but the leader must also infuse ethics into the organization and hold others accountable. |
| 5. Business leaders are less ethical today than they used to be. | Ethical concern in organizations has always been a pervasive issue. |

*Source:* Adapted from L. K. Treviño and M. E. Brown, "Managing to be Ethical: Debunking Five Business Ethics Myths," *Academy of Management Executive* 18, no. 2 (2004): 69–81.

# Box 7-2

they argue that ethical decision making is a complex process that extends beyond removing the bad apples from the organization and establishing formal ethics codes. It begins with proactive behavior on the part of top executives that infuses ethics into the fabric and culture of the organization.

In addition, the extent to which an individual behaves ethically is influenced by many factors, including one's stage of moral development, individual and personality differences, and the culture of the organization. The organization can influence some but not all of these factors. Organizations can foster more ethical decision making to a substantial extent, however, by emphasizing ethics in leader decisions, selecting and rewarding individuals who act in an ethical manner, and raising awareness of ethical concerns through training. Distinguishing ethical organizations from unethical ones is not always an easy task, as discussed in Box 7-2.

# 7-3 Social Responsibility

Whereas managerial ethics refers to an individual's responsibility when making business decisions, **social responsibility** refers to the expectation that organizations should serve both society and the financial interests of the owners or shareholders. In other words, the notion of social responsibility adds to the given economic and financial concerns the concept of **social responsiveness,** the idea that organizations must adapt to changing environmental conditions and decisions should be made to promote positive social change.

An organization's stance on social responsibility is typically embedded in its culture. This stance can and should influence both strategic and day-to-day decisions. If social responsibility is not considered, decisions may be aimed only at short-term objectives without balancing social objectives that the firm might also wish to consider. As we shall see, however, these issues are not always easy to resolve.

Business organizations have always been expected to provide employment for individuals and to meet consumer needs. Today, however, many members of developed societies also expect firms to help preserve the environment, to sell safe products, to treat their employees equitably, and to be truthful with their customers.[26] In some cases, firms are even expected to provide training to unemployed workers,

**social responsibility**
the expectation that business firms should serve both society and the financial interests of shareholders

**social responsiveness**
the perspective that organizations must adapt to changing environmental conditions, and decisions should be made to promote positive social change

contribute to education and the arts, and help revitalize urban areas. Some organizations are noted for their social positions. Firms such as Coca-Cola, UPS, and Johnson & Johnson recently earned high marks for social responsibility, whereas Bridgestone and Philip Morris earned the lowest marks.[27]

At the global level, environmental concerns have become a major social responsibility issue. Issues such as the depletion of natural resources, pollution of various forms, disposal of toxic wastes, and global warming are commonly discussed areas of concern. Fundamentally, organizations must either behave in a manner that is consistent with what is believed to be sound environmental practice or risk increased and costly regulation from governments.

**values-based management**
a system whereby organizational decisions are based on a set of established organizational values

Some organizations practice **values-based management,** a system whereby organizational decisions are based on a set of established organizational values. A values-based approach also has implications for ethical decision making. Ultimately, these values reflect the culture of the organization and the principles it holds dear. Figure 7-3 illustrates an example of such a firm—Johnson & Johnson—whose corporate reputation ranked number one in 2002 and 2003 in the Harris Interactive survey.[28] In addition, a memory device for making ethical decisions is also provided as an example of values-based management.

## Our Credo

We believe our first responsibility is to the doctors, nurses, and patients,
to mothers and fathers, and all others who use our products and services.
In meeting their needs everything we do must be of high quality.
We must constantly strive to reduce our costs
in order to maintain reasonable prices.
Customers' orders must be serviced promptly and accurately.
Our suppliers and distributors must have an opportunity
to make a fair profit.

We are responsible to our employees,
the men and women who work with us throughout the world.
Everyone must be considered as an individual.
We must respect their dignity and recognize their merit.
They must have a sense of security in their jobs,
Compensation must be fair and adequate,
and working conditions clean, orderly, and safe.
We must be mindful of ways to help our employees fulfill
their family responsibilities.

Employees must feel free to make suggestions and complaints.
There must be equal opportunity for employment, development,
and advancement for those qualified.
We must provide competent management,
and their actions must be just and ethical.

We are responsible to the communities in which we live and work
and to the world community as well.
We must be good citizens—support good works and charities
and bear our fair share of taxes.
We must encourage civic improvements and better health
and education.
We must maintain in good order
the property we are privileged to use,
protecting the environment and natural resources.

Our final responsibility is to our stockholders.
Business must make a sound profit.
We must experiment with new ideas.
Research must be carried on, innovative programs developed, and
mistakes paid for.
New equipment must be purchased, new facilities provided,
and new products launched.
Reserves must be created to provide for adverse times.
When we operate according to these principles,
the stockholders should realize a fair return.

*Johnson & Johnson*

**Figure 7-3**
*Johnson & Johnson Credo*
*Source:* Courtesy of Johnson & Johnson.

---

| Management Focus on Ethics | *A Memory Device for Making Ethical Decisions* |

Most people believe it is important that ethics take on a conscious, deliberate role in business decision making. In a nutshell, the issue of ethics boils down to asking yourself, "What price am I willing to pay for this decision, and can I live with that price?" This process can be helped by defining each letter of the word *ethics*.

**E = EXPERIENCE.** The values we carry with us into adulthood, and into business, are those that were modeled to us, usually by a parent, teacher, or some other significant adult. How people behave and the decisions they make speak much louder and are more convincing than what they say.

**T = TRAINING.** Training means training yourself to keep the question of ethics fresh in your mind deliberately.

**H = HINDSIGHT.** Success leaves clues that we need to tap into in order to help us make that tough decision. What if the problem you face was the problem of the person you admire most in life? What would he/she do?

**I = INTUITION.** What does your gut tell you is the right thing to do? Some call it conscience, or insight. How do you know when you've gone against your gut? You feel guilt, shame, remorse, have a restless, sleepless night, etc. Now the decision to be made is determining what to do about it.

**C = COMPANY.** How will your decision affect the company, the people who work with and/or for you, your customers, and your family? No matter how big or small your decision is, it affects other people in your life.

**S = SELF-ESTEEM.** The greatest ethical decision is one that builds one's self-esteem through the accomplishment of goals based on how these goals positively impact those around you.

*Sources:* Adapted from F. Bucaro, "Ethical Considerations in Business," *Manage,* August–September 2000, 14; and A. Gaudine and L. Thorne, "Emotion and Ethical Decision Making in Organizations," *Journal of Business Ethics,* May 1, 2001, 175–187.

---

The degree to which social responsibility is a relevant concern is widely debated, however. There is a second perspective that should be considered, the **social obligation** perspective. This view suggests that organizations should only be required to meet their economic and social responsibilities. As such, many economists, however, including such notables as Adam Smith and Milton Friedman, have argued that social responsibility should not be part of management's decision making process. Friedman has maintained that business organizations function best when they concentrate on maximizing returns by producing goods and services within society's legal restrictions. According to Friedman, corporations should be concerned only with the legal pursuit of profits and let shareholders address any priorities they might have on an individual basis.

**social obligation** the perspective that business organizations should only be required to meet their economic and social responsibilities

Debates between the social obligation and social responsibility perspectives often delve into philosophical arguments. As an example, the social obligation view suggests that rights to property ownership are natural or God given. As such, an individual owner or a group of owners (i.e., shareholders) have the inherent right to pursue profit as long as it is pursued in a legal manner. Proponents of the social obligation view tend to emphasize the idea that organizations should not harm society, not the idea that organizations should seek to advance society in a certain direction.

In contrast, according to the social responsibility view, individual property rights may be seen as granted by a society as a means of advancing social welfare for the entire society. Following this view, managers have a responsibility to direct the organization so that it furthers society's objectives. It should be noted, however, that these philosophical viewpoints are simplified herein. Contrary to the social obligation perspective, advocates of the social responsibility view emphasize the notion that organizations should actively seek to advance certain societal goals.

Delving deeper into this debate is beyond the scope of this text. From a pragmatic perspective, however, even if one accepts the social obligation view, one could argue that organizations should act in a socially responsible manner. There are two primary reasons why. First, not behaving in a socially responsible manner can increase the likelihood of more costly government regulation. Historically, a number of government regulations over business operations have been enacted because some firms refused to act in a socially responsible manner. Had some organizations not damaged the environment, sold unsafe products, or engaged in discrimination or misleading advertising—even when no laws were broken—legislation in these areas would not have been necessary. Government regulation is always possible when companies operate in a manner contrary to society's interests.

Second, stakeholders affected by an organization's social responsibility stance—most notably customers—are also those who must choose whether or not to purchase its goods or services. Prospective customers have become more interested in learning about a company's social and philanthropic activities before making purchase decisions. The social responsibility debate aside, many executives—especially those in large firms—have concluded that their organizations must at least *appear* to be socially responsible or face the wrath of angry consumers. As such, they are concerned not only about the actual behavior of the firm, but also about how it is perceived. Evidence suggests that consumers want the firms that produce the products and services they buy not only to support public initiatives, but also to uphold the same values in terms of the day-to-day decisions of running the company.[29]

The line between social responsibility and managerial ethics can be difficult to draw, as what may be considered by some to be socially irresponsible firm behavior may be a direct result of unethical managerial decision making. Nonetheless, while the debate over social responsibility continues, few would argue that managers should not behave ethically. However, what is morally right or wrong continues to be a topic of debate, especially when firms operate across borders where ethical standards can vary considerably. In the United States, for example, bribes to government officials to secure favorable treatment would be considered unethical. In a number of other countries—especially those with developing economies—small cash tips are an accepted means of transacting business and may even be considered an integral part of an underpaid government official's compensation.

The notion of social responsibility can be difficult to put into practice. By definition, a firm that is socially responsible is one that is able to generate both profits and societal benefits. However, exactly what is good for society is not always clear.[30] For example, society's demands for high employment and the production of desired goods and services must be balanced against the pollution and industrial wastes that may be generated by manufacturing operations. The decisions made to balance these concerns can be quite difficult to make.

Many consumers and activists in the United States have become increasingly concerned about trade deficits with other nations and job losses that occur when an organization moves a production facility abroad or a retailer stocks its shelves with imported products.[31] A number of American firms have closed production facilities in the United States and opened new ones in Mexico, China, India, and other countries where labor costs are substantially lower.[32] In 2003, China and Mexico accounted for almost one-quarter of imported apparel in the United States, followed by Honduras, Bangladesh, and El Salvador. With the expiration of world garment quotas in 2005, China's lead is expected to increase.[33] Analysts also suggest that differences in wages could spark increased global outsourcing in a broad array of professional and technical fields, such as architects, accountants, and even attorneys.[34]

Although outsourcing usually does not create legal concerns for an organization, many organizations have become more sensitive to this issue. In 2004, for example, E-Loan announced that customers would be given a choice about whether loan applications will be processed in Delhi or Dallas, with the latter taking as much as two days longer.[35] Hence, E-Loan customers can make their own decisions by balancing their concerns for speed and outsourcing.

## Summary

In many respects, an organization is defined by its culture, the shared values and beliefs held by its members. For an organization to be effective, its culture must be aligned with other characteristics of the organization, including the strategy. It is possible for leaders to shape the culture within an organization, but this process can be difficult.

The culture of an organization is likely to include values or expectations concerning both managerial ethics and social responsibility. Ethics can be viewed from a variety of perspectives and is a key component in organizational decision making. Although the extent to which social responsibility should be a concern for organizations is often debated, acting in a socially responsible manner is generally in the organization's best interest.

## Review Questions and Exercises

1. What is the difference between a national culture and an organizational culture? Are the two related? Explain.

2. What are four categories of organizational culture? Which of the four is best? Explain.

3. What is the difference between social responsibility and managerial ethics? Explain.

4. Could you argue that organizations should act in a socially responsible manner even if their leaders do not accept the notion that firms have social responsibilities?

## Quiz

1. Organizational culture can facilitate or hinder an organization's strategic actions.
   **True or False**

2. The most important influence on an organization's culture is its geographical location.
   **True or False**

3. Cultural effectiveness refers to the extent to which organizational members agree about the importance of certain values.
   **True or False**

4. The involvement culture emphasizes an internal strategic focus through stability.
   **True or False**

5. Adam Smith and Milton Friedman have argued that social responsibility should be central to the strategic management process.
   **True or False**

6. The concepts of ethics and social responsibility are interchangeable.
   **True or False**

7. The greatest influence on an organization's culture is
   a. its customers.
   b. its managers.
   c. its founder.
   d. none of the above.

8. Which of the following characteristics of culture were not identified by Deal and Kennedy?
   a. values
   b. ceremonies
   c. heroes
   d. all of the above characteristics of culture were identified by Deal and Kennedy

9. Innovation and creativity are most highly valued in which type of culture?
   a. bureaucratic culture
   b. stability culture
   c. mission culture
   d. none of the above

10. Which of the following is not a means whereby top managers can influence the organization's culture?
   a. react to critical incidents and organizational crises
   b. serve as a deliberate role model, teacher, or coach
   c. modify the procedures through which the organization recruits, selects, rewards, and terminates employees
   d. none of the above

11. The ethics perspective that considers the outcomes of a decision is
    a. the utilitarian view.
    b. the justice view.
    c. the interactive social contracts view.
    d. none of the above.

12. The idea that organizations must adapt to changing environmental conditions and decisions should be made to promote positive social change is called
    a. utilitarianism.
    b. social action perspective.
    c. social responsiveness.
    d. none of the above.

## Endnotes

1. E. Weitz and Y. Shenhav, "A Longitudial Analysis of Technical and Organizational Uncertainty in Management Theory," *Organization Studies* 21 (2000): 243–265.

2. W. J. Duncan, "Organizational Culture: 'Getting a Fix' on an Elusive Concept," *Academy of Management Executive* 3 (1989): 229–236.

3. M. Weber, *The Theory of Social and Economic Organization* (Englewood Cliffs, NJ: Prentice-Hall, 1947).

4. W. G. Ouchi, *Theory Z: How American Business Can Meet the Japanese Challenge* (Reading, MA: Addison-Wesley, 1981).

5. E. H. Schein, "Organizational Culture," *American Psychologist* 45 (1990): 109–119.

6. M. J. Rouse and U. S. Daellenbach, "Rethinking Research Methods for the Resource-Based Perspective: Isolating Sources of Sustainable Competitive Advantage," *Strategic Management Journal* 20 (1999): 487–494.

7. E. H. Schein, "The Role of the Founder in Creating Organizational Culture," *Organizational Dynamics* 12 (Summer 1983): 14.

8. J. F. Love, *McDonald's: Behind the Golden Arches* (New York: Bantam Press, 1995).

9. T. E. Deal and A. A. Kennedy, *Corporate Cultures: The Rites and Rituals of Corporate Life* (Reading, MA: Addison-Wesley, 1982).

10. G. A. Yukl, *Leadership in Organizations* (Upper Saddle River, NJ: Prentice-Hall, 2002).

11. B. Arogyaswamy and C. M. Byles, "Organizational Culture: Internal and External Fits," *Journal of Management* 13 (1987): 647–659.

12. E. H. Schein, *Organizational Culture and Leadership* (San Francisco: Jossey-Bass, 1985): 30.

13. D. Tosti and S. Jackson, "Alignment: How It Works and Why It Matters," *Training* 31 (April 1994): 58–64; T. Brown, "The Rise and Fall of the Intelligent Organization," *Industry Week* (March 7, 1994): 16–21; D. Lawrence Jr., "The New Social Contract Between Employers and Employees," *Employee Benefits Journal* 19, no. 1 (1994): 21–24.

14. M. Driver, "Learning and Leadership in Organizations: Toward Complementary Communities of Practice," *Management Learning* 33 (2002): 96–126.

15. L. Hayes, "Gerstner Is Struggling as He Tries to Change Ingrained IBM Culture," *The Wall Street Journal*, May 13, 1994, A1, A8.

16. C. Pringle, D. Jennings, and J. Longenecker, *Managing Organizations: Functions and Behaviors*, 309 (Columbus, OH: Merrill, 1988).

17. Schein, 1985.

18. T. Thomas, J. R. Schermerhorn Jr., and J. W. Dienhart, "Strategic Leadership of Ethical Behavior in Business," *Academy of Management Executive* 18, no. 2 (2004): 56–66.

19. E. Soule, "Managerial Moral Strategies—In Search of a Few Good Principles," *Academy of Management Review* 27 (2002): 114–124.

20. G. R. Weaver and B. R. Agle, "Religiosity and Ethical Behavior in Organizations: A Symbolic Interactionist Perspective," *Academy of Management Review* 27 (2002): 77–97.

21. D. J. Fritzsche and H. Becker, "Linking Management Behavior to Ethical Philosophy—An Empirical Investigation," *Academy of Management Journal* 27 (1984): 166–175.

22. C. Bialik, "Will the Music Industry Sue Your Kid?" *Wall Street Journal,* September 10, 2003, D1, D12.

23. M. Mangalindan, "For Bulk E-Mailer, Pestering Millions Offers Path to Profit," *Wall Street Journal,* November 13, 2002, A1, A17; B. Morrissey, "Spam Cost Corporate America $9B in 2002," January 7, 2003, Study by Ferris Research reprinted at http://www.clickz.com/experts/archives/emailstrategies/rept/article.php/1564761.

24. B. E. Ashforth and V. Anand, "The Normalization of Corruption in Organizations," in *Research in Organizational Behavior,* vol. 25, ed. R. M. Kramer and B. M. Staw, 1–52 (Amsterdam: Elsevier Publishing, 2003).

25. L. K. Treviño and M. E. Brown, "Managing to be Ethical: Debunking Five Business Ethics Myths," *Academy of Management Executive* 18, no. 2 (2004): 69–81.

26. M. J. Verkerk, J. DeLeede, and A. H. J. Nijhof, "From Responsible Management to Responsible Organizations: The Democratic Principle for Managing Organizational Ethics," *Business and Society Review* 106 (2001): 353–378; A. E. Randel, "The Maintenance of an Organization's Socially Responsible Practice: A Cross-Level Framework," *Business and Society* 41 (2002): 61–83.

27. R. Alsop, "Survey Rates Companies' Reputations and Many Are Found Wanting," *Wall Street Journal,* February 7, 2001, B1, B6.

28. R. Alsop, "Perils of Corporate Philanthropy," *Wall Street Journal,* January 16, 2002, B1, B4.

29. R. Alsop, 2002; A. Maitland, "No Hiding Place For the Irresponsible Business," Special Report, *Financial Times,* September 29, 2003, 1–2.

30. R. J. Ely and D. A. Thomas, "Cultural Diversity at Work: The Effects of Diversity Perspectives on Workgroup Processes and Outcomes," *Administrative Science Quarterly* 46 (2001): 229–273.

31. C. Ansberry and T. Aeppel, "Surviving the Onslaught," *Wall Street Journal,* October 6, 2003, B1, B6.

32. J. Dean, "Long a Low-Tech Power, China Sets Its Sight on Chip Making," *Wall Street Journal,* February 17, 2004, A1, A16; D. Morse, "In North Carolina, Furniture Makers Try to Stay Alive," *Wall Street Journal,* February 20, 2004, A1, A6; D. Luhnow, "As Jobs Move East, Plants in Mexico Retool to Compete," *Wall Street Journal,* March 5, 2004, A1, A8; J. Millman, "Blueprint for Outsourcing," *Wall Street Journal,* March 3, 2004, B1, B4.

33. R. Buckman, "Apparel's Loose Thread," *Wall Street Journal,* March 22, 2004, B1, B8.

34. K. Maher, "Next on the Outsourcing List," *Wall Street Journal,* March 23, 2004, B1, B8.

35. J. Drucker and K. Brown, "Latest Wrinkle in Jobs Fight: Letting Customers Choose Where Their Work Is Done," *Wall Street Journal,* March 9, 2004, B1, B3.

# Managing Organizational Processes

# Decision Making, Power, and Politics

## Key Terms

| | |
|---|---|
| bounded rationality | organizational decision making |
| Carnegie model | organizational politics |
| coalition | power |
| incremental decision model | programmed decisions |
| intuitive decision making | rational model of decision making |
| nonprogrammed decisions | satisficing |
| organizational conflict | unstructured model of decision making |

This book has emphasized the importance of strategically managing organizations, whether they are operating in the for-profit sector or the not-for-profit sector. The challenge of competitive forces, discussed in Chapter 2, Organizational Strategy and Performance, is reaching a zenith. This fact particularly impacts the first topic of this chapter, which is decision making. Because competition for resources and customers has reached the hypercompetitive level, people must make quick, accurate decisions for their organizations.

# 8-1 Decision Making in Organizations

Why do people in organizations make decisions? Primarily, decisions are required because organizations represent the merger of people, systems, and technology. Such a complicated conflagration inevitably leads to problems that beg solving or creates opportunities that need courses of action. Hence, **organizational decision making** is the process of identifying problems or opportunities and finding solutions or courses of action that further the goals of the organization.

When firms are small, such as those usually found in the existence stage of the organizational life cycle, all important decisions and most minor decisions are made by one person or a small group of people. However, as organizations add capacity to produce, and as they add employees and markets, the need for decision making increases exponentially. Modern organizations are pushing this decision-making responsibility to the lowest possible levels to increase speed and efficiency. This concept, known as empowerment, puts the responsibility for solving a problem or acting on an opportunity in the hands of those closest to the situation.[1]

As technology continues to permeate our organizations, markets and competition become global, and productivity increases accelerate, the time available for mulling over important matters in the decision-making process shrinks. Fortunately, most decisions faced by organizations are somewhat routine. Decisions made on a routine, repetitive basis addressed by company policy and procedures are known as **programmed decisions.**

**Nonprogrammed decisions** involve nonroutine, out-of-the-ordinary situations and are generally not covered by existing policy or procedure. An example of a nonprogrammed decision would be a competitive situation where an organization is faced with a serious threat from a substitute product. Think about the difficulty faced by steel producers when automobile manufacturers began to utilize plastic on a widespread basis in their new cars. This is an example of a strategic threat from the external environment that resulted in a loss of revenue. That is a serious enough issue. However, this substitution led to the utilization of plastic into other products, replacing glass, steel, and even paper.

### 8-1a The Rational Decision-Making Model

Regardless of whether decisions are programmed or nonprogrammed, everyone has a process that they follow when confronted with the need for a decision. As organization theory has evolved over the years, researchers and practitioners alike have recognized a clear need for a model for decision makers to adopt. Too many organizational managers were making decisions based only on past experience, expediency, or whatever might make them look good to their superiors.

Allowing organizational decision makers to fly by the seat of their pants works against the goals and objectives set by most firms. To overcome this problem, a rational or classical model of decision making has been developed. The **rational model of decision making** is a decision-making process that relies on a step-by-step, systematic approach to solving a problem. This model has been portrayed as

**organizational decision making** the process of identifying problems or opportunities and finding solutions or courses of action that further the goals of the organization

**programmed decisions** decisions made on a routine, repetitive basis that are addressed by company policy and procedures

**nonprogrammed decisions** decisions that involve nonroutine, out-of-the-ordinary situations and are generally not covered by existing policy or procedure

**rational model of decision making** a decision-making process that relies on a step-by-step systematic approach to solving a problem

| Step 1: Recognize and confront the situation | Step 2: Develop the solution options | Step 3: Evauate the possible outcomes of each option | Step 4: Choose the best option and implement |
|---|---|---|---|

**Figure 8-1**
*The Rational Decision-Making Model*

anywhere from a three-step[2] to a six-step[3] to an eight-step[4] process. Figure 8-1 depicts a version of the rational model based on a four-step strategic management approach.

Each step in Figure 8-1 will be explained using a practical example from the Coca-Cola Company headquartered in Atlanta, Georgia. During the early 1980s, Coca-Cola began losing market share in supermarkets to Pepsi. Although newly introduced Diet Coke had recently become the No. 1 diet soft drink, Coca-Cola executives were concerned with their competitive position in relation to Pepsi's. To make matters worse, Pepsi had been running taste test advertisements on television for several years where blindfolded consumers picked Pepsi over Coke based on taste.

Robert Goizueta, chairman of Coca-Cola, believed that the sweeter taste of Pepsi was leading to Coca-Cola's loss of market share. He initiated a secret project to tinker with Coke's formula, originally developed in 1886 by Georgia pharmacist John Pemberton. By 1984, the company was ready to try the new formula in consumer trials in more than 30 cities in the United States. With the aid of a market research firm, Coke conducted its own taste tests, with close to 40,000 people choosing New Coke over the old classic by 55 to 45%. They also chose it over Pepsi.

The introduction of New Coke and the withdrawal of old Coke came in April of 1985. To the company's surprise, the outcry over the new formula and the pulling of the old Coke was met with outrage. Less than 90 days later, the old formula was reintroduced to the market as Coca-Cola Classic. Coca-Cola's stock price went up more than $5 in one week after bringing back the old formula.[5] This example is not an illustration of a successful initial decision, as Coca-Cola's decision to introduce New Coke could only be described as a failure. However, it very clearly demonstrates how difficult important strategic decisions can be, and it reveals one firm's ability to recognize when it had made a mistake.

The following list explains the steps in Figure 8-1, as well as how they apply to the New Coke scenario at the Coca-Cola Company.

*Step 1:* Recognize and confront the situation—Decision makers should not sit on a situation that is a potential problem or opportunity for their organizations, hoping that the problem will take care of itself. Coca-Cola executives became concerned with a drop in market share in the early 1980s as Pepsi began outselling Coke in supermarkets. The company decided the problem was the taste of their product, in that Pepsi was sweeter than Coke.

*Step 2:* Develop the solution options—Strategic managers base decision-making options on their compatibility with the organization's strategy to accomplish its goals and objectives. Anything else is counterproductive. Coca-Cola owned the most recognizable brand in the world. To protect its market share and its name, Coca-Cola looked at introducing new products (like Diet Coke), changing advertising strategies (conducting its own taste tests), and actually altering the formula of its main product (introducing New Coke).

*Step 3:* Evaluate the possible outcomes of each option—Sometimes a possible solution to a situation sounds very good until it is evaluated based on the possible outcomes. As they evaluated each option, Coca-Cola executives knew they already had six brands on the shelves of stores, they believed their marketing campaign was already one of the best in the world, and they were concerned that tinkering with their tried and true formula was risky.

*Step 4:* Choose the best option and implement—Once the best option is identified based on an evaluation of possible outcomes, implement the option. After analyzing this situation for some time, Goizueta, with support from Robert Woodruff, the ninety-five-year-old former chairman of Coca-Cola, put the wheels in motion for the introduction of New Coke.

The example of decision making at Coca-Cola by its top management team demonstrates that even a rational, objective, research-based decision can be wrong. In the end, after spending more than $4 million to taste test its new formula, Coca-Cola failed in its introduction of New Coke. Some say an intangible factor, e.g., the consumer's emotional tie to the brand, was to blame for New Coke's failure.[6] Yet, Coca-Cola survived and prospered under Goizueta's leadership as its stock price increased 3,800% during his tenure. Since his death in October of 1997, however, Coca-Cola has struggled to find the right leader at the right time.[7]

Critics are quick to point out that the rational model has several flaws. For example, managers do not have complete, perfect information most of the time. They do not know all possible alternatives, and they do not understand, nor can they predict all possible outcomes of those alternatives. Decision makers also have limited mental capability, something that is not recognized by this model. The rational model is a *prescriptive* model in that it lays out a process for how decisions *should* be made. A second model that is more *descriptive,* demonstrating how decisions actually are made in organizations, will be discussed in section 8-1b.

### 8-1b The Carnegie Model

**Carnegie model** reflects a descriptive decision-making process in organizations where coalitions determine a final choice based on incomplete information, social and psychological processes, limited abilities of decision makers, and the need to find quick, satisficing solutions.

A second model of decision making is the *administrative* model, or the **Carnegie model.** Developed by organizational researchers James March and Herbert Simon from Carnegie-Mellon University, this model tries to explain how organizational decision makers actually make decisions. The result is a realistic snapshot of the limitations decision makers bring to the process, particularly in light of the tremendous number of variables involved in decision making in today's organizations.

The Carnegie model reflects a descriptive decision-making process in organizations where coalitions determine a final choice based on incomplete information, social and psychological processes, limited abilities of decision makers, and the need to find quick, satisficing solutions.[8] The Carnegie model is a good example of what happens to a behavioral theory in management when it is actually studied in practice. Rarely does one single top manager make all of the important decisions in an organization without input and buy-in from many other key managers. Although an organization may have clearly defined goals, conflict as to how to obtain those goals or whether they are actually the proper goals often develops. In these situations, coalitions can form within the organization between employees, managers, and/or shareholders to push forward a solution.[9] In contrast, the *rational* model of decision making tends to assume no conflict exists in organizations and that organizational goals are all commonly shared by immediate stakeholders.

**coalition** a group of people who band together to win some issue

Henry Mintzberg categorizes the possible reasons for coalitions in an organization and identifies the actual groups, both external and internal, that might result. He defines a **coalition** as "a group of people who band together to win some issue."[10] These possible coalitions include:

**External Coalitions**

Owners—those who have legal control of the organization

Associates—suppliers and buyers of organizational resources and products/services

Employee Associations—unions and professional associations

Publics—this term refers to general groups such as families and opinion leaders, special interests groups, and government

Directors—board members

### Internal Coalitions

Top Management Team—also referred to by some as the dominant coalition

Operators—describes the workers who actually produce the firm's product or service

Line Managers—all managers from the CEO down to first-line supervisors

Analysts of the Technostructure—systems planning and control personnel

Support Staff—specialists who work on matters of law, public relations, etc.

Ideology Supporters—those who share a set of beliefs that distinguish the organization from others[11]

This list emphasizes the fact that coalitions are powerful, yet fundamental forces to be reckoned with in any organization. The vast number of special interests, causes, needs, and other considerations that can be conjured up by this list confirms the practical approach to decision making that coalition-building represents. This is not to say that coalitions are only concerned with self-interest, but it does make one aware of the importance of coalition building in managing an organization.

A second major difference between the rational model and the Carnegie model has to do with choosing the optimal solution in the decision-making process. March and Simon have described that, in many cases, solutions to problems are arrived at through a process of **satisficing.** The concept of satisficing is choosing a course of action that is the most acceptable to the greatest number of people involved or affected. In a perfect world, this would not be the case. Decision makers would always choose whatever solution was best for the organization. Remember, organizations are groups of people who must work together to accomplish anything. Unfortunately, optimal solutions are not always going to be supported by organizational stakeholders.

Another factor involved in decision making that the rational model overlooks is the sheer limitations of human decision makers based on their bounded rationality. Although organizational decision makers are usually well-versed in their industry, trained in their jobs, and networked to opportunities and threats in the external environment, they are also limited by their own cognitive ability. So, **bounded rationality** refers to the limitations of the mind that restrict the ability of decision makers to solve problems or take advantage of opportunities. Operating within this limited framework, decision makers can make a quick list of alternatives based on past experience and personal knowledge of the situation at hand, prioritize them based on importance, and move on with a solution. Are all relevant alternatives likely to be included?

**satisficing**   choosing a course of action that is the most acceptable to the greatest number of people involved or affected

**bounded rationality**   refers to the limitations of the mind that restrict the ability of decision makers to solve problems or take advantage of opportunities

Input and buy-in from key managers aid and strengthen the decision making process.

The answer is probably not. However, the need not to spend too long deliberating a situation, the tendency to satisfice, and the personal preferences of the primary decision maker usually overrule any inclination to try to be exhaustive in identifying alternatives.

### 8-1c Incremental Decision Making

**incremental decision model** situation whereby managers make decisions that are only slightly different than the ones made by their predecessors or the ones they themselves made in the past

A different model of decision making is the **incremental decision model.** The name incremental is quite descriptive, as managers make decisions that are only slightly different than the ones made by their predecessors or the ones they themselves made in the past.[12] The idea behind the incremental model is that managers are only muddling through as they are confronted with important decision-making opportunities. Many managers practice this decision-making style because the chance for failure is reduced when they only incrementally change what has been happening for a long time. Although new courses of action may eventually develop when the incremental model is practiced, they take a long time to come about due to the small-step-by-small-step process.

### 8-1d The Unstructured Model

**unstructured model of decision making** decision making in uncertain environments as a structured sequence of activities that require smaller decisions throughout the process

While the Carnegie model emphasizes the need to recognize social and psychological processes, the unstructured model, based on the observance of actual decision makers in operating organizations, focuses more on the actual steps taken by decision makers. The **unstructured model of decision making,** developed by Henry Mintzberg, sometimes referred to as the father of strategic management, describes decision making in uncertain environments as a sequence of activities that require smaller decisions throughout the process.[13]

Mintzberg and his colleagues studied twenty-five organizational decisions as a process from beginning to end. They outlined three major phases common to the firms studied: the *identification phase,* the *development phase,* and the *selection phase.* The identification phase involved *recognizing* the problem or opportunity and gathering more information, or *diagnosing.* The development phase was focused on *searching* for alternatives or *designing* a solution that was customized to fit the situation. In the selection phase, a judgment was made, followed by *analysis, bargaining,* and eventual *authorization.* In their research, Mintzberg and his coauthors noted that sometimes major barriers would be encountered, requiring decision makers to go back and repeat steps they had already taken.

In any decision model, most critical decisions are made over a period of time. As we have emphasized in this book, the environment for most businesses changes over time, sometimes drastically. Mintzberg's model is realistic in that regard, particularly when an organization is operating in an uncertain internal or external environment, since it accounts for barriers that can arise.

### 8-1e Intuition in Decision Making

**intuitive decision making** decision-making system that involves relying on judgment and feel for a situation based on experience

A somewhat recent school of thought in the decision-making literature looks at the importance of intuition. Using intuition, or practicing **intuitive decision making,** involves relying on judgment and feel for a situation based on past experience.[14] Intuition is invaluable because it represents an informed gut reaction to a problem or opportunity, it allows decisions to be made faster as the reaction intuitively is fairly immediate, and it relies on information that has been burned into the subconscious over a long period of time.[15]

Intuition plays an important role in the decision making of Meg Whitman, president and CEO of eBay, who is featured in Box 8-1. Whitman must make decisions on critical business issues like expansion, acquisitions, personnel, and so forth. However, she has other decisions to make that involve social and cultural issues that can

# Box 8-1

Box 8-1

## Best Practices

### Meg Whitman, eBay

According to *Fortune,* the most powerful woman in business for the year 2004 was Meg Whitman, president and CEO of eBay.[16] Carly Fiorina of Hewlett-Packard had been named number one for six years in a row prior to 2004.[17] Why did Meg Whitman move up from second in 2003 to first? Part of the reason was that eBay was arguably the hottest company in the world in 2004. But perhaps even more important was the fact that Meg Whitman was the most respected woman manager in the world. One reason for that awesome reputation is her ability to manage a fast-growing business garnering worldwide attention without going on a power trip.

Whitman amassed a tremendous base of power by trying not to act powerfully. She has grown eBay from $5.7 million in revenue to just over $3 billion in about seven years. This makes eBay the fastest growing company in history, faster than FedEx, Microsoft, Cisco, Oracle, or even Wal-Mart for its first eight years of existence. Whitman takes no credit for the unprecedented success of eBay, choosing instead to constantly heap praise on her employees and loyal customers. Yet fellow executives at eBay are quick to remark that no one could have kept everything on course at the company except Meg.

The key to Whitman's tremendous tenure at eBay is rooted in her approach to power. She was quoted as saying: "Ask anyone about me, and they would never think of power."[18] Instead, Whitman would point to her unconventional power, a more subtle kind of power that continues to garner her a legion of admirers. Her credibility is key. Whitman does what she says she will do. She is also a counterintuitive strategist, a rare ability in today's uncertain environment. In a very unpowerful way, Whitman practices the art of enabling others to go out and accomplish great things for eBay. Yet, in the end, this art of enabling has made Meg Whitman the most powerful woman in business.

become quite complicated. For example, eBay permits the sale of Lizzie Borden's ax but not Jeffrey Dahmer's refrigerator.[19] Whitman finds that she must monitor chat rooms and customer emails almost daily to stay in touch with where her online market is going. Some items she has banned from sale on eBay include firearms, tobacco, alcohol, and Nazi items. Some of these decisions have been controversial since free market advocates can make an argument for selling anything legal as long as there is a market willing to purchase the product. Whitman has had to rely on her own intuition and gut feeling to try to do what is socially responsible without severely damaging her firm's ability to prosper.

# 8-2 Power in Organizations

Power is an elusive concept to grasp and formulate a formal definition for because it tends to be associated with authority, control, influence, and other similar things. Yet, power is also one of those organizational characteristics that most people know when they see it. For example, Salancik and Pfeffer,[20] researching strategic-contingency theory, asked ten managers in an insurance company to rank twenty-one people in the organization based on their influence. Only one person hesitated, asking "What do you mean by influence?" When he was told "power," he immediately joined the other nine in compiling what turned out to be very similar lists.

Mintzberg wrote about power being "in and around organizations" due to the growing body of literature on power between firms, as well as within firms.[21] This discussion of power will focus on power as it relates to the internal workings of an organization. **Power** is one's ability to achieve desired outcomes by exerting influence over others. Sometimes this influence is exerted in the form of orders or instructions to be carried out,[22] while other times it is subtly understood. A.G. Lafley

**power** one's ability to achieve desired outcomes by exerting influence over others

Box 8-2

## Career Point
### Position Power

When young, up-and-coming executives are given their first official, titled jobs, at least some position (or legitimate) power comes into play. Being named to a particular managerial spot on the organization chart automatically puts a person higher on the pecking order than some others. Many who fall into the others category are more experienced in the industry and know more about the company than the newly titled up-and-comer.

As you prepare for your first titled position in an organization, think about how you will manage your newfound position power. Meg Whitman, CEO and president of eBay (see Box 8-1), agrees with this statement made by Rajiv Dutta, eBay's CFO: "To have power, you must be willing not to have any of it."[25] This is difficult for new executives to grasp, since obtaining and exercising power is something they think they're working for in the first place.

Exercising position power requires a deft hand for a young executive. Young managers should not abdicate their power just because there are others in the workgroup who know much more about the business than they know. Conversely, they shouldn't ignore the valuable contributions these coworkers can make. Just like the green second lieutenant who comes to rely on his seasoned first sergeant, new managers must learn how to manage the knowledgeable folks they work with while continuing, where appropriate, to interject their own fresh thoughts that are not colored by years of doing the same old thing in the same old way.

Top management teams are looking for new managers who understand the core competencies of the firm, yet bring fresh new ideas to the table. They are not looking for new managers who want to be respected so badly that they impose their ideas on others, even when they are bad for the organization. Remember, in any organization, managers are respected for doing what they say they will and for advancing the goals and objectives of the firm, or, in other words, being credible and having integrity.

---

of Proctor & Gamble was recently quoted as saying, "The measure of a powerful person is that their circle of influence is greater than their circle of control."[23]

### 8-2a Individual Sources of Power

Power originates from several sources. These sources are covered in most organizational behavior courses at the collegiate level, but they are worth mentioning again here. Some of these power sources are based on a person's position in an organization, and some are based on person's individual characteristics or personality. Most of these power sources, legitimate, coercive, reward, expert, referent, and charismatic, were identified and described by French and Raven.[24]

The first source of formal power is *legitimate* power. Legitimate power is obtained by virtue of the position one holds in an organization. It is sometimes referred to as position power. Having a title or being designated a manager usually allows a person a certain amount of power based solely on the position. A second type of formal power is known as *coercive* power. Coercion means one has the ability to force someone to act in a certain way based on a fear of negative consequences if that action isn't taken. For example, one may be demoted or even fired for not following orders or doing as one was told. See Box 8-2 for a practical perspective on position power.

A somewhat more pleasant type of formal power is *reward* power, which is just the opposite of coercive power. Managers who have the ability to reward performance will usually get the results they need based on subordinates' desire to achieve the rewards. These rewards can be financial, such as salary increases or bonuses, or they can be nonfinancial, including options such as better working conditions, a nicer office, more time off, plum assignments, or promotions.

Individual sources of power include the notion of being an expert. *Expert* power refers to one's knowledge or skill that is greater than that of others in the workgroup.

This expertise about something specific to the needs of the organization brings a degree of respect and dependence from coworkers. For example, a technician from the information technology (IT) department at your company would be better suited to help you with a PC problem than your coworker in the marketing department. Eventually, if the PCs at your firm break down or lock up regularly, the computer technician may become one of the most powerful people in the organization. An example of this involved maintenance engineers at French tobacco-processing plants studied by researcher Michael Crozier. Crozier discovered that these maintenance engineers, although low on the organizational chart, were actually some of the most powerful people in the corporation due to the machinery frequently breaking down. Without the machinery operating properly, there was no production. These engineers exploited this situation by refusing to show operators how to make minor repairs, insisting that all repair work be done by the engineering maintenance department.[26]

The last personal source of power is known as *referent* power. Referent power is based on someone having admirable personality traits, so much so that others allow that person to exercise power over them because they want to please him. Referent power is a very strong kind of influence. We see its personification in advertising where sports heroes or music personalities are contracted to sell and promote products because companies understand that many people look up to these celebrities and want to be like them. Politicians will even solicit the assistance of rock and roll stars to campaign on their behalf, persuading fans to vote for the endorsed candidate.

Referent power can be taken to another level if someone possesses charisma. *Charismatic* power is a person's gift of being able to influence others by transforming their attitudes and beliefs, even in the face of contradicting information. A charismatic person may become a leader without a formal leadership position. This sometimes happens when a person does something heroic. An example would be the FedEx employee who could not open a drop box; instead of just moving on to the next one, he physically lifted the box and put it in his truck to be opened at the hub so that none of the documents or packages would be late.

### 8-2b  Departmental Sources of Power

We began the discussion on power with a reference to Pfeffer and Salancik's work on strategic contingency theory. The concept of environmental uncertainty is relevant to the idea of strategic contingencies, for over a period of time, what is strategically critical to the organization may change. The department or division that controls the critical resources or performs whatever task is most relevant will receive the most power. Pfeffer and Salancik identified five situations (see Table 8-1) where a department can exert tremendous influence.[27]

*Dependency* refers to a department needing an output from another department in order to successfully do its work. An example might be that the flight-scheduling department cannot complete its schedule without a status report on each pilot from personnel. This makes flight scheduling dependent on personnel.

| **TABLE 8-1** | Departmental Contingencies That Produce Power |
|---|---|
| Dependency | Nonsubstitutability |
| Financial resources | Coping with uncertainty |
| Centrality | |

*Financial resources* are more prized every day in organizations, and the departments that generate them are usually very powerful. Many times the sales department plays this role. When times are good and above-average returns are generated, other departments may make extra demands for more funds. In a university, the college, school, or department where enrollment is growing very fast will demand more resources to keep up with demand, but will also do so because it has amassed a certain amount of power based on its growth.

*Centrality* looks at the key function of an organization and determines what role a particular department has in that function. In a manufacturing organization, for example, the line people in the production area are usually considered to be more critical to the firm's primary activity, manufacturing, than the accounting department, which is considered to be more of a staff support group. Production would have more power in a manufacturing organization than accounting due to its central role in making the product.

*Nonsubstitutability* is a source of power that exists when the role played by a particular department cannot be filled by any other. Due to the knowledge of people in the department or their expertise due to education or training, substitutes are rare or nonexistent.

*Coping with uncertainty* is a strong base of power in today's hypercompetitive environment. Emery and Trist described a situation they labeled *turbulent fields,* where competition was so fierce that the organization believed the ground was actually moving under them.[28] A department can diffuse that uncertainty with accurate predictions or *obtaining prior information.* For example, a new product that is designed take advantage of environmental changes could be developed. Alternatively, power can be garnered through *prevention,* somehow stopping the organization from committing an error. The third method of coping with uncertainty is *absorption,* moving in after a bad situation has developed and diffusing the overall effect on the organization.

# 8-3 Politics in Organizations

This chapter has discussed decision making and power because they are closely related in any organization. Those with power have influence, and those with influence tend to be involved in decision making. There is a third force that must be added to these first two if power and decision making are to be fully understood, and that force is politics.

To some people who work in organizations on a daily basis, politics is a dirty word. They view politically astute managers or staff members as scheming, conniving, and self-serving. Yet, while some people do abuse the political process in organizations, politics is essential to progress. This is especially true for larger organizations.

Jeffrey Pfeffer has provided a good working definition of politics in organizations. According to Pfeffer, **organizational politics** are, "activities taken within organizations to acquire, develop, and use power and other resources to obtain one's preferred outcomes in a situation in which there is uncertainty or disagreement about choices."[29] This definition reveals several interesting points about politics in today's modern organizations.

First, politics are directly related to power. Pfeffer says political activities are specifically undertaken to acquire, develop, and use power. Second, politics are about obtaining preferred outcomes, which requires overcoming obstacles and differences of opinion among organizational members as to the best course of action. Third, political activities are particularly conspicuous in situations where there is uncertainty. Earlier, we discussed environmental uncertainty's effect on decision making and how organizational departments that can predict future events tend to wield much power. This definition of politics in organizations further explains that many times uncer-

**organizational politics** activities taken within organizations to acquire, develop, and use power and other resources to obtain one's preferred outcomes in a situation in which there is uncertainty or disagreement about choices

tainty and disagreement of choices lead to a situation where coalition building is usually required for a solution to be determined or a decision to be made.

So, politics in organizations is not always a negative thing. Yes, some political activity is self-serving and perhaps even subversive. Remember, organizations are composed of people, so society's problems and ills will probably be mirrored in our organizations. However, most organizational goals would never be met if it weren't for the political astuteness of key organizational leaders and power brokers. Some disputes are so great and some environments are so uncertain, that without political behavior very little would be accomplished. Imagine a decision process, for example, where an organization is trying to decide in which foreign country to pursue expansion. There are so many countries with so many diverse populations and standards of living, the choices are overwhelming. Some type of political coalition would have to be developed to push for one particular country over another to get the process moving.

Politics is a difficult behavior to define because, like power, it is one of those things that we know when we see it. Additionally, it is directly related to power, since it is the use of power to get something done. Most people dislike negative, self-serving politics and the people who practice such activity, but we need political activity whenever our organizations are faced with uncertainty and disagreement.

# 8-4  Conflict in Organizations

**Organizational conflict** occurs when two groups clash over competing goals. To understand why disagreement surfaces in organizations, we need to look at the sources of conflict. Borrowing from the work of Louis Pondy, the sources of conflict in organizations include interdependence, differences in goals and priorities, bureaucratic factors, incompatible performance criteria, and competition for resources.[30]

*Interdependence* is a term that describes how some subunits of the organization seek autonomy and pursue their own agendas of goals and objectives. This phenomenon occurs most often when the organization has diversified over a period of time. The need for interdependence identified by upper management to accomplish organizational goals can conflict with the desire for autonomy by subunits.

*Differences in goals and priorities* develop among subunits because each is engaged in a different pursuit, some with close ties to the external environment and some shielded by the internal core of the organization. A customer service center in direct contact with end users on a daily basis might have different priorities than an internal engineering department that is charged with lowering production and

**organizational conflict**
occurs when two groups clash over competing goals

Competition for scarce resources can sometimes resemble a tug-of-war in many organizations.

process costs. An example at the university level would be professors desiring reduced class sizes and teaching loads to facilitate the pursuit of academic research while the upper-level administrators seek larger class sizes and heavier teaching loads to reduce costs.

*Bureaucratic factors* can become a source of conflict in very large organizations due to the status afforded different groups according to their importance. In a firm such as General Electric, known as a proven training ground for top managers, a human resources vice president would have a difficult time of rising to the position of CEO or president. Staff jobs in human resources are considered important, but staff functions are not considered as relevant for training top managers as are line positions, such as division head or director of operations.

*Incompatible performance criteria* are a source of conflict between subunits because they may be evaluated in different ways, leading to incongruent performance outcomes. Subunits that are dependent on each other indirectly may become at odds. For example, if engineering is working to lower production costs but sales is hearing from customers that they want products with more features, conflict is likely to occur. In order to increase sales and keep customers from seeking other vendors, sales may need research and development to design new features to enhance its products. Engineering will then find itself working to redesign the manufacturing process to include the new features, probably adding costs in the long run. Performance in the sales department goes up, while cost containment programs by engineering are lost.

*Competition for scarce resources* is a ready source of conflict in most every organization operating in our modern global environment. Depending on how an organization is structured, this conflict can have several sources. If the structure is functional, as described in Chapter 5, marketing will compete with finance or research and development for scarce resources. If the structure is divisional, large operating divisions will find themselves lobbying the home office for resources. Resources are critical because organizations cannot grow without investment, and, unfortunately, there are never enough resources to meet everyone's expectations. When General Motors decided to form the Saturn automobile division in the mid-1980s, top managers knew significant financial resources would be necessary to design and build a new, world-class car. The eventual price tag was approximately $5 billion. Other divisions at General Motors suffered during this period, particularly Chevrolet. Chevrolet went from selling one-fifth of all cars in the United States in 1970 to 12.1% in 1992. Much of this lost market share was attributed to lack of new designs for its cars and continued erosion to Japanese carmakers.[31]

Not all conflict is bad for organizations. Most organizational researchers would agree that some conflict is quite constructive, as differences of opinion get out in the open and each side in a dispute becomes aware of the other's position. In Chapter 11, we will examine how organizational learning, a critical component of competitiveness in the future, is facilitated by conflict.

## Summary

Organizational decision making is the process of identifying problems or opportunities and finding solutions or courses of action that further the goals of the organization. Decisions made on a routine, repetitive basis addressed by company policy and procedures are known as programmed decisions. Nonprogrammed decisions involve nonroutine, out-of-the-ordinary situations and are generally not covered by existing policy or procedure.

The rational model is a decision-making process that relies on a step-by-step systematic approach to solving a problem. The Carnegie model reflects a descriptive decision-making process in organizations where coalitions determine a final choice based on incomplete information, social and psychological processes, limited abilities of decision makers, and the need to find quick, satisficing solutions. The concept of satisficing is choosing a course of action that is the most acceptable to the greatest number of people involved or affected. Another factor involved in decision making that the rational model overlooks is the sheer limitations of human decision makers based on their bounded rationality. Bounded rationality refers to the limitations of the mind that restrict the ability of decision makers to solve problems or take advantage of opportunities.

A different model of decision making is the incremental decision model. The idea behind the incremental model is that managers are only muddling through as they are confronted with important decision-making opportunities, improving on former decisions incrementally.

The unstructured model of decision making describes decision making in uncertain environments as a structured sequence of activities that require smaller decisions throughout the process. Using intuition, or practicing in-

tuitive decision making, involves relying on judgment and feel for a situation based on past experience.

Power is one's ability to achieve desired outcomes by exerting influence over others. Power is derived from a legitimate position, the ability to be coercive, the ability to reward, being an expert, appealing to others' desire for referent affiliation, and/or a strong charismatic personality. The department or division that controls the critical resources or performs whatever task is most relevant will receive the most power.

Organizational politics comprise activities taken within organizations to acquire, develop, and use power and other resources to obtain preferred outcomes in a situation in which there is uncertainty or disagreement about choices. Organizational conflict occurs when two groups clash over competing goals.

## Review Questions and Exercises

1. Rational decision making appears to be the optimal process for solving problems. Discuss.

2. Compare and contrast the rational model with the Carnegie model. In your opinion, which is better?

3. Explain the term *satisficing*.

4. Compare and contrast the expert basis of power with the referent basis of power.

5. Why is intuition important in decision making?

6. Is organizational politics good or bad? Defend your answer.

## Quiz

1. Organizational decision makers always have all the information they need to solve a problem or take advantage of an opportunity.
**True or False**

2. The Carnegie model emphasizes the role played by coalitions in organizational decision making.
**True or False**

3. Incremental decision making is practiced by many managers because repeating decisions of the past with only incremental changes reduces the chance for failure.
**True or False**

4. Legitimate power is also referred to as position power.
**True or False**

5. An individual can only possess expert power if she is a manager.
**True or False**

6. Practicing politics in an organization is never really needed to attain organizational goals.
**True or False**

7. Obtaining power in an organizational department can be accomplished in all of the following ways, except
a. neutrality.
b. centrality.
c. dependency.
d. coping with uncertainty.

8. The three major phases common to the unstructured decision-making model include all of the following phases, except
a. the identification phase.
b. the development phase.
c. the selection phase.
d. categorization phase.

9. Using intuition in decision making means
a. asking someone outside the firm for help.
b. relying on your gut feel for a situation.
c. hiring a consultant.
d. not making any decision at all.

10. When an organizational department performs a function that cannot be duplicated or replaced by another, it is said to have power based on
    a. centrality.
    b. financial resources.
    c. nonsubstitutability.
    d. external influence.

11. The fourth step in the rational model of decision making is
    a. develop the solution options.
    b. choose the best option and implement.
    c. recognize and confront the situation.
    d. evaluate the possible outcomes of each option.

12. The sources of conflict in organizations include all of the following, except
    a. interdependence.
    b. differences in goals and priorities.
    c. bureaucratic factors.
    d. earning above-average returns.

# Endnotes

1. J. Conger and R. Kanungo, "The Empowerment Process: Integrating Theory and Practice," *Academy of Management Review* 13 (1988), 471–481.

2. G. Jones, *Organization Theory* (Upper Saddle River, NJ: Pearson, 2004).

3. S. Robbins, *Organizational Behavior*, 10th ed. (Upper Saddle River, NJ: Pearson, 2003): 132.

4. R. Daft, *Organization Theory and Design*, 8th ed. (Mason, OH: South-Western, 2004): 449.

5. J. Fierman, "How Coke Decided a New Taste Was It," *Fortune* 115, no. 11 (1985): 80; A. Fisher, "Coke's Brand-loyalty Lesson," *Fortune* 116, no. 4 (1985): 44–46.

6. Fisher, 1985.

7. B. Morris, "The Real Story," *Fortune* 149, no. 11 (2004): 84–98.

8. J. March and H. Simon, *Organizations* (New York: Wiley, 1958); H. Simon, *The New Science of Management Decision* (New York: Harper and Row, 1960).

9. W. Stevenson, J. Pearce, and L. Porter, "The Concept of 'Coalition' in Organization Theory and Research," *Academy of Management Review* 10, no. 2 (1985): 256–268; R. Cyert and J. March, *A Behavioral Theory of the Firm* (Englewood Cliffs, NJ: Prentice-Hall, 1963).

10. H. Mintzberg, *Power In and Around Organizations* (Englewood Cliffs, NJ: Prentice-Hall, 1983): 27.

11. Mintzberg, 1983.

12. C. Lindbloom, "The Science of Muddling Through," *Public Administration Review* 19 (1959): 79–88.

13. H. Mintzberg, D. Raisinghani, and A. Theoret, "The Structure of Unstructured Decision Making," *Administrative Science Quarterly* 21 (1976): 246–275.

14. O. Behling and N. Eckel, "Making Sense out of Intuition," *Academy of Management Executive* 5, no. 1 (1991): 46–54.

15. L. Burke and M. Miller, "Taking the Mystery out of Intuitive Decision Making," *Academy of Management Executive* 13, no. 4 (1999): 91–99; A. Hayashi, "When to Trust Your Gut," *Harvard Business Review* 79, no. 1 (2001): 59–65.

16. P. Sellers, "eBay's Secret," *Fortune* 150, no. 8 (2004): 161–178.

17. A. Harrington and M. Shanley, "The Power 50," *Fortune* 148, no. 8 (2003): 103–110.

18. Sellers, 2004, 162.

19. Sellers, 2004.

20. G. Salancik and J. Pfeffer, "Who Gets Power—and How They Hold On to It: A Strategic-Contingency Model of Power," *Organizational Dynamics*, Winter (1977): 3–21.

21. Mintzberg, 1983, 1.

22. R. Dahl, "The Concept of Power," *Behavioral Science*, 2 (1957): 201–215.

23. Sellers, 2004, 162.

24. J. French and B. Raven, "The Bases of Social Power," in *Studies in Social Power: Origins and Recent Developments*, ed., D. Cartwright, 150–167 (Ann Arbor, MI: University of Michigan, Institute for Social Research, 1959).

25. Sellers, 2004, 161.

26. M. Crozier, *The Bureaucratic Phenomenon* (Chicago, IL: University of Chicago Press, 1964).

27. Salancik and Pfeffer, 1977.

28. F. Emery and E. Trist, "The Causal Texture of Organizational Environments," *Human Relations* 18 (1965): 21–32.

29. J. Pfeffer, *Power in Organizations* (Boston, MA: Pitman, 1981): 7.

30. L. Pondy, "Organizational Conflict: Concepts and Models," *Administrative Science Quarterly* 2 (1967): 296–320.

31. K. Kerwin, "Meanwhile, Chevy Is Sulking in the Garage," *Business Week*, August 17, 1992, 90–91.

# Innovation and Organizational Change

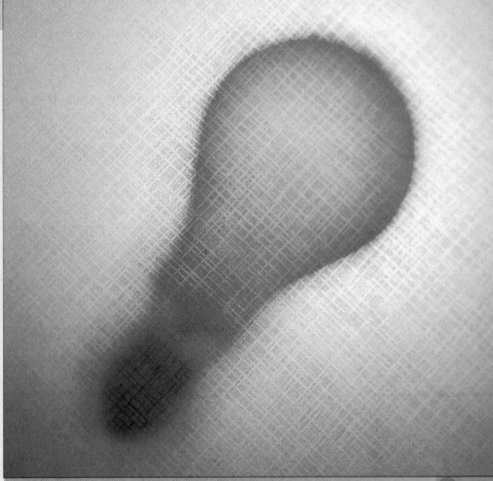

## Chapter 9

## Key Terms

action research
cooptation
evolutionary change
incremental innovation
innovation
innovative process
intrapreneurship
invention
organizational change
planned change

process-oriented innovation
product-oriented innovation
radical innovation
reactive change
reengineering
revolutionary change
reward system
systematic innovation
venture teams

Entrepreneurial activity, both within existing organizations and in the creation of new ones, has become vital in today's competitive environments of for-profit and not-for-profit organizations. Entrepreneurs create new markets, new customers, and new consumer demand. The instrument used to implement entrepreneurship is innovation.[1]

## 9-1 What Is Innovation?

Joseph Schumpeter, the German economist, heralded the work of the entrepreneur. He describes the entrepreneur's ability to transform an innovation into a viable business as creative destruction, a process whereby current methods of production are rendered obsolete.[2] Consider the example of the personal computer, a product that has rendered the typewriter unnecessary. How soon will pay telephones become obsolete due to the proliferation of cellular phones? However, just as important as the ability of the entrepreneur to enact creative destruction is the instrument of innovation.

**innovation** the transformation of creative ideas and concepts into products or services that meet the needs of customers

**invention** the creation of a new product or process

**Innovation** can be defined as the transformation of creative ideas and concepts into products or services that meet the needs of customers.[3] The process of innovation represents a managed-change effort by an organization that will be discussed in section 9-7b. Schumpeter distinguished between the types of changes that organizations experience, including invention, innovation, and imitation.[4] **Invention** involves the creation of a new product or process. When an organization utilizes an invention to create a product or service for a customer, it becomes an innovation. The adoption of an innovation by a similar firm is known as imitation.[5]

As an example, consider Thomas Edison, the famous inventor of the late nineteenth and early twentieth centuries. Edison worked tirelessly to invent the incandescent light bulb. He then transformed this invention into a true innovation when, in 1882, he flipped the switch and produced light at his Pearl Street station in New York City.[6] Not long afterward, George Westinghouse imitated Edison's innovation by building very similar electrical systems utilizing alternating current instead of Edison's choice of direct current.

George Westinghouse (1846–1914).

*Source:* Library of Congress, Prints and Photographs Division, LC-B2-1049-12

The accelerated nature of competition in today's global business environment has made innovation a critical organizational activity. Other types of organizational change have also moved to the forefront, including restructuring and reengineering, as firms attempt to become more efficient and effective in their operations. Yet it is innovation, the managed effort of organizations to get new products and services to market, that separates competitors earning above-average returns from those earning less.

# 9-2 Types of Innovation

Most innovations can be categorized in one of two ways. An innovation is either product oriented or process oriented.[7] Creating new products or services and bringing them to market creating new consumer demand is **product-oriented innovation.** This creation of a new product or service that replaces an existing one is also referred to as **radical innovation.** Product-oriented innovation also applies to **incremental innovation,** the improvement of existing products or services to enhance their marketability.[8] **Process-oriented innovation** involves the improvement of existing production processes or other organizational processes such as management, organizational reporting structures, or information processing systems. Process-oriented innovations can also be radical, such as the creation of an entirely new production process, or incremental.

Product-oriented innovations abound in today's society, as individuals and companies move into a wireless age of communication with cellular telephones that serve a wide variety of applications. Process-oriented innovations are less obvious to the public but not less novel as organizations find creative solutions to combat waste and slack in the manufacture and delivery of goods and services to remain competitive.

**product-oriented innovation** the creation of new products or services to bring them to market, creating new consumer demand

**radical innovation** creation of a new product or service that replaces an existing one

**incremental innovation** the improvement of existing products or services to enhance their marketability

**process-oriented innovation** the improvement of existing production processes or other organizational processes such as management, organizational reporting structures, or information processing systems

# 9-3 Sources for Innovative Opportunity

There is a common perception that innovation is the result of an entrepreneur having a magical moment where a bright idea ignites a creative impulse to go to work. In actuality, the process of innovation is usually a one-step-at-a-time plodding that eventually results in the creation of something new and improved out of existing knowledge. In fact, the key to organizations becoming more innovative is to practice **systematic innovation.** Organizations should support the search for changes in the environment and identify how those changes can be systematically analyzed as to their future innovative potential.

Two environments provide the backdrop for this purposeful search for change by organizations. Within these two environments, Peter Drucker has identified seven sources to monitor for potential innovative opportunities. The first environment is the firm and the industry in which it operates. This environment is home to four of the seven sources:

**systematic innovation** the search for changes in the environment and the identification of how those changes can be systematically analyzed as to their future innovative potential

- *The unexpected*—this results from an event that has not been anticipated, such as the unexpected success or the unexpected failure
- *The incongruity*—this source develops because something is not quite as it is assumed to be or ought to be
- *Innovation based on process need*—this occurs as the result of a problem within the organization that must be solved
- *Changes in industry structure or market structure*—usually a surprise to everyone in the industry causes this source

The second environment that provides sources of innovative opportunity is the general environment, a macroenvironment that is outside the scope of the firm and its industry. The remaining three sources are:

- *Demographics*—this refers to changes in population sizes, age distributions, and so forth
- *Changes in perception, mood, and meaning*—these are sociocultural changes within populations
- *New knowledge*—this is the discovery of something new, either through science or society[9]

To provide a clearer understanding of Drucker's work, examples of each source of innovation follow. These examples were cited by Drucker in his work on innovation and entrepreneurship.

- *The unexpected*—The computer was developed for the purpose of furthering science and facilitating the work of scientists. Early on, however, businesses began to demand the use of computers for such functions as payroll and accounts receivable. This was clearly not what the inventors of the computer had in mind.
- *The incongruity*—An incongruity is a discrepancy between what is and what ought to be. Large steel mills seemed to only do well during times of war. When there was a need for incremental capacity expansion, the expansion was so expensive it only allowed for short-term profits. The answer was the concept of the mini-mill, a way to provide additional capacity to meet existing demand in an affordable manner.
- *Process need*—Early telephone service in America was manual, processed by operators. Around 1909, it was projected that population growth would require the Bell company to employ every woman in America between the ages of seventeen and sixty as an operator by 1930. Within two years of realizing this limitation of manual calling, the Bell engineers had designed the automated dialing system.
- *Changes in industry or market structure*—In the 1960s, when the automobile industry went global, a struggling small car company named Volvo decided to become a world car company. It advertised its cars as sensible, sturdy, and safe transportation that was a better value than other more or less expensive models.
- *Demographics*—Improvements in public health in the Latin American region of the world led to a growth in populations, due in large part to a drop in the infant mortality rate. What followed was a tremendous growth in the urbanization of the region. Former Sears chairman, Robert E. Wood, after reading about this population explosion in the early 1950s, visited the region, studied the competition, and designed an entry strategy to take advantage of this opportunity.
- *Changes in perception*—Sometime during the early 1950s, Americans began to refer to themselves as being part of a middle class rather than a working class. William Benton, owner of *Encyclopedia Britannica,* discovered that middle class standing was achieved, in part, by attaining a high school education. In response to that discovery, he enlisted the help of high school teachers to sell his product to parents of students. If parents wanted their child to do well in school and achieve a middle-class standing, they needed encyclopedias in their homes.
- *New knowledge*—Lee de Forest, an American, invented the audion tube in 1906. This invention was the key to developing the radio. Although new knowledge many times precedes its actual application by thirty or more years, the radio was introduced to the public in the early 1920s. Its introduction, ahead of its time, was a result of the need during World War I for a wireless transmission instrument in combat zones.

Successful innovation by organizations is the result of exploiting these seven sources of innovative opportunity from the general and industry/firm environments.

Viewed from this perspective, innovation is not a technical term. Rather, it is an economic or social concept representing the process of transforming creative ideas into something that satisfies customers' needs.

# 9-4 The Innovation Process—A Life Cycle Approach

Each **innovative process** refers to how innovations are nurtured and facilitated from the early development stage to an eventual decline. This is known as a life cycle approach. The concept of life cycle has been borrowed from the biological sciences, where organisms are born, grow, mature, and eventually die.[10] Management researchers have utilized this model to study organizations, products, and the changing priorities of top managers as organizations change.[11]

The innovative process of organizations consists of six stages of life:

1. *Development*—The organization takes a creative idea, evaluates its potential, and modifies it.
2. *Application*—From this modified, creative idea, a new product or service is produced.
3. *Launch*—The new product or service is made available to the marketplace.
4. *Growth*—The launch of the new product or service is successful, and demand for it grows.
5. *Maturity*—Demand levels off as other organizations imitate the product or service.
6. *Decline*—Demand declines as new substitute products or services are embraced by the market.[12]

In today's hypercompetitive business environment, life cycles of innovations are becoming shorter and shorter. Organizations can no longer rely on a new product or service providing them with long-term profits. This is why innovation needs to be systematized through an organizational culture that promotes and rewards innovative behavior.

> **innovative process** a life cycle approach concerned with how innovations are facilitated from development to decline

# 9-5 Promoting Innovation

Organizational culture is the shared values and patterns of belief that members of a particular organization accept and practice. Culture can play a large role in developing positive or negative attitudes about innovation among organizational members. If an organization values innovative activity and behavior, that behavior will be pursued by its associates. If, however, an organization promotes a bureaucratic culture with strict adherence to standardized policies and procedures, innovation can be hindered.

Organizations that promote innovation through their unique cultures include 3M, Johnson & Johnson, Apple Computer, and Merck. As a result, these organizations lead their industries in new and innovative product and service activity. They promote innovation by communicating a sense to their associates that innovation is valued and rewarded. Managers in these organizations do not punish or discourage risk takers, giving employees an assurance that reaching for something new and creative is not a contrary activity.

When large organizations promote innovative activity, they are said to be supporting **intrapreneurship.** Intrapreneurship, also known as corporate entrepreneurship, is the term used to denote entrepreneurial activity within a corporate structure. Individual organizational members buy in to the cultural bent toward

> **intrapreneurship** entrepreneurial activity within a corporate structure

### Best Practices

#### GM and Saturn

During the 1970s, General Motors faced tremendous competition from Japanese companies that made smaller, more fuel-efficient automobiles. The gasoline crisis earlier in the decade allowed Toyota, Honda, and Nissan to take significant market share from American automobile makers, particularly GM.

To combat this threat, GM's CEO, Roger Smith, felt he had to develop an innovative group of designers who could pursue the process of new-car building without the baggage traditionally present at the firm. To accomplish this, Smith created a venture team to develop and bring to market the Saturn model. Saturn was

to be built in Tennessee, far from the rust-belt Midwest, the traditional home of GM factories and unions. This seclusion enabled team members to work outside the normal confines of a very bureaucratic organization, creating a freedom to pursue something new. The Saturn automobile, cited for its quality and dependability, was a worthy challenge to the Japanese imports.

Firms must be careful not to discourage unsuccessful innovative efforts. New product and service creation is a difficult undertaking, requiring much trial and error learning. Due to the hypercompetitive environment in which most firms exist, ideas that seemed sound and marketable in the early stages may not be viable by the time they reach application.

---

innovation by pursuing entrepreneurial ventures within the confines and for the benefit of their large organization.

**reward system** an overt mechanism of recognition and compensation to promote intrapreneurship or innovation within the firm

A company's **reward system** is an overt mechanism of recognition and compensation to promote intrapreneurship, or innovation within the firm. Employees engage in actions that are encouraged and rewarded, and they tend to avoid actions that are discouraged or punished. An important aspect of a reward system for innovation is the provision of an actual financial or nonfinancial incentive for innovative behavior. The reward serves to reinforce the promotion of innovative idea generation within the organization.

One nonfinancial method of promoting innovation is the concept of skunk works described by Peters and Waterman in their classic work, *In Search of Excellence*.[13] Excellent companies separate small teams of associates, sometimes called **venture teams**, into secluded or isolated quarters, away from the corporate office, where creative thinking and experimentation can be converted into innovative products or services. The term *skunk works* refers to this isolation from firm activities where teams can work on a specific developmental project without influence or interference. An example of a massive creative project where the product developers were isolated from the rest of the organization is presented in Box 9-1. Other organizations promote innovation through creative departments,[14] such as research and development.

**venture teams** system in which companies separate small teams of associates into secluded or isolated quarters where creative thinking and experimentation can be converted into innovative products or services

## 9-6 Reasons for Not Innovating

Some organizations never seem to introduce anything new or innovative, relying instead on the imitation and duplication of others' successes. These organizations fail to innovate due to lack of resources, failure to recognize opportunities, or a built-in resistance to change.[15]

1. *Lack of resources*—To be successful at innovation, an organization must be able to devote financial resources to the process. Likewise, individual and collective talent must be available within the organization to pursue innovative progress. These resources, people, and money, are limited in every organization. Some firms do not generate enough profit to have the excess capital needed to fund

the innovation process. No organization can finance the pursuit of all the creative ideas or innovative concepts that its employees might pursue. Discriminating decision makers must choose only those that promise the greatest potential for success.

2. *Failure to recognize opportunities*—Firms that are unskilled in the art of recognizing potentially profitable innovations lag behind others in the introduction of new products and services. Capital may be invested unwisely in projects that are mere continuations of, or minor improvements to, existing products and services, lacking innovative qualities from the beginning.

3. *Resistance to change*—Some organizations simply do not promote change. They have a built-in resistance to trying anything new that completely stifles innovation. Old, tried-and-true methods that worked in the past are considered to be intractable. And, some firms choose not to change because the operational strategy they have employed is working satisfactorily, producing profits and maintaining market share. The only problem with this approach is that most firms are trying to improve their products and/or services to their customers in an effort to grow their market share. When firms choose to not change, they tend to eventually get left behind by the competition.

# 9-7 Organizational Change

When firms innovate, organizational change is inevitable. The development of new production techniques, the creation of new products, or the implementation of new organizational structures are all innovations that demand organizational change. **Organizational change** is the adoption of any new idea, behavior, or substantive modification by an organization.[16]

> **organizational change** the adoption of any new idea, behavior, or substantive modification by an organization

## 9-7a Forces for Change

Firms constantly impact and are impacted by the general and industry environments. Change in these external environments is many times the force for change within the organization. External forces that can have dramatic effects on organizations include influences from sectors of the general environment, such as technology, political-legal, sociocultural, demographic, economic, and global.[17] Examples include widespread economic depression, aging populations, and societal changes in values. External forces are also found in the industry environment that includes the labor supply, competitors, customers, suppliers, regulators, and partners. These organizational stakeholders are in a position to affect change in a much more direct manner.

Internal forces for change exist within the organization's internal environment. These influences can come from owners, employees, shareholders, directors, or someone or some group with a serious stake in the organization's future. Many times the internal force for change is in response to an external environmental influence. For example, changes in technology, specifically the development of the personal computer and the Internet, have allowed some workers to perform their jobs at home, working individually on their own time. This has caused organizational change as employers grapple with managing the business through email rather than face-to-face communication. Box 9-2 explains how organizational change is relevant to you in embarking on your personal business career.

## 9-7b Types of Change

Just as with innovation, organizational change can be either radical or incremental. **Evolutionary change** involves a series of small, progressive steps that do not change the organization's general equilibrium.[18] **Revolutionary change** tends to

> **evolutionary change** change that involves a series of small, progressive steps that do not change the organization's general equilibrium

> **revolutionary change** change that alters or transforms the entire organization

Box 9-2

## Career Point
### Organizational Change

Some people are deathly afraid of change. Others welcome change and embrace it. When organizations experience change, individual members are threatened because it takes them out of their comfort zone. In some cases, change costs them their jobs. In particular, corporate entities of large size tend to undergo regular structural changes, commonly referred to as reorgs. Reorganizations can cause people to be moved from one position, department, or even division to another, sometimes involving relocation.

If changes in your life tend to cause you great discomfort, look for a career in an organization that experiences only gradual change. Older, larger, and more bureaucratic organizations tend to maintain a similar operational style for decades at a time. Also, firms that are dependent on extensive technology change slowly due to extremely large economies of scale that are expensive to replace.

Many people are very opposed to changes in location. If you do not want to leave a certain geographic area, try to find a position with a firm that only has local operations. Large, multinational organizations have global needs that require a global workforce.

Remember, however, no matter what organization employs you, change is a natural occurrence, driven many times by changes in the environment. When change is announced, find out everything you can about it. The more you understand the change and the need for it, the easier it will be for you to accept and even promote the change.

---

alter or transform the entire organization. Two other types of change include planned and reactive.

### Evolutionary Change

Organizations regularly undergo evolutionary change. It occurs over time, usually within the confines of the existing structure, strategy, and decision-making processes. This type of change sometimes affects only parts of the organization and many times involves changes in technology or information systems implementations. The limited reach of incremental or evolutionary change makes it simple to manage, as the existing framework of the organization is unaffected.

### Revolutionary Change

Differing greatly from the slower-moving evolutionary change, revolutionary change tends to alter an organization's essential core beliefs and structure.[19] For example, organizations that once lacked inertia and took years just to move slightly in one direction or the other can be transformed through revolutionary change, becoming nimble, responsive, and customer driven. Bill Ford, in a planned and organized manner, is trying to radically change the Ford Motor Company from a firm used to evolutionary change to one that accepts and understands the need for revolutionary change. Managing revolutionary periods of change is difficult at best. The change is so drastic that it usually catches everyone off guard and meets stiff resistance, particularly from long-term employees.

### Planned Change

**planned change** a response that is deliberately thought out and implemented in anticipation of future opportunities and threats

**Planned change** is a response that is deliberately thought out and implemented in anticipation of future opportunities and threats. Planned change can be facilitated through the efforts of a change agent, a person from within or from outside of the organization who marshals the resources and leads the other organizational members through the change process.[20] Sam Palmisano's recent initiative in the area of business on demand for IBM is an example of a planned, organization-wide integration of resources to provide a superior service to its customers.

***Managing Planned Organizational Change*** Planned change can be enacted in four general areas of an organization. They are:

- *Technology*—changes in the production process.
- *Products and services*—involves output changes.
- *Structure and systems*—focuses on administrative changes.
- *People*—changes in peoples' values, attitudes, and beliefs.[21] Organizations that value their members choose not to release at will those who can contribute to its overall success, even if there needs to be some change in their attitudes or beliefs.

Figure 9-1 reflects the four types of change that can provide a strategic advantage if properly implemented.

Organizational change is always viewed as difficult and time consuming. The need for change in an ever-changing business environment, however, is impossible to ignore. The strategic importance of successfully implementing changes in technology, products and services, structure and systems, or people is discussed below.

The first area of planned change, technology, encompasses a wide array of organizational alterations. Technology changes are usually implemented to improve efficiency or effectiveness. Examples include information systems improvements, machinery and equipment replacements, and the sequence of activities required to deliver products and services to market. Successful technology changes can increase the speed at which customer service is delivered; lower production costs, for example, by substituting automobile assembly line robotics for human labor; and raise the overall information level of the organization as more people have access to more information through technological innovations.

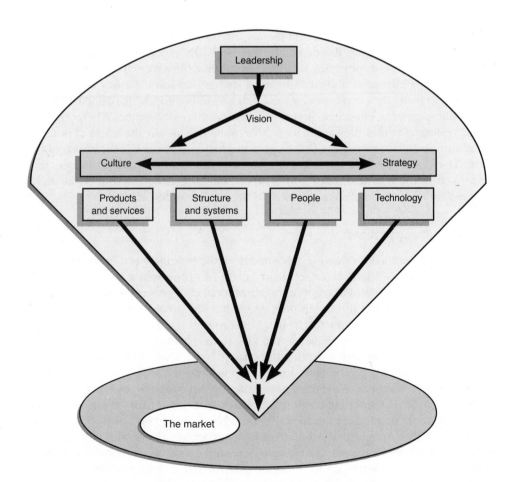

**Figure 9-1**
*The Competitive Wedge*

*Source:* J. E. McCann, "Design Principles for an Innovating Company," *Academy of Management Executive* vol. 5, no. 2 (1991): 85. Reprinted by permission of Academy of Management Executive via Copyright Clearance Center.

Changes in products or services are primarily undertaken to increase market share. These changes can be new products or services, alterations to existing products or services, or both. Nowhere is this more prevalent than at 3M, where thirty percent of revenues each year must come from new products developed within the last four years.[22] This new-product pipeline provides 3M with great public relations stories and customer loyalty.

Changes in structure and systems refer to how firms are administered. Each organization has a distinct structure that determines reporting relationships, division of work, and primary responsibilities. Organizational strategy and how it is implemented would also fall under this heading. Indeed, structural changes are often needed to support a new strategy. Too many times firms want to reorganize to improve performance when it is actually the strategic direction that is the problem. To avoid this common mistake, organizations should perform an internal audit, commonly referred to as a SWOT analysis, which details the firm's *s*trengths and *w*eaknesses and matches those with its environmental *o*pportunities and *t*hreats.

Finally, changes in the people of organizations may be the most difficult to implement, but, if successful, they can make a bigger difference in the organization than any of the other three types of change can. The people's beliefs and values are established from the beginning of an organization's existence by the founder(s). As more people are added to the staff over time, each is indoctrinated with the underlying values and beliefs the company promotes. The admonition, "That's not how we do things around here," has been spoken at businesses for centuries. However, today's business environment rewards those firms that strive for constant innovation and improvement. Innovation and improvement have to have a supportive and rewarded corporate culture if they are to flourish.

### Reactive Change

**reactive change**   change that is usually piecemeal and in direct response to a specific opportunity or threat from the external environment

As forces for change put pressure on the organization, managers can simply react to each situation as it arises. **Reactive change** is usually piecemeal and in direct response to a specific opportunity or threat from the external environment. Strategically, reactive change is a clear indication that an organization has lost its way, choosing to maintain a certain status quo, reacting to environmental conditions only when they appear to challenge directly the organization's existence. When organizational managers realize they are in a reactive mode it is usually the result of political infighting and power struggles that exist at the expense of the overall health of the firm. The best way out of the reactive mode is a return to a strategic management approach to the business that focuses on establishing goals and objectives and a process for their accomplishment based on the mission of the organization.

### 9-7c The Change Process

Because organizational culture is established from the beginning of a firm's existence, change is usually difficult to enact. Kurt Lewin has proposed a simple model for change agents to adopt in attempting organizational change. Lewin suggests that organizational change is a three-step process.[23] Step one involves *unfreezing* current behavior to reduce resistance to change. This requires making a strong case for the need for change and its importance to the long-term success of the organization. The second step is *moving,* implementing the change itself. Third, to ensure the change becomes part of the organizational landscape, a new *refreezing* process is necessary. Managers must reinforce and reward new behavior that supports the change.

Rossabeth Moss Kanter contends that Lewin's model is actually much too simple for the modern complex organization. According to Kanter, Lewin's model provides managers with a straightforward manner of approaching a very complex task, and that is why the model has survived for well over a half century.[24] Kanter's Big Three model of change involves understanding an organization's movement, the forms change can take, and the action roles necessary for the change process. She contends that organizations are never really *frozen* as depicted by Lewin's example. Rather, organizations are very fluid, moving through developmental stages that overlap.

Another way to enact change is through action research. **Action research** relies on initial organization research, followed by actions that are evaluated and serve as the basis for future change. This model usually involves planned change experts in organization development who work closely with organization managers, assisting in the implementation of an on-site intervention.[25] Some organizational change is very difficult to accomplish, and involving action research professionals from outside the organization greatly facilitates the needed change process.

**action research** a model that usually involves planned change experts in organization development who work closely with organization managers, assisting in the implementation of an on-site intervention

### 9-7d Resistance to Change

It is very difficult for managers to enact change in an organization if they do not understand why employees are so resistant to change. The primary reasons for resistance to change are uncertainty, lack of understanding and trust, differing perceptions, self-interest, and feelings of loss.[26] Uncertainty refers to the fear of the unknown experienced by a firm's employees when confronted with the need for change. They are concerned that they cannot perform under new rules or policies, they may not be predisposed to change as far as their personality is concerned, or they may believe the change will lead to a loss of jobs.

Some workplaces have developed a lack of trust toward management. This translates to a resistance to any kind of change due to years of mistrust between management and labor. Employees may simply not understand the need for change due to its being poorly articulated by management. Some resistance is a lack of agreement as to the true nature of a problem, or, put another way, a differing perception as to what really is the need for change. This is especially prone to occur if one manager, or a small handful of managers, makes a decision to enact change without input from other sources.

The self-interest of managers, and sometimes employees, is another barrier to change in any organization. Power and status that take years to acquire can be lost in one sweeping reorganization.[27] Managers protect their turf by finding excuses as to why a particular change is not going to work, even though it might actually be very good for the organization. When old methods are held to be too sacred, organizational employees may find themselves incapable of the change required to meet new external challenges.

Similar to this is the sense of loss. Employees develop strong social alliances with each other over time, and many organizational changes directly impact those

Managers who are tasked with an internal change project must overcome employees' resistance to change due to uncertainty and self-interest.

alliances. People are asked to move from one city to another, one division to another, or one continent to another, breaking up long-standing social networks. Employees effectively become removed from their comfort zones and at-work friends.

### 9-7e Overcoming Resistance to Change

Empirical research has demonstrated that participation may be the most effective mechanism for overcoming resistance to change. As people are invited to actively assist in implementing an organizational change, they tend to take ownership of the change to ensure its success. This is especially true when external leaders are included directly in organizations, such as a local banker becoming a member of the board of directors. This process, known as **cooptation,** fosters better cooperation between the firm and its external environment as the banker becomes psychologically vested in the success of the firm once he joins the board of directors. Communication is another important prerequisite to successful change efforts, as people need information about the specific need for change if they are to be persuaded to help with its implementation. Another potential change approach is that of facilitation. If employees are having trouble adjusting, facilitation is the best approach, but it can be expensive and time consuming.

For organizations facing stiff resistance, three other approaches are available, all with negative drawbacks. The first is *negotiation,* in which management agrees to give something up to accomplish the needed change. Negotiation can set a negative precedent, leading others to try the same tactic when change is needed again. A second approach is *manipulation,* used only if other tactics will not work. Manipulation can cause employees to feel they are being used by management. The third approach is *coercion,* a speedy tactic designed to overcome any kind of resistance. Coercion can leave employees angry with management, leading to future problems.[28]

### 9-7f Reengineering

One of the most difficult organizational change processes being undertaken today is business process **reengineering.** Made popular by the book, *Reengineering the Corporation,* by Michael Hammer and James Champy, reengineering is defined as "a radical redesign of business processes in a cross-functional manner to achieve major gains in cost, service, or time."[29] Similar to zero-based budgeting, the concept involves redesigning an organization's processes as if they could be done over completely from the beginning. Put another way, if the organization had a blank sheet of paper and began designing its production and service processes, what would they look like?

Reengineering is somewhat threatening to employees. Processes and steps in the value chain that have been part of the organization for decades come under close scrutiny. Jobs can be eliminated when it is discovered that value is no longer being added by a particular function or process. Reengineering has been found to be most effective in large organizations, particularly those with needs in the area of new-product development and customer service. Mature organizations that tend to operate as bureaucracies find ways to reduce overhead costs and eliminate duplication of process through reengineering efforts. At Motorola, cellular telephone production time was reduced from fourteen hours to two through a reengineering project. Reengineering is too costly, time consuming, and threatening to employees, however, to be undertaken for simple refinements or quality improvements.

### 9-7g The Learning Organization

The final organizational change process is the movement to become a learning organization. Made popular by Peter Senge, the concept of a learning organization refers to an organization continually and proactively creating, acquiring, and enacting knowledge. Then, on the basis of this new knowledge, the organization changes

**cooptation** a process in which leaders from the environment become active in the organization; for example, a banker might become a member of the firm's board of directors

**reengineering** a radical redesign of business processes in a cross-functional manner to achieve major gains in cost, service, or time

to something different.[30] The learning organization will be discussed in detail in Chapter 11.

## Summary

Most management researchers contend that organizations must innovate if they are to successfully compete in the current global business arena. Innovation is the transformation of creative ideas into products or services that fulfill customers' needs. Systematic innovation is possible through the establishment of an organizational culture that encourages and rewards innovative behavior without punishing failed attempts. Creative departments or venture teams can be vehicles by which organizations promote innovation.

To facilitate innovation, many organizations face the need for change. Resistance to change is stiff due to a variety of reasons, such as uncertainty, lack of understanding and trust, differing perceptions, self-interest, and feelings of loss.

## Review Questions and Exercises

1. Discuss the difference between invention and innovation.

2. Innovations are either process-oriented or product-oriented. Which would be more important in a service business? Why?

3. Provide an example of and explain how a change in demographics can be perceived as a source of innovation for an organization.

4. Why do you think the life cycle of innovations has become shorter than it was 40 or 50 years ago?

5. Explain the difference between evolutionary and revolutionary change.

6. Why are organizational members so resistant to change?

## Quiz

1. The adoption of an innovation by a similar firm is known as imitation.
   **True or False**

2. According to Peter Drucker, the discovery of an incongruity is finding something not quite as it is assumed to be.
   **True or False**

3. Demographic changes refer to changes in mood or perception.
   **True or False**

4. Intrapreneurship is also known as corporate reengineering.
   **True or False**

5. Reactive change is a response that is deliberately thought out by organizational managers.
   **True or False**

6. Organizational culture changes usually involve changes in values, attitudes, or beliefs.
   **True or False**

7. _____ relies on initial organizational research followed by actions that are evaluated and serve as the basis for change.
   a. Big Three research
   b. Subjective research
   c. Action research
   d. Quantitative research

8. Kurt Lewin's organizational change model involves
   a. unfreezing, moving, and refreezing.
   b. shakeout, maturity, and decline.
   c. leading, organizing, and directing.
   d. downsizing, reengineering, and rightsizing.

9. The most effective mechanism for overcoming resistance to change is
   a. overtime.
   b. participation.
   c. adding more staff.
   d. reducing benefits.

10. The innovative process for organizations includes all but
    a. launch.
    b. development.
    c. maturity.
    d. shakeout.

11. Creating new products or services and bringing them to market such that new consumer demand occurs is known as
    a. process-oriented innovation.
    b. organizational learning.
    c. product-oriented innovation.
    d. incremental innovation.

12. An example of a creative department within an organization that is focused on creative thinking and experimentation is
    a. research and development.
    b. technical engineering.
    c. operations.
    d. logistics.

# Endnotes

1. P. Drucker, *Innovation and Entrepreneurship* (New York: Harper & Row, 1985).
2. J. Schumpeter, *The Theory of Economic Development* (Cambridge, MA: Harvard University Press, 1934).
3. A. Van de Ven, "Central Problems in the Management of Innovation," *Management Science* 32 (1986): 590-607.
4. Schumpeter, 1934.
5. P. Sharma and J. L. Chrisman, "Toward a Reconciliation of the Definitional Issues in the Field of Corporate Entrepreneurship," *Entrepreneurship Theory & Practice* 23, no. 3 (1999): 11-27.
6. B. McCormick, *At Work with Thomas Edison* (Canada: Entrepreneur Press, 2001).
7. E. B. Roberts, *Innovation: Driving Product, Process, and Market Change* (San Francisco: Jossey-Bass, 2002).
8. E. B. Roberts, "Managing Invention and Innovation," *Research Technology Management* (January–February 1988): 1-19.
9. P. Drucker, 1985.
10. D. Lester and J. A. Parnell, "A Strategic Interpretation of Organization Life Cycle," *Journal of Applied Management and Entrepreneurship* 5, no. 1 (1999): 14-32.
11. N. Churchill and V. Lewis, "The Five Stages of Small Business Growth," *Harvard Business Review* 61, no. 3, (1983): 30-50.
12. L. B. Mohr, "Determinants of Innovation in Organizations," *American Political Science Review* 69 (1969): 111-126; G. A. Steiner, *The Creative Organization* (Chicago: University of Chicago Press, 1965); J. E. Ettlie, "Adequacy of Stage Models for Decisions on Adoption of Innovation," *Psychological Reports* 71 (1980): 28-36.
13. T. J. Peters and R. H. Waterman, *In Search of Excellence* (New York: Harper & Row Publishers, 1982).
14. H. Mintzberg, *The Structuring of Organizations* (Englewood Cliffs, NJ: Prentice-Hall, 1979).
15. R. Griffin, Management, 6th ed. (Boston: Houghton-Mifflin Company, 1999).
16. J. L. Pierce and A. L. Delbecq, "Organizational Structure, Individual Attitudes, and Innovation," *Academy of Management Review* 2 (1997): 27-37.
17. T. J. Dean, R. L. Brown, and C. E. Bamford, "Differences in Large and Small Firm Responses to Environmental Context: Strategic Implications from a Comparative Analysis of Business Formations," *Strategic Management Journal* 19 (1998): 709-728.
18. D. Miller, "Evolution and Revolution: A Quantum View of Structural Change in Organizations," *Journal of Management Studies* 19 (1982): 111-151; D. Miller and P. Friesen, "Momentum and Revolution in Organization Adaptation," *Academy of Management Journal* 23 (1980): 591-614.
19. A. D. Meyer, J. B. Goes, and G. R. Brooks, "Organizations in Disequilibrium: Environmental Jolts and Industry Revolutions," in *Organizational Change and Redesign*, ed. G. Huber and W. H. Glick, 66-111 (New York: Oxford University Press, 1992); M. L. Tushman, W. H. Newman, and E. Romanelli, "Convergence and Upheaval: Managing the Unsteady Pace of Organizational Evolution," *California Management Review* 29, no. 1 (1986): 29-44.
20. R. McLennan, *Managing Organizational Change* (Englewood Cliffs, NJ: Prentice-Hall, 1989).
21. J. E. McCann, "Design Principles for an Innovating Company," *Academy of Management Executive* 5, no. 2 (1991): 76-93.
22. L. D. DiSimone, "How Can Big Companies Keep the Entrepreneurial Spirit Alive?" *Harvard Business Review* 73, no. 6 (1995): 184-185.
23. K. Lewin, "Frontiers in Group Dynamics: Concept, Method, and Reality in Social Science," *Human Relations* (June 1947): 5-41.
24. R. M. Kanter, B. A. Stein, and T. D. Jick, *The Challenge of Organizational Change* (New York: The Free Press, 1992).
25. T. G. Cummings and C. G. Worley, *Organization Development and Change,* 5th ed. (St. Paul, MN: West Publishing Company, 1993).
26. A. S. Judson, *Changing Behavior in Organizations: Minimizing Resistance to Change* (Cambridge, MA: Blackwell, Inc., 1991).
27. H. Mintzberg, *Power In and Around Organizations* (Englewood Cliffs, NJ: Prentice-Hall, Inc., 1983).
28. J. P. Kotter and L. A. Schlessinger, "Choosing Strategies for Change," *Harvard Business Review* 57, no. 2 (1979): 106-114.
29. T. A. Stewart, "Reengineering: The Hot New Management Tool," *Fortune* 128, no. 4 (1993): 41-48.
30. P. M. Senge, *The Fifth Discipline* (New York: Doubleday, 1990).

# Organizational Technology

## Chapter 10

## Key Terms

computer-integrated manufacturing

continuous process production

craft technologies

engineering technologies

intensive technology

job design

job enlargement

job enrichment

job rotation

joint optimization

large-batch technology

long-linked technology

mass customization

mechanistic structure

mediating technology

nonroutine technologies

organic structure

pooled interdependence

routine technologies

sequential interdependence

slack

small-batch and unit production

sociotechnical systems approach

task analyzability

task interdependence

task variety

technical complexity

technological imperative

technology

# 10-1 Introduction to Technology

New employees coming into today's modern workplace are faced with a myriad of challenges that demand specific skills and abilities. In 1991, the United States Secretary of Labor issued a report known as the Secretary's Commission on Achieving Necessary Skills (SCANS) that outlined the basic skills required to be successful in the technologically challenging organizations of the future.

Today we are seeing those organizations in full bloom throughout developed countries. Gone are the smelly, hot, hazardous factories of the past. Modern factories are clean, highly technical, and, in many cases, even air-conditioned. Safety is a priority, and automatic, computer-managed production lines are the norm. The skills and abilities articulated in the SCANS report (see Box 10-1, Career Point) are minimum requirements in the current organizational work environment. Thinking, communicating, problem-solving individuals who understand computers as well as they do the products they make have replaced the backbreaking manual labor force of the past.

**technology**   the ways that organizations find to do something; it may include the use of machinery and equipment, production materials, computers, or skills and techniques necessary to take inputs and transform them into outputs

Modern production facilities, like the Porter-Cable plant in Jackson, Tennessee, which produces electric tools through the use of computer-integrated manufacturing techniques, thrive on technology. **Technology** is a term that describes the ways that organizations find to do something. It may include the use of machinery and equipment, production materials, computers, or practically any skills and techniques necessary to take inputs and transform them into outputs. In Chapter 1, we presented the Business System model in Figure 1-1. It demonstrates the transformation process. None of the three steps, inputs, transformation, or outputs, would be possible without technology.

**slack**   a lull in activity; or, in the case of slack resources, having excess on hand for surprise circumstances

As has been expressed in this book before, competitive pressures are at an all-time high in almost all business sectors. This pressure forces organizations to utilize technology in many new and creative ways. For example, inputs of raw material or information could be processed routinely on its way to the production or conversion processes. However, in order to reduce costs, reduce or eliminate **slack** (time, e.g., a lull in activity, and/or resources, having excess on hand for surprise circumstances), and to increase the speed at which products are produced, technology has come to play an important role in the acquisition of inputs. Therefore, several departments become involved with acquiring inputs in an effort to manage the external environment of suppliers and providers so that the organization can remain competitive. Most of the technology issues discussed in this chapter will refer to the manufacturing environment.

# 10-2 Computer-Integrated Manufacturing

Television has come to play a prominent role in our business culture due to the popularity of utilizing television as a medium for advertising. Recent advertisements have focused on the advantages some companies offer their customers through the process of **mass customization.** The companies advertising the benefits of mass customization, such as IBM, Dell, and Levi Strauss, are offering their customers a customized product from a mass-production operation. The benefit to the customer is obvious, as one commercial relates when a woman is able to design her new car in terms of features, color, interior, and so forth, on the Internet. The plus for the business supplying the product is that advanced technology is enabling firms to pursue mass customization at low, mass-production costs.[1] In particular, the competitive position of the firm is enhanced as it is able to address individual customer needs without sacrificing economies of scale.

**mass customization**   a customized product from a mass-production operation

**computer-integrated manufacturing**   an integrative process where each step of production is coordinated, including design, machinery, robotics, and engineering

Computer-integrated manufacturing, also referred to as advanced manufacturing technology or flexible manufacturing systems, is the new technology that has made mass customization possible. The system of **computer-integrated manufacturing**

# Box 10-1

## Career Point
### The SCANS Report

The SCANS report suggested the skills and abilities people would need when they went to work right after high school.[2] The report resulted in a set of skills and competencies that the commission believed each young person needed to be successful at work. In the last decade or so, we have discovered that many employers are also concerned that their new hires from colleges and universities lack some of these necessary skills.

What is important to you, as an individual who is pursuing some kind of collegiate degree program, is that these skills are *in addition* to your college education. While you may recognize certain skills that you believe you have developed or improved over the course of your college years, you will also find several that you feel need much improvement if you are to meet the minimum standards suggested by the SCANS report.

The exhibit included below briefly outlines the competencies and foundation skills recommended in the SCANS report.

These skills and competencies are articulated in much more depth in the report. While you may be put off by the fact that this report was directed at high school graduates, go over the recommendations carefully and you will probably find one or two areas where you could stand some improvement.

Many universities in the United States are reevaluating their core curriculums, even in colleges of business, to ensure that these recommendations from SCANS are not being overlooked. In particular, skills such as creative thinking, reasoning, and problem solving, or what are commonly referred to today as critical thinking skills, and communication skills such as listening and speaking are receiving serious attention. The number one skill employers seek regarding new hires is the ability to communicate orally and in writing.[3]

Success in today's high-performance economy depends on the development of the SCANS skills and competencies. The technology issues discussed in this chapter illustrate the importance of computers, machinery, systems, and people all working in an integrative manner to accomplish organizational goals. With the increased level of international business, outsourcing of certain functions, and diversity in the workplace, the SCANS recommendations from 1991 have become the mandate for today.

---

### Workplace Know-How

*Workplace competencies*—Effective workers can productively use:

- *Resources*—They know how to allocate time, money, materials, space, and staff.
- *Interpersonal skills*—They can work on teams, teach others, serve customers, lead, negotiate, and work well with people from culturally diverse backgrounds.
- *Information*—They can acquire and evaluate data, organize and maintain files, interpret and communicate, and use computers to process information.
- *Systems*—They can understand social, organizational, and technological systems; they can monitor and correct performance; and they can design or improve systems.
- *Technology*—They can select equipment and tools, apply technology to specific tasks, and maintain and troubleshoot equipment.

*Foundation skills*—Competent workers in the high-performance workplace need:

- *Basic skills*—reading, writing, arithmetic and mathematics, speaking and listening.
- *Thinking skills*—the ability to learn, to reason, to think creatively, to make decisions, and to solve problems.
- *Personal qualities*—individual responsibility, self-esteem and self-management, sociability, and integrity.

is an integrative process where each step of production is coordinated, including design, machinery, robotics, and engineering.[4] Through the use of computer-coordinated production techniques, firms are able to customize products for individual customers without completely reconfiguring production lines.

The primary technologies driving computer-integrated manufacturing are computer-aided design (CAD), computer-aided manufacturing (CAM), computer-aided materials management (CAMM), just-in-time (JIT) inventory systems, and integrated information networks throughout the organization. *Computer-aided design* utilizes computers in designing and engineering new products and parts, improving design flexibility and creativity and simplifying product design.[5] *Computer-aided manufacturing* focuses on the transformation process, as inputs are converted to outputs using production machinery controlled and integrated by computers. *Computer-aided materials management* controls the flow of inputs to the transformation process, while assisting in production scheduling and controlling inventory. *Just-in-time inventory systems* regulate the inflow of raw materials when they are needed for customer orders and production needs, as opposed to providing slack resources. Finally, the integration of manufacturing processes and techniques is made possible by the introduction of *integrated information networks* that connect all information reservoirs of the organization. Box 10-1 outlines several skills and abilities needed by workers in this computer-integrated age of manufacturing.

## 10-3 Manufacturing Technology and Technical Complexity

The conversion of crude oil into gasoline, cotton into shirts, and components into computers involves technology. However, each example utilizes starkly different kinds of technology, and each example also has very different levels of complexity. Sociologist Joan Woodward has provided organizational theorists with the most comprehensive study of the technical complexity of manufacturing firms and how each production process differs from the others.

Woodward studied firms in England during the 1950s to see how they were organized and managed.[6] She and her team of researchers went on-site to more than 100 companies, collecting data and observing manufacturing operations. The result of this extensive research project is the foundation for understanding manufacturing and its reliance on technology. In terms of structure, Woodward noted that the **technical complexity** of a production process, or how mechanistic or programmed it is, is the factor that distinguishes one type of process from another. Transformation processes that thrive on individual skills and abilities are low in technical complexity. Transformation processes that produce standardized outputs through programmable automation are high in technical complexity.

An example of a process low in technical complexity would be the making of a Rolls-Royce luxury automobile. Much of the finished product is built by hand, as craftsmen install fine wood trims, ensure doors open and close almost effortlessly, and construct sumptuous leather interiors. While this work is not technically complex as defined by Woodward, building a Rolls-Royce automobile is a complex process, requiring extensive skill and coordination. The process does, however, lack automation. Conversely, at the high end of technical complexity would be the Dupont plant in Memphis, Tennessee, that is fully automated, depending primarily on a process flow that is managed and facilitated by machines.

According to Woodward's classification of the firms she studied, there are ten categories or levels of technical complexity. These ten levels are detailed in Figure 10-1, as are the three simpler technology groups that are still used today to identify types of production technology.[7]

**technical complexity**
the measure of how mechanistic or programmed a production process is

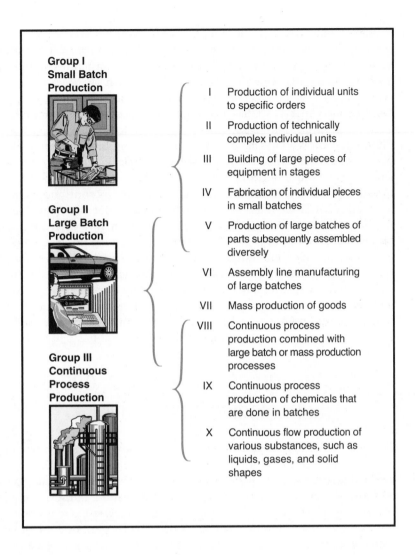

**Group I
Small Batch
Production**

**Group II
Large Batch
Production**

**Group III
Continuous
Process
Production**

I   Production of individual units to specific orders

II   Production of technically complex individual units

III   Building of large pieces of equipment in stages

IV   Fabrication of individual pieces in small batches

V   Production of large batches of parts subsequently assembled diversely

VI   Assembly line manufacturing of large batches

VII   Mass production of goods

VIII   Continuous process production combined with large batch or mass production processes

IX   Continuous process production of chemicals that are done in batches

X   Continuous flow production of various substances, such as liquids, gases, and solid shapes

**Figure 10-1**
*Woodward's Classification*

*Source:* Adapted from J. Woodward, *Management and Technology* (London: Her Majesty's Stationery Office, 1958): 11.

*Small-batch and unit production:* The first technology group, **small-batch and unit production,** is characterized by skilled individuals who make products to order. Although machinery and computers are becoming more common at all levels of technical complexity, the expertise of the small-batch producers is still more important than technology. This puts the small-batch group low on the scale of technical complexity.

Consider the craftsman who builds custom cabinetry for individual clients for their kitchens. Each area of need in the kitchen is addressed in terms of the clients' needs and the space available. The cabinets are then designed to meet both. This is especially important in small kitchens where space is at a premium. Custom cabinetmakers can build in special features that pull out or recess or extend or do whatever is necessary to make a space functional for the client.

*Large-batch and mass production:* Most people think of factories in terms of mass production. A large automotive manufacturing plant, such as the Toyota plant in Georgetown, Kentucky, best characterizes Woodward's second strategy of technology. The goal of **large-batch technology** is to increase the use of machinery and technical complexity to ensure standardization of production. The long assembly lines move cars and trucks through a series of assembly steps, many performed by robotic technology. After exiting the factory, these automobiles are delivered to dealers for retail sale.

**small-batch and unit production** production system characterized by skilled individuals who make products to order

**large-batch technology** increased use of machinery and technical complexity to ensure standardization of production

Mass production, or producing products in large batches, eventually leads to lower costs by manufacturers. Lowering production costs is critical in mature industries, such as the automobile industry, because firms are constantly competing on price. By lowering their costs of production, firms can pass on savings to consumers. In recent years, we have seen automobile manufacturers lean heavily on suppliers to lower their production costs so that the manufacturers could benefit from those savings.

**continuous-process production** the highest form of technical complexity; it automates or mechanizes a firm's production process completely

*Continuous-process production:* The example mentioned earlier of the Dupont Chemical plant is a typical continuous process production operation. **Continuous-process production,** the highest form of technical complexity, automates or mechanizes a firm's production process completely. Due to the continuous nature of production and the highly mechanized character of continuous process, any malfunction or breakdown has the potential to totally shut down the operation.

The benefits of continuous process production, however, are highly desired by businesses. Production is normally a smoothly flowing process, where human error is reduced to a bare minimum, and outputs, such as chemicals at the Dupont plant, are consistent. Most organizations utilizing this type of production, however, experience expensive maintenance costs. Any cutting of corners regarding upkeep and maintenance can be potentially hazardous, such as the tragedy at the Union Carbide pesticide plant in Bhopal, India, where more than 3,800 people died and more than 100,000 were injured in December of 1984.[8]

## 10-4 Management, Structure, and the Technological Imperative

Do managers manage organizations differently based on their technology? According to Woodward's research, there are definitely differences in some areas. Prior organizational management theories had each espoused one best way to manage. After Woodward's study, researchers began to understand that there were many ways to manage organizations, and some worked better in certain circumstances than others. For example, managers of small-batch firms had a span of control of twenty-three employees, indicating that employees in those types of firms needed wide latitude to serve their constituencies best. Mass production managers' span was forty-eight, demonstrating the standardized nature of the work. Continuous-process firms, however, were found to have a span of control of fifteen as the result of the need for closer supervision of skilled employees utilizing sophisticated technology.[9]

Structure issues were also documented by Woodward. Small-batch organizations tended to be flatter with their structures, having the fewest layers or levels of hierarchy. The work performed in small-batch organizations is individualized and highly skilled, making production performance difficult to program. Structures are relatively flat because the technical experts need to be close to the customers and responsive to change. Mass-production organizations had somewhat more hierarchical structures that encompassed wide spans of control. Mass-production tasks are much more programmable than small batch, as the process is more mechanized and predictable. Continuous-process organizations were the tallest, but their spans of control were narrower. The technical complexity of the continuous-process organization requires close supervision to avoid breakdowns or, in the case of Bhopal, disasters.

**organic structure** method of organizing for firms that require flexibility in operations and the need to be close to the customer

**mechanistic structure** the structured, centralized manner of organizing for mass-production organizations

Two types of organization systems have been posited as a response to environmental uncertainty that involve the amount of formal structure and control over employees.[10] Small-batch organizations require great flexibility for immediate responses to customers and/or unplanned events. These organizations tend to perform best when they adopt an **organic structure.** Mass-production organizations tend to perform best in a more structured, centralized manner referred to as a **mechanistic structure.** Optimal performance for continuous-process organizations is a combination of organic structure at the highest levels of the organization and mechanistic structure at the lower or operational levels.

Due to Woodward's research, organization theorists began to postulate that a firm's technology was critical to its choice of structure. Since managers managed each type of technology differently, and since firms set up similar structures in each group, (small batch, mass production, and continuous process), a concept known as the **technological imperative** emerged. Simply put, the technological imperative says that technology determines structure. While this argument is intuitively appealing, work over the last several decades in the area of strategic management has cast a bit of a pall over the technological imperative. A firm's choice of strategy and the growth of very large multinational organizations may have as much bearing on structure as technology.

**technological imperative** concept that states that technology determines structure

# 10-5 Departmental Technology and Charles Perrow

Sections 10-1 through 10-4 focused on technology, primarily in the manufacturing sector, at the organizational level. The following information moves down the organizational ladder to examine technological complexity at the departmental level. Just as Joan Woodward laid the important groundwork for study of technological complexity at the organizational level, Charles Perrow provides the definitive study of this topic at the departmental level.[11] Perrow identified two underlying dimensions of departmental tasks, variety and analyzability, that help us determine their routinization or complexity.

### 10-5a Task Variety

The first dimension of departmental activities that Perrow identified is **task variety.** Task variety defines the number of exceptions that occur during the transformation process in an organization. Put another way, when a person is working on a transformation process, how many times does something unexpected occur? If unexpected events occur frequently, the task variety is said to be high. When exceptions are infrequent, task variety is low.

A line worker who stuffs boxes with product all day would have a low task variety. While some boxes used to ship product may be damaged or perhaps an incorrect size, most of the time the task is without much variety. Engineers at NASA, however, may experience a good deal of task variety when designing new equipment to be used in space. Depending on where the mission is headed, what kind of conditions the equipment will be experiencing, and what the actual function of the equipment is can all contribute to any number of exceptions.

**task variety** the number of exceptions that occur during the transformation process in a manufacturing organization

### 10-5b Task Analyzability

Perrow's second dimension of work, **task analyzability,** concerns the extent to which search activity is required to solve a problem. An activity that is analyzable is one where a worker can follow a company training manual or policy and procedures document in performing her tasks. Activities that fall within this parameter are usually programmable. That is, the tasks can be planned ahead of time.

Some job activities are not analyzable, except in the most general sense. Too much is unknown, and experimentation and/or research are critical in determining the job's outcome. A simple example is the group of scientists who work at Merck. While they are considered some of the most talented people in their respective fields of pharmaceuticals, sometimes the outcome of their work is difficult to predict. One of Merck's most popular drugs, Vioxx, was eventually pulled from the market because

**task analyzability** the extent to which the transformation process can be analyzed, or broken down into a sequence of steps

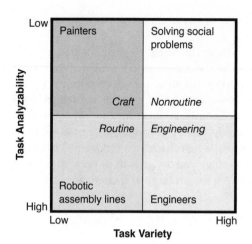

**Figure 10-2**
*Perrow's Framework*

*Source:* Adapted from C. Perrow, *Organizational Analysis: A Sociological Approach* (Belmont, CA: Wadsworth, 1970): 78.

of the discovery of bad side effects, including an increased risk of heart attacks or strokes. This was a dramatic blow to Merck's bottom line, as Vioxx was a $2.5 billion-a-year drug.[12] The value of Vioxx and other COX-2 inhibitors to the general population for pain control is such that they may be brought back to market with more strict warnings as to potential negative side effects.

### 10-5c Perrow's Four Types of Technology

Figure 10-2 identifies Perrow's framework for categorizing task analyzability and task variety when viewed in the context of four types of general technology. Perrow's four types of technology are craft, routine, nonroutine, and engineering. Figure 10-2 uses a two-by-two matrix to depict the task analyzability and task variety of each of the four types of technology.

**craft technologies** jobs that are difficult to analyze because they require individual skill and ability

**Craft technologies** are jobs that are difficult to analyze because they require individual skill and ability. While they are low in variety due to the specific skills involved, these jobs are not programmable. Craftspeople use their intellect and training in managing the various aspects of their work. If three actors were given the opportunity to audition for the role of Hamlet on the stage, each person would approach the role in his own unique style based on years of preparation and past experiences of having seen Hamlet performed by others. In a similar manner, if three painters are asked to paint a new house, each will have a different color scheme in mind based on how they visualize the finished product. Training, intellect, ability, and past experiences dramatically impact the transformational work of craftspeople.

**routine technologies** highly programmable tasks that contain little variety

**Routine technologies** are highly programmable tasks that contain little variety. Routine technologies involve tasks that have high analyzability, in that exceptions can be addressed according to programmed solutions. The production line of a 1940s automobile plant is an appropriate example because the mental image is familiar to most students of organizations. If a person's job was to attach bumpers every day of the week, every week of the year, he or she would become skilled at attaching bumpers due to the repetitive nature of the work and the lack of exception. There are obvious advantages to the routinization of work, such as lowering costs and standardizing products. In today's manufacturing environment, robotics or machinery are replacing people performing many of these kinds of jobs. By removing the possibility of human error, organizations are manufacturing products at a much lower defect ratio. The replacement of people in these jobs is one reason the economy in the United States has shifted its emphasis to service businesses.

**nonroutine technologies** tasks high in variety and low in analyzability due to the ambiguous nature of the work

**Nonroutine technologies** are the most difficult activities to analyze. These tasks are high in variety and low in analyzability due to the ambiguous nature of this work. Examples include solving a complicated prediction sales model problem for Ford, a process which involves utilizing regression analysis. Another example might be de-

Technology is critical in moving people through large spaces, such as airports and malls.

ciding how to solve the poverty problem in the United States. While we are clearly a wealthy country with many of the finest amenities of life available to us, we still have a portion of our population living in abject poverty. This kind of social problem is not only difficult to solve mentally; it is particularly difficult to solve in reality. One possible solution might be education, but education is another seriously debated issue in the United States. Those in poverty who need education the most seem to be the least likely to thrive in the educational environment.

**Engineering technologies** represent production that is high in variety, but this is offset by the ease at which tasks can be analyzed. There are many rules and laws of mathematics and science providing formulas and proven steps to take in determining the best way to handle the exceptions encountered in the transformation process. Engineers can take advantage of these laws of science while building custom products or large-scale projects. In this regard, engineering transformation processes are similar to batch production. Each project or customized product may be different, but the expertise and scientific approach needed to complete them are similar.

**engineering technologies** production that is high in variety, but the variety is offset by the ease at which tasks can be analyzed

### 10-5d Designing Departments with Routine Technology

Departments utilizing routine technologies typically employ *mechanistic* organizational structures. The departmental tasks are programmed, standardized, and highly formalized. Policy and procedure drive much of what is accomplished in this environment. The mechanistic organization, with its centralized management, hierarchy of authority, and tall structure maintains the order and control that are required for repetitive transformation processes.

This controlling, mechanistic, formal structure has some drawbacks. For example, front-line workers are not encouraged to participate in very much except the work itself. Innovative solutions that might bubble up from those actually doing the work will be lost as upper management discourages their input so that management can maintain total control of costs and decision-making responsibility. Although management might believe this structure to be the only viable one for pursuing a low-cost strategy, much more may be lost than is gained. Changing an organization with a mechanistic structure is like trying to turn a large aircraft carrier on a dime. In today's hypercompetitive environment, change is not only desired, it is almost a necessity.

### 10-5e Designing Departments with Nonroutine Technology

Departments that utilize nonroutine technology find it necessary to stay close to the customer. Because the tasks tend to have variety and are difficult to analyze, programming is not effective. This means that standardization of work is low. This environment requires an *organic* structure to be most effective. Organic departments

Box 10-2

## Best Practices
### Dell Computer

In 2000, Michael Dell and his top managers were a bit concerned about their business model. Although Dell Computer, as it was known at that time, was king of the hill among personal computer (PC) users, new competitors were creeping in the back door. Its stock price was lagging, and it had already made a lot of people "Dellionaires," but the future of the company was uncertain. Of course, we now know in retrospect that 2000 was the end of the bubble, and Dell, as it is now known, was just getting started.

By 2004, Dell had moved into the server, storage, and printer markets with a vengeance. In fiscal 1995, Dell's revenues were less than $5 billion.[13] In 2003 they were $41 billion.[14] What is Dell's secret formula for success? According to Michael Dell, the company is built on sound management principles and the integration of the latest proven technologies into every facet of its business. As an assembly operation, Dell is nothing short of sensational.

Surviving on lower margins than most technology producers, Dell's operation is a model that many try to emulate and most envy. Most of its orders are prepaid, it carries no more than a total of seven days of inventory, and it is able to assemble 84% of its orders in a customized way and ship them out in eight hours.[15] By utilizing Internet marketing where customers specify what components they want in their PCs, Dell gives them what they want, not what his company wants to make. Each component is bar coded so future repairs can be made as simply and accurately as possible.

How does Dell keep making this low-cost strategy successful? According to company managers, it's the culture. Employees are chosen with care, making every effort to ensure they are compatible with the culture. Of course, the culture is to do whatever it takes to serve the needs of the customer. It has worked pretty well for Michael Dell, whose personal wealth was valued at about $16.5 billion in 2002.[16]

---

are more fluid, meaning they can quickly adopt a new perspective or take a new direction without disrupting operations or slowing down production.

The structural characteristics of this organic environment include decentralized decision making, a low level of formalization, and a relatively flat structure with few levels of management. Employees are empowered decision makers since their technical skill and customer relations abilities often determine if customers come back. The most common example of an organic department is research and development. However, many production departments making products to order operate organically as well (see Box 10-2).

## 10-6  The Interdependence of Work

In this chapter we have examined technology, primarily manufacturing technology, from the organizational and department levels. Of particular concern has been how technology affects structure. The third piece to this puzzle is how departments are related to each other. The term for this is task interdependence. **Task interdependence** refers to the extent to which one department must rely on another to accomplish its goals. If task interdependence is low, a department can be expected to accomplish its goals with a great deal of independence. If task interdependence is high, departments can only partially accomplish their goals without assistance of some kind from another department.

To illustrate how departmental interdependence works, we turn to the leading organizational researcher in this area, James Thompson. Thompson identified three types of technology, *mediating, long-linked,* and *intensive,* and three forms of matching interdependence, *pooled, sequential,* and *reciprocal.*[17] See Figure 10-3.

**task interdependence**
the extent to which one department must rely on another to accomplish its goals

| Form of interdependence | Type of technology | Type of coordination | Cost of coordination |
|---|---|---|---|
| Pooled ▢ ▢ ▢ Piecework | Mediating | Standardization | Low |
| Sequential (Assembly line) ▢►▢►▢ | Long-linked | Planning & scheduling | Medium |
| Reciprocal (Hospital) ▢↔▢↔▢ | Intensive | Mutual adjustment | High |

**Figure 10-3**
*Interdependence and Technology Type*

## 10-6a  Pooled Interdependence and Mediating Technology

The first manufacturing technology that impacts departmental goal accomplishment is mediating. In firms that utilize **mediating technology,** departments are able to work independently within the organization by serving different needs of customers. Morgan Stanley, for example, has the capability to advise clients on a multitude of investment strategies, involving different markets such as stocks or bonds, countries such as Germany or the United States, and different exchanges such as the NASDAQ or the New York Stock Exchange. Area specialists are preferred by investors in each of these categories. However, some customers may prefer to be diversified in several areas.

To provide coordination of this type of diversified customer offering, firms employ pooled interdependence. **Pooled interdependence** means that departments can perform separate tasks from other departments but the contribution of different departments can be pooled. So, each Morgan Stanley branch office manages customer requests regarding purchases of stocks or bonds independent of other branches. The independence with which each department can operate in a pooled environment suggests the lowest need for coordination, as each branch mediates between the buyer and the broker.

The mediating technology Thompson describes can be seen in the management of a Taco Bell franchisee. The franchisee can own multiple Taco Bell locations and separately monitor the performance of each. Yet, the entire franchise operation is also monitored through the same technology, providing information on organization-wide performance as well as individual unit performance.

**mediating technology**
arrangement whereby departments are able to work independently within the organization by serving different needs of customers

**pooled interdependence**
situation that occurs when departments perform separate tasks from other departments but the contribution of different departments can be pooled

## 10-6b  Sequential Interdependence and Long-Linked Technology

Thompson's second type of manufacturing technology is long linked. **Long-linked technology** implies that each department's outputs become inputs for the next department in the production chain. The performance of the first task or department in the chain can sometimes determine whether the final output will be acceptable to the customer or not, since each step of the process is linked. W. Edwards Deming addressed this problem in the U.S. auto industry when he first started consulting with Ford Motor Company in 1981. The interrelatedness of steps in the production of cars made them particularly susceptible to poor workmanship.

Dr. Deming came to the forefront in the United States with the airing of a television program in 1979 called "If Japan Can …Why Can't We?" This program highlighted

**long-linked technology**
type of interdependence in which each department's outputs become inputs for the next department in the production chain

the total quality philosophy of Dr. Deming, particularly his work in Japan following World War II. Ford had adopted a slogan that quality was "job one," but the results of its production of automobiles did not reflect the slogan. In fact, Ford lost $1.6 billion dollars in 1980, the year before Dr. Deming began working with the firm. It took more than three years for Ford to fully adopt and understand Dr. Deming's statistical-based approach to quality, but the tools they learned served them well in the 1980s.[18]

One of the big problems facing Ford was the attitude of many of the organization's departments that they could act independently, pursuing their own goals amidst an environment of distrust and extreme bureaucracy. Thompson's term, *sequential interdependence,* illustrates the linked nature of automobile manufacturing technology. **Sequential interdependence** refers to the tasks performed by one department having a direct effect on another department. At Ford, a problem with transmissions early on in Deming's tenure brought the sequential interdependence issue to light. Ford's Batavia plant could not keep up with orders for transmissions. The company looked to Mazda to provide additional transmissions, of the same type, to take care of demand. Customers began to request Fords with the Mazda transmissions because they were less noisy. A close inspection of the Ford transmission and the Mazda transmission by a group of engineers discovered the Mazda product had less piece-to-piece variance than the Ford product. The end product for the customer, which was a Ford automobile, was perceived to be better when equipped with a Mazda transmission.[19]

While coordination by management is important, each department still acts relatively independently. Communication is needed at a higher level than the pooled interdependence model since each output becomes an input for another department.

### 10-6c  Reciprocal Interdependence and Intensive Technology

Thompson's third type of technology is known as intensive technology. **Intensive technology** refers to organizations where all departments' tasks are necessary for all other departments in serving the needs of the customer. This type of technology is characterized best by the concept of reciprocal interdependence. Reciprocal interdependence exists when department A's outputs become inputs for department B whose outputs are then used as inputs back to department A.

To demonstrate this situation, imagine a modern hospital that must coordinate several different types of health-care services to ensure the best treatment possible for its patients. Some patients may need a variety of treatment or diagnostic options to allow doctors to pinpoint the exact nature of their medical situations. These options may include x-ray, respiratory therapy, laboratory blood analysis, surgery, or any of a myriad of other hospital services. As each test or procedure is completed, the information travels with the patient to the next procedure, then back to the doctor. This process is greatly facilitated by sophisticated technology that captures the information provided at each step of the process. For example, at the Hackensack University Medical Center in Hackensack, New Jersey, technology has been woven into all phases of patient treatment, preventing doctors from making errors and saving patients' lives.[20] When medications are ordered by doctors, the drug-order entry system cross-checks it against any other prescriptions the patient may already be taking. Warnings are issued immediately when a possible dangerous mix of drugs is discovered. While expensive to adopt, this kind of technology is preventing mistakes that might have slipped through in the past.

From a management perspective, pooled interdependence is the most easily managed, as independent departments operate under the overall umbrella of the organization. Sequential interdependence requires a moderate amount of coordination, as one department's efforts serve as inputs for another. The reciprocal interdependent process is the most difficult to coordinate for management, as each department's outputs become inputs for another, which then returns its output back to the original department.

**sequential interdependence** departmental relationship in which tasks performed by one department have a direct effect on another department

**intensive technology** refers to each department's work being necessary to every other department in serving the needs of the customer

People and technology work together in a reciprocal manner in modern health care organizations.

# 10-7 People and Technology in Harmony

During the 1950s, a group at the Tavistock Institute in England began studying the relationship between people and technology in the workplace. This stream of research became known as the **sociotechnical systems approach,**[21] with *socio* referring to the human side of enterprise and *technical* the technology side. The needs of each component of this approach are different, thus posing the difficulty of designing systems where they work in harmony.

The social system of an organization thrives on people and their skills. The system is comprised of individuals and their needs, teams, culture, and how people manage people. The technical system is comprised of the technology utilized in the transformation process, whether the technology is pooled, sequential, or reciprocal; the actual physical setting of the workplace; and so forth.[22] The goal of sociotechnical research is to identify the best system for each organization to reach **joint optimization,** where people and machines work toward accomplishing organizational goals in harmony. It should be noted that joint optimization is a difficult outcome in many modern organizations operating in today's hypercompetitive environment. This is particularly true in mature industries where price is the competitive feature of a product or service.

One area of work where the sociotechnical system approach has been successful is job design. **Job design** is specifying the tasks and responsibilities expected of employees in specific positions. The type of technology employed by an organization is critical in designing particular jobs, and those jobs can change dramatically when new technology is introduced. While most jobs in manufacturing are fairly straightforward, organizations intent on cutting costs have increased job responsibilities through a process known as job enlargement. **Job enlargement** is an increase in the number of tasks per job. A better approach is **job enrichment,** where workers are given more responsibility and the authority to carry out that responsibility. Finally, some jobs require very similar skills, allowing employers to practice job rotation. **Job rotation** involves employees learning several different jobs over time, providing them with more variety in their work in an attempt to improve job satisfaction.

**sociotechnical systems approach** the relationship between people and technology in the workplace

**joint optimization** situation in which people and machines work toward accomplishing organizational goals in harmony

**job design** the tasks and responsibilities expected of employees in specific positions

**job enlargement** an increase in the number of tasks per job

**job enrichment** workers are given more responsibility and the authority to carry out that responsibility

**job rotation** job design system that involves employees learning several different jobs over time, providing them with more variety in their work in an attempt to improve job satisfaction

## Summary

Technology is a term that describes the machinery and equipment, production materials, computers, skills, and abilities necessary to take inputs and transform them into outputs. The system of computer-integrated manufacturing, an integrative process where each step of production is coordinated, including design, machinery, robotics, and engineering, has made mass customization—addressing the individual customer needs without sacrificing economies of scale—possible.

In terms of technology's impact on organizational structure, Joan Woodward noted that the technical complexity of a production process, or how mechanistic or programmed it is, is the factor that distinguishes one type of process from another. Transformation processes that thrive on individual skills and abilities are low in technical complexity. Transformation processes that produce standardized outputs through programmable automation are high in technical complexity.

Charles Perrow, analyzing firms at the departmental level, identified two underlying dimensions of tasks—variety and analyzability—that help us determine their complexity. Task analyzability and task variety are viewed in the context of four types of general technology, including craft, routine, nonroutine, and engineering.

James Thompson helps us understand how departmental interdependence works. Thompson identified three types of technology—mediating, long-linked, and intensive, and three forms of matching interdependence—pooled, sequential, and reciprocal. How dependent a department is on others determines the way they are managed and how their activities are coordinated.

A group at the Tavistock Institute in England studied the relationship between people and technology in the workplace. This stream of research became known as the sociotechnical systems approach, with *socio* referring to the human side of enterprise and *technical* the technology side. This research has been instrumental in subsequent job design efforts, tying the tasks and responsibilities expected of employees in specific positions to the need for technology.

## Review Questions and Exercises

1. Compare and contrast task variety with task analyzability.

2. Discuss the differences between Woodward's three technology groups: small-batch, large-batch, and continuous-process production.

3. Explain what Thompson meant by pooled interdependence.

4. What is the difference between mass production and mass customization?

5. Woodward's concept of technical complexity impacts organizational structure. Discuss.

6. Pick a business in your town and analyze its technological composition. Using the analyses of Woodward, Perrow, and Thompson, discuss the level of technical complexity and the impact of technology on tasks performed there.

## Quiz

1. Mass customization has been made possible by the advent of computer-integrated manufacturing.
   **True or False**

2. The concept of technology only refers to the people skills of individuals in manufacturing organizations.
   **True or False**

3. Pooled interdependence is the lowest form of interdependence among departments, according to Thompson.
   **True or False**

4. The term *mass production* usually refers to the type of technology that might be found in a chemical plant or an oil refinery.
   **True or False**

5. The organizational structure commonly found in mass-production technology organizations is organic.
   **True or False**

6. The sociotechnical system is concerned with the interaction between human needs and technology requirements in an organization.
   **True or False**

7. Which of the following is not one of Woodward's types of production?
   a. small-batch
   b. large-batch
   c. organic
   d. continuous-process production

8. The need for management coordination and control _____ as an organization's technical complexity increases.
   a. increases
   b. decreases
   c. stays the same
   d. lightly decreases

9. Which of the following is not one of Perrow's four types of technology?
   a. craft
   b. analyzable
   c. nonroutine
   d. engineering

10. The *technological imperative* states that
    a. structure determines technology.
    b. assets determine technology.
    c. technology determines structure.
    d. customers determine technology.

11. Computer-integrated manufacturing has been made possible by all of the following, except
    a. computer-aided design.
    b. computer-aided materials management.
    c. just-in-time inventory systems.
    d. piece-rate pay systems.

12. Increasing the number of tasks per job is known as
    a. job enlargement.
    b. job enrichment.
    c. job rotation.
    d. job design.

## Endnotes

1. R. Zammuto and E. O'Connor, "Gaining Advanced Manufacturing Technologies' Benefits: The Roles of Organization Design and Culture," *Academy of Management Review* 17 (1992): 701–728.
2. U.S. Department of Labor. *Skills and Tasks for Jobs: A SCANS Report for America 2000* (Washington, DC: The Department of Labor, 1993).
3. J. Moody, B. Stewart, and C. Bolt-Lee, "Showcasing the Skilled Business Graduate: Expanding the Tool Kit," *Business Communication Quarterly* 61, no. 1 (2002): 21–36.
4. R. Daft, *Organization Theory & Design,* 8th ed. (Mason, OH: South-Western, 2004): 250.
5. A. Thompson, A. Strickland III, and J. Gamble, *Crafting and Executing Strategy,* 14th ed. (New York: McGraw-Hill/Irwin, 2005): 122.
6. J. Woodward, *Industrial Organization: Theory and Practice* (London: Oxford University Press, 1965).
7. J. Woodward, *Management and Technology* (London: Her Majesty's Stationery Office, 1958).
8. "India's Night of Death," *Time,* December 17, 1984, 22–31; "It Was Like Breathing Fire," *Newsweek,* December 17, 1984, 26–32.
9. J. Woodward, 1965.
10. T. Burns and G. M. Stalker, *The Management of Innovation* (London: Tavistock Publications, 1961).
11. C. Perrow, "A Framework for the Comparative Analysis of Organizations," *American Sociological Review* 32 (1967): 194–208.
12. J. Simmons and D. Stipp, "Will Merck Survive Vioxx?" *Fortune* 150, no. 9 (2004): 91–104.
13. B. Morris, "Can Michael Dell Escape the Box?" *Fortune* 142, no. 9 (2000): 93–110.
14. D. Kirkpatrick, "Dell and Rollins: The $41 Billion Buddy Act," *Fortune* 149, no. 8 (2004): 84–88.
15. Morris, 2000.
16. J. Boorstin, J. Freedman, and C. Tkaczyk, "America's 40 Richest under 40," *Fortune* 146, no. 5 (2002): 169–176.
17. J. Thompson, *Organizations in Action* (New York: McGraw-Hill, 1967).
18. M. Walton, *The Deming Management Method* (New York: The Putnam Publishing Company, 1986).
19. Walton, 1986.
20. T. Mullaney and A. Weintraub, "The Digital Hospital," *Business Week,* March 28, 2005, 77–84.
21. E. Trist and H. Murray, *The Social Engagement of Social Science: A Tavistock Anthology,* vol. 2. (Philadelphia, PA: University of Pennsylvania Press, 1993).
22. R. Daft, 2004. Based on the following sources: T. Cummings, "Self-Regulating Work Groups: A Sociotechnical Synthesis," *Academy of Management Review* 3 (1978): 625–634; D. Hellriegel, J. Slocum, and R. Woodman, *Organizational Behavior,* 8th ed. (Cincinnati, OH: South-Western, 1998); G. Northcraft and M. Neals, *Organizational Behavior: A Management Challenge,* 2nd ed. (Fort Worth, TX: The Dryden Press, 1994): 551.

# Future Challenges

## Part 5

# Knowledge Management and the Learning Organization

## Chapter Outline

## Key Terms

adaptive

building shared visions

codified knowledge management system

cognitive structure

creative management model

explicit knowledge

information

intellectual capital

knowledge

knowledge management

learning organization

lifelong learning

mental models

personal mastery

personalized knowledge management system

servant leadership

systems thinking

tacit knowledge

team learning

Can you imagine what work was like before information and technology were as fully integrated as they are today? As an example, imagine an office manager's job in the mid-1970s. Jane, our imaginary office manager, reports to work at 8:00 a.m., grabs a cup of coffee, and chats with several coworkers for a few minutes. Later, when she settles into her office, her secretary hands her a couple of telephone messages and goes over Jane's schedule for the day. The next hour is spent dictating memos for the secretary to type and distribute. Then she remembers she needs to make sure her secretary booked that flight to Cleveland . . .

Now, fast forward thirty years to see how our new millennium office manager, Sarah, approaches her job. At 5:30 a.m. Sarah is up having a glass of juice while she checks her email from home. At 6:00 she is at the health club working out on the StairMaster, pausing only long enough to say hello to a colleague from an industry competitor. By 7:30 Sarah is in line at Starbucks and talking to one of her employees on her cell phone.

Arriving at her office building, she goes through the metal detector, smiles at the security guard, and then settles into her cubicle. Turning on her computer, she follows up on a couple of emails, then checks her schedule on her software scheduling package. As she sends out some emails to her employees, Sarah reaches for her Black-Berry to check on the details for the video conference with Shanghai . . .

# 11-1 Introduction

The pace at which the world conducts business has changed. Technology has become prevalent. People work in a very different manner today than they did thirty years ago. One reason is that the entire concept of time has been altered. Businesses have shortened all time frames, quickened the decision-making process, and compressed the time frames for bringing new products and services to market.[1]

The maturation of most markets, the ubiquity of machines and gadgets, and the need for speed has contributed to a new dynamic business environment. Because of market maturation, many firms must compete on price. This leads to organizations demanding more productivity from each employee and the elimination of people from work wherever possible. The ubiquity of gadgets and machines has helped fuel this productivity increase, as well as the elimination of people from some jobs. The need for speed has been a by-product of more productivity, hypercompetition, and machines and gadgets.

The search for competitive advantage in this fast-moving new environment has begun to focus on **information** and knowledge. Although these two terms are often used interchangeably, they are not the same thing. Information can be defined as disparate data, or facts, compiled into a useful form. Through the use of information, for example, organizations can rank their best customers as to volume, determine which products they purchase most often, and identify their primary destinations. Information, therefore, is valuable.

What is more valuable than information, however, is knowledge. Organizational **knowledge** is a conclusion drawn from different streams of information, and that knowledge can be shared by members of the organization and used to further its goals. This compiling and sharing of knowledge throughout the organization with those who need it is called **knowledge management.**

# 11-2 Knowledge Management

Knowledge management is not simply the storage of data or the publication of a policy and procedures manual. Knowledge must be systematically gathered and shared across the organization so it can be put to use by organizational members.[2] The

**information** disparate data, or facts, compiled into a useful form

**knowledge** a conclusion drawn from different streams of information that can be shared by members of the organization and used to further its goals

**knowledge management** sharing of knowledge throughout the organization with those who need it

process of making available the acquired knowledge of an organization has been greatly facilitated by the new advances in information technology.

Why is knowledge management becoming so important? Many organizations are finding that they are at a distinct competitive disadvantage without a system for capturing and disseminating knowledge. The global nature of the business environment means change is not just needed but required. When fast change is needed, information and analysis need to be available to every involved employee in the organization. The movement to reduce organizational structure levels and get people closer to customers and other stakeholders has made this need for knowledge dissemination even more important. If an organizational associate is expected to make more decisions and be empowered to act in the organization's interest, she must have access to the firm's intellectual capital. **Intellectual capital** is a term that describes the sum total of everything that is known by the people of an organization.[3]

A new dynamic that is affecting many firms today is the need for older, more experienced employees to learn from younger, newer ones.[4] Managing the knowledge of an organization requires the input of new, fresh ideas and varied experiences to the already existing traditional intellectual capital. Of course, the younger, newer employees also need to understand the existing knowledge base upon which the firm was built. By understanding where the firm has been, new innovations for the future can be fostered, some out of old ideas that never worked and some out of totally new ideas that have never been considered.

One thing is for sure: Information technology and the management of organizational knowledge have altered the structure of organizations. Even something as simple as email changes the way we do business. No longer is information passed down from the hierarchy, maybe getting to lower levels, or maybe not. Now information is shared almost laterally, which is another example of the flattening of organizational structures.[5] The Internet is a tremendous source of information that employees have access to, as is the intranet of most large organizations, which have become platforms of knowledge for everyone involved.[6] With many products and much business now conducted on the web, customers can provide instant feedback to suppliers, and that feedback needs to be available to everyone.[7]

One obstacle to knowledge management is the issue of power that is discussed in Chapter 8. Individual managers who might have spent years building power bases see the sharing of knowledge organization-wide as threat to their well-earned power status. Yet, unless knowledge can be transferred across the organization, innovative activity will suffer.[8]

## 11-3 Knowledge Management Methods

Two different kinds of knowledge are present in most organizations. The first, **explicit knowledge,** is the compilation of standardized facts that are used to manage the organization.[9] Specifications, rules, policies, and processes comprise examples of explicit knowledge. The second type is **tacit knowledge,** a type of implicit or intuitive knowledge that is usually learned through experience.[10]

Organizational managers need to base their knowledge management system on the kinds of products and/or services they provide. Those firms that build products out of standardized parts can implement a **codified knowledge management system.**[11] Codifying data, information, specifications, and procedures into an accessible and standardized system provides a reference for everyone in the organization. If a codified system can be continually updated as new standards emerge, and this can be done from all functional areas of the organization, the ultimate goal of organizational learning can be facilitated.

If the products or services produced by a firm are not of a standardized nature, a more **personalized knowledge management system** is needed. Nonstandardized

**intellectual capital** the total of everything that is known by the people of an organization

**explicit knowledge** the compilation of standardized facts, such as specifications, rules, and policies, that are used to manage the organization

**tacit knowledge** implicit knowledge that is usually learned through experience

**codified knowledge management system** method of codifying data, information, specifications, and procedures into an accessible and standardized system to serve as a reference for everyone in the organization

**personalized knowledge management system** system that captures the expertise of individuals designing and delivering customized products and services in a rapidly changing technological environment

products, or customized products, require the capturing of expertise from individuals who are designing and delivering such products in a rapidly changing technological environment. In particular, customers with needs specific to their organizations may require customized solutions that involve industry knowledge, understanding of technology, and some history of the customer's operations. Codified systems cannot capture this kind of idiosyncratic, tacit knowledge.

If you were trying to manage the intellectual capital at the computer animator Pixar, for example, you would have very little standardized information with which to work. With such diverse credits as *Toy Story, A Bug's Life, Toy Story 2, Monsters Inc., Finding Nemo,* and *The Incredibles,* Pixar has led the way in computer animation. Pixar's success has been driven by Ed Catmull and his team's creative genius, not a standardized operations manual of policy and procedures. Continuously pushing the envelope of computer graphics, Catmull's teams of project developers must constantly interact and coordinate their individual tasks to make hits such as *The Incredibles* possible.[12] The innovative ideas generated at a business like Pixar could not be captured through a codified system.

## 11-4 Knowledge Management as a Competitive Advantage

The ability of organizations to harness and manage intellectual capital, or knowledge, has been identified as a source of competitive advantage.[13] Management researchers view superior intellectual capital as an inimitable resource, that is, one that cannot be duplicated by another organization.[14] In fact, regardless of which generic strategy type (see Chapter 2) an organization pursues, the acquisition and development of knowledge can be a source of competitive advantage.[15] Indeed, the entire human capital of an organization can be developed over time through the process of organizational learning.[16]

## 11-5 The Learning Organization

**learning organization**
an organization that has developed the continuous capacity to adapt and change

Collecting, storing, and disseminating data and information and sharing it throughout the organization, or knowledge management, is valuable to its short-term success. Taking this to the next logical step, however, is the key to staying competitive for the long term. The next step is organizational learning, or becoming a **learning organization.**

Several definitions have been used to describe the learning organization. To introduce the concept, we present two straightforward definitions. The first comes from *Fortune's* Brian Dumaine: "… a consummately adaptive enterprise with workers freed to think for themselves, to identify problems and opportunities, and to go after them."[17] The second definition, similar to *Fortune*'s, is from organizational behavior researcher Stephen Robbins. According to Robbins, the learning organization is "an organization that has developed the continuous capacity to adapt and change."[18]

## 11-6 Becoming a Learning Organization

The best known proponent of creating learning organizations is Peter Senge. Senge describes the basic meaning of a learning organization as one "that is continually expanding its capacity to create its future."[19] Senge proposed five new component technologies critical to the development of a learning organization. These five technologies are personal mastery, mental models, building shared visions, team learning, and systems thinking.[20] Because Senge has been the leader in this area of organizational theory research, each of these five will be briefly explained.

**Personal mastery** involves learning to expand one's capacity to create results desired. In this context, mastery refers to becoming very proficient at something, as an artist would be to painting. Individuals in organizations must want to learn and to learn to get better continually. As organizational members become more proficient, the organization itself becomes more learned. Thus, personal learning and organizational learning develop a reciprocal relationship.

**Mental models** are the images that we utilize in our minds to understand the world. To promote organizational learning, individuals must take stock of their mental models about their firm, their markets, and their competitors. In many cases these mental images will have to be altered. This is accomplished through planning, as planning becomes learning for many people.

**Building shared visions** involves the leaders of organizations being able to translate their vision of the firm's future in a way that causes others to adopt, or share, the same vision. The goal is to bind people together through a vision they can actually relate to, rather than a vision statement that was written for the strategic plan.

**Team learning** occurs when the skill level of the team exceeds that of the individual members and when the team performs at an exceptional level. The ability to learn as a team is dependent on dialogue, the sharing of insights by team members that lead to new understanding.

**Systems thinking** is a way of thinking about the pattern of interactions that form interrelationships and shape the behavior of organizations, as well as a language for describing and understanding it. Every action that occurs in an organization has some relationship to another action which impacts something else, and so on. This is clear from the total quality movement where internal customer/supplier relationships were stressed. If department A provided an important input to department B, and department B was having trouble converting that input to what it really needed, a customer/supplier alignment would be recommended. In that situation, department A would be asked to alter its output, the input for department B, to a form that facilitates the efficiency and effectiveness of department B. This alignment process is necessary throughout an organization due to the systemic nature of organizational work. In the future, when department A wants to make a change in its output process, the people in the department will know to consider the needs of department B before making any substantial changes.

**personal mastery** learning to expand one's capacity to create results desired

**mental models** images that we utilize in our minds to understand the world

**building shared visions** component technology that involves the leaders of organizations being able to translate their vision of the firm's future in a way that causes others to adopt, or share, the same vision

**team learning** situation in which the skill level of the team exceeds that of the individual members and in which the team performs at an exceptional level

**systems thinking** a way of thinking about and a language for describing and understanding the pattern of interactions that form interrelationships and shape the behavior of organizations

Face-to-face communication, the most effective kind, is part of an effective internal customer-supplier relationship.

# 11-7 Learning Organizations Need Skilled Leaders

Senge has identified some specific skills needed by the leaders of learning organizations.[21] First, a leader must be a designer. What must be designed are the strategies, policies, and structures of organizations. In a learning organization, these important design steps will be crafted, not dictated or presupposed.[22] Once the strategies, policies, and structures are in place, a learning organization leader must focus on creating learning processes that will be adopted and fostered throughout the firm.

The second skill of a learning organization leader is that of teacher. Today's popular management literature couches management in terms of an athletic coach, one who exhorts, encourages, and teaches. The notion is that people become better at their jobs if they are motivated by a coach who can encourage them to contribute to a team effort while simultaneously improving their individual skills. In a learning organization, people need to develop the mental model of systems thinking, and leaders are responsible for setting the example and developing the culture of learning by being teachers.

The third skill of leaders in learning organizations is stewardship. Learning organization leaders have a steward's role for the organization's goals and one for the organization's employees. By being a servant to these two causes, leaders facilitate not only organizational learning, but also growth, development, and competitiveness. Many organizational leaders become consumed with the power of their position and become users of employees, not a steward of people resources. This idea of stewardship, put forth in the **servant leadership** literature, requires a commitment to a higher purpose that tends to rise above the level of the organization, representing something of higher importance.[23] To fully understand servant leadership, one must think of a philosophy of management where the leader is a servant first.

**servant leadership** a philosophy of management where the leader is a servant first

If learning organizations require dramatic culture changes, and most do early on in the process, new leaders who can facilitate such change must emerge.[24] Mintzberg suggests a need for leaders who can combine art and science, understanding the importance of analytical, strategic thinking without dismissing the contribution that can be made by being creative and artful.[25] Senge sums up the leadership require-

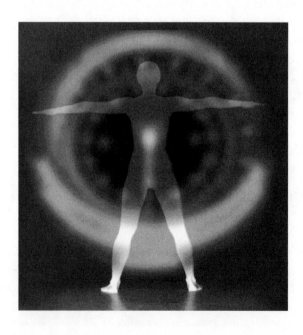

ments for learning organizations: "In short, leaders in learning organizations are responsible for *building organizations* where people are continually expanding their capabilities to shape their future—that is, leaders are responsible for learning."[26]

# 11-8 A New Paradigm for Organizations

While management theory has not progressed seamlessly through the centuries, there have been some clearly identifiable periods and movements. Traditional theories have included scientific management (efficient task performance), the bureaucratic model (authority and structure), and administrative management (universal management principles). Two important modifications to those theories are behavioral science (psychological, sociological, and cultural issues) and management science (economic-technical rationality). The concept of the learning organization reflects an attempt at a new paradigm, or framework, of organizations. For this paradigm to become reality, several traditional ways of thinking and doing in organizations must be drastically altered.

In Section 11-5, we presented the definition of a learning organization. Several things become clear when that definition is fully understood. First, our organizations must become much more **adaptive.** In the past, managers have espoused the idea of a best way to do things to produce the most for the least. In an adaptive culture, people are encouraged to change so that the organization can successfully compete as their environments change. One example of this adaptive behavior is IBM. A world leader in mainframe computers for several decades, it suddenly found itself outdated, outmoded, and out of touch with the new PC-based environment. Under the direction of Lou Gerstner, IBM became invigorated, pursuing a new strategy made possible by a dramatic cultural overhaul that has made Big Blue a world leader in on-demand technology.[27]

Two other changes that are important to learning organizations go hand in hand. The first is the flattening of organizational structure to ensure fast response and close customer contact. This change also requires empowering workers, even those at the lowest level. Tall, hierarchical structures promote rigid, policy-driven cultures where work is standardized and decision making is a process of checks and balances. This structure is epitomized at firms like General Motors, where twenty-three levels of organization structure make change slow and difficult. Modern organizations with three or four levels of structure are considered extremely flat, while those with more than ten are considered relatively tall.[28]

Flatter organizational structures and empowered employees represent drastic changes from past management philosophies. Learning organizations foster empowerment for employees as individuals improve their knowledge base, making them more ably equipped to make decisions and handle problems or opportunities as they arise. The sharing of knowledge with employees across the organization, as discussed in Sections 11-2, 11-5, and 11-6, facilitates the empowerment process.

There is no single recipe for a successful learning organization. However, the changes mentioned earlier are a good place to start if top management seeks to create an internal environment that promotes learning. Flatter organizational structures, more adaptive corporate cultures, empowered employees, and a broad sharing of knowledge are primary ingredients for a successful learning organization recipe.

A more specific list of factors that promote organizational learning is presented in Table 11-1. While some factors included in this table have been previously discussed, this ten-point set of suggestions is comprehensive, yet brief. For a look at how important learning is to an individual's career, see Box 11-1, Career Point.

**adaptive** encouraging change so that an organization can successfully compete as its environments change

**lifelong learning** a long-term self-improvement process whereby workers continue to upgrade their skills and knowledge level, making them better employees

## Box 11-1

### Career Point

The Importance of Learning

The fast-paced and fast-changing world of business has become fertile ground for a concept known as **lifelong learning.** Lifelong learning is a long-term self-improvement process whereby workers continue to upgrade their skills and knowledge level, making them better employees. This phenomenon is being driven by the constantly changing external environment, the accelerated improvements in the world of technology, and the quickly evolving discriminating consumer.

No longer do high school graduates migrate to the factory and perform the same, routine set of tasks for forty years and retire. Factories of today look very little like factories of forty years ago. Technology and demand drive production, not people. To be qualified to make a contribution in this new manufacturing environment, you must constantly upgrade your personal knowledge base, learn new skills, and understand all aspects of customer service.

In what used to be referred to as the white-collar world, an out-of-date term to be sure, we encourage the development of knowledge workers[29] to handle the staff and support functions necessary to every organization. Lifelong learning is just as important to this group as it is to those in manufacturing. New software packages, improved product designs, and constantly changing government regulations are just a few of the reasons training and learning are needed.

So, if you think graduation will mark the end of your learning phase, think again. It's called "commencement" for a reason. When you begin your search for a career position, inquire about in-house training programs, external classes and certificated programs, and even informal, on-the-job training. While a college degree seems to be a prerequisite to getting an entry job into most large organizations, the real training and learning actually occur inside the company. Indeed, noted management theorist Peter Drucker has dubbed the organization as the most important educational system in the United States.[30] The more eager you are to improve yourself, the more open it appears you are to change. For a practical business example of organizational learning, see Box 11-2, the Best Practices discussion on Google.

| TABLE 11-1 | Factors That Facilitate Organizational Learning Capabilities |
|---|---|
| 1. Scanning imperative | Interest in external happenings and in the nature of one's environment. Valuing the processes of awareness and data generation. Curious about what is "out there" as opposed to "in here." |
| 2. Performance gap | Shared perception of a gap between actual and desired state of performance. Disconfirming feedback interrupts a string of successes. Performance shortfalls are seen as opportunities for learning. |
| 3. Concern for measurement | Spend considerable effort in defining and measuring key factors when venturing into new areas; strive for specific, quantifiable measures; discourse over metrics is seen as a learning activity. |
| 4. Experimental mind-set | Support for trying new things: curiosity about how things work; ability to play with things. Small failures are encouraged, not punished. See changes in work processes, policies, and structures as a continuous series of graded tryouts. |
| 5. Climate of openness | Accessibility of information, relatively open boundaries. Opportunities to observe others; problems/errors are shared, not hidden; debate and conflict are acceptable. |
| 6. Continuous education | Ongoing commitment to education at all levels; support for growth and development of members. |
| 7. Operational variety | Variety exists in response modes, procedures, systems; significant diversity in personnel. Pluralistic rather than monolithic definition of valued internal capabilities. |
| 8. Multiple advocates | Top-down and bottom-up initiatives are possible; multiple advocates and gatekeepers exist. |
| 9. Involved leadership | Leadership at significant levels articulates vision and is very actively engaged in its actualization; takes ongoing steps to implement visions; hands-on involvement in educational and other implementation steps. |
| 10. Systems perspective | Strong focus on how parts of the organization are interdependent; seek optimization of organizational goals at the highest levels; see problems and solutions in terms of systemic relationships. |

*Source:* "Facilitating Factors" from *Organizational Learning and Competitive Advantage* by B. Moingeon and A. Edmondson. Copyright © 1996 Sage Publications.

# Box 11-2

### Best Practices

#### Google

One of the most talked-about companies in the world today is Google. With its stock price soaring, its founders Larry Page and Sergey Brin famous, and its services used by millions, Google is probably here to stay. What has been the secret of Google's success, and why are people paying $280 for a share of its stock?

The key to Google's success has been difficult for analysts to determine. While its search engine service is considered very, very good, others, such as those by Yahoo!, Amazon, and Microsoft, are also very good. Yet, in the last year, Google's market share has risen in the face of increasing competition. The key to Google's success is its ability to innovate and stay close to the customer.

Google relates well to the concepts discussed in this chapter for several reasons. First, Google's organizational structure is relatively flat, keeping employees and managers (there are currently three levels of management at Google) close to the customers. Staying close to the users of Google's services is also facilitated by the email system known as Gmail. Google customers are provided an email account through its system, Gmail, which gives the company easy and quick access to each customer.

The Gmail accounts also provide customers with a gigabyte of free online storage. Messages are easily saved and recalled with the Gmail system. Another benefit to Google is that it can target advertising from its vast array of corporate advertisers to specific customers by reading their Gmail accounts to see what they are interested in. Also, through Picassa, a desktop photo organizer, Google customers can send photographs to their family members.

Another effort at innovation is the effort to globalize Google's search engine, which is now available in eight languages, including Chinese. As the service becomes adopted by more foreign users by adding more language choices, the number of advertisers will grow as well. Advertising currently provides nearly $2 billion in annual revenues for Google. Google also provides ads to other company websites, such as seatguru.com and mobiletracker.net, for its major sponsors.

To establish the corporate culture that Google believes it needs to be successful, the company's headquarters remind one of a university setting. Offices have several people in them to resemble the atmosphere of graduate school. Employees are encouraged to make their offices resemble dormitory rooms, with hockey gear and in-line skates hanging on the walls. Google also provides three free meals a day for employees, as well as free laundry service and banking. Brin and Page hope to make new employees, many who are just out of college or graduate school, feel right at home. Meetings even start at seven minutes after the hour to emulate an academic environment.

Google is an interesting example of a company trying to continually learn about its customers, competitors, and partners. Its technological capabilities allow the spread of this knowledge both within and without the organization to be accomplished quickly. Its ability to continually innovate in areas that are favorably received by its stakeholders may ensure its eventual goal of being the next Microsoft.[31]

# 11-9 Factors That Impede Organizational Learning

Everyone who has ever held a job has heard the phrase, "That's not how we do things around here," from someone with tenure in the organization. It is a natural response when new ideas are proposed, particularly new ideas that seem somewhat threatening to employees who are comfortable with the status quo and fearful of change. This attitude seems most prevalent in organizations where programmed decision making (see Chapter 8) is prevalent.

The more programmed decisions are utilized by an organization, the more resistant to change it becomes. Many of these firms are pursuing low cost strategies that require extreme efficiency of operations in order to maximize margin. As programmed decision making becomes not only prevalent but also successful, innovation and creativity become stifled. This creates an atmosphere of complacency, and organizational learning suffers. The fear of the unknown, or that which could be learned, takes precedence, and searches for new knowledge are stifled. Even in times of crisis, organizations may not recognize a need for change, choosing instead to increase the centralization of decision making as a further deterrent to external threats.[32]

A second reason for lack of organizational learning is that some managers or people in positions of authority have worked in one environment for an extended period of time, limiting their exposure to new ideas and methods of operation. This is a particular problem at firms where the top management team has been together for many years, and therefore their collective beliefs are very similar. Known as **cognitive structure,** this system of beliefs, values, and expectations limit the way top management teams make decisions. Of particular importance is how these homogeneous managers view their external environments. A more heterogeneous team of managers might perceive environmental changes differently than one where most of the managers have similar cognitive structures.

A different model, one that works best in a learning environment, is the creative top management team suggested by Hurst, Rush, and White.[33] These authors propose a top management team that practices insight and innovation. Differing from the traditional strategic management model, the **creative management model** fosters a learning process that institutionalizes successful innovations, making them routine. This represents a drastic departure from the left-brained, analytical approach championed by the strategic management model. A top management team that is creative, imaginative, and innovative will set a positive tone for learning for the rest of the organization.

**cognitive structure**   system of beliefs, values, and expectations that limit the way top management teams make decisions

**creative management model**   theory that a top management team that is creative, imaginative, and innovative will set a positive tone for learning for the rest of the organization

## Summary

Knowledge must be systematically gathered and shared across the organization so it can be put to use by organizational members, a process known as knowledge management. Two different kinds of knowledge are present in most organizations. The first, explicit knowledge, is the compilation of standardized facts that is used to manage the organization. The second type is tacit knowledge, a type of implicit knowledge that is usually learned through experience. Firms that build products out of standardized parts can implement a codified knowledge management system. If the products or services produced by a firm are not of a standardized nature, a more personalized knowledge management system is needed.

The next step for firms managing knowledge is organizational learning, or becoming a learning organization.

The learning organization is an organization that has developed the continuous capacity to adapt and change. Five new component technologies critical to the development of a learning organization are personal mastery, mental models, building shared visions, team learning, and systems thinking.

Leaders in learning organizations must be designers, teachers, and stewards of organizational resources. In the new learning paradigm, organizations must become much more adaptive, develop flatter organizational structures, and empower employees. Over time, the more frequently programmed decisions are utilized by an organization, the more resistant to change it becomes. A top management team that is creative, imaginative, and innovative will set a positive tone for learning for the rest of the organization.

## Review Questions and Exercises

1. What are some examples of data and information that organizations would store and make available through a knowledge management system?

2. Discuss the difference between knowledge and information.

3. Explain why systems thinking is so important to the concept of the learning organization.

4. What skills are necessary for a leader who is developing a learning organization?

5. What is meant by the term *adaptive?*

6. What are some of the factors that impede organizational learning?

## Quiz

1. Organizational knowledge is a conclusion drawn from different streams of information that can be shared by members of the organization and used to further its goals.
   **True or False**

2. The term *intellectual capital* describes the sum of all long-term invested funds of the organization.
   **True or False**

3. Tacit knowledge is a type of implicit knowledge that is usually learned through experience.
   **True or False**

4. Building shared visions refers to the work of a shop-floor committee.
   **True or False**

5. Servant leadership is a concept that means the leader of an organization is a servant first.
   **True or False**

6. Cognitive structure is a system of beliefs, values, and expectations that limits the way top management teams make decisions.
   **True or False**

7. The compilation of standardized facts that are used to manage the organization is known as
   a. tacit knowledge.
   b. explicit knowledge.
   c. implicit knowledge.
   d. personalized knowledge.

8. The entire human capital of an organization can be developed over time through the process of
   a. organizational learning.
   b. input processes.
   c. output processes.
   d. cognitive structures.

9. The five new technologies to promote organizational learning proposed by Peter Senge include all of the following, except
   a. systems thinking.
   b. mental models.
   c. hierarchical structures.
   d. team learning.

10. The concept that every action that occurs in an organization has some relationship to another action which impacts something else refers to
    a. team learning.
    b. personal mastery.
    c. mental models.
    d. systems thinking.

11. Effective leaders in learning organizations need to be all of the following, except
    a. designers.
    b. teachers.
    c. intellectuals.
    d. stewards.

12. The creative management model describes a top management team that has creative and imaginative skills, which differs from what other top management team model?
    a. systems management model
    b. organizational behavior model
    c. one best way management model
    d. strategic management model

## Endnotes

1. M. Harvey and M. Ronald Buckley, "Assessing the 'Conventional Wisdoms' of Management for the 21st Century," *Organizational Dynamics* 30, no. 4 (2002), 368–378.

2. D. Garvin, "Building a Learning Organization," *Harvard Business Review* 71, no. 4 (1993), 78–91.

3. M. Hitt, R. Ireland, and R. Hoskisson, *Strategic Management: Competitiveness and Globalization*, 5th ed. (Mason, OH: South-Western, 2003): 74.

4. G. Hamel, "Reinvent Your Company," *Fortune* 141, no. 12 (2000): 98–118.

5. T. Stewart, "Managing in a Wired Company," *Fortune* 130, no. 1 (1994): 44–56.

6. T. Stewart, 1994: 46.

7. G. Hamel and J. Sampler, "The E-Corporation," *Fortune* 138, no. 11 (1998): 81–92.

8. W. Tsai, "Knowledge Transfer in Intraorganizational Networks: Effects of Network Position and Absorptive Capacity on Business Unit Innovation and Performance," *Academy of Management Journal* 44 (2001): 996–1004.

9. R. Grant, "Toward a Knowledge-Based Theory of the Firm," *Strategic Management Journal* 17 (1990): 109–122.

10. S. Berman, J. Down, and C. Hill, "Tacit Knowledge as a Source of Competitive Advantage in the National Basketball Association," *Academy of Management Journal* 45 (2002): 13–31.

11. M. Hansen, N. Nohria, and T. Tierney, "What's Your Strategy for Managing Knowledge?" *Harvard Business Review* 77, no. 2 (1999): 3–19.

12. B. Schlender, "The Man Who Built Pixar's Incredible Innovation Machine," *Fortune* 150, no. 10 (2004): 206–212.

13. T. Davenport, J. Harris, D. DeLong, and A. Jacobson, "Data to Knowledge to Results: Building an Analytic Capability," *California Management Review* 43, no. 2 (2001): 117–138.

14. S. McElivy and B. Chakravarthy, "The Persistence of Knowledge-Based Advantage: An Empirical Test for Product Performance and Technical Knowledge," *Strategic Management Journal* 23 (2002): 285–306.

15. J. Katz, "Blown to Bits: How the New Economics of Information Transforms Strategy," *Academy of Management Executive* 14 (2000): 160–162; H. Tsoukas and E. Vladimirou, "What is Organizational Knowledge?" *Journal of Management Studies* 38 (2001); 973–994.

16. A. Sheldon, "Strategy Rules," *Fast Company*, January 2001, 164–166.

17. B. Dumaine, "What the Leaders of Tomorrow See," *Fortune* 120, no. 1 (1989): 48.

18. S. Robbins, *Organizational Behavior*, 10th ed. (Upper Saddle River, NJ: Prentice-Hall, 2003): 666.

19. P. Senge, *The Fifth Discipline: The Art & Practice of the Learning Organization* (New York: Doubleday, 1990): 14.

20. P. Senge, *The Fifth Discipline*, 1990; P. Senge, "The Leader's New Work: Building Learning Organizations," *Sloan Management Review* 32 (Fall 1990): 7–23.

21. P. Senge, *The Fifth Discipline*, 1990.

22. H. Mintzberg, "Crafting Strategy," *Harvard Business Review* 65, no. 4 (1987): 66–75.

23. R. Greenleaf, *A Journey into the Nature of Legitimate Power and Greatness* (New York: Paulist Press, 1977).

24. M. Sashkin and W. Burke, "Organization Development in the 1980's, and an End-of-the-Eighties Retrospective," in *Advances in Organization Development*, ed. F. Masarik (Norwood, NJ: Ablex, 1990).

25. H. Mintzberg, *Mintzberg on Management* (New York: The Free Press, 1989).

26. P. Senge, *The Fifth Discipline*, 1990: 9.

27. D. Kirkpatrick, "Inside Sam's $100 Billion Growth Machine," *Fortune* 149, no. 12 (2004): 80–98.

28. P. Wright, M. Kroll, and J. Parnell, *Strategic Management Concepts* (Englewood-Cliffs, NJ: Prentice-Hall, 1996).

29. B. Schlender, "Peter Drucker Sets Us Straight," *Fortune* 149, no. 1 (2004); 115–118.

30. B. Schlender, 2004.

31. F. Vogelstein, "Google @ $165: Are These Guys for Real?" *Fortune* 150, no. 12 (2004): 98–110.

32. P. Nystrom and W. Starbuck, "To Avoid Organizational Crises, Unlearn," *Organizational Dynamics* 12 (1984): 53–65.

33. D. Hurst, J. Rush, and R. White, "Top Management Teams and Organizational Renewal," *Strategic Management Journal* 10 (1989): 87–105.

# Global Dynamics

## Chapter 12

## Key Terms

| | |
|---|---|
| comparative advantage | international franchising |
| cultural relativism | international licensing |
| cultural universalism | self-reference criterion |
| customization | standardization |

Most large organizations in the developed world have shifted from an emphasis on resources, products, and customers in their home countries to one that seeks to produce and distribute products worldwide. This global transformation has altered how organizations function in a variety of ways. Today more than ever, an understanding of a global orientation—including the acquisition of resources, production of goods and services, and marketing to customers across borders—is essential to organizational success. This understanding begins with the concept of culture, a concept applied to organizations in Chapter 7.

# 12-1 Culture

Each of the world's nations has its own distinctive culture, its generally accepted values, traditions, and patterns of behavior.[1] With many organizations now functioning in multiple countries and conducting business across borders, the need to understand the influence of national culture on organizational processes has never been more important. The concept of a national culture should be distinguished from that of a corporate or organizational culture, however. A national culture refers to commonalities among individuals within a country, whereas a corporate culture refers to commonalities within a single organization. In this chapter, the word *culture* refers to a national culture.

Geert Hofstede developed a popular approach for comparing and contrasting national cultures in 1980.[2] His work is based on more than 116,000 surveys of employees in more than 70 countries. Although it has been both refined and critiqued ever since, Hofstede's framework provides an excellent starting point for discussing national culture.[3] According to Hofstede, cultures can be classified along five dimensions.

The first dimension, *power distance,* refers to the degree in which individuals with less power expect and accept unequal distributions of power within a culture. Cultures like Mexico's with high power-distance emphasize hierarchies and centralization, whereas cultures with low power-distance emphasize flatter hierarchies and a more equal distribution of power.

The second dimension, *individualism,* refers to the degree to which one's self and immediate family are emphasized over the society at large. High individualism cultures such as those in Australia and the United States value freedom, individualized rewards, and privacy, whereas low individualism cultures emphasize collectivism, tradition, experience, and group harmony.

The third dimension, *masculinity,* refers to the degree to which a culture emphasizes the traditional masculine roles of assertiveness and competition. High masculinity cultures such as that in Japan value these roles, whereas low masculinity cultures emphasize cooperation and family support.

The fourth dimension, *uncertainty avoidance,* refers to the degree to which individuals within a culture seek to avoid uncertain events. Countries with cultures high in uncertainty avoidance, like France, emphasize formality and structure, whereas those low in uncertainty avoidance are more informal and relaxed.

A fifth dimension, *long-term or short-term orientation,* was a later addition to the framework.[4] Cultures with a long-term orientation, such as the culture in Korea, prioritize values focusing on the future, such as frugality, persistence, and hard work. Those with a short-term orientation emphasize such values as stability and respect for tradition.

Table 12-1 lists culture dimension scores for eleven select nations and one nation cluster.[5] Following Hofstede's framework, distinct differences can be seen among nations. The United States, for example, is the most individualistic nation. As such, factors such as employee personal time, freedom and challenge in job assignments, and salary level (as opposed to working condition) are relatively more important than in other nations. In contrast, Mexico—the United States' neighbor to the south—scored the lowest in individualism among the select twelve in the table. Japan's high scores in masculinity and uncertainty avoidance are also noteworthy, as is Israel's low score on power distance.

| TABLE 12-1 | Culture Dimension Scores for Select Nations | | | |
|---|---|---|---|---|
| **Nation** | **Power Distance** | **Individualism** | **Masculinity** | **Uncertainty Avoidance** |
| Arab countries | 80 | 38 | 53 | 68 |
| Australia | 36 | 90 | 61 | 51 |
| Brazil | 69 | 38 | 49 | 76 |
| Canada | 39 | 80 | 52 | 48 |
| France | 68 | 71 | 43 | 86 |
| Germany | 35 | 67 | 66 | 65 |
| Great Britain | 35 | 89 | 66 | 35 |
| India | 77 | 48 | 56 | 40 |
| Israel | 13 | 54 | 47 | 81 |
| Japan | 54 | 46 | 95 | 92 |
| Mexico | 81 | 30 | 69 | 82 |
| United States | 40 | 91 | 62 | 46 |
| Mean of all 53 nations and nation clusters | 57 | 43 | 49 | 65 |

In a similar vein, Ronen and Shenkar proposed eight country clusters based on cultural characteristics: Anglo, Germanic, Nordic, Near Eastern, Arab, Far Eastern, Latin American, and Latin European. The Anglo cluster, for example, includes the United States, Canada, Australia, the United Kingdom, Ireland, New Zealand, and South Africa. Ronen and Shenkar note that cultural values tend to change as a country develops economically and technologically, and are also influenced by language, religion, and geography.[6]

Other attempts to understand and categorize national cultures have also been made. Trompenaars, for example, surveyed more than 15,000 managers in twenty-eight countries over a ten-year period and proposed a five-dimensional framework.[7] In many respects, there are substantial similarities across approaches, however.

The work of Hofstede and others demonstrates the importance of taking culture into consideration, especially when decisions concern organizations or divisions across borders. In too many instances, these differences are avoided or simply ignored. The unconscious reference to one's own cultural values as a standard of judgment—the **self-reference criterion**—has been suggested as the cause of many business problems when multiple cultures are involved. Individuals, regardless of culture, become so accustomed to their own ways of looking at the world that they often have difficulty comprehending other perspectives. When organizations function in multiple countries, however, they should adjust to the culture of a host country to improve prospects for success.[8] Some adjustments are product related, such as KFC's decision to sell a spicier version of its chicken in China than it sells in the United States.

The self-reference criterion presents other problems related to organizational culture as well. Managers often believe that the leadership styles and organizational culture that are effective in their home country should work elsewhere. Because each nation has its own unique culture, organizational values and norms must be tailored to fit the unique culture of each country in which the organization operates, at least to some extent. The need to customize values and norms can create special challenges when firms from different countries become partners or even merge their organizations. There is also considerable debate on precisely how much customization is appropriate when mergers occur.

Whereas the self-reference criterion refers to the subconscious realm, a distinction should be made between the conscious perspectives of cultural universalism and cultural relativism.[9] **Cultural universalism** holds that there is a single best culture—either in theory or in practice—against which all cultures should be compared.

**self-reference criterion**
the unconscious reference to one's own cultural values as a standard of judgment

**cultural universalism**
the idea that that there is a single best culture—either in theory or in practice—against which all cultures should be compared

Box 12-1

## Career Point
### Working Abroad

Would you be excited about an international career assignment or would you rather leave the organization than take the assignment? As global business expansion continues, more managers will have the opportunity to work in other countries and experience other cultures. In addition to opening career doors within the organization, accepting an international assignment can also provide a rich cultural experience for a manager and his or her family. There are several things you can do to prepare for an international assignment.

First, seek employment with a global organization and express your interest in working abroad. There is a need for talented, energetic professionals willing to live and work abroad. Finding the right company is the best place to start.

Second, study a foreign language. Taking college courses in a language is one way to learn, but there are also numerous audio and computer-based programs designed to teach foreign languages. In general, an organization will not require language capability for an assignment and will provide immersion training to facilitate the survival skills within a given country. The more background one has prior to this training, however, the better.

Finally, consider your personal and family goals. Discuss your plans with your spouse before you pursue an international assignment. Your spouse may also need employment, and many organizations are willing to assist spouses in obtaining a rewarding experience abroad as well.

---

For example, a proponent of cultural universalism would hold that specified levels of power distance, individualism, masculinity, and uncertainty avoidance would comprise the best possible combination. These specified levels may be embodied within a certain culture, or they may represent a theoretical standard. Other cultures would be judged on the proximity of their scores to those of the superior one.

**cultural relativism**   the idea that no culture is inherently superior to any other

In contrast, **cultural relativism** holds that no single culture can be judged as inherently superior to any other culture. This perspective suggests that managers should not attempt to enforce culturally sensitive standards when functioning in other nations. Instead, management styles should be tailored to the specific characteristics of each culture.

Cultural universalism and cultural relativism can be viewed as opposite ends of a continuum. As such, individual perspectives may lean substantially in one direction or the other, but most would comprise some sort of mix of the two extremes, at least within a specified range. Hence, individual differences in perspectives on culture are not always easy to categorize or quantify.

In some respects, cultural differences appear to be diminishing as familiarity with other cultures increases. Indeed, the Internet explosion is in part responsible for some degree of cultural convergence in recent years. As individuals become more comfortable with other parts of the world, they become less resistant to other cultures. Although the introduction of high-speed travel and communication coupled with the expansion of the Internet has led to a convergence of social and other practices across nations, substantial differences among nations still remain.[10] Rather, the differences in culture that can affect organizations operating across borders will likely remain important in the upcoming years. It can also create interesting career opportunities for individuals seeking a global assignment, as discussed in Box 12-1.

It should be noted that global effects on culture are not limited to national culture, but also include organizational culture. In many respects, an organization's culture can be viewed as a subset of the national culture. Operating outside one's own country can create leadership challenges and make it more difficult to maintain a strong organizational culture. For example, leaders of some nations resist innovation and radical new approaches to conducting business, whereas others welcome such change. Such national tendencies often become a part of the culture of the organization in those countries.

## 12-1a  Influence of Religion

Cultures are comprised of and influenced by such factors as family values, educational institution, and religious orientation. It can be argued that religion is the greatest of these factors because it greatly influences many of the others. Most religions attempt to shape the morals and values of their followers, but there can be differences. There are a number of religious orientations represented in the world, but five appear to have the greatest influence on world cultures (see Table 12-2). A cursory understanding of each of these is essential to comprehending differences in world cultures.

*Christianity* has had the greatest influence in the Americas and Western Europe, although it is growing in other parts of the world as well, including Eastern Europe, Africa, and China. Christianity dates back about 2000 years, although it grew out of Judaism, an older faith. Christians follow the teachings of Jesus Christ and as such strive to live in peace, respect individual rights and responsibilities, and treat others as they would like to be treated. Christians comprise about 33 percent of the world's population.

*Islam* has had its greatest influence in the Middle East and Asia, with the largest number of Muslims (i.e., practitioners of Islam) living in the populous Asian countries of Indonesia, Pakistan, Bangladesh, and India. Islam claims about 22 percent of the world's population. Although it has roots in Judaism and Christianity, Islam dates back to the teachings of the prophet Muhammad around the year AD 600. Like Christianity, Islam teaches mutual respect and moral purity. However, Muslim practices such as the required five daily prayers and modest dress for women tend to transcend other cultural influences more than the practices of many other religions. Hence, where Muslims comprise a high percentage of a nation's population, its influence is usually more prominent in daily life, customs, and even business dealings.

*Hinduism* claims about 15 percent of the world's population, although most are situated in the Indian subcontinent. Hinduism can be traced back about 4,000 years. In general, Hindus believe that one's karma—the spiritual progression of the soul—is influenced by how one lives. Through reincarnation, individuals can make the soul more perfect with each life and eventually attain nirvana, or spiritual perfection. Hinduism supports the caste system, whereby individuals are born into a clearly defined social class that cannot readily be changed. Because Hindus place the cow in high esteem, most do not consume beef, and many are vegetarians.

*Buddhists* comprise about 6 percent of the world's population, mostly in parts of Asia. Buddhism was founded by Siddhartha Guatama in about 600 BC. Its followers believe that suffering emanates from the pursuit of pleasure, which can be suppressed by following the Noble Eightfold Path: right understanding, right thought, right speech,

| TABLE 12-2 | Influence of World Religions | | |
|---|---|---|---|
| **Religion** | **Geographical Prominence** | **Estimated Number** | **Percentage** |
| Christianity | Americas, Europe | 2 billion | 33% |
| Islam | Africa, Middle East, Asia | 1.3 billion | 22% |
| Hinduism | Indian subcontinent | 900 million | 15% |
| Nonreligious | Various, including United States and Australia | 850 million | 14% |
| Buddhism | Asia | 360 million | 6% |
| Other | Various | 600 million | 10% |

*Source:* Based on information available at www.adherents.com, accessed July 8, 2004.

Christianity has had a great influence on culture in the Americas and Europe.

right action, right livelihood, right efforts, right mindfulness, and right concentration. Although Buddhism has its roots in Hinduism, it does not support the caste system.

About 10 percent of the world's population follows one of many other religions. These religions can be very important in certain geographical locations where they might be prominent, such as the domination of the nation of Israel by followers of Judaism. Hence, the influence of religions represented in this category should not necessarily be discounted.

The *nonreligious* category is often ignored in discussions of world religion because it does not represent a religious affiliation. This group can have a strong influence on culture, however, and includes approximately 14 percent of the world's population. This is a very diverse category, including individuals who deny the existence of any god (i.e., atheists), those who are skeptical but undecided (i.e., agnostics), and those who are simply nonreligious. It should be noted that atheists represent less than 1 percent of this category, which is characterized by a general passivity towards religion. Individuals in the nonreligious category often argue for high tolerance and diversity in general. In many cases, they seek to deemphasize the influence of a religion on culture. About 7.5 percent of Americans and 15 percent of Australians identify with this group.

The influence of religion on organizational practice is often mediated by a nation's culture. In the West, for example, Sunday—a preferred day of worship for Christians—is often considered to be a day off in many lines of employment. In contrast, offices in much of the Middle East are closed on Friday, a preferred day of worship for many Muslims. Most organizations function around these culturally defined workweeks without regard to the religious preference of the managers or workers who practice other religions.

## 12-2 Global Influences on the External Environment

Differences in economies across borders can influence organizations in a number of ways. Most notably, these differences include economic and related concerns, as well as differences in social changes and trends. These areas are discussed in greater detail in Sections 12-2a, 12-2b, and 12-2c.

## 12-2a The Economy, Regulations, and Protectionism

Organizations functioning across borders must account for differences in legal systems. Bribery, for example, is an accepted practice in some countries but outlawed in others. In the United States, the Foreign Corrupt Practices Act of 1977 forbade any bribery involving representatives of any American business operating in another country even if the practice is condoned there. As a result, American managers cannot engage in bribery when operating in less developed nations where financial incentives are often provided as a matter of course.

The economic environment also varies substantially across borders, especially between developing and emerging nations, where the cost of borrowing can be as high as 100 percent annually. Excessive rates of inflation often accompany and influence these high interest rates, as was the case in parts of Latin America in the 1990s. Routine decisions such as pricing and costing become almost impossible to make under such conditions. High and unpredictable inflation rates also cause the prices of goods and services to rise and become less competitive in international trade.

Political influences, especially as they relate to regulations of business activities and restrictions on global trade, affect the effect of global economic forces on organizations. The period from the 1940s to the late 1980s was marked by increased trade protection in most countries. Many protected their industries by imposing tariffs, import duties, and other restrictions. Import duties in some developing Latin American countries even exceeded 100 percent.[11] However, this trend was also pervasive in the developed world. Countries in Europe and Asia—and even the United States— imposed import fees on a variety of products, including food, steel, and cars. In the 1980s, the United States also convinced Japanese manufacturers to impose restrictions on exports of automobiles to the United States in lieu of a tariff. Interestingly, this particular tariff may be largely responsible for Japanese automobile manufacturers' establishing a large number of production facilities in the United States, thereby blurring the concept of the foreign car among American consumers.

During this time, however, leaders from many nations recognized that all countries would likely benefit if trade barriers could be reduced across the board. After the end of World War II, twenty-three countries entered into the cooperative General Agreement on Tariffs and Trade (GATT), working to relax quota and import license requirements, introduce fairer customs evaluation methods, and establish a common mechanism to resolve trade disputes. The World Trade Organization (WTO) and the International Monetary Fund (IMF) were also established at this time. By 1994, GATT membership had expanded to more than 110 nations and was replaced by a new WTO, viewed more as an organization than as a treaty. Today the WTO contains 147 members and continues to negotiate global trade agreements, although member nations must ratify the agreements before they become effective.

A major shift in U.S. policy occurred in the late 1970s and the 1980s to reduce business regulations, eliminating a number of legal constraints in such industries as airlines, trucking, and banking. By 1990, a reversal of trade protectionism and strong governmental influence in business operations began to take place in the United States and many parts of the world. In the United States, new economic policies reduced governmental influence in business operations by deregulating certain industries, lowering corporate taxes, and relaxing rules against mergers and acquisitions. Although this trend has continued into the twenty-first century, corporate scandals and concerns over outsourcing sparked new calls for business regulation in a number of areas.

The move toward free trade was also seen in Europe, where a number of nations banded together to develop a free-trade European Community. Today, Europe is fast becoming a single market of 350 million consumers. The European Union represents the largest trading bloc on earth, accounting for more than 40 percent of the world's gross domestic product (GDP).[12] Meanwhile, the United States, Canada, and Mexico established the North American Free Trade Agreement (NAFTA) to create its own strategic trading bloc.

Many analysts believe that global business soon will be divided into several such blocs, each providing preferred trading status to other nations within the bloc. Such blocs have strengthened business relationships in North America (NAFTA), Europe (EU), Latin America, Africa, and Southeast Asia. The notion of a trading bloc can be viewed as a compromise between the protectionist model on one end of the spectrum and totally free world trade on the other. Because a bloc includes only a subset of the world's nations, and cultural and political differences among nations in a bloc are usually less substantial than those that exist among the world's nations as a whole, the trading bloc concept allows a nation to pursue free trade with its neighbors without engaging in a degree of conflict that is more likely to occur on a global scale.

This trend toward less regulation has even extended to the former communist countries. As the nations of the former Soviet bloc in Eastern Europe overturned their governments, they began to open markets and to invite foreign investment.[13] In addition, China officially remains a communist nation, but its economic development policies have taken a distinctively free market approach since the late 1990s. Nonetheless, regulation—or the lack thereof—always seems to be a key political and business issue, most recently in copyrighted products distributed electronically, such as software, music, and movies.[14]

It should be noted that trade restrictions will always exist to some extent, especially in politically sensitive areas. For example, the United States and other Western countries have banned the export of advanced technology in some circumstances. The United States prohibits the export of certain electronic, nuclear, and defense-related products to many countries, particularly those believed to be involved in international terrorism. Many of these restrictions were revised and strengthened following the terrorist attacks of September 11, 2001.[15]

### 12-2b Global Social Forces

Changes in social forces occur constantly throughout the world but can take different forms in different nations. Some social changes may occur in many or all nations, but at different times. For example, the pastime of watching television took hold in the United States in the 1950s. Because of its link to technological advances, however, it did not spread to emerging nations for several decades. Other social forces, such as preferences for clothing styles or particular sporting activities, show varying amounts of consistency across borders.

Managers in progressive organizations recognize that cross-cultural differences in norms and values require modifications in their structure and activities. Consider, for example, that business negotiations may take months or even years in countries such as Egypt, China, Mexico, and much of Latin America. Until personal friendships and trust develop between the parties, negotiators are unwilling to commit themselves to major business transactions.[16] In addition, Japanese business executives invite and even expect their clients or suppliers to interact socially with them after working hours, for up to three or four hours an evening, several times a week. Westerners who decline to attend such social gatherings regularly may be unsuccessful in their negotiations because these social settings create a foundation for serious business relationships.

Managers of American organizations should remember that their firms have exceptionally high visibility because of their American origins. As such, citizens of other countries may disrupt the business operations of American corporations as a form of anti-American activity. For example, only two months after Euro Disneyland opened in France, hundreds of French farmers blocked entrances to the theme park with their tractors to express their displeasure with cuts in European Community farm subsidies that had been encouraged by the United States, even though 90 percent of the food sold at the park was produced in France.[17]

### 12-2c Technological Change in the Global Environment

Changes in technology have had pronounced effects for organizations operating across borders, especially when the extent to which technological advances have been implemented differs markedly across nations. In developed countries, for example, technological amenities such as access to email, cellular telephone service, and reliable scheduled internal transportation services are expected as a matter of course. In less developed nations, however, Internet and cellular telephone service may be available only in certain areas and internal bus or train transportation may not be reliable. These differences must be taken into account when conducting business abroad.

The effect of technology on global business can be viewed from an economic development perspective. For years, manufacturers in technologically advanced nations established operations in developing countries to minimize production and other costs. These expansions have generally been successful for both manufacturers and the societies where they expand because they bring capital, workforce training and development, and technology to the host country. In many cases, this interaction has benefited the developing country over the long term, most notably in the cases of emerging nations such as Mexico, Brazil, India, and China.[18]

Leaders in developing nations have not always been pleased with this global business expansion, in part because anticipated economic and social benefits do not always materialize. In some cases, the expanding organization promises but does not deliver specialized business development assistance, the establishment of research and development (R&D) facilities, and the hiring of locals in managerial and other professional positions.[19] On-the-job training notwithstanding, the overall long-term contribution to the host country is sometimes questioned by leaders in the developing nations.

## 12-3 Global Influences on Organizational Mission and Direction

An organization's mission may be closely intertwined with the global environment in a number of ways. Most organizations require inputs and resources from abroad. This phenomenon is most pervasive in organizations whose headquarters are located in a small or less developed nation. Consider, for example, that virtually all of Japan's industries would grind to a halt if imports of raw materials from other nations ceased, because Japan is a small island nation and its natural resources are quite limited.

Organizational mission and global involvement are also connected through the economic concept of **comparative advantage,** the idea that certain products may be produced more cheaply or at a higher quality in particular countries due to advantages in labor costs or technology. Chinese manufacturers, for example, have enjoyed some of the lowest global labor rates for unskilled or semiskilled production in recent years, resulting in increases in the outsourcing of production to facilities there. As skills rise in the rapidly emerging nation, some companies have succeeded in extending this comparative advantage to a number of technical skill areas as well. The annual salary for successful engineers in China had risen to around $10,000 in 2002, a level well below their comparably skilled counterparts in other parts of the world.[20]

Global involvement may also provide advantages to the firm not directly related to costs. For political reasons, a firm often establishes operations in countries where a substantial proportion of sales is made. Doing so can also provide managers with a critical understanding of local markets and customs.

**comparative advantage**
the idea that certain products may be produced more cheaply or at a higher quality in particular countries, due to advantages in labor costs or technology

## 12-4 Global Corporate Strategy

The most fundamental global strategic decision concerns the extent to which an organization will become engaged in activities outside of its host country. An organization may choose to be involved only in its domestic market, or it may compete abroad at the international, multinational, or global level. The use of these three terms to represent three different levels of involvement should not be confused with their relative interchangeability in everyday conversation. In general, large organizations are more likely to emphasize competition abroad, although small organizations can also be successful pursuing activities across borders.[21]

The most conservative means of moving outside the domestic market is to become involved on an *international* basis. Such organizations operate in various countries but limit their involvement to importing, exporting, licensing, or strategic alliances. Activity at this level can be beneficial to many organizations. Exporting alone can significantly benefit even a small company. International joint ventures—a form of strategic alliance involving cooperative arrangements between businesses across borders—may be desirable even when resources for a direct investment are available. For example, in 2001, GM launched a $333 million joint venture with Russian firm OAO AvtoVAZ to provide technological support to the struggling holdover from Soviet-era industry for engineering a stripped-down version of an SUV offered by the Russian carmaker. By engaging in the joint venture, GM gained immediate access to the market but placed its reputation on the line by putting its Chevy name on a vehicle produced by a technologically weak automobile producer.[22]

Organizations with global objectives may decide to invest directly in facilities abroad. Due to the complexities associated with establishing operations across borders, however, strategic alliances may be particularly attractive to firms seeking to expand their level of involvement. Organizations often possess market, regulatory, and other knowledge about their domestic markets but may need to partner with companies abroad to gain access to this knowledge as it pertains to international markets. A number of international strategic alliances can be seen among automobile producers, including production facilities owned jointly by General Motors and Toyota or those owned jointly by Ford and Mazda.

Internal growth is usually both attractive and challenging when an organization expands outside its borders. In 2003, for example, McDonald's announced plans to expand its cadre of 566 stores in China by approximately 100 annually. By that time, however, KFC had already grown to about 900 eateries in China with plans for an additional 200 units annually. McDonald's slower growth resulted from its struggle to build a network of local suppliers, many of whom are the same ones it utilizes in the United States, whereas KFC built a network of Chinese suppliers while aggressively adapting to local tastes in an effort to speed up its growth efforts. Starbucks had fewer than 100 Chinese locations in 2003 and has found it difficult to convert a nation of tea drinkers to specialty coffee.[23]

International strategic alliances provide a number of advantages to an organization. They can provide entry into a global market, access to the partner's knowledge about the foreign market, and allow for risk sharing with the partner. They can work effectively when partners can learn from each other and when both partners share common strategic goals but are not in direct competition. However, problems can arise from international joint ventures, including disputes and lack of trust over proprietary knowledge, cultural differences between firms, and disputes over ways to share the costs and revenues associated with the partnership.

Other options are also available to a firm seeking an international presence. Under an **international licensing** agreement, a foreign licensee purchases the rights to produce a company's products and/or use its technology in the licensee's country

**international licensing**
an arrangement whereby a foreign licensee purchases the rights to produce a company's products and/or use its technology in the licensee's country for a negotiated fee structure

for a negotiated fee structure. This arrangement is common among pharmaceutical firms. Drug producers in one nation typically allow producers in other nations to produce and market their products abroad.[24]

**International franchising** is a longer-term form of licensing in which a local franchisee pays a franchiser in another country for the right to use the franchiser's brand names, promotions, materials, and procedures.[25] Whereas manufacturers are likely to pursue licensing, service industries, such as fast-food restaurants, commonly employ franchising.

If top managers are interested in a more substantial degree of activity abroad, the organization can become involved at the *multinational* level, where the organization pursues direct investments in other countries, and their subsidiaries operate independently of one another. Colgate-Palmolive has attained a large worldwide market share through its decentralized operations in a number of foreign markets.

Finally, some firms are *globally* involved, with direct investments and interdependent subdivisions abroad. Global organizations operate in multiple nations and view their markets from a global perspective, often without giving primary consideration to national borders.

Organizations pursue a global orientation for many reasons. Developing global markets can reduce per-unit production costs by increasing volume. A global strategy can extend the product life cycle of products whose domestic markets may be declining, as U.S. cigarette manufacturers did in the 1990s. Establishing facilities abroad can also enable an organization to benefit from comparative advantage, the difference in resources among nations that provide certain production cost advantages in a particular country. For example, athletic shoes tend to be produced most efficiently in parts of Asia where rubber is plentiful and labor is less costly. A global orientation can also lessen risk because demand and competitive factors tend to vary among nations.

International growth is often pursued through expansion into emerging economies in those nations that have achieved enough development to warrant expansion but whose markets are not yet fully served. Although emerging economies such as those in China, South Africa, Mexico, and parts of Eastern Europe are attractive in many respects, poor infrastructure (e.g., telecommunications, highways, etc.), cumbersome government regulations, and workforce limitations can create great challenges for the organization considering expansion.

**international franchising** a form of licensing in which a local franchisee pays a franchiser in another country for the right to use the franchiser's brand names, promotions, materials, and procedures

# 12-5 Global Influences on Business Strategy

Global competition is complex and in many cases intense. There is no simple formula for developing and implementing successful business strategies across national borders. Having a global presence does not guarantee success. Organizations must cultivate a global mindset whereby its members seek knowledge and expertise on a global scale and develop the ability to integrate it into attractive courses of action.[26] Organizations can convert global presence into global competitive advantage by adapting to local market differences as needed, exploiting economies of scale and scope that become available at the global level, tapping optimal locations for activities and resources, and facilitating knowledge transfer across its global sites so that managers at each location can learn from the others.[27]

Fundamentally, an organization has three choices when it develops a competitive strategy for a market abroad.[28] First, it may pursue **standardization,** whereby it markets the same product or service in all of its international markets. Second, it may pursue **customization,** whereby it modifies its home products or services to meet the needs of markets abroad. Finally, it may choose to develop an entirely different set of products or services for its markets abroad. If the organization pursues one of the first two options, then it must determine whether the communication

**standardization** a global strategic approach whereby the organization markets the same product or service in all of its international markets

**customization** a global strategic approach whereby the organization modifies its product or service offering to meet the needs of all of its international markets and promotional efforts should be standardized or customized as well. As a result, the organization has five options, as depicted in Table 12-3.

The first approach is to standardize both the product/service and the means of communication with the customers. This is the least expensive approach from a cost perspective, and soft drink and other beverage producers have employed this approach. One can argue that consistency across borders is critical, citing examples such as Coca-Cola, whose emphasis on quality, brand recognition, and a small world theme has been successful in a number of global markets.

The second approach is to standardize the product/service, but customize communication. A powdered soup producer may distribute the same product in both Europe and the United States, although the producer may market it as a soup in Europe and as a sauce or dip in the United States.

The third approach is to customize the product/service, but standardize communication. Automakers typically must modify their products to meet local regulations and emissions requirements. In addition, drivers in some countries drive on the right side of the road while those in other countries drive on the left. Hence, communication and promotional efforts may be largely unchanged, although the products have been modified. Using this approach in the food industry, KFC modifies the spice content for its fried chicken somewhat to adjust to palates in different countries. The promotional and communications efforts do not change, however.

The fourth approach is to customize both the product/service and the communication, an approach often referred to as "think globally, but act locally." Following this logic, an organization would emphasize the synergy created by serving multiple markets globally, but formulate a distinct competitive strategy for each specific market tailored to its unique situation.

Tailoring a business strategy to meet the unique demands of a different market requires that top managers understand the similarities and differences between the markets from both industry and cultural perspectives. For example, since the 1970s, Japanese automobile manufacturers like Honda have tried to blend a distinctively Japanese approach to car building while remaining sensitive to North American and European values. In 2000, Mitsubishi began aggressively redesigning the Montero Sport to make it a global vehicle that could sell effectively in world markets. In 2001, however, the carmaker dropped its one-size-fits-all approach and began to emphasize design factors unique to the critical American market.[29]

The final approach is to produce an entirely different array of goods and services for a new market. Although a firm can enjoy the benefits of brand recognition by extending its offerings across borders, the increased costs associated with modifying both the product or service and the message make this a less attractive option.

| **TABLE 12-3** | Global Competitive Strategy Options | |
|---|---|---|
| **Global Competitive Strategy Option** | **Product/Service Decision** | **Communication and Promotion Decision** |
| Standardize product/service and communication | Standardize | Standardize |
| Standardize product/service but customize communication | Standardize | Customize |
| Customize product/service but standardize communication | Customize | Standardize |
| Customize product/service and communication | Customize | Customize |
| Produce different products/services | New products/services | New communication and promotion for different markets |

Box 12-2

## Best Practices
### Global Success at Yum Brands

Yum Brands operates several well-known restaurant chains, including KFC, Pizza Hut, Taco Bell, A&W All American Food Restaurants, and Long John Silver's. In addition to operations in its home country, the United States, Yum Brands is heavily represented in China, Korea, and the United Kingdom. In fact, Yum operates more than 500 KFC outlets in China, and its brand is widely recognized, especially by young members of the Chinese population.

What is the key to Yum's global success? First, Yum seeks a balance between its strong American brand names and local tastes in the host country. For example, KFC's chicken is a little spicier in China than in the United States. Pizza Hut offers different condiments for its pizzas in Australia. Americans traveling abroad will recognize the products abroad, but will notice minor changes that fit well with local tastes.

Second, Yum hires local managerial talent whenever possible. For example, British managers are in charge of restaurants in the United Kingdom and Japanese managers are responsible for Pizza Hut outlets in Japan. In general, local managers are able to recruit and motivate employees more effectively than expatriates from the home country could. They are also more familiar with local customs and preferences.

---

Adopting an approach can be a difficult decision, as many firms have succeeded with different approaches. Yum Brands is an example of one such company, as discussed in Box 12-2.

Regardless of the competitive strategy choice, the intensity of competition in most markets in the developed world suggests that strategic managers should remain abreast of opportunities that may exist in emerging economies. India, for example, has enjoyed considerable growth in recent years. A number of firms have outsourced jobs in technical areas to India where trained workers are available at considerably lower wages. Economic liberalization in the country has invited additional foreign investment into the country. India's Tata Motors is helping overcome the country's reputation for poor production quality by exporting an estimated 20,000 CityRovers to the United Kingdom in 2004.[30]

India, however, has received only a small fraction of the level of foreign investment made in China, which boasts the world's largest population and has been projected as a world economic leader within the next few decades. China's entrance into the World Trade Organization, declining import tariffs, and increasing consumer incomes suggest a bright future for the nation. At present, China remains a mix of the traditional lifestyle based in socialism and its own form of a neo-Western economic development. Nowhere is this friction seen best than on the roads of the capital, Beijing, where crowds of bicycles attempt to negotiate traffic with buses and a rapidly increasing number of personal automobiles. U.S.-style traffic reports have even become pervasive in a country where the world's largest automakers are fighting for a stake in what many experts believe will be a consumer automobile growth phase of mammoth proportions.[31]

When a Western firm seeks to conduct business with one of its Chinese counterparts, managers from both firms must recognize the cultural differences between the two nations. Recently, a number of consulting and management development organizations in both China and the West have been busy training managers to become aware of such differences and take action to minimize misunderstandings that can arise from them. For example, Chinese managers are more likely than Americans to smoke during meetings and less likely to answer email from international partners. In the United States, it is more common to emphasize subordinate contributions to solving problems, whereas Chinese managers are more likely to respect the judgment of their superiors without subordinate involvement.[32]

Steeped in rich history and tradition, China offers myriad opportunities to Western organizations whose managers can adapt to its culture.

Western manufacturers such as Eastman Kodak, Procter & Gamble, Group Danone of France, and Siemens AG of Germany have already established a strong presence in China. A number of Western restaurants and retailers have also begun to expand aggressively into China, including U.S.-based McDonald's, Popeye's Chicken, Yum Brands (i.e., KFC and Pizza Hut), and Wal-Mart.[33] French-based Carrefour has been one of the most successful retailers in China with 31 stores in 2003 with continued growth projected through the middle of the decade. Product mixes in the Chinese stores tend to be similar to those in the domestic market, with adjustments made for local preferences. For a number of firms, the only attractive prospects for growth lie in emerging economies such as China, Brazil, and Mexico.[34]

## 12-6 Global Influences on the Individual Manager

As organizations become more involved in the global business environment, managers with additional skills and abilities are required to meet the challenge. Seven characteristics of effective global managers are identified in Table 12-4.[35] The first characteristic is a global mindset. Effective global managers view the environment as global, spanning national borders, cultures, languages, and modes of business practice.

Second, global managers must be highly effective communicators. When one functions in more than one culture, communication barriers resulting from language, expectations and other cultural factors are likely to arise. It is not realistic to expect that such barriers can ever be completely removed. Nonetheless, effective global managers should have the ability to minimize communication problems and transmit knowledge and ideas clearly across cultural boundaries.

Third, effective global managers understand the context of global strategic management. When strategy is viewed at a global level, a number of additional considerations are present. For example, international strategic alliances can provide an opportunity for an organization to pursue a business opportunity abroad without making a large financial commitment, but alliances are not best for every organization. Managers must understand the pros and cons of strategic options so that the most effective strategy can be developed and implemented.

| TABLE 12-4 | Characteristics of Effective Global Managers |
|---|---|

A global mindset
Effective communication skills
Working knowledge of global strategy
Ability to manage change effectively
Understanding and appreciation of cultural diversity
Ability to work effectively in flexible organizations
Comfort and ability to lead and work as a member of cross-cultural teams

*Source:* Based on P.W. Beamish, A. J. Morrison, A. C. Inkpen, and P. M. Rosenzweig, *International Management*, 5th ed. (Boston: Irwin-McGraw-Hill, 2003).

Fourth, global managers must have the ability to manage change effectively. The pace of change, especially in emerging economies, is staggering. In addition, as the geographical boundaries in which one operates become wider, the complexity of change within those boundaries also becomes greater.

Fifth, effective global managers understand and appreciate cultural diversity. They are able to approach business and daily activities in different manners when operating in different cultures, and they genuinely respect cultural differences and enjoy learning about them.

Such a diversity perspective does not necessarily suggest that a manager would not argue for some degree of consistency in practices across cultures. One can understand and appreciate different cultures while either arguing for widely divergent management approaches in different nations or for a high degree of consistency in the organization's management approach across cultures.

In addition, an understanding and appreciation for cultural diversity does not suggest that a manager lacks a strong moral compass with regard to ethical dilemmas. In contrast, an effective manager understands how individuals from multiple nations might view the same situation differently from an ethical perspective and strives to develop solutions and make decisions that are viewed as ethical and upstanding across cultures.

Sixth, because organizations functioning across borders tend to be more flexible, global managers must be able to work effectively in such an environment. Flexible organizations are generally marked by flexible structures, including reporting relationships, job responsibilities, and the like.

Finally, effective global managers must not only be able to function as a member of a team, but must also have the ability to lead and work as a member in a *cross-cultural* environment. Managing different languages, time zones, cultural mindsets, and other influences are important parts of this characteristic.

It is worth noting that familiarity with multiple cultures and/or languages from childhood can serve as an excellent foundation for developing the skills necessary to work effectively as a global manager. Although not prerequisites for success, such a background can provide a head start for someone seeking success in the global environment.

## Summary

Many opportunities and challenges for organizations can be found outside the borders of its host country. Operating effectively in multiple nations and evaluating global opportunities can only be done if managers understand cultural, economic, and social differences across borders.

The influence of the global environment on organizations is profound. Those wishing to pursue involvement outside of the host country can become involved at the international, the multinational, or the global level. International involvement is minimal and includes areas such as importing, exporting, licensing, or strategic alliances. Maximum involvement is seen with global involvement, where an organization operates interrelated divisions in various countries and serves a global market. The global environment also influences how managers perform their individual jobs.

## Review Questions and Exercises

1. What is the difference between national culture and organizational culture? Are the two concepts related? Explain.

2. How does the national culture in which an organization functions influence its activities and prospects for success?

3. What strategic options are available for an organization seeking to expand operations outside of its domestic borders?

4. How can managers be successful in a global environment?

## Quiz

1. According to Hofstede, a culture can be analyzed by considering its degree of masculinity.
   **True or False**

2. According to Hofstede's research, the United States and Mexico have two of the most individualistic cultures in the world.
   **True or False**

3. The unconscious reference to one's own cultural values as a standard of judgment is known as the cultural criterion.
   **True or False**

4. Competitive advantage refers to the idea that certain products may be produced more cheaply or at a higher quality in particular countries due to advantages in labor costs or technology.
   **True or False**

5. The most conservative means of moving outside the domestic market is to become involved on an international basis.
   **True or False**

6. It is not always clear whether or not a firm's strategic approach should be consistent across borders or should be tailored to each national market.
   **True or False**

7. Emerging markets are often more attractive than developed ones because
   a. competition is not as intense.
   b. consumer incomes in emerging markets are not a concern.
   c. the infrastructure in emerging markets is already developed.
   d. none of the above.

8. At the global level, the period from World War II to the late 1980s was marked by
   a. an increase in trade protection.
   b. a decrease in trade protection.
   c. an absence of U.S. imports.
   d. none of the above.

9. The idea that certain products may be produced more cheaply or at a higher quality in particular countries due to advantages in labor costs or technology is known as
   a. comparative advantage.
   b. competitive advantage.
   c. strategic advantage.
   d. national advantage.

10. Which of the following is not an advantage of international joint ventures?
    a. access to knowledge about a foreign market
    b. ability to eliminate risk associated with global expansion
    c. firms learn from each other
    d. entry into the foreign market is secured

11. Firms operating on an international basis limit their nondomestic activities to
    a. licensing, strategic alliances, importing and exporting.
    b. global venture management.
    c. those designed to generate less than 10 percent of organizational revenues.
    d. none of the above.

12. Which of the following skill areas is not critical to success as a global manager?
    a. communication skills
    b. ability to manage change
    c. ability to speak at least three languages fluently
    d. all of the above are critical to success

# Endnotes

1. E. Weitz and Y. Shenhav, "A Longitudinal Analysis of Technical and Organizational Uncertainty in Management Theory," *Organization Studies* 21 (2000): 243-265.

2. G. Hofstede, *Culture's Consequences: International Differences in Work-Related Values,* 2nd ed. (Thousand Oaks, CA: Sage, 2001)

3. A. A. Tavakoli, J. P. Keenan, and B. Crnjak-Karanovic, "Culture and Whistleblowing: An Empirical Study of Croation and United States Managers Utilizing Hofstede's Cultural Dimensions," *Journal of Business Ethics* 43 (2003): 49-64; R. F. Baskervile, "Hofstede Never Studied Culture," *Accounting, Organizations & Society* 28, no. 1 (2003): 1-14; B. McSweeney, "Hofstede's Model of National Cultural Differences and Their Consequences: A Triumph of Faith—A Failure of Analysis," *Human Relations* 55 (2002): 89-118.

4. G. Hofstede, 2001.

5. G. Hofstede, 2001.

6. S. Ronen and O. Shenkar, "Clustering Countries on Attitudinal Dimensions: A Review and Synthesis," *Academy of Management Review* 10 (1985): 435-454.

7. F. Trompenaars and C. Hampden-Turner, *Riding the Waves of Culture: Understanding Cultural Diversity in Global Business* (New York: McGraw-Hill, 1997).

8. P. Wright, M. Kroll, and J. A. Parnell, *Strategic Management:Concepts* (Upper Saddle River, NJ: Prentice Hall, 1998).

9. B. S. Turner, "Cosmopolitan Virtue: On Religion in a Global Age," *European Journal of Social Theory* 4 (2001): 131-152; T. Donaldson, "Values in Tension: Ethics Away from Home," *Harvard Business Review* 5, no. 10 (1996): 48-62.

10. S. C. Schneider and J. L. Barsoux, *Managing Across Cultures* (Harlow, England: Pearson Education, 2002).

11. *International Financial Statistics Yearbook* (Washington, DC: International Monetary Fund, 1989).

12. C. Rapoport, "Europe Looks Ahead to Hard Choices," *Fortune* 125, no. 50 (1992): 145.

13. F. M. E. Raiszadeh, M. M. Helms, and M. C. Varner, "How Can Eastern Europe Help American Manufacturers?" *The International Executive* 35 (1993): 357-365.

14. K. J. Delaney and C. Goldsmith, "Music Industry Targets Piracy By Europeans," *Wall Street Journal,* January 20, 2004, B1, B2.

15. "How September 11 Changed America," *Wall Street Journal,* March 8, 2002, B1.

16. P. Wright, "Organizational Behavior in Islamic Firms," *Management International Review* 21, no. 2 (1981): 86-94.

17. "World Wire: French Protest Hits Euro Disney," *Wall Street Journal,* September 20, 1993, A10.

18. B. Schofield, "Building-and-Rebuilding—A Global Company," *The McKinsey Quarterly* 2 (1994): 37-45; R. B. Reich, *The Next American Frontier* (New York: Times Books, 1983).

19. A. R. Negandhi, "Multinational Corporations and Host Governments' Relationships: Comparative Study of Conflict and Conflicting Issues," *Human Relations* 33 (1980): 534-535.

20. P. Wonacott, "China's Secret Weapon: Smart, Cheap Labor for High Tech Goods," *Wall Street Journal,* March 14, 2002, A1.

21. J. M. Geringer, S. Tallman, and D. M. Olsen, "Product and International Diversification among Japanese Multinational Firms," *Strategic Management Journal* 21 (2000): 51-80.

22. G. L. White, "GM Trusts Former Soviet Auto Maker to Build Car with the Chevy Name," *Wall Street Journal Interactive Edition,* February 20, 2001.

23. B. Dolven, "Trailing KFC, McDonald's Plans to Accelerate Expansion in China," *Wall Street Journal,* September 8, 2003, A13; G. A. Fowler, "Starbucks' Road to China," *Wall Street Journal,* July 14, 2003, B1, B3.

24. H. Merchant and D. Schendel, "How Do International Joint Ventures Create Shareholder Value?" *Strategic Management Journal* 21 (2000): 723-737; T. L. Powers and R. C. Jones, "Strategic Combinations and Their Evolution in the Global Marketplace," *Thunderbird International Business Review* 43 (2001): 525-534.

25. P. Chan and R. Justis, "Franchise Management in East Asia," *Academy of Management Executive* 4 (1990): 75-85.

26. A. K. Gupta and V. Govindarajan, "Cultivating a Global Mindset," *Academy of Management Executive* 16, no. 1 (2002): 116-125.

27. A. K. Gupta and V. Govindarajan, "Converting Global Presence into Global Competitive Advantage," *Academy of Management Executive* 15, no. 2 (2001): 45-57.

28. W. J. Keegan, "Multinational Product Planning: Strategic Alternatives," *Journal of Marketing* 1 (1969): 58-62.

29. N. Shirouzu, "Tailoring World's Cars to U.S. Tastes," *Wall Street Journal,* January 15, 2001, B1.

30. J. Slater and J. Solomon, "With a Small Car, India Takes Big Step onto Global Stage," *Wall Street Journal,* February 5, 2004, A1, A9; C. Karmin, "India, Poised for Growth, Merits Closer Look," *Wall Street Journal,* February 19, 2004, C1, C18; S. Thurm, "Lesson in India: Some Jobs Don't Translate Overseas," *Wall Street Journal,* March 3, 2004, A1, A10.

31. K. Leggett and T. Zaun, "World Car Makers Race to Keep Up with China Boom," *Wall Street Journal,* December 13, 2002, A1, A7; K. Chen, "Beyond the Traffice Report," *Wall Street Journal,* January 2, 2003, A1, A12.

32. M. Fong, "Chinese Charm School," *Wall Street Journal,* January 13, 2004, B1, B6.

33. L. Chang and P. Wonacott, "Cracking China's Market," *Wall Street Journal,* January 9, 2003, B1.

34. L. Chang, "Western Stores Woo Chinese Wallets," *Wall Street Journal,* November 26, 2002, B1, B6; B. Saporito, "Can Wal-Mart Get Any Bigger?" *Time,* January 13, 2003, 38-43.

35. A. K. Gupta and V. Govindarajan, 2002; S. H. Rhinesmith, J. N. Williamson, D. M. Ehlen, and D. S. Maxwell, "Developing Leaders for the Global Enterprise," *Training and Development Journal* 43, no. 4 (1989): 24-34; P. W. Beamish, A. J. Morrison, A. C. Inkpen, and P. M. Rosenzweig, *International Management,* 5th ed. (Boston: Irwin-McGraw-Hill, 2003).

# Integrative Cases

**Part 6**

# Walton Arts Center: Act 2

## Case A*

## John Todd
## Donald D. White**

Anita Scism expressed her excitement at a press conference announcing her appointment as President of the Walton Arts Center (WAC), in November 1998: "It's a great place. I love it!" In spite of this public statement, however, she was apprehensive about several significant challenges facing her. Foremost in her mind was the Center's need to increase revenues. "The Board of Directors (the Center's governing body) will be supportive in many ways, but I know that the primary responsibility for the Center is on my shoulders," she confided to close friends.

Three months later, Scism was still struggling with her new responsibilities. She said:

> There's a two-day strategic planning "retreat" scheduled next month for our Board members and the management team. The Board wants to review our Mission Statement. I've got a lot to do here at the Center, but I also have to begin thinking about the kinds of things that could move the Center into the future. I have seen, firsthand, the enthusiasm for the arts in the community. People want to have more exciting, unique, and diverse art experiences, and I know we need to make these dreams even more of a reality for people all around our region. And we must find more revenues. What should we be doing differently?

*Source:* Reprinted by permission from the *Case Research Journal.* Copyright 2002 by John Todd and Donald D. White, and the North American Case Research Association. All rights reserved.

*This case was prepared as a basis for class discussion rather than to illustrate either effective or ineffective management.

**Author affiliations: John Todd, University of Arkansas; Donald D. White, University of Arkansas.

# A-1 Background Information

In 1992, the Walton Arts Center, a newly constructed 1,200 seat performing arts facility, opened in Fayetteville, Arkansas. Fayetteville, a city of 53,000 population and home of the University of Arkansas, was the largest city in the fast-growing Northwest Arkansas corridor (primarily Washington and Benton counties, all within a 30-mile radius of Fayetteville) that included approximately 270,000 residents.

Scism was only the second President of the Center. Her predecessor, Bill Mitchell, was a popular and charismatic individual who was widely recognized both locally and nationally for his leadership in the arts community. He provided effective direction and inspiration for the WAC's construction and development as its first President from 1987 (pre-construction) to 1997. Under Mitchell, the Board of Directors adopted "Celebrate Imagination" as the Center's mission; a formal statement of vision, values, and goals supported that concept (see Exhibit 1). The Center experienced rapid growth, although that growth was accompanied by the growing pains of limited finances and the evolution of organizational systems and structure during its early years.

**Walton Arts Center**
Mission
Celebrate Imagination

**Vision**

The Walton Arts Center nourishes creativity and embraces cultural risk.

We ignite passion in our audiences for the full exploration of art.

We convey enthusiasm for quality.

**Values**

We value the power of ART to transform and influence the lives of all people.

We value the CHILDREN of Northwest Arkansas and their endless imagination.

We value excellence in arts EDUCATION for both children and adults, incorporating direct involvement with art and artists.

We value a continuing effort to reach out to ALL PEOPLE of Northwest Arkansas.

We value building and strengthening COMMUNITY through the arts.

We value the positive influence that our state-of-the-art FACILITY has on the cultural life of the region.

**Goals**

To build partnerships that create understanding, trust, and diverse audiences.

To build financial support that allows for expansive growth of programming and community services.

To create and invest in a balance of programs of high quality performance and visual arts.

To lead in the field of arts education.

To be an active voice for the arts in development of regional, state, and federal policy issues.

**EXHIBIT 1**

Walton Arts Center Vision Statement

# A-2 Mitchell's Departure

The years 1997 and 1998 were eventful for the Walton Arts Center, particularly because of Bill Mitchell's departure. Other performing arts organizations, over the years, had inquired about Mitchell's availability for CEO openings, because he was well known in the performing arts industry and had served as President of the National Association of Performing Arts Presenters. Mitchell and his wife were happy in Fayetteville, so he did not pursue the openings. However, changes in the Mitchell's family situation (all the children had grown up and left home) and an attractive challenge of starting over again to build a new arts center led him to seriously consider an offer in 1997.

The Center for the Arts and Sciences of West Virginia contacted Mitchell about a CEO position that would provide both new challenges and a significant increase in salary. The Center in West Virginia planned a major development, and Mitchell explored the opportunity with increasing excitement. He later explained his and his wife's decision:

> We really had no desire to leave Fayetteville. We loved it there and thought it would be where we would retire. But I'm into my fifties now, and we both thought if we were ever to make another move, this would be the right time. We hope this will be our last stop.

Thus, the "founding father" of the Center and the person who, to many, personified the WAC resigned at the end of October, 1997.

# A-3 The Replacement

Mitchell recommended that Anita Scism, then Senior Vice President, be named as Interim President, and the WAC Board of Directors accepted that recommendation. Scism, 42, was born, raised, and educated in Northwest Arkansas. She attended the University of Arkansas and had held various clerical and administrative positions with a number of local companies including a bank, a poultry company, and a law firm prior to joining the WAC in 1991. She was a quiet person, and people in the community considered her to be intelligent and personable.

Scism first had been appointed Director of Financial Affairs for the Center. She was promoted to Senior Vice President for Administration and Operations in 1994. Her primary responsibility had been to manage the Center's internal operations while Mitchell handled most of the external functions (e.g., Board relations, fund-raising, and programming). Other Vice Presidents who reported to Mitchell handled the marketing and education functions. Scism enjoyed working with Mitchell and credited him with teaching her about performing arts administration. She said, "I always worked well with Mitch, and we talked a lot about the Center and where it was going."

The Board appointed a Search Committee composed of selected Board members, secured the services of an executive search firm to locate a new President and CEO, and set the beginning salary range at $75,000 to $90,000 per year. The Search Committee developed a list of the President/CEO's responsibilities, as follows:

- Strengthening the Center's connection and service to the surrounding communities and the University of Arkansas
- Enhancing the mix of presented attractions
- Establishing the programming for the Baum Learning Center (a new hands-on arts education facility owned by WAC)
- Providing ever-greater program and learning opportunities for area students and educators
- Securing a primary role for arts and cultural activities in the future growth and development of the Northwest Arkansas region

A Connecticut-based search firm narrowed an overall field of nearly 30 candidates to five finalists. Scism was the only local finalist among the five. The consultant, in assessing Anita Scism's qualifications, said, "Any weaknesses she has come primarily from being in that 'number-two' position."

Three of the finalists for the position withdrew their applications at various stages of the interview process and a fourth was eliminated when members of the WAC search committee decided that "... his personality would not be a good fit in the community." The first candidate brought in was one of those who later withdrew. He stated that he did so because of time lags in the interview process during which he received no information, and because he received no closure from the search committee.

Finally, in November 1998, after nearly one year and with no other candidates remaining from the original pool of applicants, the Board's executive committee unanimously endorsed Anita Scism to become the new President and CEO of the Walton Arts Center. The Board itself concurred (also unanimously). Speaking at a local press conference, the Chairperson of the Board supported Scism's appointment: "She has seen the tremendous changes that have come to our region and she knows how to take advantage of those opportunities. Her collaborations in the business and education community make her an ideal ambassador for the center."

In Scism's comments to those attending the announcement of her appointment she asked the Board, Center staff members, and others in attendance for their input as she formulated her vision for the Center's future. From West Virginia, Mitchell expressed his pleasure and excitement for Scism, "It's an absolute delight to know that her leadership and talents have been recognized and will be supported. Her vision will pick up where mine left off."

# A-4 A New Management Team

The Walton Arts Center's management team experienced a number of changes between September 1997 and December 1998 (see Exhibits 2A and 2B for the organization charts before and after the changes). Anita Scism made most of these changes and as a result was leading a team that she had created. One exception, Sonny Hildebrand, was appointed by Mitchell to fill the position of Vice President for Development shortly before Mitchell's departure. Hildebrand had a sales background and extensive community contacts. The position had been vacant for much of the last year of Mitchell's tenure due to financial constraints. Just prior to his departure, Mitchell also hired Tracy Dickson, a C.P.A. with four years accounting experience. Dickson filled a newly created position of Comptroller. Sue Jones-Cearley, the original Vice President of Marketing and Public Relations, resigned in early 1998, and that position was eliminated. Scism hired Terri Trotter to fill another newly created position, Vice President of Communications. Terri reported directly to the Senior Vice President of Programs; her primary responsibilities included developing information and promotions for Center performances. She also managed promotions, advertising, patron services and public relations. Terri graduated with a master's degree in telecommunications from Indiana University in 1993 and subsequently held positions as Promotion Director of two radio stations and Director of Marketing for a special events production company.

Jenni Taylor Swain, the only remaining member of Mitchell's management team other than Scism, had served as Vice President of Education for the Center since her graduation from the University of Arkansas with a Master's of Fine Arts degree. When Jones-Cearley left, Scism assigned responsibility for both education and marketing to Taylor Swain and promoted her to Senior Vice President of Programs. The Vice President of Communications, the Visual Arts Manager, and two Education Managers re-

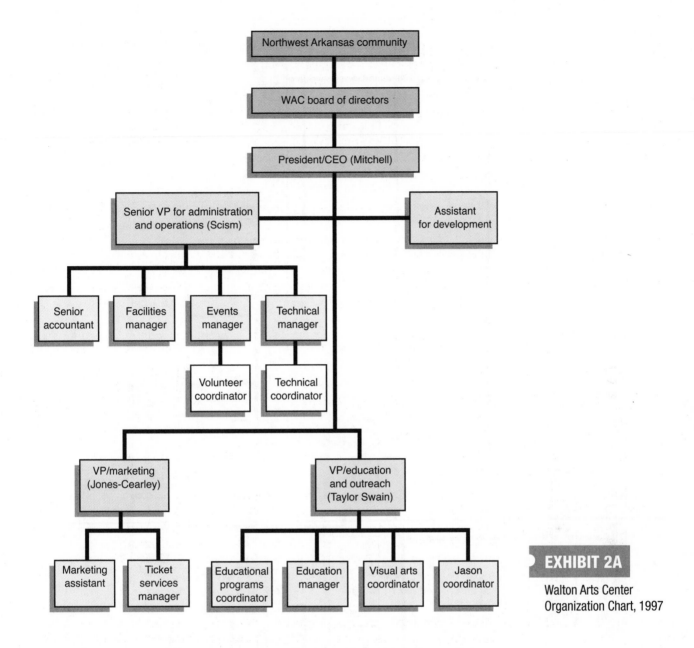

Walton Arts Center
Organization Chart, 1997

ported directly to her. This change accomplished some financial savings by reducing the number of Vice Presidents. In addition to the promotion, Scism assigned Taylor Swain primary responsibility for events programming, a function personally performed by Bill Mitchell before he resigned. Scism explained why she delegated this important responsibility despite Taylor Swain's lack of experience in either marketing or performance programming, "It takes so much time to negotiate, schedule, and handle arrangements for performances. I just felt I needed that time for overall management of the Center."

The WAC Board of Directors was also changing. Cynthia Coughlin, wife of a senior Wal-Mart executive, became the first Chairperson from outside Fayetteville. She replaced James Stobaugh, President of a local Fayetteville bank. Coughlin resided in Bentonville, a community some 25 miles north of Fayetteville and headquarters to Wal-Mart Stores, Inc. She had served as a Board member for six years and had actively supported extending Center activities to regional communities outside of Fayetteville. Board members served three-year terms and could only be reappointed twice,

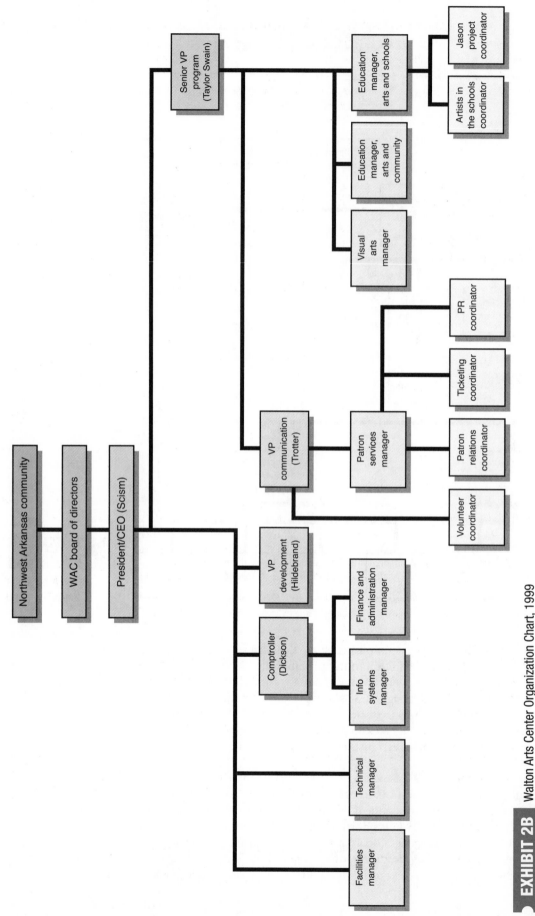

**EXHIBIT 2B** Walton Arts Center Organization Chart, 1999

thereby serving up to nine years on the Board. The remaining original Board members, most of whom were very active and influential in WAC activities, were scheduled to complete their ninth year of service in 1999. With several new Board members to be appointed then, the Board's approach to oversight and decisions after that was uncertain.

# A-5 Center Finances

## A-5a Contributions

The financial situation for the Center had improved in some respects over the past two years. Two large contributions by Northwest Arkansas families, who were already Center benefactors, increased the Center's endowment funds and further supported its educational activities. Because of a special interest in education, one of the families earmarked its contribution for the Baum Learning Center, a 17,000-square foot facility previously acquired by the WAC for hands-on education of arts such as pottery, photography, theater, music, painting, and drawing. Renovation of the Learning Center building to prepare it for WAC usage had been halted in late 1996 due to a lack of funds, and the contribution allowed construction to be resumed. Scism hired an Education Manager for the Learning Center and hoped to open it soon, although there was not yet enough money to furnish it. A limited number of classes were offered temporarily in other facilities pending completion of the Baum Learning Center. The new Education Manager explained how the Learning Center would contribute to WAC's educational mission: "We will be able to broaden what we offer because people can get dirty and use messy material and have a proper art-making space."

## A-5b Endowments

Significant increases in the value of endowment investments, primarily because of stock value appreciation, accelerated the growth of the WAC's endowment funds during 1997 and 1998. As reflected by the Statement of Financial Position at June 30, 1998 (Exhibit 3), the value of these restricted funds increased to over twelve million dollars—from just over eight million dollars two years earlier. Although the principal of the endowment funds could not be spent by the Center, the increased endowment indirectly created more financial stability in the Center operations. The WAC Foundation, governed by an independent Board, supplemented the budgeted transfer of endowment earnings to Center operations with a special "one-time" transfer of approximately $75,000. The Foundation authorized the special transfer in order to provide badly needed working capital and financial stability for the Center. That transfer enabled the staff to lessen its preoccupation with day-to-day financial problems. The Foundation also paid directly for new Center equipment totaling over $200,000.

## A-5c Sponsorships

Approximately seventy sponsors, primarily businesses, banks, and a considerable number of Wal-Mart vendors, provided significant funding for specific WAC events and programs. The area media also provided increasing amounts of in-kind marketing services in order to publicize WAC performances. One of the sponsors expressed his company's reason for financially supporting the WAC:

> The Walton Arts Center has dramatically improved the quality of life for families in
> Northwest Arkansas by bringing additional opportunities for cultural experiences
> and education for all people in our community. . . . We at Pace Industries believe

> **EXHIBIT 3** Walton Arts Center Statement of Financial Position—June 30, 1998

| | Total | Unrestricted | Temporarily Restricted | Permanently Restricted |
|---|---|---|---|---|
| **Assets** | | | | |
| Cash | $ 1,151,084.45 | $ 513,845.67 | $ 637,238.78 | $ — |
| Investments | 11,543,545.60 | — | 3,213,545.60 | 8,330,000.00 |
| Accounts receivable | 41,982.11 | 36,670.77 | 5,311.34 | — |
| Prepaid expenses | 11,295.50 | 11,295.50 | — | — |
| Unconditional promises to give | 391,311.22 | — | 391,311.22 | — |
| Deposits | 448.00 | 448.00 | — | — |
| Property and equipment, net | 1,679,545.13 | 1,679,545.13 | — | — |
| Leasehold improvements, net | 3,344,524.18 | 3,344,524.18 | — | — |
| Total assets | $ 18,163,736.19 | $ 5,586,329.25 | $ 4,247,406.94 | $ 8,330,000.00 |
| **Liabilities and Net Assets** | | | | |
| Accounts payable | $ 162,793.11 | $ 162,793.11 | $ — | $ — |
| Wage payable | 310.38 | 310.38 | — | — |
| Deferred revenue-ticket sales | 581,834.62 | 581,834.62 | — | — |
| Total liabilities | 744,938.11 | 744,938.11 | — | — |
| **Net Assets** | | | | |
| Unrestricted | 4,841,391.14 | 4,841,391.14 | — | — |
| Temporarily restricted | 4,247,406.94 | — | 4,247,406.94 | — |
| Permanently restricted | 8,330,000.00 | — | — | 8,330,000.00 |
| Total net assets | 17,418,798.08 | 4,841,391.14 | 4,247,406.94 | 8,330,000.00 |
| Total liabilities and net assets | $ 18,163,736.19 | $ 5,586,329.25 | $ 4,247,406.94 | $ 8,330,000.00 |

that we should support any organization that has such a positive impact on the quality of life in our community.

Other sponsors cited the importance of the WAC's cultural leadership in recruiting top-quality employees for their companies from a nationally competitive market.

### A-5d A Profitable Year

The Statement of Activities (Exhibit 4) showed an increase in unrestricted net assets (a rough equivalent to profit) of $95,724 for the fiscal year ended June 30, 1998. Revenue from sponsorships more than doubled over the previous year to $369,302, although the increase was primarily in-kind marketing services with offsetting marketing expenses. Ticket sales increased by nearly $280,000 over the previous year. Grants, rentals, and class fees also increased. Altogether, operating revenues increased 25% over the previous year, continuing the growth experienced by the Center since its beginning. Since WAC's fiscal year corresponded with the season performance schedule, most of the revenue increases resulted from plans formulated and programs developed prior to Mitchell's departure.

Several expenses increased along with the additional revenues. For example, artist fees and faculty fees rose with ticket sales (see Exhibit 5 on page 210 for the Statement of Functional Expenses). Salaries increased by $100,000, including a $30,000 bonus authorized by the Board for the employees, partially as a reward for the prior year's "profit." Before the bonuses and salary increases, several employees were paid below the bottom limit of pay ranges that had been set two years earlier. First to be

| EXHIBIT 4 | Walton Arts Center Statement of Activities Year Ended June 30, 1998 |

|  | Total | Unrestricted | Temporarily Restricted | Permanently Restricted |
|---|---|---|---|---|
| **Revenues** | | | | |
| Contributions | $  3,160,741.42 | $   165,643.49 | $   695,097.93 | $ 2,300,000.00 |
| Sponsorships | 369,302.00 | 369,302.00 | — | — |
| Ticket sales | 942,826.00 | 942,826.00 | — | — |
| Ticket services and handling fees | 43,922.41 | 43,922.41 | — | — |
| Class fees | 182,210.16 | 182,210.16 | — | — |
| Concessions | 19,998.48 | 19,998.48 | — | — |
| Rentals | 181,548.72 | 181,548.72 | — | — |
| Grants | 445,368.88 | 445,368.88 | — | — |
| Advertising | 49,050.00 | 49,050.00 | — | — |
| Technical services | 30,691.08 | 30,691.08 | — | — |
| Other income | 36,372.98 | 35,938.94 | 434.04 | — |
| Investment income | 514,981.33 | 13,207.53 | 501,773.80 | — |
| Gains (losses) on investment sales | 2,584,181.23 | — | 2,584,181.23 | — |
| Unrealized gains (losses) | (1,372,944.12) | — | (1,372,944.12) | — |
| Net assets released from restrictions | — | 633,880.08 | (633,880.08) | — |
| Total revenue | 7,188,250.57 | 3,113,587.77 | 1,774,662.80 | 2,300,000.00 |
| Expenses | | | | |
| Program services | 1,424,958.00 | 1,424,958.00 | — | — |
| General and administrative | 1,570,870.42 | 1,570,870.42 | — | — |
| Fund raising | 15,813.67 | 15,813.67 | — | — |
| Loss on disposition of equipment | 6,221.33 | 6,221.33 | — | — |
| Total expenses | 3,017,863.42 | 3,017,863.42 | — | — |
| Increase (decrease) in net assets | 4,170,387.15 | 95,724.35 | 1,774,662.80 | 2,300,000.00 |
| Net assets at beginning of year | 13,248,410.93 | 4,745,666.79 | 2,472,744.14 | 6,030,000.00 |
| Net assets at end of year | $ 17,418,798.08 | $4,841,391.14 | $4,247,406.94 | $ 8,330,000.00 |

upgraded were the salaries of vice presidents where the largest gaps were apparent; however, others also received pay increases. Though some complained that the raises were long overdue, most employees welcomed the attempt to at least bring salaries up to the lower ends of those ranges. The search for a new President also contributed to increased expenses during the period. Overall, expenses for the year ended June 30, 1998 increased by about 25% over the previous year's expenses.

# A-6 The Downturn

The monthly internal financial reports for the first six months of the June 30, 1999 fiscal year, however, showed a different picture from the success of the preceding year (see Exhibit 6 on page 211 for the Summary Budget to Actual, prepared on a cash basis). As of December 31, 1998, several revenue sources were significantly below budgeted expectations, particularly sponsorships, class fees, grants, and contributions. Even though revenues still exceeded expenses by $179,281, that "profit" was inflated by the full season ticket sales being included in revenue (cash basis)

## EXHIBIT 5 | Walton Arts Center Statement of Functional Expenses Year Ended June 30, 1998

| | Program | General and Administrative | Fund-Raising | Total |
|---|---|---|---|---|
| Artist fees | $ 740,339.16 | $ — | $ — | $ 740,339.16 |
| Licenses | 585.00 | 522.10 | 270.00 | 1,377.10 |
| Software rental and licenses | — | 2,561.63 | — | 2,561.65 |
| Bad debt expense | 1,400.00 | 14,900.00 | — | 16,300.00 |
| Faculty fees | 58,604.70 | — | — | 58,604.70 |
| Bank charges | 25,849.95 | 61.16 | — | 25,911.11 |
| Investment fees | — | 55,481.90 | — | 55,481.90 |
| Insurance | — | 22,151.50 | — | 22,151.50 |
| Equipment rental | 2,650.00 | 99.68 | 1,051.20 | 3,800.88 |
| Repairs and maintenance | 9,586.55 | 46,959.45 | — | 56,546.00 |
| Landscaping | — | 14,843.55 | — | 14,843.55 |
| Depreciation | — | 167,759.31 | — | 167,759.31 |
| Miscellaneous | — | 1,989.00 | — | 1,989.00 |
| Special events | 7,301.37 | 11.19 | 3,780.92 | 11,093.48 |
| Marketing | 271,778.47 | 3,648.30 | 8,116.48 | 283,543.23 |
| Meetings | 56.22 | 998.60 | 13.95 | 1,068.77 |
| Postage | 13,072.19 | 10,899.80 | 330.00 | 24,301.99 |
| Supplies and stationery | 30,227.96 | 54,651.84 | 1,366.23 | 86,296.03 |
| Printing and copies | 121,163.47 | 3,983.42 | 575.31 | 125,722.20 |
| Telephone | — | 15,333.65 | — | 15,333.65 |
| Utilities | — | 124,259.58 | — | 124,259.58 |
| Contractual services | 81,782.44 | 46,677.72 | 44.94 | 128,505.10 |
| Service contracts | — | 26,646.65 | — | 26,646.65 |
| Sponsorship allowance | 6,970.24 | — | 208.32 | 7,178.56 |
| Volunteers | 1,547.66 | — | — | 1,547.66 |
| Transportation | 20,000.00 | — | — | 20,000.00 |
| Travel | 22,313.79 | 25,296.11 | 56.34 | 47,666.24 |
| Shipping | 4,510.83 | — | — | 4,510.83 |
| Ticket program | 4,473.00 | — | — | 4,473.00 |
| Property taxes | — | 4,270.21 | — | 4,240.21 |
| Legal | — | 235.00 | — | 235.00 |
| Accounting | — | 10,500.00 | — | 10,500.00 |
| Other consultants | — | 38,178.70 | — | 38,178.70 |
| Staff training | 695.00 | 10,877.71 | — | 11,572.71 |
| Dues and subscriptions | — | 2,311.14 | — | 2,311.14 |
| Publications | — | 1,301.35 | — | 1,301.35 |
| Training | — | 1,551.00 | — | 1,551.00 |
| Salaries | — | 631,666.27 | — | 631,666.27 |
| Payroll tax expense | — | 56,620.08 | — | 56,620.08 |
| Employee benefits | — | 63,454.94 | — | 63,454.94 |
| Temporary employees | — | 110,167.96 | — | 110,167.83 |
| Total | $ 1,424,958.00 | $ 1,570,870.42 | $ 15,813.67 | $ 3,011,642.09 |

while a large portion of accompanying expenses were not to be paid until after the performances in the last half of the fiscal year. Endowment transfers had also been advanced in order to provide additional working capital. Unless revenues increased in the last half of the year, there would clearly be a significant operating deficit at the end of the year. Since the local economy continued its strong growth pattern, Scism

| EXHIBIT 6 | Walton Arts Center Summary Budget to Actual—July 1, 1998 to December 31, 1998 |
| --- | --- |

| | FY99 Budget | YTD Budget | YTD Actual | % of Total Budget | FY98 Actual | FY97 Actual |
| --- | --- | --- | --- | --- | --- | --- |
| **Revenues** | | | | | | |
| Education Endowment | 39,000 | 39,000 | 39,000 | 100% | — | — |
| Operations Endowment | 181,000 | 60,000 | 60,000 | 33% | 165,000 | 163,000 |
| Long-Term Maintenance | 84,000 | 60,000 | 78,228 | 93% | 88,623 | 97,906 |
| Maintenance Endow | 88,000 | 88,000 | 88,000 | 100% | 61,000 | 59,000 |
| Contributions—Member | 171,100 | 72,600 | 53,259 | 31% | 140,951 | 169,267 |
| Special Events | — | — | — | | 50,627 | — |
| Sponsorships | 324,200 | 144,200 | 73,350 | 23% | 147,723 | 166,535 |
| Sponsors-In-Kind | 192,000 | 84,750 | 40,604 | 21% | 213,460 | — |
| BLC Class Fees | 42,220 | 20,120 | 16,406 | 39% | 26,736 | — |
| Class Fees/Registrations | 201,000 | 73,000 | 60,432 | 30% | 155,474 | 170,462 |
| Ticket Sales | 798,680 | 640,000 | 650,777 | 81% | 941,127 | 653,376 |
| Incentive Ticket Sales | 11,420 | 9,000 | 5,248 | 46% | — | — |
| Sponsor Ticket Sales | 35,070 | 30,000 | 27,270 | 78% | — | — |
| Ticket Services | 47,000 | 20,000 | 22,590 | 48% | 50,011 | 39,641 |
| Interest | 7,000 | 3,600 | 6,747 | 96% | 13,208 | 2,359 |
| Concessions | 18,000 | 9,000 | 12,179 | 68% | 19,998 | 16,430 |
| Event Rentals | 127,850 | 69,500 | 78,509 | 61% | 1784,509 | 166,594 |
| Leases | 45,520 | 2,800 | 21,886 | 48% | — | — |
| Grants | 384,065 | 118,532 | 96,044 | 25% | 454,144 | 346,895 |
| Other Income | 120,198 | 77,758 | 128,234 | 107% | 49,023 | 72,978 |
| Technical | 17,000 | 8,820 | 9,225 | 54% | 30,691 | 14,469 |
| Arts Partners | 20,000 | 20,000 | 21,735 | 109% | 20,645 | 20,145 |
| Program Advertising | 54,000 | 35,400 | 34,886 | 65% | 49,050 | 47,325 |
| **Total Revenues** | 3,008,323 | 1,706,080 | 1,626,610 | 54% | 2,862,000 | 2,206,382 |

| **Expenses** | FY99 Budget | YTD Budget | YTD Actual | % of Total Budget | FY98 Actual | FY97 Actual |
| --- | --- | --- | --- | --- | --- | --- |
| Program | 1,274,950 | 640,817 | 707,874 | 56% | 1,176,954 | 954,548 |
| Administrative | 346,637 | 190,685 | 180,783 | 52% | 364,345 | 320,288 |
| Personnel | 1,053,183 | 526,292 | 454,808 | 43% | 861,909 | 755,625 |
| Professional Services | 60,045 | 26,045 | 29,713 | 49% | 86,146 | 28,062 |
| In-Kind Marketing | 192,000 | 84,750 | 38,214 | 20% | 215,440 | — |
| **Total Expenses** | 2,926,815 | 1,468,889 | 1,411,392 | 48% | 2,704,794 | 2,058,523 |
| Capital | 26,700 | 26,700 | 35,937 | 135% | 129,784 | 37,947 |
| Contingency | 54,808 | — | | 0% | — | — |
| **Total Expenses and Capital** | 3,008,323 | 1,495,589 | 1,477,329 | 48% | 2,834,578 | 2,096,470 |
| Excess Revenue over Expense | — | 210,492 | 179,281 | | 27,422 | 109,912 |

believed that the deficit could be avoided, partially because commitments for funds not yet received covered some of the differences between actual and budgeted revenues.

Scism also reduced the staff in order to cut expenses. Scism set an example for everyone by pitching in to do whatever was needed. Taylor Swain told of one incident: "I was driving by the arts center one day and I saw her out mowing the lawn. I said, 'What is she doing now? That's Anita out there!'" The administrative and personnel expense reductions are reflected in the difference between the 1999 YTD Budget and YTD Actual (Exhibit 6). ("FY98 Actual" amounts in Exhibit 6 varied somewhat from the "Unrestricted" amounts in the audited Statement of Activities in Exhibit 4;

these variations were due primarily to the differences between cash and accrual bases, to adjustments and reclassifications made by the auditors, and to differences in Exhibit 2 the way that Foundation transfers to the Center were recorded.)

## A-7 Events Programming

Performing arts events received the greatest attention among the various Center activities. Bill Mitchell personally selected most programs while he was President. Anita Scism assigned this responsibility to the Senior Vice President of Programs, Taylor Swain, after Mitchell left.

The WAC's most loyal patrons were primarily motivated to support programs that reflected their love of the arts and those programs that stimulated artistic talents and interests in others. These individuals came primarily from the university faculty and the business and professional community. A recent survey found that more than 60% of the Broadway Series patrons had a college degree or higher educational level.

## A-8 Programming Criteria

Scism described the criteria used in programming decisions: "Prime concerns for any program are 'Does this program fit into what we are trying to do or say at the Walton Arts Center? Does the performance have integrity? What horizon are we hoping to expand or broaden for our audiences?' Artistic vision leads most programming decisions."

One of the Board members explained his personal priority for the WAC:

One of the challenges in the future is to constantly revise the programming to reflect current interests and keep the blend vital. There are audiences out there we have yet to discover and we won't until we offer something that attracts their attention. But at the same time, we have to offer the things that keep our current audiences coming back.

Scism described the important role of education in programming decisions: "Since our inception, the key component to our mission at the Walton Arts Center is education." University faculty members and Helen Walton, matriarch of the Walton family, especially promoted the educational merits of programming, which in turn influenced the selection of programs. Programs catering to school children received high priority attention, and the presentation of these programs for student groups brought over 60,000 children to the Center each year. The opening of the Nadine Baum Learning Center and sponsoring of six-week residencies for artists in local schools were expected to further expand the educational programs of the WAC. Also, statewide delivery of selected arts education programs, utilizing the university's technology, had been discussed. In addition to its arts education activities, the Center was the only arts-based center in the nation to provide an interactive site for the JASON Project, a technology-based science education experience for students.

## A-9 Program Results

The Center budgeted for each performance event's ticket sales and subsequently collected information about ticket sales, corporate sponsorships, and artist fees for each event. The data allowed a computation of what was termed "net income" (revenues minus artist fees) as well as a comparison of ticket sales to budget for each event. This information was provided to the management team each month.

Of the twenty-six events presented, six plays drove the very successful 1997–1998 ticket sales. These plays collectively accounted for 76% of the Center's ticket sales for the year's twenty-six events, and approximately $370,000 revenues (including sponsorships) in excess of artist fees. Each play produced ticket sales of more than $100,000, and nearly all performances were sold out. Of $200,000 sponsorships that could be identified with specific events, the six plays collectively generated half of that revenue. The plays included *A Chorus Line, To Kill a Mockingbird, Joseph and the Amazing Technicolor Dream Coat, Damn Yankees, Carousel,* and *West Side Story.* All six plays were very profitable, especially the first three. *A Tuna Christmas,* The New York City Opera, The Coasters/Drifters/Platters, and The Kingston Trio also were profitable, collectively selling $116,000 of tickets and $47,000 of sponsorships, with $108,000 of artist fees. Revenues from four other events collectively exceeded the associated artist fees by approximately $17,000. In contrast, artist fees for the other twelve events collectively exceeded the revenues they generated by $40,000 and also produced ticket sales far below budget. Artist fees for The Kadinsky Trio, Dorsey/Jones, Street Sounds, and Ballet Florida exceeded not only the actual revenues for each event but also the budgeted revenues.

Jenni Taylor Swain explained why some shows lose money: "Not all of our shows make money, so to speak, so they are subsidized by contributions from sponsors and by revenues brought in by the more popular shows. Because they fulfill part of our artistic mission, it's important for us to bring those in."

The former Vice President for Marketing expressed another viewpoint prior to leaving: "Education is our number one priority. . . . Some of our performances are brought in for education and they just won't sell . . . I mean, a Brazilian flute player just won't pay his own way. I think Education is kind of out there on its own."

Programs anticipated to generate the greatest revenues during the 1998–1999 performance season included: *The King and I, Spirit of the Dance, A Funny Thing Happened on the Way to the Forum, Fiddler on the Roof,* and *Idols of the King.* Most tickets for these performances were priced in the $24–$28 range. All of the plays presented before December 31, 1998 (the others were to be presented during the Spring) were financially successful. In addition, *STOMP* (a popular, non-traditional percussion performance) was presented under a special revenue-sharing arrangement with the producers, and it generated as much profit as most of the other Broadway events. A comparison of 1998–1999 total ticket sales to the previous year showed a decrease, although this was somewhat misleading since *STOMP* tickets were not included in the current year's sales. (Net profit from *STOMP* is shown in "Other Income" because of the percentage split structure of that contract.) Five other events during the first part of the season showed losses, and approximately half of all the programs fell short of budgeted ticket sales by 10% or more. Diavolo, a dance troupe scheduled the Saturday after Thanksgiving, produced the largest single loss when only 87 seats were sold for the event. For the first six months of the 1998–1999 fiscal years, sponsorships were down and direct expenses were up from comparable events during the previous year. Lack of sponsor support also forced a reduction in the number of "golden-oldies" concerts from three presented in recent years to only two (Don McLean and The Temptations) scheduled in the Spring of 1999.

# A-10 Looking Ahead

Anita Scism considered the Center's status in early 1999:

> The best part of my job is all the fun and creativity. I'm still as excited and committed as the day I got the job. I believe that the organization is stronger as a result of staff restructuring and management team appointments. I also believe that my style of delegating authority to the staff and building teamwork has been effective through the transition.

Asked about the development of her vision for WAC, she said: "It hasn't been forgotten, but the past three months have been so hectic that I had to delay it. It's on the floor, literally," she noted with a smile as she pointed to a stack of papers on the floor, "but I know it should include more event partnerships with arts groups in our community and at the University. The possibilities seem endless when I consider all their talent and enthusiasm." Reflecting on her experience as President, she said:

> There's just so much to do that it is exhausting. With the staff cutbacks on top of everything else, I just haven't had enough time. I haven't got out and joined the Chamber of Commerce or made many new business contacts, but I've felt accepted by most of the people I have come into contact with. I guess there's a natural transition of following Mitch and building credibility in the business community by any new person, and maybe particularly a woman for some people.

Scism was also concerned about a proposed 700 to 1,500 seat performing arts center, projected to cost up to $15,500,000, to be located in Bella Vista and operated by a newly formed arts organization. Bella Vista was a community just north of Bentonville, headquarters for Wal-Mart Stores, Inc., and home to a number of Wal-Mart managers and executives. One of the supporters of the proposed center said: "We want this arts center to be accessible to the whole area. It's definitely not just a Bella Vista thing. We're hoping to kick off the fund raising drive soon."

# AstroTech Fuel Systems

## Case B

H. Richard Eisenbeis
Sue Hanks
Phil Sheehan*

*Source:* Reprinted by permission from the *Case Research Journal.* Copyright 2001 by H. Richard Eisenbeis, Sue Hanks, and Phil Sheehan, and the North American Case Research Association. All rights reserved.

*Author affiliations: H. Richard Eisenbeis, Colorado State University, Pueblo; Sue Hanks, Colorado State University, Pueblo; Phil Sheehan, Colorado State University, Pueblo.

# B-1 AstroTech Fuel Systems—Part A

Shortly after responsibility for completion of AstroTech's AutoFlow project had been removed from under Jim McGee's direction, the staff at the Fuel Systems division was informed that Roger Banter, the absentee General Manager of the Fuel Systems Division, would make one of his rare visits to the Texas facility. Jim anticipated that Banter's visit was to propose that the heavy focus currently placed on Engineering should now be shifted to Marketing. But, during his visit and much to Jim's surprise, Banter made it a point to visit privately with him. As usual, Banter wasted no time on trivialities:

> Jim, I've discussed your situation with Corporate Headquarters and suggest you call your previous boss about the possibility of a transfer back to your old job in Utah. You've not yet gotten a black eye in the company; but I'm concerned that if you stay here any longer, you will. Otherwise, any potential you might have for a promising career in this organization could very well be nothing more than wishful thinking.

As Banter stood and prepared to leave, Jim said:

> Wait a minute! I feel I've made significant improvements to the engineering and quality systems here. I've developed a number of new products, increased the department's capability level and brought many of our poorly designed products up to specifications. I'd like to know what it is that I've done wrong. I've invested a lot of energy here. Although I admit I've not gotten along well with the staff even though I've tried. I like it here and would like to stay.

Banter hesitated for a second, turned, and said:

> After all this is settled, you and I will sit down and talk, even if I have to come to Utah to do it.

Banter quickly exited, and Jim was left alone in his office in a state of confusion and astonishment. Jim believed that he had always been good about recognizing his own mistakes and weaknesses and being able to accept the truth. But, he found it extremely difficult to accept blame for things he didn't believe he was guilty of. Many thoughts raced through his mind as he considered his next move.

## B-1a AstroTech and the Fuel Systems Division

AstroTech, one of the United States' foremost and largest corporations, was involved in virtually all facets of manufacturing auxiliary equipment for the aerospace and airline industries. During the decade of the 1990s, annual revenues for the corporation exceeded $4 billion. Although in a "cutting edge" industry, the organization had tended to conform most closely to the divisionalized bureaucratic structure (Exhibit 1); however, it seemed to be transitioning toward a more organic structure.

The Fuel Systems product line had been acquired by AstroTech three years previously from a small, independent manufacturer of fuel systems serving the aeronautical industry. AstroTech's stated objective for this new division, consisting of 60 employees, was that it was a first step toward becoming the major supplier of aircraft fuel systems for the aerospace and aircraft industry. Although most of the original rank and file employees were retained, Fuel Systems management was replaced by AstroTech personnel immediately upon acquisition. New and old employees alike believed that because of the facility's location and the generous salary and benefit packages that "this is the closest we'll ever get to living in paradise." They were all committed to seeing that the undertaking become a profitable and permanent facility within AstroTech.

During its three years as a division of AstroTech, Fuel Systems had generated between $6 and $8 million in revenues annually. When compared to other units within the corporation—the smallest of which generated over $200 million in revenues

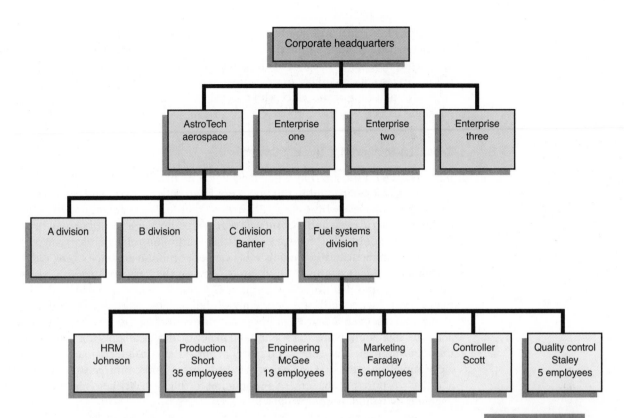

**EXHIBIT 1**

Organizational Chart before
Phalen's Departure from the
Fuel Systems Division

annually—some thought it a stretch of the imagination to assign Fuel Systems "division" status. Instead, they thought it should have been designated as a product line attached to one of the other divisions. Whereas top-of-the-line products manufactured by Fuel Systems sold in the range of $6,000/unit, more sophisticated, state-of-the-art units manufactured by competitors ranged from $10,000 to $60,000/unit. But, because Fuel Systems' product line was unique to AstroTech and because it was perceived as having substantial long-range growth and profit potential, the unit was separated from the rest of the corporation and accorded divisional status. A downside to this was that because it represented a relatively small investment compared to other divisions, Fuel Systems received only minimal oversight from corporate headquarters.

### B-1b  Jim McGee and AstroTech

Jim had begun his career with AstroTech Corporation at AstroTech's Composite Systems Division in Utah. Years of dedication and hard work earned him the challenging and satisfying position of Manager of Engineering and Quality. Although he was viewed by most as being a task master, he was respected for soliciting input from colleagues and subordinates before making decisions that would affect their welfare. Given his success in the Composite Systems Division, it came as no surprise to others when was Jim selected by the Corporation's Human Resource Department in conjunction with the corporate Vice-President of Technology to head the Engineering Department of the Fuel Systems Division. Jim welcomed his promotion and new responsibilities and was assured that he would play a key role in the success of the operation. Although he had been with AstroTech for ten years and had advanced rapidly in the corporation, unbeknownst to Jim, he was not in the least prepared for the challenges he would face and the compromises that would have to be made if he were to survive in his new position and in the corporate arena.

Prior to this most recent promotion, Jim's career with AstroTech had been marked by a continuous stream of accomplishments and promotions in Utah and at a previous assignment in Virginia. Although most of his experience was in mechanical and materials engineering, he had acquired a solid foundation in aerospace-related engineering and quality systems applicable to electronics-dominated fuel systems. Jim prided himself on his tenacity, his ability to motivate and his ability to resolve complex problems. He was optimistic that the successful completion of this assignment would further enhance his career with the corporation.

### B-1c  The Concern for Quality Control

Jim had been on the job only a few days when he became painfully aware that interpersonal relationships within the unit were far from what had been conveyed to him during his interview with George Phalen, the division's president. Jim knew that the division was struggling and that he was part of a team charged with turning it around, but he was astonished at the extent of quality control improvements that would have to be made immediately if the unit was to meet corporate goals. Not only did he find that many of Fuel Systems product lines were on the verge of becoming obsolete, but he also found that none of them met FAA specifications. Records indicated that the previous owner had almost certainly altered data to pass FAA inspections.

Jim also discovered that Phalen was far more interested in increasing unit output and sales than identifying and solving the major quality problems that had come with the acquisition. He was convinced that if major system design changes were not initiated immediately, the division's works-in-progress would continue to be substandard and that Corporate management's reputation for high quality aerospace systems and engineering would be compromised.

Jim was concerned that Phalen minimized the importance of the need for upgrading these systems. It appeared to Jim that many at AstroTech ignored the fact that the division could be fined and/or shut down if its internal quality control systems did not comply with FAA regulations and that individuals could even be imprisoned for severe infractions. Mindful of the magnitude of the issues involved, Jim knew he could help the fledgling business meet quality expectations if he could somehow get through to Phalen that the current quality control systems were substandard. Jim also realized that he needed to do this without creating negative publicity for the corporation or without ruffling Phalen's feathers.

During the first few weeks on the job, Jim assessed the strengths and weaknesses of the division's quality control systems until he was sure of what needed to be done to meet quality standards. Shortly thereafter, at a bimonthly staff meeting, Jim attempted to offer suggestions on how to improve the division's control systems but was quickly cut off by Phalen's comment:

> Don't waste your time on that; what we need here are new products. That's why we brought you in, and that's what you need to focus on.

Phalen then went on to describe how he and the Director of Operations, Ben Short, had "whipped the Engineering Department into shape" during the three months the department operated without a manager prior to Jim's arrival. Both Phalen and Short stated that before they became personally involved, the Engineering Department personnel "were poorly managed and sloughed off."

### B-1d  George Phalen

George Phalen had been employed by AstroTech about five years prior to the Fuel Systems acquisition. He had been hired at the corporate level and was reputed to have had close ties with one of the corporate Vice Presidents. Phalen had risen very quickly within the firm and left no doubts of his desire to someday manage at the corporate level. Upon being chosen to manage the Fuel Systems division immediately after it was acquired, he saw this as a major opportunity to favorably impress managers at the top level of the organization. Because Fuel Systems was out of the mainstream of the organization and received little or no oversight from corporate headquarters, Phalen was able to manage with minimal accountability. From the onset, he appeared to have become obsessed with power. He ran a tight ship and insisted that tasks be completed immediately and be done his way regardless of subordinate suggestions or company policy. The fact that Phalen consistently overestimated sales projections contributed substantially to an ongoing pressure situation for the unit. In addition, Phalen had had no experience in dealing with the FAA. However, away from the plant, he was described as being very likeable and sociable, and a good family man and neighbor.

### B-1e Ben Short

Short was a long-time employee with the organization and was considered by upper management to be an excellent production manager. He was transferred from another division to Fuel Systems to head up production immediately after Fuel Systems had been acquired by the parent organization. Short was looked upon as a "pure operations person," that is, highly production oriented and "one who got things done." He was extremely loyal and dedicated toward achieving the new division's goals and objectives. Short was described by others in the plant as "being so firmly anchored as to be able to withstand a tornado."

Short made it clear to Jim that he believed engineers needed to be ridden hard to get results; and if they couldn't or wouldn't perform, they should be fired. He said:

> After all, the success of this business depends upon quick sales. We don't have time to baby people. There are lots more engineers out there where these guys came from. You design the products and I'll build them; it's that simple. We straightened everything out for you before you got here, so stay on top of those guys or you'll lose the momentum. You have to show them who's boss, or they'll walk all over you.

Jim was taken aback by Phalen's and Short's comments concerning his department's priorities and how to motivate engineering personnel. In addition, he noticed that on occasion Short was extremely gruff and aggressive with production workers. This was not a good sign in light of the fact that personnel from Engineering would be required to work closely with Production. The production departments with which Jim had been associated elsewhere in AstroTech were very professional and collegial, as well as productive. He was certain that his engineers would resign should they be subjected to Short's harsh leadership, and he knew that he couldn't afford to lose the few engineers he had.

### B-1f Fuel Systems Engineering Department

In analyzing the situation, Jim asked engineering personnel about how the unit functioned prior to his arrival. He learned that he was the fourth Engineering Manager since AstroTech purchased the business three years earlier. Although it concerned Jim that two of the previous engineering managers had had successful careers with AstroTech until joining the division, he remained optimistic that he would be successful. He thought:

> After all, since I've been able to overcome some major obstacles in two larger divisions, I should be able to do the same in this, the smallest division.

Jim was particularly concerned about the lack of depth of his technical staff. While they were very dedicated, only 3 of the 13 members possessed engineering degrees. In addition, the group was currently in the process of developing or modifying over 20 products, a ratio deemed "aggressive" in any business. Also, given the limited resources at his disposal, Jim was convinced that Phalen and Short's emphasis on high volume production would result in the division's demise. His most pressing concern, the lack of the highest level of quality control systems, intensified his resolve to improve them.

As he became more familiar with the existing systems, Jim realized the magnitude of the task before him. The previous owner had run the business as a "garage shop" with very few formal control systems and had done little to train his people in FAA or aerospace regulations. In further discussions with Phalen and Short, it became evident to Jim that only he understood the full impact of noncompliance with these regulations. He found it ironic that although Phalen and Short had created an overwhelming myriad of development programs during their brief, but "successful," stint in engineering, they had little knowledge of the level of work required to develop and qualify highly technical products that would meet stringent FAA regulations and customer expectations.

As weeks grew into months, Jim attempted to simultaneously keep up with new product development and the improvement of system quality processes. In addition, he devoted considerable time to addressing problems associated with existing product lines. Several of these designs failed to meet specifications and mandated immediate redesigns. As a result, department personnel were asked to put in extensive overtime. Jim, himself, exceeded 75 hours per week on a regular basis. He believed that leading by example was the catalyst that motivated his personnel to work these overtime hours without complaining. Although the department had jelled as a team, Jim observed the workload was wearing on individuals who began taking shortcuts that he feared would create future problems.

It was evident to Jim that he could not design the necessary quality control systems required, develop new products, and service existing product lines with the limited personnel and resources at his disposal. This being the case, Jim approached Phalen and insisted: (1) that he be permitted to change priorities from developing new products to servicing existing product lines and (2) that he be given more technical personnel to enable him to focus more on meeting quality standards. Irritated by Jim's demands, Phalen accused him of not being able to manage his people. He said:

> Jim, you need to sit on these people and kick them into gear to get work out of them. It's about time you quit letting them manage you. I need these products, and you're overdue. My advice to you is to get your department under control.

Jim was becoming more concerned by Phalen's refusal to realize the seriousness of the situation. Jim thought:

> He simply doesn't want to hear about it. To hell with product development, I'll just have to do what I know is right.

In a subsequent staff meeting, it was announced that annual sales for the division were substantially below projections and that the division was continuing to "bleed red ink." Controller Willard Scott emphasized that the division had not once met sales projections or turned a profit in the three years since becoming part of AstroTech and that "It's high time we find out why." When individual staff members were asked for their opinions, a consensus emerged that the main reason for the division not reaching Phalen's goals was that they were unrealistic. It was obvious to Jim that Engineering was not the only unit having serious problems. Phalen countered their concerns with:

> That's pure nonsense! If Engineering would develop the products they are assigned to and if Marketing would generate the sales that they've committed to, achieving these goals would be a piece of cake. You people just need to work smarter. If you don't have the right people, then get rid of the ones you have and find the right people.

As was typical of Phalen's staff meetings, he then began pitting staff members against one another by blaming the failure of one unit to meets its goals on one or more of the other units. Phalen would simply make a series of accusations and then sit back and watch the fireworks. At times, just when it appeared as if problems were near being resolved, Phalen would make new accusations to rekindle the flames. These staff meetings were notorious for lasting 3–4 hours, and the badgering and yelling that occurred usually precluded any constructive thought. The end result was exhaustion and frustration especially considering the workload that awaited staff in their respective departments. Phalen would also meet one-on-one with staff members and initiate rumors purposely designed to create conflict. He had once boasted to Jim, "I believe in managing with chaos. You must keep people on their toes and guessing in order to keep the upper hand."

## B-1g Staff Concerns

In the ensuing months, the staff secretly met on several occasions to discuss the plight of the division and how to best deal with Phalen's unorthodox management tactics. Because Phalen had a history of creating untenable situations for people and then firing them, claiming to his superiors that the person was dishonest or incapable, extreme caution was necessary. With the division performing as poorly as it was, the staff was concerned that, once again, Phalen would attempt to buy himself time by blaming various personnel for the division's woes and terminating them. At the end of one long, frustrating day, Jim's top mechanical engineer approached him and said:

> Jim, I've had enough. This place is just too crazy, and nobody outside of Engineering has a clue about what it takes to develop these products. I've decided to accept a position with another company.

Jim was devastated. The engineer's resignation had been preceded by two top draftsmen for essentially the same reasons.

It was at this time that Jim found an unexpected ally in Short who also began to distance himself from Phalen. Both Jim and Short agreed to use their contacts elsewhere in the corporation to discreetly let people know that all was not well at the Texas facility.

The resignation of key people and the fact that the Engineering unit continued to fall behind did have one positive effect. Jim was finally able to persuade Phalen to give him permission to hire additional personnel as well as to replace those who had left. Jim was fortunate to be able to hire three, very capable, new engineers. He was now confident that the unit would be able to meet performance expectations and would become a force to be reckoned with in the marketplace. But, he also knew that they must focus on the most critical projects if this was to become a reality. Jim was a strong believer in the old adage, "You can do many things poorly, or you can do a few things well."

## B-1h The Morale Survey

But, focusing on the most critical products was not to be the case. Phalen insisted that his original performance expectations for the division and the Engineering unit remain unchanged. By the end of Jim's first year, frustration at all levels of the division was clearly evident. People were tired of the excessive workload and the perceived lack of Phalen's desire, or possibly his ability, to fix things. This frustration was further aggravated by the fact that Phalen was the only person who ever went home on time and rarely put in more than a 40-hour week. Morale was at an all-time low. But, spirits were lifted when it was rumored that the division was slated for an employee morale survey. Upon receiving confirmation that the survey was to be administered, the staff agreed among themselves to be honest in their responses and make Corporate Headquarters aware of Phalen's exploitive leadership style and the negative impact it continued to have on productivity and employee morale. Even though the engineering staff members were aware that their answers would be collected separately from the rest of the plant and, therefore, identifiable, they resolved that the Phalen "issue" had to be addressed and agreed to give identical responses to questions in spite of potential consequences.

One month later when the results of the survey were returned, Phalen had not fared well. Although negative comments occurred randomly, one set of particularly negative comments were sequentially numbered. It didn't take Phalen long to determine that these had originated in the Engineering Department and to identify the most negative comments as Jim's. With few exceptions, the other staff groups had failed to live up to their part of the agreement. Phalen called Jim into his office and laid out the entire list of his responses, including Jim's request for a new General Manager, and asked him point-blank:

Are these your comments and would you explain to me why you wrote them?

Noting that Phalen was uncharacteristically calm, Jim responded:

George, I was pretty upset over the way you were handling things when we filled out the surveys. As you are aware, we have a big difference in opinion over what the priorities should be in Engineering, as well as what we should ship and not ship and when.

The discussion did not last long.

Shortly after the survey and perhaps as a result, Phalen fired the Director of Marketing, confidently claiming that, "I made more sales on my last public relations trip than he did during the entire year." The subsequent search for a replacement led to the addition of Dick Faraday as the Director of Marketing. Like most of the management staff, Faraday came from another AstroTech division. He had a very confident air about him and was quickly able to prove his expertise. Rumors quickly emerged that Phalen had handpicked Faraday to become his heir apparent, and the two bonded quickly. Within a few weeks of his arrival, it was apparent that Faraday sided with Phalen in virtually all matters concerning personnel, product development and service, and quality control.

As the weeks passed, Phalen increased his demands on the Engineering Department and intensified his personal attacks on Jim. For the first time since coming to AstroTech, Jim had serious concerns about job security and his future with the company. He addressed these concerns by working feverishly to stay ahead of Phalen's demands, but contrary to Phalen's wishes, insisted on keeping the FAA and quality issues as his top priority because of the potential legal and ethical ramifications of shipping substandard products. Should loss of life occur as a result of inadequate quality control systems, Jim believed that he would ultimately be held responsible. Once in the past the Corporation had gained notoriety for not adhering to quality specifications in the aircraft industry with near disastrous results. Jim knew that the potential for a similar tragedy existed if quality control was not maintained at the highest level. Because of his emphasis on quality, it was inevitable that development projects would slip—and they did.

Jim often received the support of staff members from other departments and occasionally Short. Arron Staley, the Quality Manager, initially backed Jim but quickly came under fire by Phalen for it. Although Staley continued to back Jim privately, he became much less supportive of him in public. Jim frequently reminded himself that the others, including Short, had not been fully honest when they failed to make their concerns known on the survey.

## B-1i Product X

A major conflict arose when Engineering detected a design flaw in Product X that was under long-term contract. Having experienced no problems with the product, the customer was unaware of the flaw. Jim announced the existence of the flaw in a staff meeting and recommended that shipments be delayed until the customer could be informed. Phalen immediately rejected Jim's proposal and demanded that the division keep shipping the product until the "real problem" was identified. However, with the exception of Phalen and Faraday, the staff members agreed that AstroTech should fix the problem and immediately inform the customer of the product's limitations. In support of Phalen, Faraday emphatically disagreed and stated that he would continue to ship the product until Engineering could come up with an acceptable solution. A heated discussion over the product continued for the entire afternoon, but nothing was accomplished—neither side was willing to make concessions. Much to Jim's dismay, Staley remained quiet during the discussion. However, two weeks later, having had enough of Phalen and Faraday's attempts to compromise product quality, Staley resigned.

Because of Jim's previous experience with quality systems and control, Phalen decided that Staley's position would not be filled and assigned responsibility for product quality to Jim's department. Unfortunately for Jim, the Quality Department was even more understaffed than the Engineering Department. Jim had argued emphatically that a replacement for Staley was critical, but Phalen and Faraday denied Jim's request on the grounds that they could not afford to replace him at that time.

After several weeks of debate, the issue of the faulty design of Product X reached a point where Jim felt that he had no alternative but to apprise the customer. Furthermore, as the Manager of Engineering and Quality, Jim believed that informing the customer was well within his area of responsibility. Jim met privately with Phalen to make one final attempt to get his permission to do so. Surprisingly, Phalen agreed and gave Jim discretion on how best to approach the customer. Fearing that Phalen would change his mind, Jim acted immediately without attempting to inform Faraday. He knew, given the stand that Faraday had taken in previous discussions, that he would do all he could to change Phalen's mind.

When Jim informed the customer about the deficiencies of Product X, its management expressed concern but were appreciative. Company representatives assured Jim that they would continue to order the product once the design flaws were corrected. Faraday's response was as expected. Upon learning of Jim's actions, he immediately demanded a staff meeting. Jim was shocked when Phalen claimed that he had not given permission. This was the final straw for Jim. After two hours of heated accusations and counter accusations, Jim once more re-stated the actual chain of events and rebuked Phalen for his failure to admit that he had given Jim his authorization. Phalen finally admitted, "Jim you're right. I did give you my consent." Jim looked at Phalen in disbelief and disgust and, exhibiting behavior that was entirely out of character, stormed out of the meeting.

In the weeks following the Product X meeting, Phalen and Faraday increased their personal attacks on Jim and exerted even more pressure on Engineering to develop additional products. Faraday even began adding products to the list for which there were no customer orders, in an attempt to show that Marketing was doing its job "of creating the vision needed for the unit to achieve its stated sales goals." Unfortunately, these new demands took resources away from critical projects already underway which caused Engineering to fall further behind. Jim pressured Phalen and Faraday to prioritize projects so that a "critical few" could be completed, but they insisted that efforts continue on all projects.

Shortly thereafter, word was received from Corporate Headquarters that the division had six months to prepare for a major FAA quality audit—the first of its kind for the new division. Jim argued that it was imperative that the Division pass this audit if it was to continue manufacturing and shipping aerospace products. The staff finally agreed that it would be necessary to completely overhaul the existing quality control systems. The task of developing new and revamping old systems was placed solely on Jim. Although he realized the importance of completing this task, he also knew that the amount of time involved would conflict even more with Phalen's push to bring new products to market.

As weeks grew into months, the strong support Jim received from his technicians and engineers gave him confidence that he was acting in the best interests of the

Corporation. However, his anxiety concerning job security and career advancement continued to increase.

### B-1j An Unexpected Visitor

The debates and personal attacks during staff meetings had risen to an unprecedented level, and Jim had given up all hope that Corporate Headquarters would act on the survey results. Willard Scott, the Controller who had frequently complained in staff meetings of being forced to "work the books," accepted a transfer to another unit within AstroTech. Only Jim, Short and Jill Johnson, the Human Resource Manager, remained of the staff who had completed the morale survey. Jim was convinced that he could not withstand the combined attacks of Phalen and Faraday and that his days with the Corporation were numbered.

Staff members were stunned, but pleasantly surprised, when one day without warning, a Senior Vice President from New York showed up and terminated Phalen because of his "continued inability to meet division objectives." The out-and-out relief felt by Jim and Short was offset by Faraday's visible disappointment. His displeasure intensified when the Senior Vice President announced that Phalen's position would not be filled because of the small size of the Fuel Systems Division. Instead, all five of the staff department heads would report directly to Roger Banter, the General Manager of a much larger division based in Indiana (Exhibit 2).

Faraday and Short knew Banter from previous assignments and were familiar with his reputation in the corporation as a strong, fair leader. The staff was generally

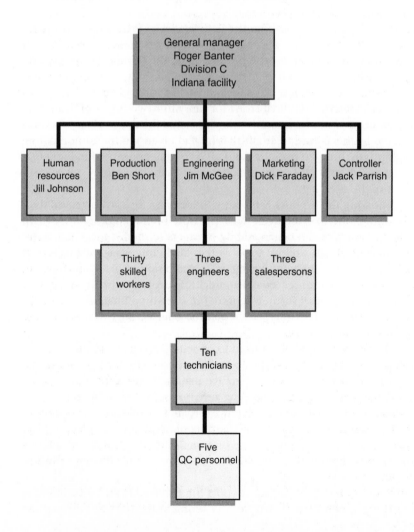

**EXHIBIT 2**

Organizational Chart after Phalen's Departure from the Fuel Systems Division pleased with his selection as the person to head the division. However, when Banter informed them that his contact with them would be through weekly teleconferences, they were disappointed that he was to be an absentee manager. Upon being informed of Banter's expectations for the division, the staff met to discuss how to avoid further conflict and resolved to make a fresh start. They agreed that they would forego one-on-one discussions with Banter unless they were initiated by Banter himself and that they would interact with him only during staff meetings. But, it soon became apparent to all that Faraday communicated more frequently with Banter than anyone else did and that these exchanges were not always initiated by Banter. Although Faraday had been the driving force behind the "group communication agreement," he ignored the agreement more than anyone.

### B-1k  FAA Inspection Anxieties

Even though the FAA audit was only two months away, Faraday again began to openly criticize Jim for spending too much time designing and revamping the quality control systems and not spending enough time developing new products. Because the Engineering Department was failing to develop new products that would sell, there was a growing concern among the staff about the Division's future. They began to agree with Faraday. Nevertheless, Jim persisted in his attempts to convince the others of the importance of the audit; but because they were not knowledgeable of the time commitments and tradeoffs between new product development and implementation of the quality control systems, he met with minimal success. Jim was especially disturbed by lack of support from Short. Jim believed it ironic that Short had been responsible for AstroTech's Quality Control prior to Staley's arrival.

Staff members who had previously blamed Phalen's leadership style as being responsible for low productivity and failure to develop new products had now shifted the blame to Jim and his engineering group. This shift of blame was instigated by Faraday. Pressures on Jim to change his priorities increased and individuals from other departments began to distance themselves from him and his group. In spite of this increasingly hostile environment, the engineering and quality control personnel continued to show Jim strong support. He also received encouragement from production operators who preferred his leadership style to the autocratic styles of Short and Faraday.

A new Controller, Jack Parrish, was finally hired to replace Willard Scott who had quit the division several months before. Parrish was a young CPA who openly discussed his desire to make a positive impact on the division in order to prove his mettle with Corporate Headquarters. Soon after joining the Fuel Systems division, Parrish claimed that the Engineering Department was "out-of-control" because of its overcommitment to quality. Faraday, capitalizing on Parrish's allegations, called a staff meeting to discuss them. He began by saying, "Jim, I no longer have confidence in your ability to manage your department." He then gave the group a detailed explanation why he believed the Engineering's priorities were the major cause of the division's inability to meet its goals. When Jim attempted to defend his priorities, it was evident that those few from other departments who had previously supported him no longer did. After Jim had had his say, Faraday quickly ended the meeting.

Even without the support of the other staff members, Jim was still convinced he was right. He was upset that his priorities and his management abilities were being questioned. Recognizing that he was in a tough spot, he decided it was time to consult one-on-one with Banter and get his opinion. He knew that to successfully plead his case with Banter he had to be completely open and honest and to avoid implying that other staff members were guilty of any wrongdoing. In his conversation with Banter, Jim said:

> My main reason for calling is to ensure that you're aware of the staff's concern
> relative to my performance. They've stated that they've lost confidence in my

ability to set priorities and to manage the Engineering Department. Perhaps you can offer me some guidance. I'd like to discuss this with you in detail at your earliest convenience.

Other than this, little of substance was said. However, Jim expected to hear from Banter before too much time had passed.

At the next staff meeting, Jim told the group that he had shared their concerns with Banter. The entire staff was angered by his disclosure. Faraday quickly accused Jim of breaking the trust of the group members by going to Banter without their permission. In defense Jim said:

First off, Banter is my direct boss, and I should be able to talk to him about issues concerning my personal performance. Secondly, you're the ones who said I was performing poorly. All I did was inform Banter of your opinions. How can you find fault in this?

As usual, Faraday was the first to censure:

He may be your boss, but you should have discussed these issues with us before you called him. Here again, you've shown that you can't be trusted.

Jim looked at everyone in disbelief, noticing that most staff members refused to make eye contact. He then said:

This whole thing is ridiculous. I've got work to do.

With this, Jim left the meeting.

Frustrated, Jim shared the gist of the meeting with a senior engineer who said:

Jim, this is absurd! Everyone knows the hours we're working and that you're the first one in at 5:00 a.m. and you're lucky to leave by 7:00 p.m. We're in here 7 days a week. Why aren't they here during those hours to work with us as a team? What do they expect from us anyhow?

Actually, Short did spend considerable time in the facility, but Faraday, Parrish, Johnson and their departmental personnel didn't come close to the time Engineering invested in these projects.

## B-11 The AutoFlow

During the ensuing weeks, Faraday continued to denigrate Jim to the staff for calling Banter as well as for informing the customer months before about the flaws in Product X. Faraday further aggravated the situation by calling a meeting initiating the development of another new product, the AutoFlow, which would be one of the largest projects ever undertaken by the division. Because of its size and complexity, Engineering estimated a major design effort of 15–18 months to develop and qualify. Nevertheless, Marketing demanded that the product be operational and fully qualified by the FAA within six months. Given their concerns about the future of the division and the perceived sales potential of the AutoFlow, the staff sided with Faraday. Once more, Jim believed he was being set up to fail. His initial reaction was that he saw no possible way to meet this schedule but added that Engineering would do its best to complete the project "as soon as possible." He also reminded them that the division had never developed and qualified a new product in less than 12 months.

Jim's working relationships with other staff members had become strained to the breaking point, and he was now clearly the odd man out. He found it hard to believe that his status had fallen from being "one-of-the-group" to "most-wanted-out-of-the-group" in such a short period of time. Faraday's calls to Banter increased and it was evident that he had gained Banter's confidence. Furthermore, no matter what information Jim volunteered in staff meetings, Faraday was quick to discredit or discount it; and there was little support from the rest of the staff, most notably, Short. In fact, the relationship between Short and Jim had deteriorated to the point where on one occasion they became entangled in a very public and violent debate on the production floor. Accusations were exchanged and the debate escalated with Short losing control and physically attacking Jim. The two were immediately separated by nearby workers and an "emergency" staff meeting was called.

McGee and Short explained to the rest of the staff that they were under a lot of pressure at the time of the incident. The altercation arose over who was to pick up a corporate executive at the local airport. McGee had initially been designated to meet this person and bring him to the plant. When time approached for the executive's arrival and McGee was not to be found, Short made arrangements to meet the visiting dignitary. About the time Short was to leave for the airport, McGee appeared on the scene. Each insisted that he was responsible for bringing the corporate officer to the facility. The argument that ensued resulted in Short connecting with a strong right hand that ended up with McGee having to pick himself up off the floor. By the end of the meeting, the staff agreed that the incident would be kept under wraps and not leaked to colleagues in other divisions or to Corporate Headquarters. Jim knew that he could have Short fired, or even arrested. However, because of his past friendship with Short and understanding the pressures they were all under, Jim decided to "sweep it under the carpet." But, it was clear that irreparable damage had been done.

## B-1m Thanks for Nothing

The FAA audit took place two weeks later and lasted for four days. Fortunately, all of Jim's hard work paid off and the division passed with flying colors. The Engineering and Quality Department personnel were ecstatic. Although Short threw a plant-wide party for Jim to celebrate the effort and its success, after the party Faraday immediately called a meeting that included Jim, Parrish, Short and himself. Its purpose was not to apologize for being unduly critical of Jim or to congratulate him further but quite the opposite. He got right to the point:

> Jim, we'd like you to know that we believe you obviously put too much effort into the audit preparation. Even though you got an "A" we needed only a "C." The wasted effort could have been better applied to new product development.

Jim then reminded the group that the FAA inspector had given them the high grade because of the extensive effort for compliance on the part of "the facility." Although the auditor was well aware of the quality problems inherited from the past owner, he agreed to limit his audit to the present and to base it the processes designed by Jim's group, which ensured that quality standards would continue to be met in the years to come. Jim's argument—that the audit would have failed had the facility not been able to show strong potential for continuous process improvement—fell on deaf ears.

## B-1n Almost Accomplishing the Near Impossible

The six-month deadline for completion of the AutoFlow project arrived all too soon. Engineering had put in a Herculean effort and had completed the design, but the project was still in the qualification phase. What made the feat even more remarkable was that Engineering had accomplished the task with very little assistance from Marketing. Although Marketing was responsible for submitting to Engineering a preliminary product specification based on the customer's needs, no such specification was ever provided. Because Jim and his group knew that any delay in the project would eventually be blamed on them, they created a specification and copied it to Marketing. When they received no feedback, they interpreted it as tacit approval to proceed. Six months later, irritated when Jim informed him that an additional 2–4 weeks would be required to complete the project, Faraday scheduled a staff teleconference with Banter. During the conference he made it a point to say:

> I would be selling the AutoFlow units now if I had had a completed design from Engineering, but as usual they're behind schedule.

After Jim had answered a few technical questions from Banter about the status of the project, the conference ended.

### B-1o While the Cat's Away

Having not taken any time off during the 18 months he had been with the Division, Jim scheduled a 3-day vacation for his family. He looked forward to getting away from the stress; but because of the pressure to complete the AutoFlow project, he informed the staff at its next meeting that he was canceling his vacation in order to speed up completion of the project. Jim was surprised when Short said, "Don't be crazy. You need some quality time with your family. Go! You've earned it." Knowing how much his family was looking forward to time away, Jim was pleased that the staff appreciated his hard work and encouraged him to go.

When he returned, Jim was furious when he learned that during his absence the staff had called Banter and reiterated their lack of confidence in Jim's ability to manage and to complete the AutoFlow project. Faraday had also reaffirmed his belief that he could sell hundreds of the units as soon as they were qualified. He had told Banter that he had three customers with approved budgets waiting for this product and three more that were very interested and that he could easily have sold over a million dollars of the AutoFlow unit within the next six months if Jim had finished the design on time. Faraday had also convinced Banter to have the AutoFlow project reassigned to Short's unit.

During the next scheduled teleconference after Jim's return, Jim tried to change Banter's mind by pointing out that the AutoFlow was one of the most ambitious projects ever undertaken by the Division and that its completion was only two weeks away. However, Banter's decision—to remove the project from Jim's control—stood. Jim attempted to discuss the issue privately with Banter but was unable to contact him by phone or to arrange a meeting. Jim experienced deep feelings of anxiety, rejection, frustration, anger and . . . betrayal.

True to Jim's prediction, Short's unit was able to complete the project within two weeks and prototypes were submitted to FAA for approval. Initial units were fabricated for Marketing and sent to pre-selected airlines for performance verification and to generate sales for the new product line. Although still smoldering from losing the AutoFlow project, Jim was extremely proud of his engineering team. They had labored against all odds, working seven days a week for six and a half months, to develop this new product in record time. Field tests had proven that the units exceeded even the engineering team's expectations. Furthermore, the AutoFlow surpassed performance standards of their competitor's product and also sold for less. In spite of all this, Marketing had yet to secure a single contract for this new, superior product. With the year rapidly coming to a close, sales goals for the division appeared more and more out of reach.

### B-1p Abandoned and Alone or Where Do I Go from Here?

Jim's thoughts returned to Banter. In the few hours since Banter's departure, many questions continued to weigh heavily on Jim:

> Why is it that no one is willing to give me credit for my accomplishments here at Fuel Systems? The FAA would have shut us down had it not been for my efforts and persistence. Besides, I was able to accomplish these things with few resources and under adverse circumstances. Where did I fail? What could I have done differ-

ently? Was I wrong for not compromising my concerns for quality? Should I leave the division and return to Utah and my old job, or should I stay here and fight it out? What does the future hold should I choose to stay? While staying would carry risk, would not my leaving be viewed as an admission of my incompetence and reduce my chances for advancement within the corporation?

This last point was the toughest one for Jim to swallow.

# B-2 AstroTech Fuel Systems—Part B

Although the manufacture of fuel systems was an area in which AstroTech lacked expertise, the product line was very profitable and much in demand in the airline industry. AstroTech's original strategy for acquiring Fuel Systems was to gain familiarity with manufacturing this line of products with an ultimate goal of acquiring the industry's major producer. Unknown to Fuel Systems employees, this new venture was to serve as a pilot study and training ground to assist in determining whether AstroTech should indeed enter this segment of the market. In addition, given that Fuel Systems was in essence an experimental unit and isolated from the rest of the company, should the corporation find that it was not in its best interests to compete in this market, the unit could be disposed of easily. The venture allowed AstroTech to test the waters with a modest investment.

In spite of the failure of the Fuel Systems division to ever show a profit, AstroTech believed in the long-term profit potential of this product line. It decided to purchase the industry's largest manufacturer of fuel systems, thereby making AstroTech the market's principal supplier. However, as AstroTech was in the process of putting together a buyout offer, the manufacturer was acquired by one of AstroTech's major competitors.

The strategists at corporate headquarters were then faced with deciding what should be done with the division and its employees.

# I'm from the Government— and I'm Here to Help You

## Case C

### Karl Borden
### Jim Cooper*

Jay Carlos had been thinking that everything was going just a tad too well to last. For the first time in a long time, there were no fires to put out. After five business start-ups and 20 years as an entrepreneur, he knew that crisis management is the rule rather than the exception in small business. His premonition was realized when the phone rang and Kris, the Program Services Director for his chain of homes for the mentally retarded said "An OSHA[1] inspector named Olive Stone just walked in the door and wants to review our blood-borne pathogen policy and employee hepatitis vaccination procedure. What should I do?"

*Author affiliations: Karl Borden, University of Nebraska, Kearney; and Jim Cooper, King Faud University.

# C-1 Industry and Company Background

It was in the mid-1970's that the national attitude toward the mentally retarded started changing. Prior to that time, most mentally retarded adults were cared for either in their parents' or another relative's home, or were placed in large state hospitals along with the mentally ill. As parents aged or relatives were unavailable, most retarded eventually wound up residing in the large state institutions. "Treatment" consisted largely of chemical restraints (drugs) to inhibit aggression, and confinement to protect the public from their occasionally erratic and antisocial behavior.

Gradually, however, a more enlightened attitude toward the mentally retarded developed. Social service professionals recognized that the mentally retarded were capable of living fuller lives, that most of their socially maladaptive behaviors derived from emotional immaturity and arrested developmental processes, and that a more normalized living environment not based on a medical model could be a less expensive alternative to hospital care.

An industry was created as the market responded to state governments' calls to contract with non-profit or profit-making private institutions willing to provide specialized behavioral treatment in a more normalized home environment for the retarded. As with most industries, market niches and specializations developed. Some homes specialized in the profoundly retarded, those with the lowest level of mental abilities and in need of the greatest degree of physical care. Others specialized in the severely, moderately, or only mildly retarded. Some homes were owned and operated by large, nation-wide corporations, usually chains of nursing homes that had decided to enter the new market; others were developed by church-affiliated or philanthropic non-profit foundations, and still others were small businesses developed by psychologists or other entrepreneurs who saw an opportunity for profitable investment.

East Hampshire Homes was one of the latter. Jay Carlos and his wife Leigh were a businessman/entrepreneur and registered nurse, respectively, in Concord, New Hampshire, when a local delegation of parents and relatives of institutionalized mentally retarded adults approached them. It was they (the relatives) who proposed to the Carloses that they build a home for the mentally retarded as a business venture, with the hope that the result would be a facility available to their institutionalized sons and daughters.

Jay and Leigh Carlos knew little about the mentally retarded, but were always interested in investment opportunities. After six months of study, they decided the potential return was worth the risk. Two years, $250,000 in investment capital, and numerous regulatory and legal hurdles later, they opened their first home. Fifteen years later, they were operating a small two-home chain with a total of 23 beds, over 100 employees, and an adult day-care program for their residents. In addition, the site was already acquired for the next eight-bed home, and ground would soon be broken on an expanded day-care center.

# C-2 Blood-Borne Pathogens and Hepatitis B[2]

Leigh Carlos, RN, MSN, FNP[3], as head of East Hampshire's medical services, was responsible for company compliance with federal, state, and local health and safety regulations. As such, she had carefully considered the risks associated with blood-borne pathogens in general and with hepatitis B in particular.

East Hampshire's homes were not "skilled nursing" facilities. That is, while they employed nurses (mostly Licensed Practical Nurses) and oversaw the medical and physical well-being of their residents, they did not provide round-the-clock, skilled nursing care. Unlike a hospital or nursing home, injections were unusual and staff contact with blood or other bodily fluids was rare.

Risk of exposure to blood-borne pathogens such as hepatitis B was, Leigh felt, far less than in an acute-care or nursing facility. It was, however, higher than in other work environments. East Hampshire Homes had developed, over the years, into an organization that specialized in mild-to-moderate mentally retarded residents with severe behavioral dysfunctions. Many of its residents exhibited violent behavior patterns, which were controlled with a combination of medications and behavioral programming directed by company psychologists. When residents did become physically aggressive they had to be physically restrained, and in some instances staff were in danger of resident biting or scratching behavior that could result in exposure to the hepatitis pathogen.

Leigh took the risk of such exposure seriously. As the organization's population of residents with such behavioral disorders grew, she addressed the question of staff risk in a businesslike manner. First, she carefully investigated Federal occupational safety regulations to determine what the company's obligations were. Then, within the scope of those regulations, she developed what she thought was a cost-effective compliance policy to provide for an adequately safe environment for her employees.

The OSHA (Occupational Safety and Health Act) regulations appeared to provide her with a significant amount of discretion. From 29 CFR 1910.1030(a):

> For Ambulatory Residential Facilities: It is the employer's responsibility to determine which job classifications involve occupational exposure. The employer is only required to make the vaccine available and provide the other protections . . . to those employees having occupational exposure. Occupational exposure is defined as reasonably anticipating exposure to blood or other potentially infectious materials as the result of performing one's job duties.

Leigh believed that her employees were significantly less at risk than those of acute care facilities. In addition to the lack of skilled nursing services, the East Hampshire client population was a relatively stable one. Of the 23 beds, only one or two typically turned over to a new resident each year. Staff turnover rates, on the other hand, were typical of the industry at 35–40% per year. Leigh therefore reasoned that the way to control exposure to the pathogen was by immunizing all of the residents and requiring that all potential new residents be tested for hepatitis B before being admitted to any East Hampshire facility. A positive test result would preclude admission. If no residents brought the pathogen with them, there would be no possibility of staff exposure from that source.

Of course, some risk of exposure from other staff members still existed, but Leigh reasoned that this risk was no greater than that faced in the normal course of employment in our society. The risk was the same as for an employee at the grocery store, the bank, or any other place of work. This normal risk, she felt, did not call for any special action by East Hampshire beyond the vaccination of residents.

# C-3 Jay's Story

"Kris, I'm not sure what we should do here. We don't have an employee vaccination program, and our understanding has been that we don't need one. I think we need some quick legal advice. You say the OSHA inspector named Olive Stone is in the office now? OK. Keep her waiting there . . . tell her the home office is consulting on our response and we'll be right back to you. I'm calling our attorney right now. Offer her coffee and be polite."

Jay immediately called his attorney, Fred Fleagle. Fred had been the Carloses' business attorney for four years, since leaving office as the state Attorney General and running a losing race as the Republican candidate for U.S. Senator. He was very politically connected in the state and had excellent contacts with his former colleagues in the state bureaucracy, an important consideration, the Carloses felt, in an industry as heavily regulated by state and Federal agencies as theirs.

Fred's response to the situation was immediate: "Don't let her inspect without a search warrant," he said. "Understand that you're not trying to be difficult or contrary, but without a search warrant you have no ability to limit the scope of her inspection and you have no idea what she is looking for. Politely ask her to return another day with a search warrant so that we have a legal trail to follow if we object to her findings and want to appeal."

Jay said he would do that, and Fred emphasized remaining polite and cooperative but firm about the need for a warrant. Jay then suggested that he might himself call the person in the state department office who oversaw financial and contractual relationships between the state Department of Health and Welfare and homes for the mentally retarded. "After all, they may have some guidance for us here. If OSHA is going to require hepatitis vaccinations for all employees of homes like ours, that will cost the state millions of dollars. Their own legal department might want to become involved." Fred thought that was a good idea.

Jay called Kris, the Program Director, back and gave him instructions for the OSHA inspector. He emphasized being polite but firm. Then he called the head of the state agency overseeing group homes for the mentally retarded, Mr. B. Yuri Kratt. Jay had known Yuri and worked with him for over 10 years now, ever since Yuri had been promoted into the job, and their relationship was a good one as Jay had worked hard to develop positive working relationships with key state department representatives. Yuri listened to Jay's story and immediately agreed that the implications of OSHA requiring employee hepatitis vaccinations were substantial for the state's budget, as such a cost would form part of the underlying cost structure of the industry which, eventually, the taxpayers of New Hampshire paid for. He said he would call their own legal department and see if they had any advice and would like to intervene in East Hampshire's defense.

## C-4 One Hour Later

Jay felt he had now done what he could do for the short term and that the situation, while not a pleasant one, was at least under control. He had never before had any contact with OSHA inspectors, but his general impression from media reports and business colleagues was not a positive one.[4] He had heard many horror stories about the agency overstepping its authority. But he had no personal experience with such actions, and was inclined to believe that, since East Hampshire had carefully followed the regulations and procedures required on this matter, they would be okay. He did take the time to pull a file folder with his notes from several years earlier when he and Leigh had considered the matter and implemented the screening policy. What he found reassured him that they were in compliance. His attorney's advice had been followed, and his contacts in the state department were thinking of providing assistance.

The phone rang. "Jay, Yuri here. I have some bad news for you. I want you to listen carefully to what I'm saying. And then I want you to make another phone call. First, our legal department will not help you. They say flatly that they will not under any circumstances tangle with OSHA. We're staying out of it. Period. And that's from the top—Legal made a quick call to the Director and he says the same. Don't touch OSHA.

"Second, I want you to call Warren Belle at New Horizon Homes over in Manchester. You know Warren. He has a story to tell you. I can't tell it—but he can. Just call him."

## C-5 Warren's Story

Jay put the phone down with some concern. Yuri hadn't sounded the same during the second phone call. He was clearly speaking between the lines, and what he seemed to be saying was that the state bureaucrats themselves were afraid of OSHA. Warren Belle at New Horizon Homes was an East Hampshire competitor, but competition in this industry was often on friendly terms. Jay had known Warren for several years. He made the call.

Warren was in the office and took the call, listening to Jay recount the morning's events. When he heard the word OSHA he stopped him. "Jay—I've got only one thing to say, and I suggest you listen to it. Do whatever they ask you to do. Do it now. Do it exactly the way they ask you to do it. Do it no matter what it costs. Don't fight. And don't listen to your lawyer.

"Jay," said Warren, "OSHA came by here two months ago. We had exactly the same policy in effect that you do now. We did exactly what you have done and called our attorney, and he gave the exact same advice to require a warrant. The OSHA inspector came back the next day with a warrant and six of his buddies. They started at one end of our building and went to the other, and within a few hours we had accumulated $13,500 in fines. One of the fines was for $2,500 because we had not posted a detailed list of the chemical ingredients in the Dawn Dishwashing Soap in the kitchen. Then the inspector said 'Are you ready to do what we want, or do we have to come back tomorrow to accumulate another $13,000 in fines?' We wound up doing what they wanted, which was to implement a vaccination program, and we still had to pay the $13,500 in fines."

"But Warren," said Jay, "the regulations are clear. We're an exception and don't have to have the vaccination program if our people aren't at risk. You know that a hepatitis B vaccination series costs $180 per person. Taking into account staff turnover, such a program would cost us almost $30,000 per year."

"Jay, do you know how OSHA gets its budget?" asked Warren. "Were you aware that they have almost no budget other than what they collect from fines?[5] Do you know they get to retain the fines they collect to finance their own operations? Do you know that there is no statutory limit to the amount of the fine they can levy for even the smallest offense?[6] Do you know that there is no appeal outside the agency other than a full-blown and expensive court case?[7] Do what they say. Do it now. Don't mess around with these guys. They're like a goon squad. You don't fight—you just hand over your wallet and hope they don't beat you up."

Jay hung up the phone with a different perspective.

## C-6 Fred's Advice

Jay knew he had another call to make immediately. He picked up the phone and dialed Fred Fleagle's number again. Fred took the call right away, and Jay told him Warren's story.

"Well, Jay," said Fred, "I have to admit that I've heard some nasty stories about OSHA. But after you called this morning I rechecked the regulations on this thing just to refresh my memory and to make sure your policy fits. It couldn't possibly be clearer. Your policy is directly in line with the regulations. Admittedly there is room for some interpretation of what constitutes an 'at risk' employee, but the regulation leaves that interpretation in the hands of the employer. I think you're absolutely in the right here and should stand up for your rights. If they come back with a warrant, let them in. If they wind up fining you or demanding that you implement a vaccination program, we'll just take them to Federal court. And we'll win."

"Yes. And tell me, Fred, how long will that take, and at $150 per hour what will it cost me to win?"

"Well, Jay, it could take some years to come to an absolute conclusion. And I won't say it would be cheap. The government has access to plenty of staff lawyers of course and you can't get your costs back even when you prevail."

"That doesn't sound encouraging, Fred."

"Yeah, Jay, but damn it, this is the sort of thing that someone has to stand up to. It's the kind of big government bullying that I ran for the Senate to try to put an end to. You know, that's another option for us. I'm pretty politically connected in this state. We have a Republican Governor, one Republican Senator, and a Republican Statehouse. I could make a few phone calls—see if we can't get these OSHA guys to call off the dogs. Whattya want me to do?"

## Endnotes

1. OSHA (the Occupational Safety and Health Administration) was created as a Federal agency by the Occupational Safety and Health Act of 1970 (Public Law 91-596). The ambitious goals of the agency are "To assure safe and healthful working conditions for working men and women; by authorizing enforcement of the standards developed under the Act; by assisting and encouraging the States in their efforts to assure safe and healthful working conditions; by providing for research, information, education, and training in the field of occupational safety and health; and for other purposes." To these ends, the Agency has broad authority to institute, interpret, and enforce occupational health and safety regulations, including substantial power to levy and collect fines. The agency (as of 2001) employs over 2,100 inspectors, working out of over 200 local offices spread throughout the country, and conducts surprise visits to job sites (the OSHA Act provides for a $1,000 fine for anyone revealing that an OSHA inspection is about to occur).

2. Health professionals may be aware that since this case occurred, the Federal government has moved to require widespread hepatitis B vaccination for both employers and students in public schools and universities. As of the incident recounted in this case, however, such was not the case.

3. MSN=Masters of Science in Nursing; FNP=Family Nurse Practitioner

4. Jay's impressions are not uncommon. OSHA itself recognizes its public image problem. The OSHA website (see http://www.osha.gov) states frankly (as of October, 2001) "in the public's view, OSHA has been driven too often by numbers and rules, not by smart enforcement and results. Business complains about overzealous enforcement and burdensome rules. Many people see OSHA as an agency so enmeshed in its own red tape that it has lost sight of its own mission. And too often, a "one-size-fits-all" regulatory approach has treated conscientious employers no differently from those who put workers needlessly at risk.

5. This comment by Warren is not strictly true. OSHA does have its own budget. Fines, however, are retained by the agency and add to their operational resources.

6. Warren's statement is not quite correct. The Occupational Safety and Health Act of 1970 (Public Law 91-596, 91st Congress, S.2193, December 29, 1970) states: "Any employer who willfully or repeatedly violates the requirements of section 5 of this Act, any standard, rule, or order promulgated pursuant to section 6 of this Act, or regulations prescribed pursuant to this Act, may be assessed a civil penalty of not more than $70,000 for each violation, but not less than $5,000 for each willful violation." On November 5, 1990, Pub. L. 101-508 amended the Act by increasing the penalties for willful or repeated violations of the Act in section 17(a) from $10,000 for each violation to "$70,000 for each violation, but not less than $5,000 for each willful violation," and increased the limitation on penalties in sections (b), (c), (d), and (i) from $1000 to $7000 for serious and other-than-serious violations, failure to correct violative conditions, and violations of the Act's posting requirements. For all practical purposes, however, short of a full-blown civil case against the government, the Agency determines what constitutes either a "serious" or a "willful" violation, and also determines what constitutes "each" violation (every day a condition exists could potentially be a new violation with additional maximum penalties).

7. The Occupational Safety and Health Act of 1970 states "Any person adversely affected or aggrieved by an order of the Commission issued under subsection (c) of section 10 may obtain a review of such order in any United States court of appeals for the circuit in which the violation is alleged to have occurred or where the employer has its principal office, or in the Court of Appeals for the District of Columbia Circuit, by filing in such court within sixty days following the issuance of such order a written petition praying that the order be modified or set aside."

# AAA Construction: A Family Business in Crisis

## Case D

### Donald L. Lester, PhD*

Thirty-year-old David Robbins looked at his grandmother, Joyce Hudson, across the kitchen table in early December of 1998 and said, "Grandmother, if we don't have $250,000 by next week, AAA may not make it."

Joyce sat stunned. David had been president of AAA (pronounced "Triple A") Construction, Inc. since the summer of 1998. His grandparents, Jack and Joyce Hudson, had started the company in 1962, and in July of 1998 Jack had died. In October of 1998, at David's request, Joyce had put a first mortgage on her home, which had been built and paid for ten years earlier, to provide a $150,000 infusion of cash for AAA.

Now, just two months later, Joyce looked across the table at her beloved grandson in her spacious home in upscale Germantown, Tennessee, a suburb of Memphis. She wondered if David could get AAA back on track the way her husband Jack always managed to do; she questioned David's insistence on firing Lewis Harris, the non-family manager that had secured an important line of credit for AAA which was lost when he was let go; and she hoped that AAA would become a comfortable, family-based business again, not a hostile workplace.

As she looked down, about to cry, she heard David say, "Grandmother?"

*Source: CASE Journal* 1, no. 2 (2005): 20–35.

*Author affiliation: Middle Tennessee State University.

# D-1 Early History

AAA Construction, Inc. was a repair/rebuild general contractor located in Memphis, TN. The company specialized in insurance-related construction work, such as fire damages, water damages, burglary damages, and vehicle damages to residential and commercial buildings. It was founded as AAA Home Service in 1962 by M. L. "Jack" Hudson. Jack Hudson had been a carpenter for several years, eventually rising to the level of superintendent for a large general contractor. Prior to 1962, his experience included the construction of schools, hospitals, college dormitories, and city halls.

For the first two years Hudson continued to work as a superintendent during the day, while calling on insurance adjusters, preparing estimates, and making repairs to homes during the evening. His wife, Joyce, fielded phone calls AAA received during normal working hours. She served in this role, as well as office manager and sometimes bookkeeper, for over twenty years.

AAA grossed $38,000 its first year. By 1964, there was enough business to warrant Jack Hudson's full-time involvement. The couple leased a small commercial location in east Memphis, and by year's end had six employees.

# D-2 The Insurance Repair Industry

The claims management process used by the insurance companies was activated when a homeowner (or someone who owned commercial buildings/property) filed a claim with their agent. The agent assigned the claim to a contractor chosen from a preferred list. Being first on that preferred list was the goal of all contractors in this industry, including AAA Construction.

A call from an insurance company for AAA to inspect a claim resulted in an estimator inspecting the damage and preparing an estimate for the insurance company and the property owner. If the property owner agreed to allow AAA to make the needed repairs, a contract was executed. The estimator wrote work orders, ordered the material, and turned the work orders over to the superintendent. At the completion of all of the work orders, the job was turned over to the bookkeeper for billing.

The claims process was more complicated when the damage was severe, such as an extensive fire or tornado damage. In those instances, several contractors would competitively bid the job. Property owners always had the final say as to who repaired their property.

Upon completion of repairs, agents or claims managers would issue checks directly to preferred contractors, rather than mailing them to the property owners. Preferred contractors were simply those that each insurer had the most confidence in and the ones they believed best served the needs of their policyholders. During the 1960's these preferred contractor relationships were solidified within the Memphis market. Of the three leading insurance repair companies, Quality Construction was the primary contractor for Aetna, Dawkins Construction was the primary contractor for Nationwide, and AAA Construction was the primary contractor for State Farm and Allstate, whose agents were writing policies on the middle class to upscale properties in the Memphis market.

# D-3 AAA Management and Organization

Managing insurance repair work required extensive coordination between trades. The construction superintendent at AAA, for example, might have between 150 and 200 ongoing jobs at different stages of completion, as opposed to new construction contractors who might work one or two large jobs at a time. Most insurance repair work carried gross profit margins between 40 and 50%, while new construction projects typically earned gross profit margins between 10 and 15%. Insurance repair jobs were smaller in scope than new construction projects.

Many duties within the company were shared. Each construction estimator was expected to see claims, prepare estimates, oversee work-in-progress, and order needed materials for jobs. AAA reflected the attitude of its founder, Jack Hudson, when it came to operational management. Sales and promotions were paramount. Planning, follow up, and attention-to-detail were considered tiresome. Long-time estimator Frank Wicker commonly referred to AAA as a "jot-'em-down store where we grab a keg of nails and some lumber and go to work, not thinking through the entire job on the front end."

AAA's Hudson was described by State Farm agent George Hurt as "a guy everybody liked with an outgoing personality and a way of exuding confidence that encouraged people in business to trust him." Hudson divided his time between promoting AAA to local insurance agents in the Memphis market and estimating repair work. He bought lunch for an insurance agent or adjustor almost every day of the week. He and Joyce purchased a lakefront property in northern Mississippi, frequently inviting adjusters to join them for boating and fishing on weekends. Hudson believed these promotional activities were the key to the long-term success of AAA.

Hudson also believed if promotional efforts were working and sales and work in progress were strong, most management problems solved themselves. Money would eventually come in, suppliers would be paid, and employees would feel secure about their futures with the firm. However, when Jack perceived work in progress was not up to his expectations, he demanded that employees increase their promotional efforts and also asked them to double up on duties in order to survive. If these moves did not initially prove successful, Hudson would begin to lay off personnel and reduce the company's operational capability.

## D-4 Influences on AAA's Sales History

From its inception in 1962 until 1998, AAA's sales were somewhat volatile due to increased competition, changes in strategy, and extreme weather conditions (see Exhibit 1).

The year 1973 was a pivotal one for AAA. The first major change in strategy occurred when the promotional emphasis was shifted from agents to adjusters. Prior to 1973, AAA had never billed over $500,000 in annual revenue. Agents controlled relatively small claims ($500 or less), whereas adjusters had unlimited authority. 1973

| EXHIBIT 1 | AAA's Sales History from 1973 to 1998 | | |
|---|---|---|---|
| 1973 | $755,000 | 1986 | 1,820,000 |
| 1974 | 770,000 | 1987 | 1,810,000 |
| 1975 | 702,000 | 1988 | 2,275,000 |
| 1976 | 980,000 | 1989 | 3,310,000 |
| 1977 | 776,000 | 1990 | 2,225,000 |
| 1978 | 1,060,000 | 1991 | 2,425,000 |
| 1979 | 1,320,000 | 1992 | 1,732,000 |
| 1980 | 1,690,000 | 1993 | 1,758,000 |
| 1981 | 1,540,000 | 1994 | 2,340,000 |
| 1982 | 1,995,000 | 1995 | 2,849,000 |
| 1983 | 1,930,000 | 1996 | 2,307,000 |
| 1984 | 2,660,000 | 1997 | 2,736,000 |
| 1985 | 2,672,000 | 1998 | 3,014,000 |

was also the year Hudson tried to disengage from the company to pursue other interests. He returned after a few months.

Other examples of strategic changes included two unsuccessful diversification attempts in the late 1960's (automotive body shop, aircraft reclamation service) and forays into heating and air conditioning repairs in 1990 and the plumbing business in 1987. In 1983, AAA opened a general contracting division to do new construction, in addition to maintaining its insurance repair work focus. This effort was made possible by the state raising its per-job ceiling to $1 million in 1978. In 1979 AAA Home Service became AAA Construction, Incorporated and moved to a new, much larger facility in an industrial park on Old Getwell Road in southeast Memphis.

The primary weather influence on sales is reflected in 1989's figures when a major ice storm caused extensive damage in the Memphis area.

## D-5 The Rise of Lewis Harris

AAA had always been a family business. For example, two brothers-in-law of Hudson were former partners and over thirty family members worked at one time or another at AAA from 1962 until 1999. However, two non-family members came to AAA in 1990 to take on key roles. Lewis Harris, a former insurance agent, became the office manager and assumed a role as Jack Hudson's personal liaison to local insurance companies. Emmo Hein came to AAA in January of 1990 as a construction estimator.

Harris became Hudson's most trusted advisor. Harris was adept at collecting money, smoothing over problems with insurance companies, and keeping AAA's employees content by providing a sympathetic ear to their concerns. He had an outgoing personality, and the employees trusted him. He also spent a good deal of time entertaining AAA's clients after office hours, spending several thousand dollars a month on the corporate American Express card. Having been a former insurance agent himself, Harris understood how the industry worked and what the agents and adjusters were looking for in a contractor.

Hudson, in his late 60's by the mid-1990's, had confidence in Harris's ability to handle the day-to-day administration of AAA. Harris was fairly close to Hudson in age, and they had been friends for many years. Harris was a sincere, dedicated, hard-working employee who appreciated Hudson for giving him the opportunity to work at AAA. Harris was the first non-family manager at AAA in over 25 years.

## D-6 David Robbins and Dave Allen: The Next Generation

While Harris was serving in his management role at AAA, Hudson's grandson, David Robbins, was learning how to estimate construction costs. Robbins described AAA's core competence as the ability, "to provide timely estimates to insurance adjustors, convince the homeowners to let AAA make the repairs, and collect the money as fast as possible."

Robbins was in his early twenties when he went to work for AAA Construction in 1992. Jack and Joyce Hudson had two sons die in childbirth, and Robbins was treated like the son they never had. As Charlie Paseur, long-time AAA painter said in 1994, "that boy (David) has always gotten whatever he wanted, and if he wants to run AAA he will."

Robbins was a frequent visitor to his grandparents' lake property, pulling his ski boat bought by Jack and Joyce behind his company truck. He regularly invited insurance adjusters to join him, becoming close friends with some in the process. In 1995 Dave Allen, the husband of Hudson's granddaughter Faith, joined AAA as an estimator.

According to Emmo Hein, "Dave Allen and David Robbins became an informal alliance, speaking as one voice regarding company decisions. They used their influence with Mr. Hudson to get several of their friends hired as full-time employees or subcontractors." Hudson focused his efforts on sales and promotions, constantly re-inforcing the importance of each to Robbins and Allen.

## D-7 The Heir Apparent

Robbins' parents divorced when he was very young. His dad lived out of state and rarely visited. According to Robbins, "Granddaddy Jack was the guy who was always there for me. He and Grandmother have been the most important people in my life." Robbins dressed, walked, and learned to view sales as the cure-all for whatever ails a company, just like his grandfather. After high school, Robbins tried his hand at a couple of jobs in the construction industry before going to work for AAA. As Joyce Hudson reflected in early 1996, "Not only was David our grandson, he was our first grandchild, and we clearly put him on a pedestal." Robbins was friendly and outgoing, like his grandfather, and he and Allen quickly developed close ties to some key insurance adjusters in the Memphis community. Sales grew at AAA, but net profit lagged (see the Case Appendix).

In December of 1997 Hudson was diagnosed with cancer. From December until his death the next summer he became increasingly withdrawn from AAA's operations. By early 1998 Harris was the defacto president of AAA, but Robbins and Allen, both much younger than Harris, began to question Harris's leadership. Allen, who had a college degree in chemistry, was known to comment frequently that running AAA Construction was a "no-brainer."

## D-8 A Rivalry Develops

According to Carolyn Jolly, AAA's bookkeeper in 1998, "A natural rivalry developed between David Robbins and Lewis Harris. Two separate camps evolved as Dave Allen sided with David while most of the office staff, particularly Emmo Hein, remained loyal to Lewis Harris." The employees of AAA knew that Hudson had a lot of confidence in Harris, but they also knew Robbins was family. Hein remarked, "Robbins did not like spending time in the office, so Harris was left to make the routine decisions."

Robbins was very close to his grandmother Joyce. Since she had not been actively involved in the business since 1987, and with her husband gravely ill, Robbins was her primary source of information about AAA. He continued to assure his grandmother that he would always "take care of her." Joyce felt secure financially, however, because her husband had life insurance, her home and her lake house were paid for, and, according to Robbins, the only problem with AAA Construction was Harris and his excessive spending on promotional activities.

Harris tried to bring some form of professionalism to the family atmosphere at AAA because he was dealing with collections and cash flow on a daily basis. Robbins did not like Harris questioning his actions, whereabouts, or spending habits. Robbins wanted to exercise the same free-wheeling, externally focused sales approach to the business as his granddaddy. As Hudson became sicker, Harris's job became more difficult, as was evident in early 1998.

A year-long, serious dispute between AAA and the state of Tennessee over workmen's compensation payments reached a crisis stage. Hudson asked Harris to try to settle the matter. While in Nashville meeting with state officials, Harris had a mild stroke. During his recovery, Robbins and Allen took on more responsibility and continued to undermine Harris. They successfully encouraged Hudson to delay any settlement with the state, which was going to be around $100,000.

In July of 1998, Jack Hudson passed away. Joyce Hudson, now the sole owner and treasurer of AAA Construction, immediately named the only two family members still employed full-time at AAA, David Robbins and Dave Allen, as president and vice president respectively. Both Robbins and Allen were given substantial increases in pay.

Harris remained as office manager, committed to fulfilling a promise he made to Hudson a few months earlier to "take care of things at AAA so Joyce would not have to worry about the company." After recovering from his stroke in September of 1998, Harris reached a settlement with the state insurance commissioner, but Robbins refused to honor the agreement, saying he wanted "to contest the issue further."

Haris had established a new banking relationship for AAA in 1992 through a banker friend of his. In thirty years, it was the first line of credit AAA had ever been able to negotiate. The banker believed that the continued involvement of Harris was critical to AAA's survival. After Hudson passed away, the banker made it clear to Robbins and Joyce Hudson that his bank would call AAA's $100,000 line of credit if Harris left the company for any reason.

Hein related that, "After Mr. Hudson died, Joyce was consumed with grief. She had been away from the business for over a decade, but, being the sole owner of AAA, it was her responsibility to mediate the power struggle. She regularly sided with David Robbins and Dave Allen, including David's decision to fire Harris. She did this knowing that AAA's banker had threatened to call the outstanding line of credit if Harris was fired." In October of 1998, David Robbins fired Lewis Harris. Harris tried to contact Joyce to make sure the decision had her blessing, but she refused to talk to him.

After Harris was fired, Joyce went back to work at AAA Construction two or three days a week for the first time in ten years. True to their word, the bank called the $100,000 line of credit, and AAA did not have the funds to pay. When Robbins asked Joyce for help, she mortgaged her home for about half of its value, to secure the funds needed to clear the line of credit. This reduced her net worth, which included AAA's property and buildings, to just over $500,000. The business, however, was left without a line of credit and cash poor.

## D-9 Joyce Analyzes AAA's Situation

Joyce was discouraged by the state of financial affairs at AAA during the fall of 1998. The company had cash flow problems and was on notice from some of its creditors. The work in progress and the accounts receivable, however, were somewhat encouraging, though not as high as they had been in the two prior years. She remembered that there had been many times in the past when AAA was short of cash, but this period seemed to be the worst she had ever seen. To investigate this problem, Joyce began to review the outstanding receivables to see what was collectable and what might be disputed. She discovered that small, nagging complaints on many jobs had not been addressed.

For moral support to help her through the crisis of losing her husband and trying to work through the cash flow problem at AAA, Joyce turned to her daughter Jackie Raines. Raines and her husband Richard had been living with Joyce for about three years by the fall of 1998. Although Raines had never been employed at AAA, Joyce had always trusted her advice. Raines believed that the company her daddy built had to remain viable to protect Hudson's legacy. Her advice was for Joyce to trust Robbins' judgment and do whatever it took financially to keep AAA viable. Raines agreed with Robbins that Harris was the company's biggest problem. She also suggested that Joyce consider bringing Allen's uncle, a management consultant in California, to Memphis to review AAA's operations and provide some action steps.

Robbins and Allen focused the company's promotional efforts on independent insurance adjustors, and the strategy proved to be successful. Romine and Associates, a firm that represented insurers of lower priced housing and commercial property, became their largest account. In the fall of 1998, Romine and Associates moved their entire operation into vacant offices on AAA's property.

The adjusters at Romine and Associates never questioned any of AAA's estimates or bills to property owners. Robbins and Allen enjoyed great latitude when it came to selling work to policyholders represented by Romine. Although the repair work involved low-cost housing and older commercial property, Robbins was convinced it was a niche market that AAA could dominate. The owner of Romine and Associates was just a few years older than himself, and they had become good friends.

# D-10 At a Crossroad

By December, the cash flow situation became more severe. Without a line of credit, AAA's repairmen could not complete jobs fast enough to maintain a positive cash flow. Robbins, a young family man, again turned to his grandmother.

Joyce weighed Robbins' request for more operating capital for several days. Since returning to AAA on a part-time basis, she had clear evidence of two things. First, AAA was selling a lot of repair work due to the relationships Robbins and Allen had established with Romine and Associates. Joyce had known Romine and Associates for years. She knew that they managed claims on residential and commercial property that was slightly depreciated. This was clearly a different market than the properties insured by State Farm and Allstate, business that was not a large part of AAA's revenue stream any more. Second, she believed the repair work, and AAA Construction, were not being managed properly. The low-cost market served by Romine and Associates could be profitable, but it required much tighter job management.

This lack of management was, as Joyce put it, "Due to David's insistence on spending most of his time 'out in the field' instead of in the office." With the firing of Harris, the office staff had been left to manage themselves. Joyce felt she had to assume the role of office manager immediately.

Joyce also believed AAA had fallen victim to an abrupt change in management and strategic direction without having had time to adjust. Her husband had "just let things go during his last six or seven months," and the cash flow problem that ensued was, in part, a result of that neglect. And, as she explained, "David and Dave had to learn how to juggle all of the responsibilities of managing AAA just as Jack and I did. It takes time." Also, Joyce believed Allen's uncle from California represented an objective third party whose assessment of AAA's operations would be taken to heart by everyone.

Conversely, Joyce, who was 69 years old, also knew her future was financially secure, and that AAA Construction was the only thing that would seriously threaten that security. Without the two most recent monthly financials to review (Robbins had told her the bookkeeper was just too busy to prepare them), Joyce was unsure exactly why cash flow had become such a severe problem. While two-thirds of her wealth consisted of the buildings and land now occupied by AAA Construction, they were actually owned by the company, of which she was the sole stockholder.

As a final consideration, Joyce was well aware of the importance of the company to her family. The business had always distinguished the Hudson family from its other relatives. Owning AAA had clearly set them apart. She wasn't sure if she was ready to let go of that distinction.

# Case D Appendix

Financial Statements for AAA Construction—Income Statements, 1996–1998

|  | 1998 | 1997 | 1996 |
|---|---|---|---|
| Revenues | 3,014,937.00 | 2,736,096.72 | 2,307,271.20 |
| *Job Costs* | | | |
| Material | 509,087.00 | 483,889.28 | 370,649.88 |
| Labor | 632,447.00 | 429,948.25 | 323,959.72 |
| Subcontracts | 697,015.00 | 776,737.90 | 770,996.20 |
| Misc. | 67,793.00 | 51,951.48 | 29,116.36 |
| Sub-total | 1,906,342.00 | 1,742,526.91 | 1,494,722.16 |
| Gross Income | 1,108,595.00 | 993,569.81 | 812,549.04 |
| Misc. Income | 144,843.00 | 6,359.63 | 9,091.80 |
| **Total Income** | 1,253,438.00 | 999,929.44 | 821,640.84 |
| *General Expenses* | | | |
| Admin. Salaries | 399,595.00 | 325,357.66 | 284,574.02 |
| Promotion | 15,898.00 | 78,685.07 | 52,620.83 |
| Vehicle Exp. | 175,492.00 | 113,304.27 | 98,169.15 |
| Bad Debts | 168,927.00 | 41,216.39 | 2,353.16 |
| Contributions | 0.00 | 350.00 | 375.00 |
| Depreciation | 47,751.00 | 42,454.86 | 25,652.25 |
| Insurance | 138,604.00 | 107,610.24 | 139,240.81 |
| Interest | 50,663.00 | 25,510.53 | 37,847.90 |
| Legal and Acctg. | 10,832.00 | 12,231.70 | 10,346.01 |
| Office Supplies | 16,274.00 | 17,089.06 | 12,165.80 |
| Rent—equipment | 4,276.00 | 2,873.34 | 4,272.90 |
| Rent—real estate | 50,600.00 | 49,400.00 | 45,700.00 |
| Maintenance | 6,580.00 | 12,389.81 | 4,138.25 |
| Small tools | 7,431.00 | 10,866.85 | 8,725.59 |
| Taxes/licenses | 112,657.00 | 85,882.48 | 67,380.17 |
| Telephone | 29,075.00 | 24,363.08 | 19,023.55 |
| Utilities | 11,609.00 | 12,561.54 | 10,471.86 |
| Misc. | 75,537.00 | 26,207.28 | 24,882.71 |
|  | 1,321,801.00 | 988,354.16 | 847,939.96 |
| **Net Income** | -68,363.00 | 11,575.28 | -26,299.12 |

### Balance Sheet for AAA Construction—Assets, 1996–1998

|  | 1998 | 1997 | 1996 |
|---|---|---|---|
| *Current Assets* | | | |
| Cash | $304.00 | $631.74 | $558.56 |
| Contracts Receivable | 214,693.00 | 322,669.08 | 323,442.32 |
| Other receivables | 5,760.00 | 3,203.25 | 3,582.23 |
| Unbilled cost of work in process | 223,389.00 | 191,838.79 | 182,162.06 |
| **Total Current Assets** | 444,146.00 | 518,342.86 | 509,745.17 |
| *Properties and Equipment* | | | |
| Land | 96,656.00 | 96,655.75 | 96,655.75 |
| Automotive equipment | 176,799.00 | 151,012.22 | 114,531.43 |
| Other depreciable assets | 241,934.00 | 232,467.24 | 220,026.48 |
| **Total** | 515,389.00 | 480,135.21 | 431,213.66 |
| *Less Accumulated* | | | |
| depreciation | 300,469.00 | 252,718.39 | 213,582.65 |
| Net Fixed Assets | 214,920.00 | 227,416.82 | 217,631.01 |
| *Other Assets* | | | |
| Cash surrender value of life insurance | 10,000.00 | 17,490.02 | 15,490.02 |
| **Total Assets** | 669,066.00 | 763,249.70 | 742,866.20 |

## Liabilities and Equity

| | 1998 | 1997 | 1996 |
|---|---|---|---|
| **Current Liabilities** | | | |
| Notes payable/bank | $15,735.00 | $0.00 | $0.00 |
| Bank overdraft | $34,603.00 | $ 63,852.16 | $42,436.23 |
| Accounts payable | $236,546.00 | $149,892.05 | $178,109.93 |
| Accrued expenses | $ 3,460.00 | $ 5,122.26 | $6,666.01 |
| Accrued federal income tax | $ 0.00 | $ 2,128.63 | $0.00 |
| Accrued franchise & excise tax | $ 0.00 | $ 3,221.39 | $0.00 |
| Long-term liabilities/current | $ 0.00 | $ 76,983.76 | $ 76,820.01 |
| **Total current liabilities** | $290,344.00 | $301,200.25 | $304,031.00 |
| **Long-term debt** | | | |
| Notes payable/bank | $ 35,205.00 | $225,069.50 | $244,738.60 |
| Less current maturities | 15,735.00 | 76,983.76 | 76,820.01 |
| **Total long-term liabilities** | 19,470.00 | 148,085.00 | 167,918.59 |
| **Other liabilities** | | | |
| Loan from affiliate | 207,713.00 | 168,031.51 | 133,291.24 |
| Notes payable to officer | 100,851.00 | 26,882.29 | 26,882.29 |
| **Total other liabilities** | 308,564.00 | 194,913.80 | 160,173.53 |
| **Stockholder's equity** | | | |
| Common stock (1,000 shares of $50 par value authorized, 100 shares issued and outstanding, including 48 shares in the treasury) | 5,000.00 | 5,000.00 | 5,000.00 |
| Paid-in capital | 26,245.00 | 26,244.66 | 26,244.66 |
| Retained earnings | 110,437.00 | 178,799.73 | 170,491.72 |
| **Total** | 141,682.00 | 210,044.39 | 201,736.38 |
| **Less treasury stock** | | | |
| At cost | 90,994.00 | 90,994.48 | 90,994.48 |
| **Total stockholder's equity** | 50,688.00 | 119,049.91 | 110,741.90 |
| **Total liabilities and stockholder's equity** | 669,066.00 | 763,249.70 | 742,866.20 |

# Kerrie's Challenge: Leading an Unpopular Change

## Case E

**Kathleen Gurley**
**Assad Tavakoli***

*Author affiliations: Kathleen Gurley, Fayetteville State University; Assad Tavakoli, Fayetteville State
University.

# E-1 Kerrie's Challenge: Leading an Unpopular Change—Part A

Kerrie Peterson did not sleep well the night after the quarterly financial review and planning session with Chief Executive Officer Tom Wilkes and other general managers of Access. Times were starting to change for Access, a Fortune 100 company in the financial services industry. The company had experienced strong profits and revenue growth over the last three years partly due to the positive economic climate of the Clinton era. It was then June 2000, and the projection for the third quarter indicated a significant decrease in revenues. The CEO had taken a very strong position that the general managers, as heads of the various business units, had to be proactive and cut their operating costs so that the company still reported a profit at the end of 2000. By the end of the meeting, each of the general managers had committed to specific cost reduction targets. Kerrie had agreed to a cost reduction goal of 15 percent of her operating budget. When Kerrie left the meeting, she felt confident that the corporate lending business unit could meet this goal. But as she lay awake in bed, she knew it would be an uphill battle just to convince her senior management team that the goal was realistic.

Kerrie had been general manager (GM) for the corporate lending business unit for two years. The business unit provided lending products, e.g., credit cards, loans, equipment leases, and financial planning services to small and medium-sized companies. The number of small businesses had grown over the previous two years, and their needs for financial support to expand their businesses had made this market very attractive. The promotion to GM for corporate lending had been a significant increase in leadership responsibility for Kerrie. Kerrie joined Access only ten years earlier, leaving a top management consulting firm to accept the position as head of strategic planning at Access. Kerrie had been given her first line position in 1995 as GM of a small, but unprofitable business unit. Kerrie got noticed by top management when she was able to turn around the business and achieve a net profit margin of 10 percent.

On the way to work the day after the review and planning meeting, Kerrie recalled the early days in her new role as GM of corporate lending. When Kerrie received the promotion, Tom Wilkes shared with Kerrie his assessment of her strengths and developmental areas. Kerrie remembers that he said she was viewed as being very bright in terms of identifying market opportunities and in developing the appropriate strategies to build the business. Her weak side was her limited leadership experience. Tom had said that she still had to prove that she had the leadership capability to inspire others and to align a large organization behind a vision. He suggested that the corporate lending business unit was a good opportunity for her to develop and demonstrate this capability. She knew this cost reduction effort would be seen as a test of her leadership ability.

When Kerrie took over as GM, she took time to get to know and assess the capabilities of each member of her senior management team. The two most senior members of team were Sam Wright and Harry Long. Sam was the vice president of account management, which was the largest division of the business unit with five thousand account managers geographically dispersed across the country. The account managers were the primary point of contact for approximately ten to fifteen companies and were responsible for everything from answering routine inquiries to providing their clients financial advice. Sam had been in his position for five years and was well respected by his employees. He previously headed up new accounts and had been with Access for eighteen years. Kerrie was aware that Sam had thought he should get the promotion to the GM position, and it seemed that the disappointment had left him a bit resentful and even negative at times. Harry, on the other hand, seemed to have accepted the fact that he would never be GM. He had been the vice president of marketing and advertising for the last ten years and was very comfortable in that position.

Kerrie had not been impressed with the other three members of her team, and when she had the opportunity, she made changes in those three positions. Kerrie promoted Peter Brown to run the new accounts department because she had been impressed with his forward thinking when she worked with Peter on a project when she was in strategic planning. Kerrie hired Tiffany Morris as head of strategic planning. She came with high recommendations from the same consulting company where Kerrie had worked. Sheila Chen had been in the product development group of corporate lending and had led a very successful new product introduction. Kerrie rewarded her by promoting her to vice president of product development. Kerrie was pleased with the composition of her team at this point, but she also recognized that there was considerable disparity in age, education, and experience among team members and it would take time for them to work together as a team. Exhibit 1 summarizes the team members' backgrounds.

Kerrie reflected on their first annual business planning process. Initially in that meeting, the atmosphere had been competitive among the team members. Each

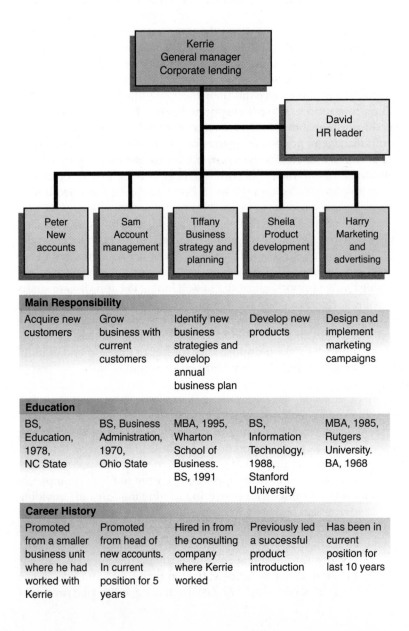

| | Peter New accounts | Sam Account management | Tiffany Business strategy and planning | Sheila Product development | Harry Marketing and advertising |
|---|---|---|---|---|---|
| **Main Responsibility** | Acquire new customers | Grow business with current customers | Identify new business strategies and develop annual business plan | Develop new products | Design and implement marketing campaigns |
| **Education** | BS, Education, 1978, NC State | BS, Business Administration, 1970, Ohio State | MBA, 1995, Wharton School of Business. BS, 1991 | BS, Information Technology, 1988, Stanford University | MBA, 1985, Rutgers University. BA, 1968 |
| **Career History** | Promoted from a smaller business unit where he had worked with Kerrie | Promoted from head of new accounts. In current position for 5 years | Hired in from the consulting company where Kerrie worked | Previously led a successful product introduction | Has been in current position for last 10 years |

**EXHIBIT 1**

member was touting his/her accomplishments and trying to win investment dollars for his/her function. Kerrie had to be very persistent in her expectations that the team members could move beyond their own self-interests and make decisions that were in the best interest of the business unit as a whole. She used her consulting skills to try to keep the discussions fact based and to make sure there were clear decision-making criteria. Over time, she felt that the team had made progress, but she also realized that this cost reduction effort would require tough decisions, and she wondered if the team was up to the challenge.

## E-1a  Senior Management Team Meeting

When Kerrie arrived at her office, she asked Betty, her executive assistant, to call a meeting of the senior management team for 10:00 a.m. She told Betty to tell the team members that the meeting was urgent and took priority over other commitments. The meeting started promptly. Kerrie's unspoken thoughts during the meeting are shown in italics in the following dialogue from the meeting.

> **Kerrie:** I want to thank you all for clearing your calendars to make this meeting. I would have given you more advanced notice of the meeting but the topic is urgent. On Monday, in the financial review and planning session, I learned that the results for the second quarter are starting to show the impact of the recession that the economy appears to be facing. The projection for third quarter is even more dismal. Tom Wilkes wants us to take action now, instead of waiting for profits to fall any further. As leaders of this business, we must take steps to keep our costs in line with revenues. The GMs in the meeting have all agreed to a goal of reducing operating costs by 15 percent by the end of the year. I know this goal sounds very aggressive, but we are one of the largest business units, and we must do our part to achieve this goal. I don't have to remind you that we all have a lot at stake personally. If the financial community isn't convinced that we can manage this downturn, our stock price will suffer and that means our stock options and bonuses decrease in value. I am looking for this team to work with me to develop and implement the action plan required for our business unit to meet the goal.

> **Sam:** We've been through this drill before lots of times. It means we freeze all jobs that are open, reduce travel expenses, and eliminate all nonessential purchases. From what I have been reading, many experts believe this downturn will be over in six months. How did you all come up with a 15 percent cost reduction goal? Isn't that cutting so deep that we endanger the continued growth of the business?

Kerrie felt a bit challenged by Sam, especially because she knew there wasn't a clear, quantitative study to back the 15 percent goal.

> **Kerrie:** *Sam always acts like he has all the answers.*

> **Kerrie:** We are seeing the impact of the recession already. Look at our own business unit results for this quarter. We are below our profit target by almost 10 percent. We can't wait until the business is in serious trouble. Currently our operating budget is $500 million, and we must reduce that amount by $75 million by the end of the year. Are there other questions about the goal?

There was a brief silence, and then Tiffany spoke.

> **Tiffany:** The predictions I have seen indicate that the recession will last for at least a year. I think we should take a more strategic approach and look for opportunities to drive costs out by reengineering business processes.

> **Sam:** Your strategic approach will take too long. Didn't you hear Kerrie say that we need to meet this goal by the end of the year?

Kerrie could see the old pattern of behavior between Sam and Tiffany starting to occur—tit for tat. Even though Tiffany had an impressive academic background, she often felt her views were not respected because of her age. Sam had sometimes complained that Tiffany was pushy.

**Kerrie:** We need to use both approaches. We should implement short-term cost saving measures immediately. Not hiring new employees, reducing travel expenses and nonessential purchases will reduce operating costs by approximately 5 percent, but that still leaves us with another 10 percent to achieve. We must start identifying opportunities to make our processes more cost effective. That's the only way we can meet this goal.

**Harry:** We looked at outsourcing the production part of our marketing campaigns before. We run an internal print shop that produces the marketing materials for our mail campaigns. The print shop has worked hard to benchmark with external print shops and reduce its own costs to be competitive. I really hope we aren't going to revisit this option. It would really discourage the print shop team, and I know we would lose productivity.

**Kerrie:** *Harry is protecting his turf. He probably won't ever change.*

**Kerrie:** We need to consider all options.

**Sam:** Are there any costs we can take out of the marketing budget? We could be more selective in the marketing campaigns we conduct.

**Harry:** If you recall, we went through a rigorous cost-benefit analysis of all the marketing campaigns during our business planning sessions. All of the campaigns show a considerable return of investment. Do we really want to curtail marketing campaigns that will build business and increase revenues? Isn't that just shooting ourselves in the foot?

**Kerrie:** This discussion isn't going to be easy. We have to be open-minded. I want us to focus on the cost structure of our core business processes and think about how we can do these processes more effectively. Maybe we need to accelerate our use of the Internet to streamline our processes.

**Peter:** I support this approach. I am having trouble signing new accounts because our costs are higher than our competitors. The time is right to make changes that will benefit the business over the long term.

Kerrie was relieved to feel some support in the room, and she wasn't surprised it came from Peter.

**Sam:** Just how do you propose taking costs out of our business processes now that you have been in our business unit for almost two years?

**Peter:** In the last business unit I worked in, we reorganized the account management function. Instead of numerous account managers across the country calling on accounts in person, we began servicing accounts more effectively over the phone and through the Internet. We actually found that our customers preferred accessing their account directly through the Internet versus having to call an account manager to get answers to their questions. There is a lot of opportunity to streamline account management.

**Sam:** The account management function in your previous business unit is quite different than ours. We provide consulting services that require our account managers to have a thorough understanding of our customers' businesses. That just isn't possible over the phone. Before we start changing our core business processes, why don't we reevaluate our decision to enlarge the business strategy group? We have built a new competitive intelligence function, and I don't believe they are adding a great deal of value. I get much of the same information about our competitors from my account managers.

Kerrie could see that Sam was feeling threatened as he tried to shift the attention to another part of the business unit.

**Tiffany:** That's pretty shortsighted. I don't think you have even tried to take advantage of the reports the competitive intelligence group has issued. Have you ever read them?

Kerrie was getting a bit angry with Tiffany.

**Kerrie:** *This kind of response doesn't help me or the other senior managers to see her as a mature member of the team.*

Kerrie recalled that she had to help Tiffany hold her own in team meetings before. Kerrie felt it was time for her to learn a more effective way of defending her position.

**Kerrie:** OK, you two. We must listen to all options and not get defensive. I haven't heard from Sheila. Any thoughts?

Kerrie wasn't surprised that she had to ask Sheila for her opinion. Sheila lacked the confidence to speak up and make her opinions heard.

**Sheila:** We are very close in rolling out a new lending product. I hope our current financial situation doesn't prevent us from moving ahead with this product. It is important to be in the market with this product before our competitors. Couldn't we also look at growth opportunities that will increase revenues and not just cost-reduction strategies?

**Kerrie:** Growing the business is still very critical, but we can't depend solely on our projected revenue growth. If the recession deepens as predicted, we may not see the increased sales expected from this new product or our other initiatives.

**David:** If we are serious about reorganizing the account management function, we need to recognize its potential impact on employees. To manage this change effectively and minimize the negative effect on employee morale, we should develop a change management plan that will help employees deal with this change.

**Kerrie:** I think you are right, David. Let's talk about this topic after the meeting. I would like your help.

I want to move quickly in developing our action plan. I will schedule another meeting next week. I would like all of you to think about other opportunities that we overlooked today. I also want to start to scope out the potential cost savings on a few of the ideas we discussed. Harry, I want you to go back and look at the estimated cost savings that were projected if we outsourced the print shop. Tiffany, I want you to look at eliminating the competitive intelligence group, and Sam, please start scoping out the potential savings associated with reorganization of the account management function.

There is one other idea I want to investigate and that is greater use of the intranet. I know we have moved some of our reports that we used to mail out hard copy and have made them available through the intranet. There may be other reports or applications we could distribute electronically as well. Peter, will you look into this strategy? What I want to see on my desk by Monday on all of these strategies are the following: (1) anticipated dollar savings, (2) number of employees potentially impacted, and (3) major risks or drawbacks. Are there any questions? One other reminder—we need to keep this work confidential. Until we have a clearer direction, I don't want the whole workforce to be disrupted and lose focus.

The meeting adjourned after two hours. When Kerrie got back to her office, she felt worn out and discouraged with the way the team had responded to this new challenge. She wondered how she could have handled the situation differently. The more she thought back on the interaction in the meeting, the more she realized she needed to have a better understanding of the resistance that almost all of the team members were expressing. She decided to meet with David, the human resources leader (HRL), and get his help. She also wanted to get David started on developing that change management plan he mentioned in the meeting.

When she met with David, he was very concerned that Kerrie and the team were not addressing the impact that this cost reduction goal would have on employees and their morale. He felt strongly that Kerrie should give a lot of thought about how to communicate the goal to the organization. Kerrie realized that her focus had been mainly on getting the senior management team on board and making timely decisions on the appropriate actions to take. She promised David that she would spend time on drafting a message to the organization. Kerrie told David that she was glad that he brought up the need for a change management plan in the meeting. Kerrie wanted David to explore options on how the business unit handles any employees who may become surplus. In particular, she asked David to look at the feasibility of offering an early retirement package that would reduce the number of employees that would have to be laid off.

She then shifted the focus of the conversation and told David that she needed his help in interviewing the senior team members and getting a sense of how they felt about the cost reduction effort. Kerrie felt that the team members would be more open with David than if she called each one of them into her office to discuss the situation. David had been the HRL for the business unit for the last five years, and he had worked with all the senior team members on various human resources issues. He seemed to get along with all the members of the team. David reluctantly agreed. His interview notes are shown in Case Appendix A-1.

The week went by quickly. On Monday morning, Kerrie was anxious to get the cost estimate reports from her team members. By noon, all the reports were on her desk. As she expected, only one of the options had the potential of meeting the cost reduction target, and that was the reorganization of account management. Kerrie also saw in her mail David's notes from the interviews with the senior management team. As she read the notes, she felt very alone. She thought to herself, "You are a star that everybody loves when the business is doing well, but when times get tough, everybody's first response is to take care of themselves." Kerrie realized that she, too, preferred strategizing about growth opportunities rather than leading an unpopular change effort. Kerrie needed to decide how to handle the decision-making process with her team and how to get their buy-in on the decision. The next meeting was scheduled for 1:00 p.m.

## Case E Appendix

### Interviews with the Senior Management Team

David, the HRL for the business unit, interviewed the members of the senior management team. The notes from these interviews are provided in this case appendix.

#### Sam, Account Management

Sam is really concerned with moving too quickly to reorganize the account management function just to meet the cost reduction goal. Sam still sees the goal as a short-term effort to make the balance sheet look good. When the economy picks up, the CEO will shift back to putting the pressure on growing the business. Sam said, "Our executives want to have their cake and eat it too. Cut costs this month and grow the business next month. But if we reduce the account management workforce, we will feel the impact through reduced revenue growth." His concern is that his account managers will become preoccupied with the reorganization and the possibility of losing their jobs, causing business results to suffer. His function has key goals, related to business growth, that they have to achieve to ensure the business meets its financial goals. Sam understands that having best-in-class economics is critical. He knows his customers are pushing for lower cost services, so he supports the overall cost reduction efforts. He just doesn't think it is smart to target the part of the organization that can produce growth. Sam also has concerns about Kerrie's leadership. He thinks she seems to be reluctant to make the tough decisions. She operates based on a team approach to decision making, which takes a lot of time. Sometimes he wonders if Kerrie already knows the outcomes she wants. She seems to go through the process of involving the team just to build political support.

### Tiffany, Business Strategy and Planning

Tiffany has tried hard to develop an organization that is capable of identifying the leading-edge trends and new opportunities for the business. She feels like the rest of the senior management team is using the cost reduction initiative as a strategy to reduce her function's influence. The competitive intelligence group is relatively new. She just hired the director from a consulting company that performed competitive intelligence in the financial services industry. She felt good about being able to attract what she felt was a critical competency for the organization. Tiffany said, "You know it is really difficult to bring about significant change in an organization because even though you are making progress, given the right opportunity, the organization will revert. Some members of the senior management team have seen my team as a thorn in their side. They haven't openly debated the data we presented. Instead, they have played the game well. I think they now smell blood." Tiffany is also disappointed in Kerrie. She expected Kerrie to take a stronger position in supporting the importance of the competitive intelligence group to the business. She and Kerrie had formulated the role of the group together based on clear examples of where this expertise had been missing. She feels Kerrie should take a stronger leadership role and provide clearer direction for the team.

### Harry, Marketing and Advertising

Harry has the experience of looking at the pros and cons of outsourcing the production of the mail campaigns at least two times previously. The first time the concern over quality and ensuring compliance with privacy guidelines and regulations prevented moving forward. The second time the controls and quality seemed to be sufficient, but the cost savings were minimal. There also was a concern that an outside vendor would not be as responsive as the internal group. Harry knows from many years of experience that marketing is not an exact science and its downstream services have to be able to respond to changes quickly. Based on the previous cost comparisons with external vendors, Harry has made significant process improvements in the print shop and an investment in new printing equipment. He believes that his operation is pretty close to best-in-class economics—given a true apples-to-apples comparison.

### Sheila, Product Development

Sheila believes that the outsourcing of the production of the mail campaigns or the reorganization of account management has the most potential. She feels that the option of eliminating the competitive intelligence group is really just shifting the work from one group to another. The competitive intelligence work still has to be done, and it will probably fall on her group as an added responsibility with no additional head count. Sheila says, "The reorganization should make a significant change in the way work is done—a strategic change to the work flow or process. We can't reduce head count without improvement in the process and without any efficiency gains."

**Peter, New Accounts**

Peter is one of the strongest supporters for reducing costs. He is finding it more and more difficult to gain new customers when the services provided don't justify the cost of the product for a lot of potential customers. Peter learns a great deal about competitive products and their value proposition from his field sales force. His function looks to the senior management team to take steps to strengthen the value proposition and make the product more attractive in the market. Peter believes that reorganizing the account management function is the best option and could result in significant savings. He believes Sam won't be open to even surveying his customers to determine the services that are most important to them. Peter is convinced that the customers are open to new ways to service their accounts. Peter commented, "We have to take this cost reduction goal seriously. It is critical for our business. I don't think the whole team is open about where there are opportunities for cost reductions in their part of the organization."

In addition to the various senior management team members' individual perspectives, the following common themes occurred:

- In general the team was angry about receiving a new cost reduction goal when they are close to halfway through the year.
- Several of the team members questioned whether or not the team would and could make this decision as a team. A few members felt that Kerrie should make the call on where the reorganization effort should focus.
- Three members wondered whether they could openly push back on Kerrie's direction. If they did, they weren't sure the impact it would have on their relationship with Kerrie and their own performance review.

# E-2 Kerrie's Challenge: Leading an Unpopular Change—Part B

Kerrie Peterson, the general manager of the corporate lending business unit, has set a 15 percent cost reduction goal for her business unit because of early signs of a recession in the general economy. The corporate lending business unit provides lending products, e.g., credit cards, loans, equipment leases, and financial planning services to small and medium-sized companies. Kerrie and her senior management team have met once to generate ideas how to meet the cost reduction goal set for their business unit. The senior management team was composed of Kerrie's direct reports, who include Sam, the vice president of account management; Harry, the vice president of marketing and advertising; Peter, vice president of new accounts; Tiffany, head of business strategy and planning; and Sheila, head of new product development. David was the human resources leader for the business unit. At the end of the meeting, the team had generated several options, and Kerrie had assigned each option to one of her direct reports to calculate the potential savings and risks associated with the option. When Kerrie received the information on all of the options, it was clear that only one of the options had the potential of meeting the goal.

## E-2a Formation of the Redesign Team

At the next meeting of the senior management team, Kerrie shared the cost estimates for all the options under consideration and told the team that she could only see one option that could deliver the cost reductions needed. She informed the team that she had made the decision to proceed with the redesign of the account management function. She asked the team if they had any questions or concerns. Most of the team felt the choice was obvious. Sam expressed concern that the redesign could cause a high turnover in his workforce. Kerrie pointed out that the senior management team had a key role in leading this change and helping employees accept the change with minimum disruption.

David suggested that the senior management team form a redesign team to analyze the current role of the account managers (AMs) and determine how to increase the efficiency of this function. Peter suggested that the redesign team benchmark with other companies and talk with customers to gain a better understanding of what they expect from their AMs. Sam also agreed that it was time to invest in updating the information technology utilized in his function and supported looking at how the Internet could be used to better service their customers. The charter for the redesign team was finally agreed upon. It was to develop a team-based design for the account management function, which utilizes new information technology and optimizes the allocation of resources. The goal for the team was to reduce the cost of account management by $60 million. The other $15 million required to meet the goal was expected to come from other routine cuts in spending.

Kerrie agreed to send out a letter to all members of the business unit explaining the situation the business unit faced and announcing the formation of the redesign team. The senior management team talked about the composition of the team and decided on the critical functions that should be represented on the team. Kerrie said she would include the list in her letter. David raised the question of how the redesign team members would be selected. Initially the senior management team assumed it would be up to them to select and assign individuals to the team. David pointed out that often the same people get appointed to special task forces. He suggested letting employees express interest in serving on the team and then having the senior management team select the team from this pool of volunteers. Peter said he felt it was important that the team was made up of the best employees and not just those individuals who were bored on their jobs. Sam felt that there would be considerable interest shown by the account managers in being on the team since they were in the employee group most affected by the redesign. After some discussion, the senior management team agreed that they would encourage their better employees to consider joining the team. David volunteered to draft a list of criteria that the senior management team could use in selecting the final redesign team members.

The senior management team also discussed the impact that this change would have on employees in the organization. From the early cost reduction estimate, the team knew that they were faced with a significant reduction in personnel. Kerrie asked the team to freeze all new job openings until the redesign was completed. David reported that the human resources division was working on a special early retirement for divisions in the company that were being downsized. The team asked David to develop a plan to help any displaced employees find other positions within the company. The senior management team was hopeful that most of the reduction in personnel would result from normal attrition or internal transfers.

Kerrie sent out the letter to employees the next day, and the response was slow at first, but the senior management team was pleased with the list of employees who had volunteered by the deadline. The management team met on Friday and selected the redesign team. Each of the senior management team agreed to inform the employees from their function. David pointed out that the redesign team needed guidance on the methodology for analyzing the business processes in account management. He suggested bringing in an outside consultant to conduct a three-day training session for the team. Kerrie supported David's suggestion and asked David to arrange for the training. Kerrie decided it was important to keep everyone informed, so she issued another letter to the business unit announcing the formation of the redesign team. Her letter is shown in Exhibit 2.

About two weeks later the redesign team met offsite for three days with an external consultant to learn the methodology and develop a project plan. Kerrie and the senior management team met with the redesign team on the third day. The redesign team raised several concerns about how the initiative was structured. First, there was no one from finance on the team, and everyone on the team agreed that it was critical

Date:       June 1, 2001
To:         All Employees
From:       Kerrie Peterson
Subject:    Formation of Account Management Redesign Team

Last month, I communicated the challenge we face in reaching the cost reduction goal set for our business unit. The goal is forcing us to go beyond just reducing travel expenses or other discretionary spending. It is requiring us to rethink how we operate the business and to identify breakthrough ideas to significantly reduce our operating costs. To help us meet our goal, the senior management team agreed to form a redesign team composed of dedicated resources for the next six months. As you may recall, we asked people who were interested in the assignment to volunteer.

I am happy to announce that we have completed the selection of the team members and we are very pleased with the talent and experience that will be on the team. The following individuals will compose the account management redesign team:

| | |
|---|---|
| John Williams | marketing |
| Frank Simons | AM northeast |
| Sue McCarthy | customer service |
| Jack Furner | AM west |
| Ann Chu | business strategy |
| George Martin | product development |
| Sally Fields | AM southeast |
| Peter Block | AM midwest |
| John Taylor | information technology |

This team is chartered to recommend ways that we can better utilize our account management resources while not sacrificing customer service and satisfaction. The account managers play a critical role in growing and sustaining our revenue growth. We need to find better ways of leveraging their talent so we can expand faster and with a lower cost base.

I expect everyone in the organization to give this team his/her support. The team will be gathering information from various sources within our organization. If the team asks you for information, I expect you to treat the request as though it was coming from me personally and respond in a timely manner.

If you have questions about the charter or the work of the team, you can talk with the senior management team member to whom you report or send me an email. The redesign team will be giving regular updates to the senior management team, and we will keep you informed of its progress.

to have finance involved up front. Second, the team members wanted to collect data from operations, which provided the back office support to the AMs. The team did not feel empowered to interview employees outside of their own business unit. An organization chart for Access is shown in Exhibit 3. The team asked Kerrie to help resolve these issues. Kerrie agreed to talk to the head of operations and explain the purpose of the redesign initiative and ask him if could arrange for the redesign team to interview some of his employees. Kerrie asked Sam to talk with the finance group that supported corporate lending and ask them to support the team.

In addition, the redesign team was concerned about the results of the interim employee satisfaction survey. This survey was conducted on a regular basis throughout the company. The following results in Exhibit 4 for the corporate lending business unit were of particular concern.

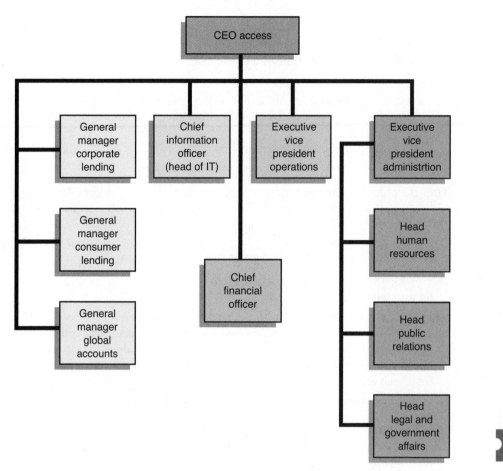

**EXHIBIT 3**

**EXHIBIT 4** Employee Satisfaction Survey—Corporate Lending Business Unit

| Survey Statement | Year end 2000 % Agreement | Interim 2001 % Agreement | Change +/- |
|---|---|---|---|
| Access has a sincere interest in its employees. | 72% | 65% | −7% |
| When changes occur, my leader communicates the effect the change will have on me. | 68% | 58% | −10% |
| Management treats employees with respect and dignity. | 75% | 68% | −7% |
| My leader is open and honest in providing information. | 72% | 68% | −4% |
| Management communicates important information in a timely manner. | 78% | 62% | −16% |
| I am rewarded based on my contribution to business success. | 64% | 59% | −5% |
| Teamwork is a priority in this organization. | 76% | 65% | −11% |

Written comments included:

- The cost reduction initiative is just another way for management to ensure they will get their big bonuses at the end of the year.
- No one has asked my opinion on where cost savings could be achieved.
- We heard the announcement about the formation of the redesign team but since then we have been left just waiting for the other shoe to drop. Management should communicate more.
- I enjoy my job at Access and feel I have contributed to the business, but I have started to look for another job because of the uncertainty.

After the meeting with the redesign team, Kerrie went back to her office and cancelled her meetings for the rest of the day. She asked Betty to call David and see if he could join her in her office. David stopped by Kerrie's office about 30 minutes later. When he entered Kerrie's office, he found her reading a *Harvard Business Review* article on leading change that he had given her two weeks ago.

**David:** I see you are reading the article I sent you. You wanted to see me; what's on your mind?

**Kerrie:** I am very disappointed with the interim employee survey results. Two of the questions where our scores dropped significantly are related to communicating on a timely basis. I have issued two letters, the first about the cost reduction goal and the second on the formation of the redesign team. They couldn't have been more timely. What do employees expect?

**David:** When I have spoken with employees, they don't seem to understand why the cost reduction effort is needed. Many of them don't feel any slowdown in the demands on them. They don't spend time every month looking at the profit or loss report like you do. I get the feeling they think management is creating this crisis just to get more work out of them.

**Kerrie:** Don't they listen to the news on TV? They have been talking about the coming recession for the last three months.

**David:** People can listen to the national news but assume it won't affect them. It is the denial stage of their response to change. For them to understand the urgency, they must hear the message several times in many different ways. Just written announcements to the organization aren't that effective. Many employees don't even read them.

**Kerrie:** I imagine people are feeling a lot of uncertainty, especially in account management. I don't know what more I can tell them. It will take the redesign team some time to conduct their analysis and make their recommendations.

**David:** I believe most employees are feeling the uncertainty, not just in account management. This is the time that employees need to see and hear from their leaders. It is important that there is a consistent message that they hear from all members of the senior management team.

**Kerrie:** Are you suggesting that I should hold more "town hall" meetings with various groups of employees and communicate the need to meet this cost reduction goal?

**David:** That would definitely help.

**Kerrie:** How will I handle the questions for which there is no answer, yet? Couldn't meetings like that make it seem like I'm not being direct and open with them?

**David:** These meetings are never easy, but they certainly are better than formal letters. Besides that's why they pay you GMs the big money! Is there anything else you need from me at this point?

**Kerrie:** No, I need to think about how I want to handle the communications. Next time the senior management team meets, I will include the topic on the agenda.

After David left, Kerrie thought about her own leadership style. She wondered if she had what it takes to establish the credibility with employees during these trying times. She did reach the conclusion that she needed to communicate more with employees.

## E-2b  The Data Collection Phase

It took the redesign team about a month to conduct the data collection, which consisted of customer interviews, competitive benchmarking and a task analysis of the account managers to determine how they were spending their time. The key findings from the customer interviews are shown in Exhibit 5.

The results of the competitive benchmarking uncovered several surprises both for the redesign and the senior management teams. Several competitors appeared to be ahead of Access in utilizing the Internet and phone to replace face-to-face meetings, which resulted in a significant reduction in the cost of the account management function. The team only selected companies that offered a similar line of services and were servicing the small and middle-sized businesses. The data gathered is in Exhibit 6.

The third component of the data collection was the task analysis survey that all account managers were asked to complete. The results of the survey are shown in Exhibit 7.

This analysis pointed out that the AMs were spending a considerable amount of time on nonvalue-added administrative work such as attempting to return calls to customers, scheduling visits to customers, and making travel arrangements. Another

---

**EXHIBIT 5** | Customer Satisfaction Interviews

| Key Services Provided by AMs | Level of Satisfaction with AM's service |
|---|---|
| • Returning telephone calls on a timely basis | • Very dissatisfied |
| • Providing accurate information | • Somewhat dissatisfied |
| • Resolving problems or complaints | • Satisfied |
| • Providing financial guidance that reflects an understanding of my business | • Very satisfied |
| • Keeping me abreast of new products and services | • Very satisfied |

---

**EXHIBIT 6** | Access and Competitive Benchmarking

| Benchmarking Factor | Access | Company A | Company B | Company C |
|---|---|---|---|---|
| No. of customers per AM by size of account | Small: 15 Medium: 8–10 | Small: 20 Medium: 15 | Small: 15 Medium: 5 | Small: 30 Medium: 10 |
| Account management costs as a percent of revenue | 30% | 25% | 40% | 20% |
| No. of visits per year to customer sites | 4 visits | 1 visit | monthly | 1 visit for medium |
| Average response time to customer inquiries | 2–3 days | 24 hours | 3–5 days | 4 hours |
| Internet access to account information | No | Yes | No | Yes |
| Role of AM: generalist or team leader of specialists | Generalist | Team leader | Generalist | Generalist |
| Location of AM | Geographically dispersed | Regional centers | Geographically dispersed | Regional centers |

| EXHIBIT 7 | Account Managers Task Analysis Survey | | |
|---|---|---|---|

| Task Description | % of Time Spent on Task | Value Added by the Task |
|---|---|---|
| 1. Attempting to return calls (telephone tag) | 12 | Low |
| 2. Answering questions on status of customers' accounts by telephone | 5 | Medium |
| 3. Analyzing customer account activity to identify suggested improvements | 2 | High |
| 4. Tracking down information to respond to customer complaints | 8 | Medium |
| 5. Scheduling visits to customers' sites | 5 | Low |
| 6. Making travel arrangements for customer visits | 3 | Low |
| 7. Researching and networking to consult with customer on various topics | 20 | High |
| 8. Developing consulting recommendations and presentations for customers | 15 | High |
| 9. Conducting face-to-face meetings with customers | 10 | High |
| 10. Traveling | 15 | Low |
| 11. Completing other administrative functions, including weekly status reports | 5 | Medium |

task that took a considerable amount of time was doing the research required to respond to customers' inquiries. To understand this task better, the redesign team interviewed several AMs. The AMs explained that the product line and services offered by Access have grown in complexity, and it was almost impossible to be an expert in every area. Because the AMs were expected to respond to the customer, the AMs often had to use the internal network to find the information required. This research took a lot of time and often frustrated the AMs because their contacts within Access had other priorities and did not always call back in a timely manner. A few of the AMs also offered the opinion that the frequent visits, which they were expected to make to the customer site, were not adding value. Sometimes it felt like an imposition on the customer. If they did not have new information or recommendations, the customers did not want to waste their time on routine updates.

During these interviews, the AMs asked a lot of questions about how their role would be impacted by the redesign. The rumors floating around were that their role would be reduced to a phone center job. The AMs also complained about the task analysis survey that they were expected to complete. Comments included:

"Management doesn't trust us to manage our time effectively—they think they have to check up on us."

"Why are we the only ones completing the survey?"

"Why are other parts of the organization not completing the survey too?"

The redesign team shared a summary of the data collected in their monthly meeting with the senior management team. Sam was very interested in the benchmarking data and asked the redesign team a number of questions. Peter was more interested in the results of the customer interviews. He wanted to know how many customers were interviewed and why they were "somewhat dissatisfied" with the accuracy of the information they received. The redesign team members responded that they had interviewed more than 10 percent of the customer base, which totaled

| EXHIBIT 8 | Account Management Comparison |
| --- | --- |

| Current AM Role | Future AM Role |
| --- | --- |
| Answering routine inquiries from customers on the status of their account | Analyzing customer account activity and recommending improvements |
| Generalist—expected to know all product lines | Project leader for a team of experts |
| Frequent visits to customers to maintain relationships | Visits centered around well-prepared updates for the customer |

more than 80 interviews. The team explained that the main cause of inaccurate information appeared to be due to timing. New information is posted to the customers' accounts daily so information may be accurate one day, but out of date the next day. Peter pointed out that if customers had direct online access to their own accounts, that many of these complaints would be eliminated. Kerrie was surprised with the task analysis and the amount of time spent on low and medium value-added tasks.

Toward the end of the meeting, Kerrie encouraged the team to create a design for account management that would be motivating to employees. She emphasized that the team should not just redesign the role to be more cost effective, but also look for ways that the job could be more rewarding and less frustrating than the current role of the AM. Kerrie suggested that the team develop a vision of the new role and a comparison between the current and future roles.

After the meeting with the senior management team, the redesign team began formulating its recommendations for the account management function. Exhibit 8 is the comparison that the team developed, as Kerrie had requested.

Although the redesign team had made good progress on the vision of the future, they knew that they could expect a lot of resistance from the AM workforce, and it would be difficult for the AMs to see the positive aspects of the new role. The rumors and negative perceptions of the redesign that were building in the AM workforce were indications of the reactions that could be expected from the AMs. The redesign team knew they would not be successful in gaining the buy-in from the AMs without the help and leadership of the senior management team.

When it was time for the monthly meeting between the redesign team and the senior management team, the redesign team presented its vision for the AM role and specific recommendations on how to make the transition. The redesign team expressed its concern that the new vision had to have senior management's support and sponsorship. Kerrie thanked the team members for all their hard work and praised them for their innovative thinking. Kerrie then turned to her senior management team and told them it was then their turn to lead and make the change happen. Kerrie said the senior management team would meet the following week to develop an implementation plan. As Kerrie left the meeting, she wondered if her senior management team was up for the hard work that still needed to be done.

On the way home from work that night, Kerrie reflected on that sleepless night after the quarterly review meeting. She was pleased with the progress that the redesign team had made and felt confident that its vision was moving the account management function in the right direction. But Kerrie was still uneasy about implementing the change. She thought about her own role in leading the change and wondered what leadership style would be most effective at this point in the change process. She thought about Sam and how she and other members of the senior management team could support him during the transition. Kerrie realized that the next meeting for the senior management team was critical. She decided that when she got home, she would list the key issues that the team should address in its meeting to plan for implementation.

# The Zone Reorganization: Developing a Strategy for Managing Change

## Case F

## Stuart Rosenberg*

"How in the world do you take four offices that have different cultures and consolidate them into one location?"

On May 14, 2003, Christine Brooks, the regional claims manager for a national insurance company, asked herself this question as she drove to an all-day meeting that she had scheduled at the White Plains, New York, office with all forty-six claims managers from the Westchester region. As the regional manager, Christine was in charge of implementing a major zone reorganization, in which the four offices under her responsibility would be consolidated into one location before the end of the year. The firm that she worked for had long been one of the country's most prestigious and most profitable insurance companies, but as a result of industry deregulation and continuing weakness in the economy, corporate management had decided to bolster the competitiveness of the company and undertake a number of cost-cutting moves, one of which included the Westchester zone reorganization. Since the announcement of this change three months earlier, there was a considerable amount of uncertainty in the work environment, and Christine recognized that to facilitate the transition it would be prudent to bring together her managers to develop the most effective strategy for managing the change.

*Author affiliation: Dowling College.

# F-1 The Evolution of the Insurance Industry

The insurance industry in the United States dates back to the early days of the nation, with the charter of a company named the Philadelphia Contributorship for the Insurance of Houses from Loss by Fire. In the early nineteenth century, as the population increased and people left the security of farms to live in the city, more people needed life insurance. The need for financial protection further increased due to factors such as westward expansion, the Civil War, and the outbreak of yellow fever and tuberculosis.

The industry was first regulated in the 1850s due to the insolvencies of many companies. These insurers had set very low rates to gain an edge in an increasingly competitive industry, but the loss of protection for their customers resulted in the establishment of state insurance regulatory bodies. In the 1869 case of *Paul v. Virginia,* the U.S. Supreme Court ruled that insurance is a local transaction and not a matter of interstate commerce, thereby granting regulatory power over insurance exclusively to the individual states and precluding any involvement by the federal government.

Changes in the way people live and work necessitated new coverages. In the late 1800s, disability insurance had become an important source of revenue for insurers. By 1920, most of the states had passed laws concerning workers' compensation as well as legislation requiring motorists to purchase automobile insurance. The public outcry for additional financial protection was a direct outcome of the Great Depression, and in the 1930s, the Social Security Act, Blue Cross (for physician care), and Blue Shield (for hospital care) all came into being; insurance companies also entered the health market to provide coverage. In addition, the Depression resulted in the Glass-Stegall Act of 1933, which constrained the structure and the conduct of the U.S. banking system, by enforcing a separation between retail banks and investment banks.

After World War II, competition among insurers continued to increase. Innovations occurred in all lines of business, companies began to offer package policies, and large life insurance companies entered the property and casualty market. In addition, innovations could be seen in the industry's investment strategies, which it developed to create stronger growth opportunities within the financial sector of the U.S. economy.

# F-2 The Financial Services Modernization Act of 1999

A groundswell of support for the structural deregulation of the financial sector increasingly took hold in the 1980s and 1990s. Many people believed that industry turf battles impeded the provision of financial services and that the Depression era legislative and regulatory restrictions on competition and innovation would prevent the growth of the economy in the twenty-first century. With a broader array of financial products to choose from, the strict regulatory separations between banks, securities firms, and insurance companies had created a burden for consumers in deciding what to do with their money. They had to decide how much to place into a savings account in one financial institution, how much to invest in stocks in a second financial institution, and how much to spend on an insurance policy in a third financial institution.

Many people also felt that the thrift failures of the 1980s and the bank failures of the 1990s were caused by the inability of firms to diversify and respond to the changing financial needs of consumers. This, too, served as a catalyst for deregulation, and with the passage of the Gramm-Leach-Bliley Act of 1999, the artificial separation of financial institutions embodied in Glass-Stegall was removed. The segmentation that had existed within the financial sector had created an artificial homogeneity among banks, among securities firms, and among insurers. This homogeneity prevented economies of scope and, consequently, it limited innovation and the pursuit of strategic opportunities. Deregulation created a brand new ball game in the financial sector, with new competitors and a heightened risk of merger activity.

Clearly, banks were no longer limited in their ability to offer securities or insurance policies to their customers, and securities firms and insurance companies were able to provide full-service banking. Because of deregulation, the various companies in the financial sector could expand into new products and new services.

Christine Brooks's employer was one such firm. The company had grown from relatively modest beginnings as a regional provider to become one of the country's largest insurance companies. After deregulation, the company established new banking operations, which enabled it to offer customers checking accounts, mutual funds, money market accounts, certificates of deposit, credit cards, loans (including home mortgage loans, home equity loans, and home equity lines of credit), and leases. The company even offered customers retirement planning services, which was certainly an indication of how aggressive corporate management had become in its operating strategies given the changed environment in financial services.

The company's flagship insurance operations were divided among different zones across the country. At the end of 2002, these zones contained a total of 820 offices that performed the primary function of processing claims on the insurance policies that the company had underwritten. Insurance was clearly the foundation of the company, and it was from this base that corporate management wanted to transform the firm to improve its position as one of the leading firms in the newly deregulated financial marketplace.

## F-3 The Economic Downturn

The downturn that began in the technology sector in 2000 soon spread to other sectors of the economy, and by 2001 the United States was mired in a recession following ten years of growth. The recession hit the financial sector hard. Despite increased premium revenues, Christine Brooks was aware of corporate management's uneasiness caused by a substantial after tax net operating loss in 2001. Although the overall weakness in the market had driven a decline in the company's stock portfolio that caused it to suffer a loss by its noninsurance affiliates, the lion's share of the loss came from substantial underwriting losses related to insurance.

The stagnant economy in 2002 helped contribute to another difficult year in the company. Premiums paid by policyholders were insufficient to cover the cost of claims and operating expenses. Lower interest rates hurt investment income, and it was insufficient for covering insurance underwriting losses. This forced the company to raise auto insurance rates for the first time in several years as a means of absorbing some of its losses. Due to the huge underwriting losses and the continued reduction in the value of the company's stock portfolio, there was a significant decline in total assets.

## F-4 The Announcement from Corporate Management

The economy was well into its third consecutive troublesome year in early 2003, when the mandate came down from corporate management that the insurance company's zones would be reorganized. As for the Westchester region, this would entail a business restructuring from four separate claims offices to a single claims office. Although the employees in the four locations all reported to Christine, over the years each of the offices had developed its own unique identity and a distinctive corporate culture, and the managers were very concerned about how their staffs would adjust to the consolidation.

The smallest of the four offices was the Chappaqua claims office, which had 75 employees. The employees in this office consisted of claims representatives and their managers, as well as support staff. These job functions were identical in all four offices. Geographically, Chappaqua was the furthest north in Westchester, and of the four offices, it occupied the only building that the company owned. Corporate management had recently begun to look for a buyer for the building, which had sixty thousand square feet of office space.

The office that was furthest south was called the Fordham claims office. It was located in a building on Fordham Road in the Bronx, across the street from Fordham University. The company leased thirty thousand square feet of office space to house a staff of 125 employees.

The New Rochelle claims office also had 125 employees. It was located in a busy commercial area, where the company leased forty thousand square feet of office space. Although the leases for the New Rochelle and the Fordham offices were not scheduled to expire at the same time, corporate management was confident that the company could make arrangements with the landlords to terminate the leases early.

Corporate management had decided that the Westchester region would be housed in the White Plains claims office. There were 300 employees in the White Plains office, which was a growing industrial corridor in Westchester County. The company had a long-term lease on eighty thousand square feet of office space in White Plains, and the corporate office determined that it was the optimal location for the Westchester region. Christine Brooks's office was in the White Plains office.

## F-5 The Manager Survey

Following the announcement of the zone reorganization, Christine created a brief survey that she distributed to all of her managers to be completed and returned one week prior to the May 14 meeting. She hoped that the survey, which protected the anonymity of the managers, would be a catalyst for generating a lively discussion surrounding the issues of the business transformation and for developing the action plan that she would propose to corporate management.

The results of the survey revealed several key findings. Almost all of the managers indicated that they were either very satisfied or somewhat satisfied with their jobs. Moreover, a high percentage of the managers assessed the level of job satisfaction among their employees as either very satisfied or somewhat satisfied. Notwithstanding this apparent vote of confidence, the managers were decidedly split on other, more specific questions. While a majority of them rated their work environment as positive, the percentage was clearly less than the percentages indicated for job satisfaction, with more than a quarter of the managers expressing negative or mixed opinions. A third of the managers indicated that they felt that there was high turnover in their staffs and a little more than half of them felt that the compensation and benefits were competitive. Although the managers indicated by a margin of almost three to one that corporate management had an appropriate plan for change, there were nearly as many managers who believed that the company had not effectively managed that change as there were who did believe it.

The survey results to these questions are shown in Exhibit 1. The number of managers who responded to each option is shown along with the percentage. Forty-six managers responded to the survey. The percentages might not total 100 due to rounding.

## EXHIBIT 1    Selected Survey Results*

1. How would you assess your overall level of satisfaction with your job?

| | | |
|---|---|---|
| Very satisfied | 21 | 46% |
| Somewhat satisfied | 24 | 52% |
| Somewhat dissatisfied | 1 | 2% |
| Very dissatisfied | 0 | 0% |
| | 46 | 100% |

2. How would you assess the overall level of satisfaction of your staff with their jobs?

| | | |
|---|---|---|
| Very satisfied | 7 | 15% |
| Somewhat satisfied | 32 | 70% |
| Somewhat dissatisfied | 5 | 11% |
| Very dissatisfied | 1 | 2% |
| No response | 1 | 2% |
| | 46 | 100% |

3. Do you feel that your work environment is a positive one?

| | | |
|---|---|---|
| Yes | 33 | 72% |
| No | 9 | 20% |
| Undecided/Mixed | 4 | 9% |
| | 46 | 101% |

4. Do you feel that you have had high turnover among your staff?

| | | |
|---|---|---|
| Yes | 15 | 33% |
| No | 30 | 65% |
| No response | 1 | 2% |
| | 46 | 100% |

5. Do you feel that the company's compensation and benefits are competitive?

| | | |
|---|---|---|
| Yes | 25 | 54% |
| No | 13 | 28% |
| Undecided/Mixed | 8 | 17% |
| | 46 | 99% |

6. Do you feel that the company has an appropriate plan of action for the future?

| | | |
|---|---|---|
| Yes | 30 | 65% |
| No | 10 | 22% |
| Undecided/Mixed | 6 | 13% |
| | 46 | 100% |

7. Do you feel that the company has effectively managed change?

| | | |
|---|---|---|
| Yes | 24 | 52% |
| No | 19 | 41% |
| Undecided/Mixed | 3 | 7% |
| | 46 | 100% |

* The manager survey included other questions, most of which dealt with demographic information, that are not shown here.

# F-6 The Strategy Meeting

The managers had a good idea of what to expect at the meeting, and everyone appeared to be in good spirits as they entered the White Plains conference room at 9:00 a.m. Christine wanted the day to go well; coffee and muffins were provided in the morning, and at noon, deli sandwiches were brought in. Six round tables had been set up around the room, and when everyone had settled in, Christine began her opening remarks.

> We should use the survey as a tool to guide our discussion, but I encourage you to talk about any issues that you feel are important as they relate to managing your staffs through this change.

Christine indicated that she was pleased with the fact that the responses to the questions on job satisfaction had been so favorable. After some brief comments on these first two questions, Christine noted that the responses to the other questions in the survey were more diverse, and she actively solicited feedback on each of them, one at a time.

For the question dealing with the work environment, those managers who felt it was positive commented that the company's strong history formed a good framework for undertaking change. There was a vocal minority, however, who commented that as the company had grown, its family-oriented work environment had disappeared. These managers felt that communication of new processes had deteriorated. They expressed the helpless feeling that as first-line managers, they had little control over their circumstances. One manager commented that shortly after the staff learns a new procedure, it changes. The managers repeated more than once their unhappiness with the requirement that they reinterview for their positions in connection with the zone reorganization. Christine reminded them that this requirement was a corporate mandate and she promised to get clarification from her superiors.

Regarding turnover, some of the managers noted that the tightness in the job market was helping to minimize this problem, but others also commented that their employees genuinely liked working in the company. Others accurately stated that much of the staff consisted of long-term employees who had already been through several changes at the company. One of the managers suggested that the real issue with turnover was at the first-line manager level. Christine took note of this. Those managers who were experiencing turnover in their ranks indicated the following reasons: low morale in the claims environment, limited growth opportunities (which reflected the significant tenure of much of the staff and which helped in part to create the morale problem), and the inability or unwillingness of staff to relocate to White Plains.

When the conversation turned to compensation and benefits, several managers commented that the compensation system tended to be competitive for tenured staff, but not for newer staff. After some managers indicated their own wish lists for benefits that they wanted, the bulk of the discussion on compensation linked to the issue of turnover. Christine addressed the fact that another insurance company had recently moved into the next office building in White Plains and had poached staff. In fact, one of Christine's managers had left for this competitor and had recruited his entire staff.

In connection with corporate management's plan for change, some of the managers acknowledged that continued success in the financial sector was dependent on the company's expansion into banking products, while others expressed concerns about losing sight of the core property and casualty business. Some managers revisited their earlier comments on communication, and they blamed corporate management for all of the uncertainty that was plaguing their staffs. When it was noted that mixed messages and a lack of honesty were commonplace throughout the organization, Christine told the managers that they were having their meeting so that they could make the transition as easy as possible for their employees.

The discussion on change naturally led to the final question on change management. Some managers felt that the company was doing what it needed to do to facilitate change, but other managers continued to complain about disorganization and poor communication. This second group indicated that the company had undertaken too many changes too quickly and that rapid growth had negatively affected the company's efficiency and its financial strength. After one manager said that it seemed as though corporate management made changes just for the sake of change and that the company was making the wrong decision to house everyone in one location, Christine interrupted. She reminded the managers again that the change was going to happen; it was up to everyone in the room to help manage the change as seamlessly as possible.

# F-7 The Decision Point

Christine took a deep breath and smiled reassuringly.

From my perspective, we can manage the zone reorganization in one of two ways. One choice is that we can move the three offices all at once. We would probably do it over a weekend and hopefully have everyone up and running on Monday morning. I know that facilities can make this happen if we decide to manage the change this way. A lot of the feedback that you've provided indicates that our employees are being affected by a lot of uncertainty right now. It may be a shock if we move everyone over a weekend, but it would be a brief shock.

The other choice is to manage this transition in a piecemeal fashion. Many of you were critical of the organization doing things too quickly. If we move one office first, we may learn some things to make the second and third moves easier. But then again, if we take too long to complete this transition, we may continue to lose staff, particularly if the economy picks up.

I want to get back to corporate with a recommendation. I think they'll be amenable to either of these options. The key for me, though, is to manage the change in the way that you feel would be best for your people.

# Murata Chemicals

## Case G

Jeff Hicks
Padmakumar Nair
Celeste P. M. Wilderom*

*Author affiliations: Jeff Hicks, School of Business, Public Administration & Technology, University of Twente, the Netherlands; Padmakumar Nair, School of Management, University of Texas, Dallas; Celeste P.M. Wilderom, School of Business, Public Administration & Technology, University of Twente, the Netherlands.

## G-1 On a Clear Day in Tokyo, You Can See Mt. Fuji . . .

Shigeru Mori stood admiring the perfectly symmetrical and snow-covered peak of Mt. Fuji, rising above the Kanto plain some 90 kilometers away from his 33rd floor office in Tokyo's Shibuya district. "If only things in here were as clear as the view out there," he thought to himself, returning his gaze back inside to the latest financial results for Murata Chemicals.

## G-2 Background

Since its establishment in 1946, Murata Chemicals has been one of Japan's leading suppliers of specialty chemicals and adhesives for industrial applications. In the 1970s, Murata made a series of breakthrough discoveries of anticorrosion chemical formulations that helped oil refineries, steel mills and other customers lower their maintenance costs by as much as 10%. Since then, and for more than 30 years, Murata has maintained its leadership in Japan's specialty chemicals market, attributing much of its success to its engineering team, an entrepreneurial group with unequaled technical expertise and a hands-on consultative style that impresses clients. Murata sales engineers are known to carry with them a set of coveralls. During client visits, even senior engineers of the sales team will not hesitate to don the coveralls and go straight onto the factory floor to investigate a problem firsthand.

## G-3 Clouds on the Horizon

Despite their leadership position, Mr. Mori, vice president of corporate planning, had become increasingly anxious about Murata's future. He felt they had strayed far from the entrepreneurial culture upon which their success had been built, and that this very success had reduced the flexibility of his management team's thinking. With responsibility for all new business development initiatives, Mr. Mori was particularly concerned that the company's ability to identify and develop new products was not keeping up with the changing customer base, as new industries with new product needs replaced the older textile and heavy manufacturing operations that continued to move offshore. A chart covering nearly half of the bulletin board on his wall showed how the percent of total revenues from products introduced within the last five years had continued to fall. "I want that chart big enough so that every person that walks into this office will have to notice it," he had said to his secretary, Ms. Asano, who had sent it to the local graphics shop for enlargement, twice, before he was satisfied with the size.

The drop in new product revenue was especially noticeable in the corrosion treatment division (CTD). From Mr. Mori's perspective, an increasing number of the new product and service ideas developed by the research division and the younger engineering staff were being rejected by CTD, not because of a lack of technical merit or market potential, but simply because they called for developing new products or attracting new customers that did not fit neatly into the current operating plans. But despite his desire for improved performance from the CTD, Mr. Mori was also aware of the strong and proud culture that existed there. For years, the CTD had been the cash cow for the entire business, and while the percentage had fallen in recent years, the CTD still brought in some 40% of Murata's total sales. Last year, in an attempt to spur innovation, Mr. Mori had convinced three of the best and brightest engineers from another division to accept a temporary one-year transfer to the CTD. But even two months after the transfer, it was clear that the three had made little progress in assimilating into the CTD, and they were transferred back to their former division.

Despite this setback, Mr. Mori was determined to bring about change in the organization, and within the CTD in particular—the challenge was to find something around which he could build a case for change that was compelling from a business standpoint, and that avoided or minimized any defensive reaction on the part of Mr. Yamada, the Director of the CTD, and his team.

## G-4 The Case for E-Biz

"I've got it!" said Mr. Mori, turning suddenly away from the window and startling Ms. Asano, who had just brought in afternoon tea. "E-business! That's it. It's e-business. Asano san, please set up a meeting with Yamada san and his senior team—this week if at all possible. We'll need at least 90 minutes. I'll send you an agenda later today. And can you get me the phone number for Taguchi san at KL Associates? Thanks."

"Would you like KL to be included in the meeting as well?" asked Ms. Asano.

He hesitated a moment before answering "No, just internal people."

"Okay, I'll let you know when the meeting time is set," said Ms. Asano on her way out.

"E-business," he reasoned to himself, "plus the involvement of some external consultants from KL—that ought to be enough to shake things up a bit. But I also know how Yamada san feels about consultants—that their output is just paper, and too conceptual. I do think we need their help with the technology, though. I'll just have to emphasize this point and get his reaction."

The following afternoon, Mr. Mori met with the CTD management team. He reiterated the importance of CTD to Murata's overall business, and then introduced the topic of e-business, pointing out Murata's current lack of initiatives in the area. He followed with a rough outline of his e-business proposal, and asked that CTD take a leadership role in this important new area. "I think we all agree that e-business is an important area, but my proposal is clearly just an outline," he said. "What I'd like you to do is take this as the starting point, and see what ideas you can come up with." Finally, he offered to fund the initial planning phase from his own discretionary budget. The members of the CTD reacted positively, and after a relatively brief discussion, they reached an agreement to go ahead. Mr. Mori put Mr. Yamada in charge of the new e-business initiative, and asked him to get started right away in identifying the appropriate next steps.

"Yamada san, just one more thing," added Mr. Mori as the meeting adjourned. "What do you think about involving some external consultants?" he probed.

"I don't think they can learn our business during the course of a project," said Mr. Yamada. "And you remember when we brought in those consultants last year—all those recommendations about culture change, communications—nothing concrete. In fact, I don't believe a single one of their recommendations was ever implemented."

"I know your opinion on this, and basically, I agree," answered Mr. Mori. "However, the one thing that does concern me about this particular opportunity is the technology—we don't have any experience with any of it—hardware, software, or the technical architecture. Even the simple home page we have out there now is being taken care of by a vendor."

"Okay. Actually I was wondering about this when you were presenting your outline—you're right about the technology being new to us," said Mr. Yamada. "If they can come in and show us how to use e-business effectively—some concrete ideas we can truly implement—then I can agree. Do you know anyone we can call on?"

"Yes, I know one of the top people over at KL Associates. He's got some clever young guys working for him. I'll give him a call and ask him if they'd like to bid for the work."

That afternoon, Mr. Mori contacted Jun Taguchi, an acquaintance of his who was in charge of the Japan practice of KL Associates, a management consulting firm. After giving a brief overview of their plans, Mr. Mori added, "Taguchi san, you should also know that there are those within Murata—Yamada san in the corrosion treatment division in particular—who do not fully agree with bringing in outside consultants. We had a bad experience last year with some consultants, and that project is still fresh in his mind. He does not report to me directly, although he does for this project, since it falls under new business development. So please understand, I'm willing to help you, but you will have to turn in a strong proposal, with a competitive price—we want some solid new ideas for e-business that we can actually and successfully implement—not just a set of high-level concept slides prepared by consultants. Most importantly, make sure your technical capabilities are strong and well represented. We'll be starting next year's budgeting process within the next eight weeks or so and I'll need to know some approximate amounts for any investments we may need to make. As a result, we'll need to get started with this project right away. I guess that's about it. Please call me if you'd like any additional information."

Mr. Taguchi thanked Mr. Mori for the opportunity, and immediately called Ms. Asano to arrange a date for their proposal presentation to Mr. Mori. He then contacted Mr. Sugimoto, leader of KL's strategy practice, explaining, I've just talked with Mori san at Murata Chemicals. They need help with a new e-business initiative. We'll need some strong technical talent but I think we have a good shot at this one. Come over to my office and I'll fill you in, then let's get started on the proposal right away."

By the following afternoon, Mr. Sugimoto had assembled a team of three consultants, two from the e-business technology practice, and a third from the business strategy practice. Working through the weekend, the team completed a draft proposal which they presented to Mr. Mori and Mr. Yamada on Monday afternoon, making sure to stress their technical capabilities and their focus on producing implementable recommendations. After some minor revisions requested by Mr. Mori, the proposal was accepted and Murata's e-business initiative was officially under way.

# G-5 Project Launch

For the first two weeks of the project, Mr. Sugimoto and his team concentrated on market research—industry size and growth, key segments and competitors. Mindful of their promise to deliver implementable recommendations, the team also began a series of interviews with Mr. Yamada and the members of the CTD to understand more about Murata's capabilities.

I believe e-business provides a great opportunity for Murata, and especially for the CTD," began Mr. Yamada during his interview with the KL team. "We have great products and solid operational support, yet even in our strongest segments, our market share is still only about 30 percent. Using the Internet as an additional sales channel, I see no reason why we couldn't push penetration to as high as 40 or even 50 percent." Other CTD members gave similarly optimistic views.

At the end of the second week, Mr. Taguchi held an informal project status meeting with Mr. Sugimoto and the rest of the KL team. "The Murata people seem pretty excited about the potential opportunity," began Mr. Taguchi. "How are the interviews going?"

"Well, actually, that's becoming a cause for concern," said Mr. Sugimoto. "Let me explain. Now that we know more about the company, we believe—and by the way, the customers agree—that Murata's real strength lies in the hands-on consultative style and technical expertise of their sales engineers. And that is just not something you can deliver over the Internet. In fact, we're beginning to wonder just how much impact—if any—that e-business or Internet technology can have in growing sales and market share of their current products to the levels they're clearly hoping for. Yamada san's talking about hitting 50 percent market share."

"You mentioned you had a couple of preliminary ideas?" asked Mr. Taguchi.

"Yes," said Mr. Sugimoto, "but I'm afraid they won't be getting very far—I shared them with Yamada san today and he wasn't at all impressed. One is for a new Internet ad campaign using some of the popular B2B exchange sites, and another for an online system that customers could use to request and schedule routine maintenance calls," Mr. Sugimoto explained.

"And Yamada san didn't like them?" asked Mr. Taguchi.

"Not at all. And that's unfortunate because they're good ideas—for the advertising one, we know their customers spend a lot of time on the Internet, mostly on procurement sites, so we're confident we'd be reaching our target audience. And for the online scheduling tool, both the customers and the Murata sales people we talked to were quite positive on the idea."

"But Yamada san didn't like either idea? Did he say why?" asked Mr. Taguchi.

"He said, and I quote, 'Why would we throw away an opportunity to go out and see the customer face to face, even if it was just to schedule a maintenance appointment?'"

"He's got a good point. So what did you say to that?" asked Mr. Taguchi.

"I explained that both of these were pragmatic ways for them to begin building their skills in e-business," answered Mr. Sugimoto. "Here's what I suspect: he's just looking for some way to leap into online sales, but I just don't believe they're ready for it. They're only seeing the sales side of this—a new channel for selling just exactly what they're selling today."

"Look, I know you and the team have worked hard," said Mr. Taguchi, "but I also know our first major presentation is coming up at the end of next week. What if we were to relax this whole capability constraint just a little? Say we try to come up with some ideas that are more innovative and with a higher priority on sales potential, whether they currently have the capability or not. Now, I'm not suggesting we mislead them—any gaps between what's required and what their current capability is—these gaps will have to be clearly documented. But at least it would get closer to what they're apparently looking for. What do you think?"

"It's not ideal, but I have been considering the same thing. Besides, at this point, I don't see any other way forward," agreed Mr. Sugimoto. "I've already told our team that we'd probably be working over the weekend. I'll reserve an off-site location for us to get away and do some brainstorming."

"Perfect," said Mr. Taguchi. "And tell the team I'll treat them all to a nice dinner when we're finished for the day."

Across the hall, Mr. Yamada and other members of CTD were finishing their traditional Japanese *bento* boxed lunches. "I think they're simply overlooking the obvious," said Mr. Yamada. "Our products and brand are strong, and with Internet sales as a new channel, I have to believe there are many more customers we could reach. With all the pressure we're under for increased sales, the two ideas they brought to us today—advertising and maintenance scheduling? That's just not what we need. Why do they seem so cautious?"

By Saturday evening, the spirits of the KL team had lifted somewhat. Their all-day session had produced what they felt to be two very attractive options that Murata was sure to embrace. The first involved the purchase and resale—under the Murata brand—of a new line of bulk chemical products, with discounts available for purchases made via a new online ordering system. Compared to Murata's mainstay specialty chemicals, most of which were made to order, the process of selecting and using bulk chemicals was far simpler—something the customers could do on their own, without consulting with a Murata engineer, thus making online purchase by customers a viable alternative. The second idea called for the development of a new Internet-based service targeting small businesses, a potentially large market segment, but one currently underserved by Murata, mostly because the low purchase volume of the typical small business could not support the cost of an in-person Murata sales team. According to the new plan, small business customers paying a monthly fee would have access to detailed information about chemicals and chemical usage through a website that was also integrated with a call center staffed with technicians who could provide simple diagnostic and troubleshooting advice.

# G-6 Project Impasse

Friday's planned presentation had been divided into two parts. First, KL would present the final results of their market research activities, followed by the presentation of a list of potential opportunities that the group would then discuss. The meeting started off smoothly enough, and the Murata team seemed pleased with thoroughness of the market research report. But soon after KL began the second half of the meeting and the presentation of their new ideas, it became clear that Mr. Yamada was not pleased with the results.

"Excuse me. I'm very sorry to interrupt," began Mr. Yamada. "And I know these are just preliminary recommendations, but I don't think you're going in the right direction at all. Bulk chemicals? Sales to small businesses? That simply is not the business of Murata Chemicals," he said, shaking his head. "We built this business into what it is today by selling made-to-order, specialty chemicals—not bulk chemicals—to the largest customers—not the small ones—who have the willingness and the ability to pay for a premium, high quality product. These ideas you've presented take us too far away—in the opposite direction, in fact—from the very products and services on which our success has been built. We can open this up for discussion, but as it stands now, I'm sorry but I can't support this set of recommendations."

After a prolonged silence, Mr. Taguchi tried to restart the discussion, but to no avail. From Mr. Mori's perspective, the reaction of the Mr. Yamada and the CTD was precisely what he had hoped to avoid. Mr. Yamada and the CTD felt the consultants had ignored the obvious—sales of existing products over the Internet—and instead had spent too much time developing other alternatives that were too far removed from their core business. For their part, the consultants were frustrated and felt they were working under multiple and contradictory mandates that, as the project went on, seemed to have less and less to do with e-business.

"Taguchi san," began Mr. Mori, "I think we're at an impasse here. Let's adjourn for today. Can you and Yamada san please come to my office first thing in the morning? We obviously need to have a serious discussion about how—or if—we can move this project forward."

# Glossary

**above-average returns** returns on investment that are much higher than the average for the industry

**action research** a model that usually involves planned change experts in organization development who work closely with organization managers, assisting in the implementation of an on-site intervention

**adaptive** encouraging change so that an organization can successfully compete as its environments change

**agency problem** a situation in which a firm's top managers (i.e., the agents of the organization's owners) do not act in the best interests of the shareholders

**balanced scorecard** an approach to measuring performance or organizational effectiveness based on an array of quantitative and qualitative factors, such as return on assets, market share, organizational capacity, customer loyalty and satisfaction, speed, and innovation

**best practices** processes or activities that have been successful in other organizations

**boundary-spanning** the interaction by members of an organization with outsiders in order to obtain information relevant to the organization

**bounded rationality** refers to the limitations of the mind that restrict the ability of decision makers to solve problems or take advantage of opportunities

**buffering** a process for managing uncertainty whereby an organization establishes departments to absorb uncertainty from the environment

**building shared visions** component technology that involves the leaders of organizations being able to translate their vision of the firm's future in a way that causes others to adopt, or share, the same vision

**bureaucracy** an organizational structural form with highly specific rules and standard operating procedures

**business unit** an organizational entity with its own unique mission, set of competitors, and industry

**business-level strategy** a strategy formulated for a business unit that identifies how it will compete with other businesses within its industry

**Carnegie model** reflects a descriptive decision-making process in organizations where coalitions determine a final choice based on incomplete information, social and psychological processes, limited abilities of decision makers, and the need to find quick, satisficing solutions.

**centralization** an organizational decision-making process whereby most substantial decisions are made by managers at higher levels within the organization

**CEO duality** a situation in which the CEO also serves as the chair of the board

**closed system** system in which organizations have no interaction with other entities

**coalition** a group of people who band together to win some issue

**codified knowledge management system** method of codifying data, information, specifications, and procedures into an accessible and standardized system to serve as a reference for everyone in the organization

**cognitive structure** system of beliefs, values, and expectations that limit the way top management teams make decisions

**comparative advantage** the idea that certain products may be produced more cheaply or at a higher quality in particular countries, due to advantages in labor costs or technology

**competitive advantage** a state whereby a business unit's successful strategies cannot be easily duplicated by its competitors

**competitive benchmarking** the process of measuring a firm's performance against that of the top performers, usually in the same industry

**computer-integrated manufacturing** an integrative process where each step of production is coordinated, including design, machinery, robotics, and engineering

**concurrent control** a measure that seeks to correct a problem while it is occurring

**context** the nature of the internal environment driving the organization and the external environment impacting the organization

**contingency theory** a perspective that suggests that the most profitable firms are likely to be the ones that develop the best fit with their environments

**continuous-process production** the highest form of technical complexity; it automates or mechanizes a firm's production process completely

**cooptation** a process in which leaders from the environment become active in the organization; for example, a banker might become a member of the firm's board of directors

**core competencies** an organization's key capabilities and collective learning skills that are fundamental to its strategy, performance, and long-term profitability

**corporate governance**  the board of directors, institutional investors, and block holders who monitor firm strategies to ensure managerial responsiveness

**corporate profile**  identification of the industry(ies) in which a firm operates

**corporate restructuring**  a corporate strategic approach that includes such actions as realigning divisions in the firm, reducing the amount of cash under the discretion of senior executives, and acquiring or divesting business units

**corporate-level strategy**  the broad strategy that top management formulates for the overall organization

**craft technologies**  jobs that are difficult to analyze because they require individual skill and ability

**creative management model**  theory that a top management team that is creative, imaginative, and innovative will set a positive tone for learning for the rest of the organization

**crisis management**  the process of planning for and implementing the response to a wide range of negative events that could severely affect an organization

**crisis**  any disruption that physically affects an organization, its basic assumptions, or its core activities

**cultural relativism**  the idea that no culture is inherently superior to any other

**cultural strength**  the extent to which organizational members agree about the importance of certain values

**cultural universalism**  the idea that that there is a single best culture—either in theory or in practice—against which all cultures should be compared

**culture**  the commonly held values and beliefs of a particular group of people

**customization**  a global strategic approach whereby the organization modifies its product or service offering to meet the needs of all of its international markets

**decentralization**  an organizational decision-making process whereby most decisions are made at the lowest possible levels in the organization

**Delphi technique**  a forecasting procedure whereby experts are independently and repeatedly questioned about the probability of some event's occurrence until consensus is reached regarding the particular forecasted event

**differentiation strategy**  a generic business unit strategy in which a business produces and markets to the entire industry products or services that can be readily distinguished from those of its competitors

**distinctive competence**  unique resources, skills, and capabilities that enable an organization to distinguish itself from its competitors and create a competitive advantage

**diversification**  the process of acquiring companies to increase a firm's size

**divestment**  a corporate-level retrenchment strategy in which a firm sells one or more of its business units

**downsizing**  a means of organizational restructuring that eliminates one or more hierarchical levels from the organization and pushes decision making downward in the organization

**employee stock ownership plan (ESOP)**  a formal program that transfers shares of stock to a company's employees

**engineering technologies**  production that is high in variety, but the variety is offset by the ease at which tasks can be analyzed

**environmental scanning**  collecting and analyzing information about relevant trends in the external environment

**ethical relativism**  the idea that ethics is based on accepted norms in a culture

**evolutionary change**  change that involves a series of small, progressive steps that do not change the organization's general equilibrium

**explicit knowledge**  the compilation of standardized facts, such as specifications, rules, and policies, that are used to manage the organization

**external growth**  a growth strategy whereby a firm acquires other companies

**factors that determine life cycle stage**  factors that include situation, which refers to the overall makeup of the firm, including its size, number of owners or shareholders, how customers influence decisions, the heterogeneity of its markets, and so forth; decision-making style, or how decisions are made in organizations and how participatory that process is; structure, which refers to how a firm establishes its reporting relationships, divides responsibilities, and organizes itself for operations; and strategy, which is top management's plan to attain its desired outcomes for the organization based on its mission and goals

**feedback control**  a measure that seeks to correct a problem after it has occurred and prevent it from happening again

**feedforward control**  a measure that anticipates problems and is initiated prior to an occurrence of an activity

**first-mover advantages**  benefits derived from being the first organization to offer a new or modified product or service

**five-stage organization life cycle**  includes the following stages: existence, the first or birth stage when firms first come into being; survival, the second stage of development where firms can remain for an indefinite period of time, begin to grow, quickly becoming much larger, or fail to progress at all and go out of business; success, the third stage of development characterized by maturity of operations, bureaucracy, large size and scope; renewal, the fourth stage of development, in which mature organizations attempt to return to a leaner form, renewing growth and becoming more flexible and responsive to customers; and, decline, the fifth stage, in which organizations tend to focus inward with power and politics hampering growth and development

**flat organization**  an organization characterized by relatively few hierarchical levels and a wide span of control

**focus** the concentration of strategic efforts on an identifiable subset of the industry in which it operates, as opposed to the market as a whole

**formal organization** the official structure of relationships and procedures used to manage organizational activity

**formalization** the extent that decisions and procedures are driven by established rules and policies

**functional strategies** strategies created at functional levels (e.g., marketing, finance, production, etc.) to support the business and corporate strategies

**functional structure** a form of organizational structure whereby each subunit of the organization engages in firm-wide activities related to a particular function, such as marketing, human resources, finance, or production

**generic strategies** strategies that can be adopted by business units to guide their organizations

**geographic divisional structure** a form of organizational structure in which jobs and activities are grouped on the basis of geographic location—for example, Northeast region, Midwest region, and Far West region

**goals** desired general ends toward which efforts are directed

**gross domestic product (GDP)** the value of a nation's annual total production of goods and services

**growth strategy** a corporate-level strategy designed to increase profits, sales, and/or market share

**hierarchy of authority** the reporting relationships and the span of control of organizational members

**horizontal growth** an increase in the breadth of an organization's structure

**horizontal structure** an organizational structure with fewer hierarchies designed to improve efficiency by reducing layers in the bureaucracy

**hypercompetitive environment** an environment that is global in nature, extremely competitive in terms of innovation, quality, and price, and fertile ground for alliances between competitors in order to amass large amounts of capital

**imitation** an approach to managing uncertainty whereby the organization mimics the strategy and structure of a successful key competitor

**incremental decision model** situation whereby managers make decisions that are only slightly different than the ones made by their predecessors or the ones they themselves made in the past

**incremental innovation** the improvement of existing products or services to enhance their marketability

**industrial organization (IO)** a view based in microeconomics theory that states that a firm's profitability is most closely associated with industry structure

**industry** a group of competitors that produces similar products or services

**industry life cycle** the stages (introduction, growth, shakeout, maturity, and decline) through which industries are believed to pass

**informal organization** the norms, behaviors, and expectations that evolve when individuals and groups come into contact with one another

**information** disparate data, or facts, compiled into a useful form

**information asymmetry** situation that occurs when one party has information that another does not

**information symmetry** situation that occurs when all parties to a transaction share the same information concerning that transaction

**innovation** the transformation of creative ideas and concepts into products or services that meet the needs of customers

**innovative process** a life cycle approach concerned with how innovations are facilitated from development to decline

**inputs** resources gathered from the open environment

**integration** a state whereby individuals identify with the organization and actively work with and learn from each other to achieve organizational goals

**integrative social contracts view of ethics** perspective suggesting that decisions should be based on existing norms of behavior, including cultural, community, or industry factors

**intellectual capital** the total of everything that is known by the people of an organization

**intended strategy** the original strategy top management plans and intends to implement

**intensive technology** refers to each department's work being necessary to every other department in serving the needs of the customer

**internal growth** a growth strategy in which a firm expands by internally increasing its size and sales rather than by acquiring other companies

**international franchising** a form of licensing in which a local franchisee pays a franchiser in another country for the right to use the franchiser's brand names, promotions, materials, and procedures

**international licensing** an arrangement whereby a foreign licensee purchases the rights to produce a company's products and/or use its technology in the licensee's country for a negotiated fee structure

**intrapreneurship** entrepreneurial activity within a corporate structure

**intuitive decision making** decision-making system that involves relying on judgment and feel for a situation based on experience

**invention** the creation of a new product or process

**job design** the tasks and responsibilities expected of employees in specific positions

**job enlargement** an increase in the number of tasks per job

**job enrichment** workers are given more responsibility and the authority to carry out that responsibility

**job rotation** job design system that involves employees learning several different jobs over time, providing them with more variety in their work in an attempt to improve job satisfaction

**joint optimization** situation in which people and machines work toward accomplishing organizational goals in harmony

**judgmental forecasting** a forecasting procedure whereby employees, customers, suppliers, and/or trade associations serve as sources of qualitative information regarding future trends

**justice view of ethics** perspective suggesting that all decisions will be made in accordance with preestablished rules or guidelines

**knowledge** a conclusion drawn from different streams of information that can be shared by members of the organization and used to further its goals

**knowledge management** sharing of knowledge throughout the organization with those who need it

**large-batch technology** increased use of machinery and technical complexity to ensure standardization of production

**learning organization** an organization that has developed the continuous capacity to adapt and change

**leveraged buyout (LBO)** a takeover in which the acquiring party borrows funds to purchase a firm

**life cycle stages** identifiable periods of the life of an organization that have distinct characteristics

**lifelong learning** a long-term self-improvement process whereby workers continue to upgrade their skills and knowledge level, making them better employees

**liquidation** a retrenchment strategy of last resort whereby a firm terminates one or more of its business units by selling its assets

**long-linked technology** type of interdependence in which each department's outputs become inputs for the next department in the production chain

**low-cost–differentiation strategy** a generic business unit strategy in which a business unit maintains low costs while producing distinct products or services industry-wide

**low-cost strategy** a generic business unit strategy in which a larger business produces, at the lowest cost possible, no-frills products and services industry-wide for a large market with a relatively elastic demand

**macroenvironment** the general environment that affects all business firms in an industry, which includes political-legal, economic, social, and technological forces

**managerial ethics** an individual's responsibility to make business decisions that are legal, honest, moral, and fair

**mass customization** a customized product from a mass-production operation

**matrix structure** a form of organizational structure that combines the functional and product divisional structures

**mechanistic structure** the structured, centralized manner of organizing for mass-production organizations

**mediating technology** arrangement whereby departments are able to work independently within the organization by serving different needs of customers

**mental models** images that we utilize in our minds to understand the world

**mission** the reason for an organization's existence; the mission statement is a broadly defined but enduring statement of purpose that identifies the scope of an organization's operations and its offerings to the various stakeholders

**multiple scenarios** a forecasting procedure in which management formulates several plausible hypothetical descriptions of sequences of future events and trends

**nonprogrammed decisions** decisions that involve nonroutine, out-of-the-ordinary situations and are generally not covered by existing policy or procedure

**nonroutine technologies** tasks high in variety and low in analyzability due to the ambiguous nature of the work

**objectives** specific, verifiable, and often quantified versions of a goal

**open systems** systems in which organizations interact with the elements of their environments

**organic structure** method of organizing for firms that require flexibility in operations and the need to be close to the customer

**organization life cycle** the pattern that describes the birth, growth, maturity, and decline of organizations

**organizational capacity** an organization's ability to remain effective and sustain itself over the long term

**organizational change** the adoption of any new idea, behavior, or substantive modification by an organization

**organizational conflict** occurs when two groups clash over competing goals

**organizational control** determining the extent to which organizational effectiveness is attained and taking corrective measures to improve effectiveness if needed

**organizational culture** shared values and patterns of beliefs that are accepted and practiced by members of a particular organization

**organizational decision making** the process of identifying problems or opportunities and finding solutions or courses of action that further the goals of the organization

**organizational differentiation** the means by which organizational activities are grouped into subunits and by which hierarchies are established to manage them

**organizational effectiveness** the extent to which an organization utilizes its resources effectively to accomplish its goals and objectives

**organizational politics** activities taken within organizations to acquire, develop, and use power and other resources to obtain one's preferred outcomes in a situation in which there is uncertainty or disagreement about choices

**organizational structure** the formal establishment of reporting relationships, management responsibilities, and coordination of work

**organizations** entities that gather people together into formal groups, providing the necessary structure, context, and culture to pursue common goals

**outputs**  the products and services that are produced through the value-added transformation process

**personal mastery**  learning to expand one's capacity to create results desired

**personalized knowledge management system**  system that captures the expertise of individuals designing and delivering customized products and services in a rapidly changing technological environment

**personnel ratios**  measures of the percentage of people in different areas of the firm, such as administration, support staff, and operations

**planned change**  a response that is deliberately thought out and implemented in anticipation of future opportunities and threats

**pooled interdependence**  situation that occurs when departments perform separate tasks from other departments but the contribution of different departments can be pooled

**population ecology**  a perspective on organizations that emphasizes the diversity among organizations that perform similar functions and utilize common resources

**power**  one's ability to achieve desired outcomes by exerting influence over others

**process-oriented innovation**  the improvement of existing production processes or other organizational processes such as management, organizational reporting structures, or information processing systems

**product divisional structure**  a form of organizational structure whereby the organization's activities are divided into self-contained entities, each responsible for producing, distributing, and selling its own products

**product-oriented innovation**  the creation of new products or services to bring them to market, creating new consumer demand

**professionalism**  the amount of formal education and training needed by employees to do their jobs

**profit center**  a well-defined organizational unit headed by a manager accountable for its revenues and expenditures

**programmed decisions**  decisions made on a routine, repetitive basis that are addressed by company policy and procedures

**radical innovation**  creation of a new product or service that replaces an existing one

**rational model of decision making**  a decision-making process that relies on a step-by-step systematic approach to solving a problem

**reactive change**  change that is usually piecemeal and in direct response to a specific opportunity or threat from the external environment

**realized strategy**  the strategy top management actually implements

**reengineering**  a radical redesign of business processes in a cross-functional manner to achieve major gains in cost, service, or time

**related diversification**  A process whereby an organization acquires one or more businesses not related to its core domain

**religious view of ethics**  perspective that ethical dilemmas should be evaluated by considering personal or religious convictions

**resource-based view**  the perspective that firms must base an evaluation of competitive strengths on their collection and use of valuable, rare, inimitable, and nonsubstitutable resources and strive to convert those resources into a sustainable competitive advantage

**retrenchment strategy**  a corporate-level strategy designed to reduce the size of the firm

**revolutionary change**  change that alters or transforms the entire organization

**reward system**  an overt mechanism of recognition and compensation to promote intrapreneurship or innovation within the firm

**rights view of ethics**  perspective that evaluates organizational decisions on the extent to which they protect basic individual rights

**routine technologies**  highly programmable tasks that contain little variety

**satisficing**  choosing a course of action that is the most acceptable to the greatest number of people involved or affected

**scientific management**  a method of discovering the right way to perform tasks

**self-directed work teams**  a group of workers acting as a team who come together to perform tasks and take responsibility for performing work as a unit rather than having an individual supervisor

**self-interest view of ethics**  perspective suggesting that benefits of the decision maker(s) should be the primary considerations when faced with an ethical dilemma

**self-reference criterion**  the unconscious reference to one's own cultural values as a standard of judgment

**sequential interdependence**  departmental relationship in which tasks performed by one department have a direct effect on another department

**servant leadership**  a philosophy of management where the leader is a servant first

**slack**  a lull in activity; or, in the case of slack resources, having excess on hand for surprise circumstances

**small-batch and unit production**  production system characterized by skilled individuals who make products to order

**social obligation**  the perspective that business organizations should only be required to meet their economic and social responsibilities

**social responsibility**  the expectation that business firms should serve both society and the financial interests of shareholders

**social responsiveness**  the perspective that organizations must adapt to changing environmental conditions, and decisions should be made to promote positive social change

**sociotechnical systems approach**  the relationship between people and technology in the workplace

**span of control** the number of employees reporting directly to a given manager

**specialization** describes how organizational tasks are divided; the more narrow the task, the more specialized the job

**stability strategy** a corporate-level strategy intended to maintain a firm's present size and current lines of business

**stakeholders** individuals or groups who are affected by or can influence an organization's operations

**standardization** a global strategic approach whereby the organization markets the same product or service in all of its international markets

**strategic alliances** a corporate-level growth strategy in which two or more firms agree to share the costs, risks, and benefits associated with pursuing existing or new business opportunities; often referred to as partnerships

**strategic group** a select group of direct competitors who have similar strategic profiles

**strategic management process** the continuous process of determining the mission and goals of an organization within the context of its external environment and its internal strengths and weaknesses, formulating and implementing strategies, and exerting strategic control to ensure that the organization's strategies are successful in attaining its goals

**strategy** top management's plans to attain outcomes consistent with the organization's mission and goals

**subsystem** functional departments or divisions that are responsible for specific performance objectives of the organization

**subunit orientation** a state whereby individuals identify and communicate almost completely with those in their divisions, not the organization as a whole

**sustainable competitive advantage** situation when a firm's strategy is unduplicated by competitors, allowing it to enjoy strategic benefits over an extended period of time

**synergy** situation that occurs when the combination of two organizations results in higher efficiency and effectiveness than would otherwise be achieved by the two organizations separately

**systematic innovation** the search for changes in the environment and the identification of how those changes can be systematically analyzed as to their future innovative potential

**systems thinking** a way of thinking about and a language for describing and understanding the pattern of interactions that form interrelationships and shape the behavior of organizations

**tacit knowledge** implicit knowledge that is usually learned through experience

**takeover** the purchase of a controlling quantity of shares in a firm by an individual, a group of investors, or another organization; takeovers can be friendly or unfriendly

**tall organization** an organization characterized by many hierarchical levels and a narrow span of control

**task analyzability** the extent to which the transformation process can be analyzed, or broken down into a sequence of steps

**task interdependence** the extent to which one department must rely on another to accomplish its goals

**task variety** the number of exceptions that occur during the transformation process in a manufacturing organization

**team learning** situation in which the skill level of the team exceeds that of the individual members and in which the team performs at an exceptional level

**technical complexity** the measure of how mechanistic or programmed a production process is

**technological imperative** concept that states that technology determines structure

**technology** the ways that organizations find to do something; it may include the use of machinery and equipment, production materials, computers, or skills and techniques necessary to take inputs and transform them into outputs

**time series analysis** an empirical forecasting procedure in which certain historical trends are used to predict variables such as a firm's sales or market share

**top management team** the team of top-level executives—including members of the board of directors, vice presidents, and various line and staff managers—all of whom play instrumental roles in managing the organization

**turnaround** a corporate-level retrenchment strategy intended to transform the firm into a leaner and more effective business by reducing costs and rethinking the firm's product lines and target markets

**uncertainty** a state whereby decision makers lack current, sufficient, reliable information about their organization and cannot accurately forecast future changes

**unrelated diversification** a process whereby an organization acquires businesses unrelated to its core domain

**unstructured model of decision making** decision making in uncertain environments as a structured sequence of activities that require smaller decisions throughout the process

**utilitarian view of ethics** perspective suggesting that anticipated outcomes and consequences should be the only considerations when evaluating an ethical dilemma

**values-based management** a system whereby organizational decisions are based on a set of established organizational values

**venture teams** system in which companies separate small teams of associates into secluded or isolated quarters where creative thinking and experimentation can be converted into innovative products or services

**vertical growth** an increase in the number of levels, or in the height of the organization's hierarchical chain of command

# Name Index

Names are referenced to the pages and the end-of-chapter notes where they are cited. For example, 241$n$13 indicates that the author is cited on page 241, note 13. The full reference appears in the Endnotes section at the end of that chapter. A page number followed by an italic $n$ with no note number (e.g., 241$n$) indicates that the author is cited in an on-page note.

## A

Adizes, I., 94$n$16
Aeppel, T., 118$n$31
Agle, B. R., 113$n$20
Alsop, R., 116$n$27, 116$n$28, 118$n$29
Anand, V., 114$n$24
Ansberry, C., 118$n$31
Arogyaswamy, B., 107$n$11
Ashforth, B. E., 114$n$24
Ayton, P., 46$n$48

## B

Baden-Fuller, C., 92$n$6
Bain, J. S., 20$n$4
Baliga, B. R., 66$n$31
Ball, D., 40$n$28
Ball, J., 40$n$19
Bamford, C. E., 143$n$17
Barnard, C., 10$n$21
Barney, J., 4$n$2, 4$n$3, 20$n$5, 20$n$6
Barsoux, J. L., 184$n$10
Barton, L., 48$n$61
Baskervile, R. F., 182$n$3
Beamish, P. W., 194$n$35
Beatty, S., 40$n$16
Becker, H., 113$n$21
Bedeian, A., 93$n$14
Behling, O., 128$n$14
Berman, S., 20$n$7, 171$n$10
Bertalanffy, L. von, 5$n$4
Bialik, C., 113$n$22
Boin, A., 47$n$53
Bolt-Lee, C., 153$n$3
Boorstin, J., 160$n$16
Boudette, N. E., 22$n$13
Bouza T., 40$n$24
Bresser, R. K. F., 20$n$8
Brockmann, E. N., 27$n$32
Brooks, G. R., 144$n$19
Brown, K., 118$n$35
Brown, M. E., 114$n$25
Brown, R. L., 143$n$17
Brown, T., 107$n$13
Buckley, M. Ronald, 170$n$1
Buckley, N., 40$n$27
Buckman, R., 118$n$33
Burke, L., 128$n$15
Burke, W., 174$n$24
Burnett, J., 47$n$51
Burns, T., 156$n$10

## C

Butler, J. E., 20$n$5
Byles, C. M., 107$n$11

Cameron, K., 92$n$5, 93$n$12, 94$n$17, 94$n$21
Camillus, J., 8$n$13
Campbell-Hunt, C., 25$n$24
Carey, S., 26$n$26
Carlton, J., 41$n$32
Carpenter, M. A., 63$n$20
Carraher, S., 93$n$10, 93$n$11
Cartwright, D., 130$n$24
Chakravarthy, B., 172$n$14
Chan, P., 191$n$25
Chang, L., 193$n$33, 194$n$34
Chang, S., 78$n$7
Chen, K., 193$n$31
Chen, S., 65$n$24
Child, J., 59$n$12, 74$n$1, 76$n$3, 78$n$9
Chrisman, J., 100$n$31, 100$n$32, 138$n$5
Chua, J., 100$n$31, 100$n$32
Churchill, N., 93$n$13, 94$n$19, 141$n$11
Clair, J. A., 47$n$52
Coase, R., 85$n$15
Cockburn, I. M., 21$n$10
Conger J., 66$n$35, 124$n$1
Costello, J., 42$n$38
Crandall, W. R., 47$n$56
Crnjak-Karanovic, B., 182$n$3
Crozier, M., 131$n$26
Cummings, J., 37$n$6
Cummings, T. G., 147$n$25, 163$n$22
Cummins, C., 37$n$7
Cyert, R., 58$n$4, 126$n$9

## D

D'Aveni, R., 4$n$1, 66$n$32
Daellenbach, U. S., 106$n$6
Daft, R., 125$n$4, 154$n$4, 163$n$22
Dahl, R., 129$n$22
Das, T. K., 63$n$20
Davenport, T., 172$n$13
David, F., 44$n$44
Davis, P., 100$n$34
Deal, T. E., 107$n$9
Dean, J., 118$n$32
Dean, T. J., 143$n$17
Deephouse, D. L., 24$n$22
Delaney, K. J., 188$n$14
Delbecq, A. L., 143$n$16

DeLeede, J., 115$n$26
DeLong, D., 172$n$13
Dienhart, J. W., 110$n$18
DiSimone, L. D., 146$n$22
Dolven, B., 190$n$23
Donaldson, T., 183$n$9
Down, J., 20$n$7, 171$n$10
Downs, A., 94$n$16
Driver, M., 107$n$14
Drucker, J., 118$n$35
Drucker, P., 138$n$1, 140$n$9
Dumaine, B., 83$n$12, 172$n$17
Duncan, R. B., 43$n$41
Duncan, W. J., 106$n$2
Dunne, N., 66$n$29

## E

Eckel, N., 128$n$14
Ehlen, D. M., 194$n$35
Eisenstadt, A. S., 84$n$13
Ellison, S., 40$n$20, 40$n$28
Ely, R. J., 118$n$30
Emery, F., 132$n$28
Epstein, L. D., 58$n$7
Ettlie, J. E., 141$n$12

## F

Fahey, L., 46$n$49
Fama, E. F., 65$n$26
Farrell, M., 77$n$5
Fayol, H., 9$n$18
Ferguson, T. D., 24$n$22
Ferguson, W. L., 24$n$22
Ferrell, W. R., 46$n$48
Ferrier, W. J., 23$n$16
Ferris, S., 67$n$36
Fierman, J., 125$n$5
Finegold, D., 66$n$35
Finkelstein, S., 66$n$32
Fisher, A., 125$n$5, 126$n$6
Florian, E., 5$n$6
Follett, M. Parker, 10$n$20
Fong, M., 193$n$32
Forte, M., 27$n$32
Fowler, G. A., 41$n$33, 190$n$23
Franklin, J. H., 84$n$13
Freedman, J., 160$n$16
Freeman, J., 35$n$3
French, J., 130$n$24
Friedman, A. L., 57$n$2

# Subject Index

Page numbers in italics identify illustrations. An italic *t* next to a page number (e.g., 241*t*) indicates information that appears in a table.